D1290469

D1227472

Johann Sebastian Bach.

Engraved by L. Sichling after G. Haußmann

J. S. BACH

ALBERT SCHWEITZER

ENGLISH TRANSLATION BY
ERNEST NEWMAN

In Two Volumes
VOLUME I

Dover Publications, Inc., New York

This Dover edtion, first published in 1966, is an
unabridged and unaltered republication of the work
originally published by Breitkopf and Härtel in
1911.

Library of Congress Catalog Card Number: 66-20414

Manufactured in the United States of America
Dover Publications, Inc.
180 Varick Street
New York, N. Y. 10014

TO

FRAU MATHILDE SCHWEITZER

IN GRATEFUL REMEMBRANCE

TRANSLATOR'S FOREWORD.

Within the last few years Bach research has made a notable advance. Among the books that have contributed to this progress, that of Dr. Albert Schweitzer takes a leading place. It is equally valuable on the æsthetic and the practical sides; its convincing demonstration of the pictorial bent of Bach's mind must necessarily lead to a reconsideration not only of the older view of Bach as a mainly "abstract" musician, but of the æsthetics of music in general; while the chapters on the right manner of performing Bach's works throw many a new light on this obscure subject. Most of all are correct ideas on this latter point invaluable now, when Bach is beginning, as one hopes, to win his due popularity among not only musicians but music lovers as a whole.

The present translation has been made from the German version of Dr. Schweitzer's book (1908), which is itself a greatly expanded version of a French original published in 1905. The text, however, has been largely altered and added to at Dr. Schweitzer's request. The English edition is thus fuller and more correct even than the German.

Like most other translators I have found it convenient — and indeed necessary — to preserve the word "clavier" to cover all the seventeenth and eighteenth century instruments — the harpsichord, clavichord, clavicembalo, &c. — of the type now represented by the pianoforte.

For the benefit of the English reader I have given all the references to Spitta's "Life of Bach" in the corresponding pages of the English edition of that book, published by Messrs. Novello & Co.

The index to the German original of Dr. Schweitzer's book being hardly adequate, I have prepared a fuller one of my own, which I hope will increase the usefulness of the volumes.

ERNEST NEWMAN.

PREFACE TO THE GERMAN EDITION (1908.)

In the autumn of 1893 a young Alsatian presented himself to me and asked if he could play something on the organ to me. "Play what?" I asked. "Bach, of course", was his reply. In the following years he returned regularly for longer or shorter periods, in order to "habilitate" himself — as they used to say in Bach's day — in organ playing under my guidance.

One day in 1899, when we were going through the chorale preludes, I confessed to him that a good deal in these compositions was enigmatic to me. "Bach's musical logic in the preludes and fugues", I said, "is quite simple and clear; but it becomes cloudy as soon as he takes up a chorale melody. Why these sometimes almost excessively abrupt antitheses of feeling? Why does he add contrapuntal motives to a chorale melody that have often no relation to the mood of the melody? Why all these incomprehensible things in the plan and the working-out of these fantasias? The more I study them the less I understand them."

"Naturally," said my pupil, "many things in the chorales must seem obscure to you, for the reason that they are only explicable by the texts pertaining to them."

I showed him the movements that had puzzled me the most; he translated the poems into French for me from memory. The mysteries were all solved. During the next few afternoons we played through the whole of the chorale preludes. While Schweitzer — for he was the pupil — explained them to me one after the other, I made the acquaintance of a Bach of whose existence I had previously had only the dimmest suspicion. In a flash it became clear to me that the cantor of St. Thomas's was much more than an incomparable contrapuntist to whom I had formerly looked up as one gazes up at a colossal statue, and that his work exhibits an unparalleled desire and capacity for expressing poetic ideas and for bringing word and tone into unity.

I asked Schweitzer to write a little essay upon the chorale preludes for the benefit of French organists, and at the same time to enlighten us as to the nature of the German chorale and the German church music of Bach's epoch, as we knew too little of them to enter thoroughly into the spirit of the cantor's music.

He set to work at this. A few months afterwards he wrote to me that it was necessary to include the cantatas and Passions in his essay, since the vocal works explained the chorale works, and *vice versâ*. "Your essay", I replied, "will simply be so much the more valuable to us."

The remarks upon the chorale and the church service in Bach's time grew into an epitome of the history of Protestant church music; the observations upon the nature of Bach's musical expression became a chapter upon "Bach's tone-speech"; a short literary portrait of the composer was seen to be desirable; then there came chapters on the practical performance of Bach's works; and so the essay upon the chorale preludes grew, in the space of six years, into a complete book upon Bach. The author sent me each chapter as it was written. When I wrote a preface to the book in Venice, on 20th October 1904, it was with the joyous feeling that the work would open up for us a free road to Bach.

Now, as I sketch the preface to the German edition, I cannot rid myself of a certain feeling of embarrassment. Is it not presumption for me, a Frenchman, to draw the attention of Germans to a work upon Bach?

I may partly plead in excuse that in a limited sense I am the joint originator of the book. It was at my request that Schweitzer undertook the work; it was I who induced him to persevere with it when the difficulties of the undertaking increased and began to look, at times, almost insurmountable.

I believe, therefore, that it is not only my right but my duty to prepare the way for this book in Germany — if that be necessary — since it seems to belong to a special category in the German literature of the arts. I rank it among the works the significance of which consists in the fact that while they are founded on a thorough professional knowledge, they treat their subject from the standpoint not of a single art but of art and science in general. Schweitzer is a philosopher through and through, as is shewn by his work on Kant; at the same time he is a theologian with a profound historical faculty, as may be seen from his well-known and comprehensive studies in the life of Jesus and in the literature of that subject; more-over he is an exceptionally good organist, — one of the most skilful and experienced players that any conductor could desire to have at the organ during the performance of a Bach cantata or Passion.

The not unreasonable complaint is sometimes heard that our æstheticians are so seldom executive artists also, and therefore cannot view things from the standpoint of the musician. There is no community of feeling between the philosophy of art and creative and executive art. For this reason works by practical men who are at the same time conversant with philosophical æsthetic are always an event in the literature of music. To read Schweitzer's *Bach* is not only to get to know the composer and his work, but to penetrate also into the essence of music in general — the "art *per se*". It is a book with "horizons". Who could have supposed that a study of the great master of the "Zopf" epoch would throw a light on the modern — even the most modern — problems of music, as is done in the three chapters — "Poetic and Pictorial Music", "Word and Tone in Bach", and "Bach's Musical Language" — with which Schweitzer prefaces his discussion of the cantatas and the Passions?

An introductory note by a Frenchman to a German book on Bach may further show that we on this side of the Vosges have also some rights in the composer. We have won them by the veneration we have felt for him. Our Bach worship does not date from yesterday. For a generation now our organists have been almost exclusively occupied with Bach; he is the master who has revealed afresh to us the true art of the sacred instrument. People speak of a new French organ school: it is founded on Bach. It was a curious dispensation of Providence that at the very time we were being led to Bach by the Belgian Lemmens — who had become acquainted with the classical organ-art through old Hesse, of Breslau — there arose an organ-builder after Bach's own heart, who gave us organs that made us the envy of Bach enthusiasts in every land. Cavaillé-Coll's instruments have revealed to us the beauty of the master's preludes and fugues; with these organs Bach has made his entry into our cathedrals and churches.

If he has not as yet taken his due place in our public concert life, that is to be accounted for on purely external grounds. Our public is enthusiastic for Bach, our singers and instrumentalists not less so. I myself have had proof of this during my ten years' conductorship of the "Concordia", when we performed many cantatas, the Magnificat and the *St. Matthew Passion.*

There are German artists whose works we admire, while at the same time we know that they will never be domesticated among us. When we try to appropriate them to ourselves, we feel that a certain something remains that, — how shall I say it? — does not come to us from the soul. We never have this feeling with Bach; there seem to be bonds of affinity between his art and ours.

The correctness of this feeling is confirmed by the interest and the admiration that Bach himself evinced for contemporary French art. What he thought of Couperin and the others is shewn by the copies that have come down to us in his handwriting and that of his pupils. His first biographer, Forkel, whose information came from Bach's own sons, expressly says that the composer thought a great deal of the old French organists, — whose works have now at last been rescued from oblivion. And Zelter himself, the old Bach enthusiast and grumbler, rather wrathfully proves to his friend Goethe that his idol did not escape the influence of the French, "especially of Couperin". His works seem to Zelter to be covered with a kind of elegant "tinsel" that must be attributed to foreign art. He would have liked to skim it off and show the true German Bach underneath.

The present-day German admirers of Bach do not share Zelter's view of the "tinsel". The finish, the elegance and the formal charm of Bach's work do not strike them as a disavowal of the German spirit. We, however, who aim at form and plastic clearness in every art, find ourselves again in Bach. And when Schweitzer, without being at all one-sided, again and again insists upon the "pictorial" as the fundamental tendency in Bach's music, he only makes it clear to us what it is that attracts us to it. The time will come when Bach will be one of the most popular of composers in France, — not merely because we can discover in him traces of French influence and of our own sense of form, but because Bach is on the whole the most universal of artists. What speaks through his works is pure religious emotion; and this is one and the same in all men, in spite of the national and religious partitions in which we are born and bred. It is the emotion of the infinite and the exalted, for which words are always an inadequate expression, and that can find proper utterance only in art. For me, Bach is the greatest of preachers. His cantatas and Passions tune the soul to a state in which we can grasp the truth and oneness of things, and rise above everything that is paltry, everything that divides us.

By thus conquering artistic and religious mankind, Bach fulfils a mission to our time, which will never rise above the barriers that the past has erected unless the great souls of the past come to its aid. We are made one by what we admire in common, revere in common, comprehend in common.

Paris, 20th October 1907.

CHARLES MARIE WIDOR.

CONTENTS.

Volume I.

CHAPTER I.

THE ROOTS OF BACH'S ART.

Some artists are subjective, some objective. The art of the former has its source in their personality; their work is almost independent of the epoch in which they live. A law unto themselves, they place themselves in opposition to their epoch and originate new forms for the expression of their ideas. Of this type was Richard Wagner.

Bach belongs to the order of objective artists. These are wholly of their own time, and work only with the forms and the ideas that their time proffers them. They exercise no criticism upon the media of artistic expression that they find lying ready to their hand, and feel no inner compulsion to open out new paths. Their art not coming solely from the stimulus of their outer experience, we need not seek the roots of their work in the fortunes of its creator. In them the artistic personality exists independently of the human, the latter remaining in the background as if it were something almost accidental. Bach's works would have been the same even if his existence had run quite another course. Did we know more of his life than is now the case, and were we in possession of all the letters he had ever written, we should still be no better informed as to the inward sources of his works than we are now.

The art of the objective artist is not impersonal, but superpersonal. It is as if he felt only one impulse, — to express again what he already finds in existence, but to express it definitively, in unique perfection. It is not he who lives, — it is the spirit of the time that lives in him. All the artistic endeavours, desires, creations, aspirations and errors of his own and of previous generations are concentrated and worked out to their conclusion in him.

In this respect the greatest German musician has his
analogue only in the greatest of German philosophers.
Kant's work has the same impersonal character. He is
merely the brain in which the philosophical ideas and
problems of his day come to fruition. Moreover he uses
unconcernedly the scholastic forms and terminology of the
time, just as Bach took up the musical forms offered to
him by his epoch without examining them.

Bach, indeed, is clearly not a single but a universal
personality. He profited by the musical development of
three or four generations. When we pursue the history of
this family, which occupies so unique a position in the art-
life of Germany, we have the feeling that everything that
is happening there must culminate in something consummate. We feel it to be a matter of course that some day
a Bach shall come in whom all those other Bachs shall
find a posthumous existence, one in whom the fragment of
German music that has been embodied in this family shall
find its completion. Johann Sebastian Bach, — to speak
the language of Kant — is a historical postulate.

Whatever path we traverse through the poetry and the
music of the Middle Ages, we are always led to him.

The grandest creations of the chorale from the twelfth
to the eighteenth century adorn his cantatas and Passions.
Handel and the others make no use of the superb treasures
of chorale-melody. They want to be free of the past. Bach
feels otherwise; he makes the chorale the foundation of
his work.

If we pursue, again, the history of the harmonisation of
the chorale, we are once more led up to him. What the
masters of polyphonic music, — Eccard, Prætorius and
the others — strove after, he accomplishes. They could
harmonise the melody only; his music at the same time
reproduces the text.

So it is, again, with the chorale preludes and the chorale
fantasias. Pachelbel, Böhm and Buxtehude, the masters
in this field, created the forms. But it was not given to

them to quicken the forms with the spirit. If all their struggles towards the ideal were not to be in vain, a greater man had to come, who should make his chorale fantasias musical poems.

Out of the motet, under the influence of Italian and French instrumental music, came the cantata. From Schütz onwards, for a whole century, the sacred concert struggles for its free and independent place in the church. People feel that this new music is cutting the ground of the old church service from under their feet. It forces itself further and further out of the frame of the service, aiming at becoming an independent religious drama, and aspiring towards a form like that of the opera. The oratorio is being prepared. At this juncture Bach appears, and creates cantatas that endure. A generation later it would have been too late. As regards their form, his cantatas do not differ from the hundreds upon hundreds of others written at that time, and now forgotten. They have the same external defects; they live, however, by their spirit. Out of the ardent will-to-create of generations that could not themselves give birth to anything durable, there has come for once a will equal to the ideal that hovered before the two previous generations, and that triumphs in spite of all the errors of its epoch, purely by the grandeur of its thought.

At the end of the seventeenth century the musical Passion-drama demands admission into the church. The contest rages, for and against. Bach puts an end to it by writing two Passions which, on their poetical and formal sides, derive wholly from the typical works of that time, but are transfigured and made immortal by the spirit that breathes through them.

Bach is thus a terminal point. Nothing comes from him; everything merely leads up to him. To give his true biography is to exhibit the nature and the unfolding of German art, that comes to completion in him and is exhausted in him, — to comprehend it in all its strivings and its failures.

This genius was not an individual, but a collective soul. Centuries and generations have laboured at this work, before the grandeur of which we halt in veneration. To anyone who has gone through the history of this epoch and knows what the end of it was, it is the history of that culminating spirit, as it was before it objectivated itself in a single personality.

CHAPTER II.

THE ORIGIN OF THE TEXTS OF THE CHORALES*.

BIBLIOGRAPHY.

PHILIPP WACKERNAGEL: *Das deutsche Kirchenlied von der ältesten Zeit bis zu Anfang des XVII. Jahrhunderts.* 5 vols. 1864—1877.
WILHELM BÄUMKER: *Das katholische deutsche Kirchenlied in seinen Singweisen.* 3 vols. 1883, 1886, 1891. (The second volume is a revised edition of Severin Meisters' *Das deutsche katholische Kirchenlied.*)
ALBERT KNAPP: *Evangelischer Liederschatz.* 2 vols. 1st ed. 1837; 3rd ed. Stuttgart, 1865. (Contains 3130 hyms from all periods.)
WILH. FRIEDR. FISCHER: *Kirchenliederlexikon.* 2 parts. Gotha, 1878. Supplemental volume 1886.
HOFFMANN VON FALLERSLEBEN: *Geschichte des deutschen Kirchenliedes bis auf Luthers Zeit.* 1854. 3rd ed. 1861.
FRIEDRICH ZELLE: *Das älteste lutherische Hausgesangbuch (Färbefass. Enchiridion* 1524). Göttingen 1903.
FRIEDRICH SPITTA: *Ein feste Burg ist unser Gott. Die Lieder Luthers in ihrer Bedeutung für das evangelische Kirchenlied.* Göttingen 1905. *Studien zu Luthers Liedern.* Göttingen 1907.
ED. EM. KOCH: *Geschichte des Kirchenlieds und Kirchengesangs der christlichen, insbesondere der deutschen evangelischen Kirche.* 8 vols. 3rd ed. Stuttgart, 1866—1877.
E. WOLF: *Das deutsche Kirchenlied des XVI. und XVII. Jahrhunderts.* Stuttgart 1894.
PHILIPP DIETZ: *Die Restauration des evangelischen Kirchenlieds.* Marburg, 1903.

It was the custom in the Catholic church, in the earliest times, for the congregation to take a direct part in the singing during the service; to it belonged the doxologies,

---

* The chorale preludes of Bach are cited in the well-known Peters edition of the organ works.

the Amens, the Kyries and the hymns. At the end of the sixth century and the beginning of the seventh, however, this privilege of the faithful, which had been secured by Ambrose, was taken from them by the Gregorian reform, which substituted the singing of the priests for that of the congregation.

In Germany, however, this reform was not adopted in its entirety. The people still preserved a few of their privileges, especially in the Easter service, when they joined in the Kyrie and the Alleluia. The result was that it became the custom to insert German verses among the lines of the liturgy in these places. In this way the German sacred song gained admission into the religious service under cover of the Kyrie and the Alleluia. Throughout a long period of time these ejaculations formed the obbligato verse-ending to every hymn sung in the church. Hence these songs were called "Kirleisen" (i. e. Kyrie songs.).

The oldest Easter-hymn dates back as far as the twelfth century. It runs thus:

> Christ ist erstanden
> Von der Marter alle.
> Des sollen wir alle froh sein,
> Christ soll unser Trost sein,
> Kyrioleis.
>
> Halleluja, Halleluja, Halleluja.
> Des sollen wir alle froh sein,
> Christ soll unser Trost sein,
> Kyrioleis.

The Mystery Plays that had such a vogue in the fourteenth and fifteenth centuries also helped the German hymn to conquer the church. The mixed Latin-German Christmas cradle-songs have a quite uncommon charm. The poetry of them is of the most primitive kind imaginable. The words are put together less with regard to the sense than to the sound and the rocking rhythm; yet the bright Christmas enchantment that surrounds them affects us no less than it did the generations that have vanished.

In Bach's organ chorales there are two of these old Christmas songs: —

> In dulci jubilo,
> Nun singet und seid froh.
> Unsers Herzens Wonne
> Liegt in praesepio,
> Und leuchtet als die Sonne
> Matris in gremio.
> Alpha et O, Alpha et O.   (V, Nr. 35.)

> Puer natus in Bethlehem,
>   In Bethlehem,
> Unde gaudet Jerusalem,
>   Jerusalem.
> Halle, Hallel.

> Ein Kind geborn zu Bethlehem,
>   Zu Bethlehem,
> Des freuet sich Jerusalem.
>   Halle, Hallel.

> Cognovit bos et asinus,
>   Asinus,
> Quod Puer erat Dominus,
>   Dominus.
> Halle, Hallel.

> Das Öchslein und das Eselein,
>   Eselein,
> Erkannten Gott den Herren sein,
>   Halle, Hallel.
>   (V, Nr. 46.)

In time, translated Latin hymns came to be admitted into German sacred poetry; the Credo, the Pater noster, the ten commandments, the Seven Last Words, and various Psalms, in metrical paraphrases, were also incorporated in it.

When the Reformation of the sixteenth century threw the doors of the churches open to German poetry, it was under no necessity to set to work to compose appropriate hymns, but could choose what suited it from the treasures of the fourteenth and fifteenth centuries. Luther, with that wonderful artistic feeling for diction that even Nietzsche had to acknowledge in him, undertook to revise the old possessions for the new Church, and to alter and improve them as might be required. At the same time he himself continued the work of the Middle Ages by re-fashioning Latin hymns, psalms, liturgical chants and biblical fragments into hymns for the German service. The German Reformation had this advantage over the French, that it found a spiritual song already existing in the popular tongue, and therefore a ground upon which it could build; but its great good fortune was that it possessed, in Luther, a man who would not permit the old wood to be cut down, recognizing with sure prescience that the new song must grow up in the shade of the old. On the other hand the sacred folk-song withered away in the Romanesque countries, because it had no root in the Middle Ages, and had to exist as best it could upon the Psalter, as it does to the present day.

At the first glance it may seem incomprehensible that Calvin, by making the Psalter the hymn-book of the people, should from the very beginning condemn his church to infertility. He obeyed the instinct of the Romanesque spirit, and pronounced the judgment that was decreed on the French Reformation even before it came into being. Later on, German chorales and English hymns were borrowed to be added to the Psalter.

The first German hymn-book, the so-called *Erfurt Enchiridion*, appeared in 1524, and was probably compiled by Luther's friend Justus Jonas. It was issued simultaneously, curiously enough, by Trutebulsch at the imprimerie of the Dyeing Tub, and in Maler's imprimerie of the Black Horn. The sole surviving copy of the Maler issue was destroyed by fire in 1870 at the bombardment of Straßburg. Fortunately it had been reproduced in facsimile in 1848. The Trutebulsch hymn-book has been recently brought out in a new edition. *

---

* Friedrich Zelle, *Das älteste lutherische Haus-Gesangbuch (Färbefass-Enchiridion 1524)*; Göttingen, 1903. In his masterly Introduction

In accordance with the practice of the time, this first hymn-book was shamelessly pirated everywhere, among other places at Nuremberg, where the printer Hans Hergott so zealously pirated Luther's writings from the very beginning that Luther, on the 26th September 1525, had to petition the town-council "to forbid the Hergötlein to pirate".* Among the twenty-six songs of the *Erfurt Enchiridion* are eight German translations of psalms, including "Aus tieffer not schrey ich zu dir", a series of hymns done into German,** the two mediæval Easter hymns "Christ lag yn todes banden" and "Jhesus Christ unser Heyland, der den Tod überwand", the old hymn upon the ten commandments, three hymns by Paul Speratus, including the well-known "Es ist das heyl uns kommen her", and some of Luther's hymns, including the "New lied von den zween Mertererern Christi zu Brussel". "Ein feste Burg" does not appear in this hymn-book.***

Besides Luther and Paul Speratus (1484—1551) there may also be mentioned, as the earliest writers of sacred poems, Nicolaus Decius (died in 1541) and Nicolaus Sel-

---

the editor gives a survey of the various Lutheran hymn-books that appeared in Luther's life-time. The title of this first small hymn-book runs thus: *Eyn Enchiridion oder Handbüchlein eynen jetzlichen Christen fast nützlich bey sich zu haben zu stetter übung und trachtung geystlicher Gesenge und Psalmen Rechtschaffen und künstlich verteutscht. 1524.* Below, on the title-page: *Mit diesen und dergleichen Gesenge sollt man byllich die yungen Kinder auffertziehen.*

* Zelle, p. 23.
** *Veni redemptor gentium = Nu kom der Heyden heyland.*
  Veni sancte spiritus = Kom heyliger Geyst herre Gott.
  A solis ortus cardine = Chrystum wir sollen loben schon.
  Veni creator = Kom Gott schepfer heyliger Geyst.
  Grates nunc omnes reddamus = Gelobt seystu Jesu Christ.
  As well as the sequence:
  Media in vita =Mytten wir im leben seynd, and John Huss's hymn:
  Jesus Christus nostra salus = Jesus Christus unser Heiland, der von uns den Zorn Gottes wand.
*** For the latest research into the much-debated date of origin of this hymn see Friedrich Spitta, *"Ein feste Burg ist unser Gott": Die Lieder Luthers in ihrer Bedeutung für das evangelische Kirchenlied;* Göttingen, 1905.

nekker (1530—1592). The last hymn-book to appear in
Luther's life-time was published in 1545 in Leipzig by
Valentin Babst; this, in its numerous reprints and pirated
editions, remained the standard for all evangelical hymn-
books until the end of the sixteenth century.

In Bach's organ chorales are found such of these oldest
hymns as were also included in the later hymn-books: *

A. SACRED SONGS OF THE MIDDLE AGES:

(1) Easter Hymns.
Christ ist erstanden (V, No. 4).
Christ lag in Todesbanden (V, No. 5; VI, Nos. 15 and 16; cantata
No. 4).
Jesus Christus unser Heiland, der den Tod (V, No. 32).

(2) Christmas Hymns.
In dulci jubilo (V, No. 35).
Puer natus in Bethlehem (V, No. 46).

(3) "Improvements" of mediæval song-paraphrases.
Da Jesus an dem Kreuze stund (The Seven Last Words. V, No. 9).
Dies sind die heilgen zehn Gebot (V, No. 12; VI, Nos. 19 and 20).
Vater unser im Himmelreich (V, Nos. 47 and 48; VII, Nos. 52
and 53).
Wir glauben all an einen Gott (VII, Nos. 60, 61 and 62).

(4) Hymns translated from the Latin.
Der Tag der ist so freudenreich (*Dies est laetitiae*. V, No. 11).
Christum wir sollen loben schon (*A solis ortus cardine*. V, Nos. 6
and 7).
Erstanden ist der heilge Christ (*Surrexit Christus hodie*. V, No. 14).
Herr Gott dich loben wir (*Te Deum laudamus*. VI, No. 26).
Komm Gott Schöpfer, heiliger Geist (*Veni creator spiritus*. VII,
No. 35).
Komm heilger Geist, Herre Gott (*Veni sancte spiritus*. VII,
Nos. 36 and 37).
Nun komm der Heiden Heiland (*Veni redemptor gentium*. V, Nos. 42
and 43; VII, Nos. 45, 46 and 47; cantatas Nos. 61 and 62).

B. HYMNS BY LUTHER.

(1) Translations.
Jesus Christus unser Heiland, der den Zorn Gottes (*Jesus Christus
nostra salus;* Hymn of John Huss, Passion hymn. VI, Nos. 30,
31, 32 and 33).
Gelobet seist du Jesus Christ (*Grates nunc omnes reddamus;* Christmas hymn. V, Nos. 17 and 18).

* In the following list the Roman figures indicate the numbers
of the volumes in the Peters Edition of Bach's organ works.

(2) Biblical paraphrases.

Aus tiefer Not schrei ich zu dir (Psalm 130: *De profundis*. VI,
Nos. 13 and 14; cantata No. 38).
Ein feste Burg (Psalm 46. VI, No. 22; cantata No. 80).
Mit Fried und Freud ich fahr dahin (The Song of Simeon, Luke II.
V, No. 41).

(3) Original Hymns.

Christ unser zum Jordan kam (Baptismal hymn. VI, Nos. 17
and 18; cantata No. 7).
Vom Himmel hoch da komm ich her (V, No. 49, and pp. 92—101;
VII, Nos. 54 and 55).
Vom Himmel kam der Engel schar (V, No. 50).

C. TRANSLATIONS AND PARAPHRASES FROM VARIOUS
AUTHORS.

Allein Gott in der Höh sei Ehr (*Gloria in excelsis*, by Nicolaus
Decius, [died. 1541]. VI, Nos. 3—11).
Christe du Lamm Gottes (*The Agnus Dei in its simple form*.
V, No. 3).
O Lamm Gottes unschuldig (The Agnus Dei expanded into three
verses, by Nicolaus Decius. V, No. 44; VII, No. 48).
An Wasserflüssen Babylon (Psalm 137, *Super flumina*, by Wolf-
gang Dachstein. VI, Nos. 12a and 12b).
Christ der du bist der helle Tag (*Christe qui lux es et dies*. V,
pp. 60 ff., Partita).
In dich hab' ich gehoffet Herr (Psalm 31, *In te Domine speravi*,
by Adam Reissner, [died. 1562]. VI, No. 34).
Meine Seele erhebt den Herrn (*The Magnificat*. VII, Nos. 41
and 42; cantata No. 10).
Kyrie, Gott Vater (*Kyrie fons bonitatis*. VII, Nos. 39a and 40a).
Christe, aller Welt Trost (*Christe unite Dei Patris*. VII, Nos. 39b
and 40b).
Kyrie, Gott heiliger Geist (*Kyrie ignis divine*. VII, Nos. 39c
and 40c).

The really creative period of the hymn begins at the end
of the sixteenth century. The whole of German poetry is
impelled upon the religious path. While France, under a
monarchy conscious of its own goal, is developing into a
strong national state, in which there springs up a brilliant
literature, fostered by an art-loving court, Germany is on
the way to complete ruin. The nation as such disappears,
and with it that national feeling without which no true
literature is possible. When the country relapsed into
barbarism during the Thirty Years' War, the only thing

of the soul that survived was religion. In its bosom poetry took refuge. Thus Germany, in its bitterest need, created a religious poetry to which nothing in the world can compare, and before which even the splendour of the Psalter pales. The hymns of that time are a mirror of contemporary events. When the plague ravages, in 1613, the eastern parts of Germany, Valerius Herberger sings his joyous dirge "Valet will ich dir geben, du arge falsche Welt" (VII. Nos. 50, 51);* Martin Rinkart's (1586—1649) "Nun danket alle Gott" (VII. No. 43), is composed while the bells are ringing out the conclusion of peace in 1648.

These hymn-writers are by no means talents of the first order. Nevertheless the sincerity of devout feeling and the grave beauty of a diction formed by a constant reading of the Bible keep the average of the songs fairly high. Perhaps all these poets wrote too much. It happens, too, with the sacred poem as with the lyric: in one inspired song the poet, become for the moment a genius, will express magically what in other songs he could only stammer out. And this one song will live. Johann Rist (1607—1667) composed six hundred and fifty-eight songs; of these five or six survived in the hymn-books **.

Among these hymn-writers were two mystics, — Philipp Nicolai (1556—1698) and Johann Franck (1618—1677). To these Bach felt himself particularly drawn, for they, like himself, were steeped in the atmosphere of the Song of Songs. He wrote a cantata on Nicolai's "Wie schön leuchtet der Morgenstern" (No. 1), and another on his "Wachet auf, ruft uns die Stimme" (No. 140), also basing

---

* *"Valet will ich dir geben"; Ein andechtiges Gebet, damit die Evangelische Bürgerschaft zu Frauenstadt Anno 1613 im Herbst, Gott dem Herrn das Hertz erweichet hat, daß er seine scharffe Zorn-ruthe, unter welcher bey zweytausend Menschen schlaffen sind gangen, in Gnaden hat niedergelegt. So wol ein tröstlicher Gesang, darinnen ein frommes Hertz dieser Welt Valet giebt. Beydes gestellet durch Valerium Herbergerum, Predigern beym Kripplein Christi.* Leipzig, 1614.

** We may mention also Paul Flemming (1609—1640), Johann Heermann (1585—1647), and Simon Dach (1605—1659).

an organ chorale on the latter (VII. No. 57). He treated Franck's "Jesu meine Freude" in a motet and in two organ chorales (V. No. 31 and VI. No. 29). The communion hymn of the same poet, "Schmücke dich, o liebe Seele", inspired him to a cantata (No. 180) and to that splendid chorale fantasia (VII. No. 49) that sent Schumann into ecstasy when he heard Mendelssohn play it on the organ.

But even in that epoch there are premonitions of decline. Subjectivity of feeling and a didactic point of view invade religious poetry, and deprive it of that naive, simple objectivity that alone can create true congregational songs for the church service. At the commencement of the period of decay, when feeling and diction are already becoming super-subtilised, there appears on the scene, as if to check the decline, the king of hymn-writers, Paul Gerhardt (1607—1676). His actions show that he was an adherent of the Lutheran scholastic, that brought about the real Reformation with such startling rapidity. The reformed Electoral Prince Friedrich Wilhelm had required the Berlin preachers to sign a declaration by which they pledged themselves, for the sake of peace, to treat with moderation the doctrinal differences between the Reformed and the Lutheran churches. Paul Gerhardt, in spite of friendly advances from the Prince, could not be induced either to sign the declaration or to make a verbal promise, and consequently had to relinquish his office. The gentle-hearted man, it is true, had never employed in the pulpit the violent kind of polemic to which the Electoral Prince wanted to put an end; he regarded, however, the promise that was demanded of him as a sort of treachery to the faith of his fathers.* Of his hundred and twenty hymns, more than twenty have found a place in the hymn-books. They breathe a vigorous,

---

* Among the plentiful literature on the subject of Paul Gerhardt which appeared in his commemoration year (1907), Paul Wernles' *Religionsgeschichtliche Volksbücher* (Halle), calls for special mention. We know little more than is narrated above of the life of the poet. It is noteworthy how unequal Gerhardt's work is; he often uses other poems as models.

simple piety, and are expressed in a popular diction of excellent quality. Even in the life-time of the poet some of them came into use in the church, while in Bach's time many had become public property. Bach was an admirer of Gerhardt, and repeatedly employed verses from his hymns in his cantatas. In the *St. Matthew Passion* he makes use of five verses from "O Haupt voll Blut und Wunden" and one from "Befiehl du deine Wege".*
The really creative period of the church song, however, had come to an end by Bach's time. Pietism did indeed produce some spiritual poetry; but for Bach's work, so far as the chorale strophes are concerned, this is of little importance.** He seized upon the copious treasures of the past that lay to his hand in the hymn-books. The following figures will give an idea of the increase of the riches at his disposal: the little Erfurt hymn-book of 1524 contained twenty-six songs; that of Babst, in the first edition, a hundred and one; Crüger's (that was in use in Berlin for almost a century), in its first edition (1640) two hundred and fifty, and in its forty-fourth edition (1736) thirteen hundred; the Lüneburg (1686), two thousand; the Leipzig (1697) over five thousand.

We know from the inventory that has been preserved that the eight volumes of the Leipzig hymn-book were in the possession of Bach. *** What became of the volumes, the leaves of which he must so often have turned over, is not known.

---

* *St. Matthew Passion*, Nos. 21, 23, 63 (2 verses), and 72; No. 53. The hymn "O Haupt voll Blut und Wunden" is derived from St. Bernard of Clairvaux's "Salve caput cruentatum".
** The hymn-book of Johann Anastasius Freylinghausen was the first to include pietistic poems (*Geistreiches Gesangbuch, den Kern alter und neuer Lieder enthaltend;* Halle, Part. I 1704; Part II 1714). It was, indeed, the most widely circulated of all the hymn-books of the eighteenth century, and its contents increased, in the many editions it went through, from six hundred and eighty numbers to more than fifteen hundred.
*** Spitta, II, 278, and III, 267. The full title of this hymn-book runs: *A ndächtiger Seelen geistliches Brand- und Gantz-Opfer, das*

It was unfortunate for Bach's work that the old chorale took so prominent a place in it; for this reason it was included in the censure which Rationalism, in the name of purified taste, pronounced upon the church hymn of the past. For the second half of the eighteenth century Bach's cantatas and Passions did not exist; they had gone into exile with the old church hymn. Only after the reaction instituted by Ernest Moritz Arndt (1769—1860), Max von Schenkendorf (1783—1817) and Philipp Spitta (1801—1859), against the neglect of the hymn-book, had once more brought the old poems into repute, were the conditions established under which a new epoch could again comprehend the old master and the piety that gave birth to his works. Thus it is no accident that it was the son of the poet of "Psalter and Harp" who made it his life-task to reveal Bach to the world.

CHAPTER III.

THE ORIGIN OF THE MELODIES OF THE CHORALES.

BIBLIOGRAPHY.

A. KÖSTLIN: *Luther als der Vater des evangelischen Kirchengesangs.* (*Sammlung musikalischer Vorträge und Aufsätze*); Breitkopf und Härtel, Leipzig, 1881.

PH. WOLFRUM: *Die Entstehung und erste Entwicklung des deutschen evangelischen Kirchenlieds in musikalischer Beziehung.* Leipzig, 1890.

JOHANNES ZAHN: *Die Melodien der deutschen evangelischen Kirchenlieder aus den Quellen geschöpft und mitgeteilt.* Gütersloh, 1889—1893, 6 vols.

FRIEDRICH ZELLE: *Das älteste lutherische Haus-Gesangbuch.* Göttingen, 1903.

KÜMMERLE: *Enzyklopädie der evangelischen Kirchenmusik.* Gütersloh, 1886.

ist ein vollständiges Gesangbuch in acht unterschiedlichen Teilen. Leipzig, 1697. The *Vollständige und vermehrte Leipziger Gesangbuch* of L. F. Werner (1733), containing 856 songs, must also be mentioned in connection with Bach.

Luther acted with regard to the melodies on the same principles as he had done with regard to the text; he took whatever old melody suited his purpose and "improved" it, — only the improvement was often more drastic in the case of the tune than in that of the words, for it was his first care to see that the melodies were singable and easily grasped.

In 1524, — the crucial year for German church-music — Conrad Rupff and Johann Walther,* two eminent musicians, were for three weeks Luther's guests, acting as his "house-precentory" (Kantorei im Hause). Köstlin, in his essay on *Luther als der Vater des evangelischen Kirchengesanges*, depicts the trio at their work.** "While Walther and Rupff sat at the table, bending over the music sheets with pen in hand, Father Luther walked up and down the room, trying on the fife the tunes that poured from his memory and his imagination to ally themselves with the poems he had discovered, until he had made the verse-melody a rhythmically finished, well-rounded, strong and compact whole."

Thus the sacred songs of the Middle Ages preserved their own melodies, and the Latin hymns were translated in such a way that the new words fitted the old melodies, just as in the *Enchiridion* of 1524. Often, indeed, the poem was so constructed as to fit the "tone" of some sacred song that was already well known.***

---

* Johann Walther was born in Thuringia in 1496; from about 1523 he belonged to the Torgau precentory of the Electoral Prince. When, in 1530, lack of funds compelled the prince to give it up, Walther, encouraged by Luther, organised a precentory maintained by the corporation. After the battle of Mühlberg (1547), which made him the sovereign of a new territory, Moritz of Saxony founded a Kapelle in Dresden, of which he appointed Walther the head. He presided over this until 1554. He then returned to Torgau, where he died in 1570.

** Köstlin, p. 306.

*** The summary given on pp. 9 and 10 of the provenance of the texts of the old songs applies also to the melodies.

Since we rarely know the history of a melody before it became attached to a hymn, the name of which it henceforth bears, it is difficult to decide which melodies were adopted and which composed by the musicians of the Reformation. In any case we must not under-estimate the number of the latter. Johann Walther in particular seems to have employed a rich inventive gift in the service of religion. To what extent Luther himself was a composer of melodies cannot be determined. Contemporary testimonies, on the strength of which a number of tunes are attributed to him, are much too vague to prove anything positively. The melody of "Ein feste Burg", that may with certainty be attributed to him, is woven out of Gregorian reminiscences. The recognition of this fact deprives the melody of none of its beauty and Luther of none of the credit for it; it really takes considerable talent to create an organic unity out of fragments.*

In his melody to the German Gloria ("Allein Gott in der Höh sei Ehr"), Nicolaus Decius openly makes use of the "Et in terra pax" from the "Gloria paschalis". There was nothing strange in this to the men who had been brought up in the singing-schools of the catholic Church; it would indeed be surprising if they had thought it so. We may recall the fact that the mediæval hymn in its turn derives from the Gregorian use.

Nicolaus Hermann, cantor of Joachimsthal, in Bohemia, who was both poet and musician, wrote some very good chorale melodies. To him we owe "Lobt Gott ihr Christen allzugleich" and "Erschienen ist der herrlich Tag".** On the whole the number of musicians who wrote melodies for the church was not large, — not because at that time there were no musicians capable of the work, but rather because

---

* On this question cf. W. Bäumker's article in the *Monatshefte für Musikgeschichte,* 1880. For a counterblast to the excessive stress laid by Bäumker on the external derivation of the melody see H. A. Köstlin's essay *Luther als der Vater des evangelischen Kirchengesangs* (*Sammlung musikalischer Vorträge,* Leipzig, 1881, pp. 313 ff.).
** Bach V, Nos. 40 and 15.

their services were not called for. For a new melody to become a true folk-melody, of the kind that would gain immediate acceptance everywhere, was a difficult process, requiring a long period of time. It was much more natural to impress existing melodies into the service of the Church, — sacred melodies at first, and then, when these did not suffice, secular ones. The Reformed Church made the most abundant use of this latter source *.

Among the church tunes there are as few indigenous melodies as there are among those of the people; all have had an external origin. The learned August Gevaert has expressed the opinion that the oldest Catholic church-music was transplanted into the church from the pagan streets **.

For the Reformation it was a question of much more than acquiring serviceable melodies. While it brought the folk-song into religion, it wished to elevate secular art in general. That the object was conversion rather than simple borrowing is shewn by the title of a collection that appeared at Frankfort in 1571: *Gassenhauer, Reuter- und Bergliedlein, christlich, moraliter and sittlich verändert, damit die böse und ärgerliche Weise unnütze und schampare Liedlein auf Gassen, Feldern und in Häusern zu singen mit der Zeit abgehen möchte, wenn man geistige gute, nütze Texte und Worte darunter haben möchte.* ("Street songs, cavalier songs, mountain songs, transformed into Christian and moral songs, for the abolishing in course of time of the bad and vexatious practice of singing idle and shameful songs in the streets, in fields, and at home, by substituting for them good, sacred, honest words.")

Believing, as he said, that "the devil does not need all the good tunes for himself", Luther formed his Christmas-

---

* For the secular originals see F. M. Böhme, *Altdeutsches Liederbuch: Volkslieder der Deutschen nach Wort und Weise aus dem XII. bis zum XVII. Jahrhundert.* Leipzig, 1877.

** August Gevaert, *Der Ursprung des römischen Kirchengesangs*, — a paper read before the Belgian Academy of Arts, 27th Oct. 1889. German translation by H. Riemann, Leipzig, 1891.

hymn "Vom Himmel hoch da komm ich her" out of the melody of the riddle-song "Ich komm aus fremden Landen her" — in which the singer propounds a riddle and takes her garland from the maiden who cannot solve it*. Afterwards, however, he had to let the devil have the melody back again, for even after its conversion it haunted every dancing-place and every tavern. In 1551 Walther ejected it from the hymn-book, replacing it by the tune to which Luther's Christmas hymn is sung to this day **.

Reversions of this kind, however, were the exception. The majority of the melodies that were dignified by admission into the church were able to maintain themselves in their new station, and may justly feel aggrieved that in all these centuries the tooth of time has not been able to make away with the scanty documentary evidence of their secular origin. It would have been difficult to detect the secular element in them, for age confers on all music a dignity that gives it a touch of religious elevation. A mystic bond embraces and unites antiquity and religion; one clever writer maintains, not without reason, that we could mislead all the purists of church music by putting before them an old secular motet with an accompanying sacred text.

To give a few examples, — Heinrich Isaak's melody to "Inspruck, ich muß dich lassen," became the chorale "O Welt ich muß dich lassen" *** and the foot-soldiers' song at the battle of Pavia, — the "Pavier-tone" — became the

---

* See Fr. Zelle, *Das älteste lutherische Haus-Gesangbuch*, Göttingen, 1903, pp. 48—50, where the melody is given in the form in which it was first used as a church melody (in Klug's *Gesangbuch*, 1531).

** Böhme was the first to conjecture that the ground of the ejectment of the first melody was its profane power of resistance. See Zelle p. 49. The new melody — the one now current — (Bach V, No. 49 and pp. 92 ff.) is found in a Leipzig hymn-book as early as 1539.

*** See Bach's *St. Matthew Passion*, chorales Nos. 16 and 44. Today this melody is usually denoted by the song "Nun ruhen alle Wälder". It first appears as a chorale tune in the Nuremberg hymn-book of 1569.

chorale "Durch Adams Fall ist ganz verderbt" (Bach V, No. 13); the chorale melody "Von Gott will ich nicht lassen" (Bach VII, No. 56), is derived from the love-song "Einmal tät ich spazieren"; the chorale "Ich hab mein Sach Gott heimgestellt" (Bach VI, No. 28) borrows its melody from another love-song, "Es gibt auf Erd kein schwerer Leid"; the melody "Helft mir Gottes Güte preisen" (Bach V, No. 21) had been one of the Table-songs (1572) of Joachim Magdeburg.

In 1601 Hans Leo Hassler (1564—1612) published at Nuremburg a *Lustgarten neuer teutscher Gesänge, Palletti, Galliarden und Intraden mit vier, fünf und acht Stimmen,* ("Pleasure garden of new German songs, balletti, galliards, and intrades, for four, five, and eight voices"). Twelve years later, one of these melodies, — the love-song "Mein G'mut ist mir verwirret von einer Jungfrau zart" — appeared as a chorale tune to the funerary hymn "Herzlich thut mich verlangen" (Bach V, No. 27), while at a later date, allied with Paul Gerhardt's poem "O Haupt voll Blut und Wunden", it became the most important melody of Bach's *St. Matthew Passion.*

Any foreign melody that had charm and beauty was stopped at the frontier and pressed into the service of the evangelical service. This was the lot of the melody of "In dir ist Freude" (Bach V, No. 34), which came from Italy in 1591 with the *Balletti* of Giovanni Gastoldi. So again with the little French song "Il me suffit de tous mes maux", which appeared in 1529 among the *Trente et quatre chansons musicales* of the celebrated Parisian music-engraver Pierre Attaignant; it was utilised for the hymn "Was mein Gott will, das g'scheh allzeit" *. One wonders if Bach had any

---

* It was, however, quite a tragic love-song, as will appear from the opening verse:
  Il me suffit de tous mes maulx, puis qu'ils m'ont livré à la mort.
  J'ay enduré peine et travaulx, tant de douleur et décomfort.
  Que faut-il que je fasse pour estre en votre grace?
  De douleur mon cœur est si mort s'il ne voit votre face.

suspicion of this fact when he harmonised the splendid melody for the *St. Matthew Passion!* *

Other French folk-tunes came at a later date into the German chorale by way of the Huguenot Psalter. As the Calvinist church found no sacred folk-songs already in existence, it was compelled to borrow even more largely than the German Church. O. Douen has shown, in his interesting work on *Clément Marot et le Psautier Huguenot***, the process by which the melodies were compiled for the Psalter. Even Calvin had to laugh, — for the only time in his life — when he saw the most frivolous tunes walking along, chastely and devoutly, hand in hand with the lofty poems of David and Solomon.

The Huguenot Psalter appeared in its definitive form in 1562. As early as 1565 Ambrosius Lobwasser, Professor of Law in Königsberg, published a German version of the Psalms, adapting them to the hundred and twenty-five melodies of the French work. These tunes thus became known, and were at once incorporated in the German chorale books. The splendid melody of "Wenn wir in höchsten Nöten sind" (Bach VII, No. 58), comes from the Huguenot Psalter; it was probably a French folk-song originally ***.

Only the shameless curiosity that characterises our boasted historical sense can rejoice at these discoveries. The musician does not trouble himself about them, and forgets them as soon as they are told to him; for they tell him no more than what he already knew by instinct — that all true and deeply-felt music, whether secular or sacred, has its home on the heights where art and religion dwell.

Happy are the chorales of whose origin nothing is known! This was the good fortune of the melodies to Nicolai's

---

* *St. Matthew Passion*, No. 31.
** Etude historique, littéraire, musicale et bibliographique; 2 vols, 1878 and 1879.
*** Philipp Wolfrum gives a comprehensive résumé of the origin of the songs in his *Die Entstehung und erste Entwicklung des deutschen evangelischen Kirchenlieds in musikalischer Beziehung;* Leipzig, 1890.

"Wie schön leuchtet der Morgenstern" and "Wachet auf, ruft uns die Stimme" (Bach VII, No. 57). Both songs appear for the first time in 1598 in the appendix to a treatise on the glories of the future life. When the treasures of melody to be drawn upon were at last exhausted, there came the epoch of the composer. The copious spiritual poetry of the seventeenth century called them to the work. There was scarcely an evangelical musician of that time who did not compose melodies for the church. Almost all the masters whose names adorn the history of polyphonic choral music call for mention also in the history of the origin of the chorale melodies. And it was with the melodies as with the poems: while a great many of a composer's tunes were destined to perish, he managed to breathe the breath of eternal life into a few of them, or at any rate into one, which will shine in imperishable beauty in our hymn-books as long as the evangelical hymn exists. The most notable of these writers is Johann Crüger (1598—1662), of St. Nicholas's church in Berlin, who devoted his art to the poems of Paul Gerhardt and Johann Franck. The most beautiful of his melodies, such as "Jesu meine Freude", "Schmücke dich, o liebe Seele", "Nun danket alle Gott", occupy a place of honour in Bach's work; the very first chorale in the *St. Matthew Passion*, — "Herzliebster Jesu" — is by Crüger.

The spirit, however, which dominated music about the beginning of the eighteenth century made it incapable of developing the true church-tune any further. German music got out of touch with German song, and fell further and further under the influence of the more "artistic" Italian melody. It could no longer achieve that naïveté which, ever since the Middle Ages, had endowed it with those splendid, unique tunes. Moreover the secular music that was then flourishing in the towns and at the courts lured it on to new problems, and it could no longer find its sole satisfaction in a self-denying co-operation with religious poetry.

When Bach came on the scene, the great epoch of chorale creation was at an end, like that of the sacred poem. Sacred melodies were indeed still written; but they were songs of the aria type, not true congregational hymns; an indefinable air of subjectivity pervaded them. In this matter Bach too was subject to the laws of his epoch. When in 1736 Schemelli, cantor at the castle of Zeitz, published through Breitkopf a large hymn-book, containing nine hundred and fifty-four numbers, he approached the famous cantor of St. Thomas's church to beg his co-operation. Bach undertook, we are told in the preface to the book, not only to revise the figured basses, but to compose melodies for the hymns that lacked them. Since in this hymn-book, as in the others, the names of the composers are not given, we cannot be perfectly sure which or how many tunes are by Bach. Those, however, which we can ascribe to him with some certainty, since they cannot be traced to an earlier date, are rather sacred arias than chorales. This description applies, however, only to their character, not their beauty; for their peculiar loveliness comes from the fact that they are the work of an artist brought up on the German chorale, writing under the influence of the formally perfect Italian melodic form. Any one who has been thrilled by the strains of "Komm süßer Tod" or "Liebster Herr Jesu" knows how unspeakably grand these melodies are*. We must not attempt, however, to sing them as congregational songs, or to arrange them for four voices, for then they wither at once, like the water-lily that has been torn from its home. The heaviness and dullness that settle on them nowadays when they are treated as chorales, show clearly that they are not true chorales.

After Bach, the bonds between the chorale and the sacred song are completely broken. The melodies that Emmanuel Bach, Johann Joachim Quantz, Johann Adam Hiller and Beethoven wrote, in artistic rivalry, to Gellert's

---

* The best known edition of these melodies is that of Zahn, *Vierundzwanzig geistliche Lieder für eine Singstimme* (Gütersloh).

poems only show what a distance separated them all from the chorale.

In the epoch of Rationalism, it is true, the melodies were not diluted to the same extent as the text; but there was still a hard struggle until the old melodies were again rehabilitated everywhere, and were no longer jostled in the chorale books by the characterless tunes of the later epoch. Now that this has been achieved, the dispute today is as to whether we shall retain the old chorales with the uniform note-values in which we have received them from the eighteenth century, or whether we should restore to them their original rhythmic variety. A definite decision, indeed, is hardly possible. Each "pro" that can be adduced from historical, artistic, or practical considerations is at once opposed by a "contra" of equal force in its way. Bach is concerned in this controversy to the extent that those who advocate the uniform polished form of chorales can plead that, although the opposite tradition had a powerful following all round him, he felt no artistic compulsion to revert to the old rhythmic form of the chorale, and so there is no cogent objection, from the purely musical point of view, against the chorale as we have received it from his hands. Against the enthusiasts for the rhythmic melodies the old master can plead as St. Paul once did against the Corinthians who knew all things so much better, that he too thinks he is possessed by the spirit.

Here are the three typical forms of "Ein feste Burg": * —

1) Original form of Luther's chorale.

---

* Friedrich Zelle discusses the history of this melody in his *"Studien über 'Ein Feste Burg'"* (Gärtner, Berlin, 1895—1897).

2) Luther's chorale in a hymn-book of 1570 (See Wolfrum, p. 216)

3) Luther's chorale in the form used by Bach.

CHAPTER IV.

THE CHORALE IN THE CHURCH SERVICE.

BIBLIOGRAPHY.

GEORG RIETSCHEL: *Die Aufgabe der Orgel im Gottesdienste bis in das XVIII. Jahrhundert;* Leipzig, 1892.

R. v. LILIENCRON: *Über den Chorgesang in der evangelischen Kirche;* Berlin, 1881.

A. G. RITTER: *Zur Geschichte des Orgelspiels, vornehmlich des deutschen, im XVI. bis zum Anfang des XVIII. Jahrhunderts;* Leipzig, 1881. Vol. I. Text. Vol. II. Musical examples.

See also the works mentioned in the bibliographies to chapters II and III.

How was the congregational song introduced into the church service at the time of the Reformation? It is usual to look upon the question as very simple, and to suppose that the people had little by little come to sing the melody while the organ played it. Did the sacred instrument really teach the congregation in this way?

We may read through all Luther's writings without finding a single place where he speaks of the organ as the

instrument accompanying the congregational singing *.
Moreover he, the admirer of true church music of every
kind, gives no directions as to how the organ is to coöperate
in the service. It is really incredible, however, that in the
few places where he mentions the organ at all, he speaks
of it not enthusiastically but almost scornfully! He does
not look upon it as necessary or even desirable in the
evangelical service, but at most tolerates it where he finds
it already.

His contemporaries shared his view. We need not be
astonished that the Reformed Church dealt drastically
with the organs and banished them from the churches. In
the Lutheran and even in the Catholic churches at that
time it fared almost the same. It had always had, indeed,
its adversaries. No less a person than St. Thomas Aquinas
had declared war on it, not regarding organ music, or
indeed instrumental music in general, as calculated to
stimulate devotion. In the sixteenth century, however,
complaints against it arose on all sides, and the Council of
Trent, (1545—1563), which dealt with all the doubtful
questions relating to the church and its service, was compelled to enact severe regulations against the erroneous and
too prevalent employment of the organ in worship. Catholics and Protestants alike at that time imposed on it a
term of penance, in order that it might alter its ungodly
nature, in default of which the Church would excommuni-
cate it.

It had fully merited this disgrace. The character of the
tasks allotted to it may be seen from the *Cæremoniale
Episcoporum* issued by Pope Clement VIII in the year

---

* The following remarks are in the main a repetition of the
views of Geo. Rietschel, expressed in his masterly essay on *Die
Aufgabe der Orgel im Gottesdienste bis in das XVIII. Jahrhundert*
(Leipzig 1892). Rietschel is the first to have thrown a light on this
question, since, instead of spinning theories, he lets the documents, —
church regulations, prefaces to hymn-books, sermons at the dedi-
cations of organs, and funeral orations on organists — speak for
themselves.

1600. The organ preludised in order to give the tone to the priest or the choir. It further gave out the liturgical songs and hymns in alternation with the choir, one verse being sung and the next played on the organ. It was never used, however, to accompany the choir. The primitive structure of the organs of that time quite forbade this; their heavy keys did not permit of polyphonic playing, while their crude, untempered tuning made it as a rule impossible to play on them in more than one or two keys. Since therefore they could not coöperate, the choir and the organ functioned in turns. When the organ had completed its verse, the text, in accordance with the above-mentioned regulations of the Pope, was either recited loudly by a chorister, or else sung, which latter was recommended as the better course *.

With the organ employed in this independent way, abuses could not fail to creep in. As the organist was unable to play polyphonically on his instrument, he was tempted to amuse himself with quick running passages in his preambles to the verses or during the course of these. Still worse was it when he indulged in well-known secular songs, which seems to have been a wide-spread practice. In 1548 an organist in Strassburg was dismissed from his post for having played French and Italian songs during the offertory **.

At a later date the organ unwarrantably deprived the choir of many of the hymns, taking almost everything upon itself. The extent to which this had become prevalent appears from an incident that happened to Luther, which

---

* *Cæremoniale Episcoporum: Papst Clemens VIII.* 1600. Cap. 28: De Organo, Organista et Musicis seu cantoribus et norma per eos servanda in divinis. "Sed advertendum erit, ut quandocuncque per organum figuratur aliquid cantari seu responderi alternatim versiculis Hymnorum aut Canticorum, ab aliquo de choro intelligibili voce pronuntietur id quod ab organo respondendum est. Et laudabile esset, ut aliquis cantor conjunctim cum organo voce clara idem cantaret."
** Rietschel, p. 41.

he tells in his best style in the *Table Talk*: "When I was a young monk in Erfurt", he says, "and had to make the rounds of the villages, I came to a certain village and celebrated mass there. When I had dressed myself and stepped before the altar in my fine attire, the clerk began to strike the *Kyrie eleison* and the *Patrem* on the lute. I could with difficulty keep from laughing, for I was not used to such an organ; I had to make my *Gloria in excelsis* conform to his *Kyrie*."

It seemed so much a matter of course at that time to substitute the organ for the choir in the liturgy that this clerk, in default of an organ, simply had recourse to the lute!

In the Evangelical church the rôle of the organ had for a long time now been the same as in the Catholic church. It preambled to the hymns of the priest and the choir and alternated with the latter; only now the congregational song is merely an addendum, to which the organ preambles and wherewith it alternates. In Wittenberg it preambled to almost all the vocal pieces, whether of priest, choir or people, and shared with the choir in the rendering of the *Kyrie*, the *Gloria* and the *Agnus Dei*. We learn this from Wolfgang Musculus, who in 1536 attended the Concordia conferences at Wittenberg, and described the singing at the service in the Wittenberg parish church on the fifth Sunday after Easter *.

This explains the curious injunction which we find in the church ordinances of the fifteenth and sixteenth centuries, namely that the organ "shall *strike* into the song in the churches". It means that certain verses are to be played by the organist alone, the congregation being silent. At the same time the caution is given that this must not happen too often, but at the most two or three times in the one hymn. It is so laid down in the "Strassburg Church-ordinance" of 1598,** and, in exactly the same way, in the

---

* Rietschel, p. 13; Luther's *Tischreden*, ed. Erlanger, p. 399.
** Rietschel, p. 21 ff.

"Nuremberg Congregation ordinance" of 1606. At first, and for another three generations at least, there was no question of the organ *accompanying* the congregational singing.

How did the choir stand with regard to the congregational chorale? Did it take the place of the organ, guiding and supporting the song of the people? A glance at the earliest hymn books appointed for the service shows us that this solution also did not occur to Luther.

The above-mentioned * *Erfurt Enchiridion* of Justus Jonas was a hymn-book not for the church but for the home, as, indeed, its title expressly indicates. The melody alone was noted over the poem, so that the father of the household could give it out to the children and the servants. The Strassburg reformer Catharina Zell hoped that "a poor mother should go to sleep, and, if at midnight the crying child had to be rocked, sing it a song of heavenly things;" this would be the right kind of lullaby, and would please God more than all the lullabies played on the organ in the Catholic church **.

The *Church chorale book* published at Wittenberg in 1524 by Luther and Walther, while the *Enchiridion* was being printed at Erfurt, makes no reference whatever to congregational singing. It merely consists, in fact, of the vocal parts of chorales written in four and five parts, and the cooperation of the faithful is barred at the outset by the fact that the chorale melody lies in the tenor, not in the soprano ***. These vocal parts, — which were probably engraved by Luther's friend, the painter and wood engraver Lucas Cranach — are those of chorale motets sung by the choir, and therefore having a cantus firmus, as was customary in the religious and secular music of that time.

---

* See p. 7.

** Catharina Zell, in the preface to her *Gesangbüchlein* of 1534. See Rietschel, p. 26.

*** The title of this edition of the vocal parts runs: *Geystliche Gesanck-Büchlein:* Wittenberg, 1524. It contains thirty-eight hymns.

Luther was not only a reformer but an artist. The logical outcome of his reforming ideas would have been a remodelling of the church service on the lines of the simple home service, in which case the congregational chorale would have been the only music used in the church. This, indeed, is the line we find him pursuing in his first drastic treatise on the service *. But, as in most men of genius, there was a fatal side to his greatness that prevented him from thinking out his ideas to their logical conclusion, and made him endow a thing and its antithesis with equal life. He was an admirer of the contrapuntal music of the Netherlands school. He regarded artistic music as one of the most perfect manifestations of the Deity. "When natural music is heightened and polished by art", he said once, "there man first beholds and can with great wonder examine to a certain extent, (for it cannot be wholly seized or understood) the great and perfect wisdom of God in His marvellous work of music, in which this is most singular and indeed astonishing, that one man sings a simple tune or tenor (as musicians call it), together with which three, four or five voices also sing, which as it were play and skip delightedly round this simple tune or tenor, and wonderfully grace and adorn the said tune with manifold devices and sounds, performing as it were a heavenly dance, so that those who at all understand it and are moved by it must be greatly amazed, and believe that there is nothing more extraordinary in the world than such a song adorned with many voices." The wonders of contrapuntal polyphony have never been so admirably described before or since **.

His favorite composers were Josquin des Près (1450—1521), the court musician to Louis XII. of France, and Heinrich

---

* *Ordnung des Gottesdienstes in der Gemeine;* 1523.

** The passage is to be found in the so-called *Lobrede Luthers auf die Musik*, which, however, — as H. Holstein showed in 1883 — is simply a preface which he orginally wrote in Latin to Johann Walther's *Lob und Preis der himmlischen Kunst Musica* (2nd ed. 1564). See Rietschel, p. 36.

Isaak's pupil Ludwig Senfl (died 1550), who was successively in the service of the courts of Vienna and Munich. His remark upon Josquin is well-known: "He is the master of the notes; they have to do as he wills; other composers have to do as the notes will." On one occasion, when a motet of Senfl's was being performed in his house, he called out: "I could not write such a motet if I were to tear myself to pieces, just as he, for his part, could not preach a sermon like me" *.

The musician in Luther could not tolerate the banishment of choir and art-song from the church, as many people desired, or the restriction of the choir to leading the congregational singing. "And I am not of the opinion" he says in the preface to Walther's chorale parts of 1524, "that on account of the Gospel all the arts should be crushed out of existence, as some over-religious people pretend, but I would willingly see all the arts, especially music, in the service of Him who has given and created them" **.

A licence was thus granted to the art in the Lutheran service; it took its place in the ritual as a free and independent power. All the phases of the development of music in general are to be clearly seen in the Lutheran service. Finally, when the motet, under the influence of Italian art, was transformed into the cantata, bringing not only instrumental music but an undisguised opera-style into the church, the service actually came to be interrupted by a sacred concert, which was looked upon as its culminating point. It was at this juncture that Bach came on the scene. On the covers of his scores he writes, not "cantata", but "concerto".

Thus had Luther not been an artist, Bach would never have been able to write his sacred concert-music for church purposes and as part of the church service. Would

---

* Luther's *Tischreden*, ed. Irmischer, B. 62.
** Friedrich Zelle, *Das älteste lutherische Hausgesangbuch;* Göttingen, 1903, p. 10.

he nevertheless have written it in any case? What would he have done had he been born in Zürich or in Geneva?

At first, then, the congregational chorale was not supported either by the organ or by the choir, but sung *unisono* without accompaniment, precisely as in the Catholic church at the end of the Middle Ages.

We must not over-estimate the number of the congregational chorales that were sung during a service. Where a choir existed, the congregation took little part in the singing, being restricted to the *Credo*, — sung between the reading of the Gospel and the sermon — and perhaps a communion hymn. In Wittenberg — so it appears from the account given by Musculus, — the congregation as a rule did not sing, but left even the chorales to the choir. In other places, — Erfurt, for example, — it was customary for the people to sing alternately with the choir between the Epistle and the Gospel, in such a way that the choir sang the sequence and the people joined in with a German chorale appropriate to the time of the year. Five or six chorales in the year sufficed for this, since the same chorale was used on each Sunday during that particular period.

In the churches that had no choir, more importance attached to the congregational singing, since in that case the *Kyrie*, the *Gloria* and the *Agnus Dei* were sung in the corresponding German chorales. But here again, as a rule, fifteen or at most twenty chorales, which had been laid down, once for all, for their particular Sundays, sufficed for the whole year.

On closer inspection we get the impression that the congregational singing, instead of gaining ground, was in the course of the sixteenth century driven back by the art-singing and by the organ, the pretensions of the latter increasing everywhere, in spite of all ordinances *.

There was thus good cause for the attempt that was made, at the end of the first century of the Reformation, —

---

* Rietschel, p. 49.

not indeed by a musician but by a priest — to improve the
position of the chorale. In 1586 the Würtemberg court
preacher Lucas Osiander published his *Fünffzig geistliche
Lieder und Psalmen, mit vier Stimmen auf kontrapunkt-
weise, für die Kirchen und Schulen im löblichen Fürstentumb
Würtemberg, also gesetzet, dass eine gantze christliche Gemein
durchaus mitsingen kann.*" ("Fifty sacred songs and psalms,
for the churches and schools in the worshipful principality
of Würtemberg, set contrapuntally in four parts in such a
way that the whole Christian congregation can always join
in them"). This was the first real chorale book in our
sense, except that it was written for the choir instead of
for the organ. The fact that Osiander relies only on the
choir, not on the organ, for the leading of the congregational
singing, proves that the instrument in his time had no
concern whatever with the latter *.

In his preface he expresses his confidence that he has
made things easier by removing the melody from the
tenor to the soprano, and thinks that when the laity
recognise the tune they will joyfully take part in it**.

Was not his confidence misplaced? It was indeed only a
half-measure, a false compromise between polyphony and
melody. If he wanted polyphony, he should have allowed
the whole congregation to sing in chorus in four parts,
as was the custom later in Switzerland; on the other hand,
if he wished to do without polyphony, he should have let
the choir sing in unison, acting, as it were, as precentor,
somewhat in the way the village cantors in his day led the
chorale without choir or organ, simply by the unison singing
of the school children. His desire, however, was to reconcile
artistic singing and popular singing, and instead of a
solution he achieved only an unstable compromise. For

---

* Friedrich Zelle, *Das erste evangelische Choralbuch Osianders,
1586*; Berlin, 1903.

** The fact that among the thirty-eight songs in Walther's
vocal parts of 1524 two have the *cantus firmus* in the soprano does
not, of course, imply that the congregation was expected to take
part in these two.

what support could the harmonies of a choir — and the choirs at that time were very weak in numbers — give to a *cantus firmus* sung by a mass of people?

Hans Leo Hassler also tried to make a forward step in this direction, and published, besides his splendid *Cantiones sacrae* and *Sacri concertus* (for performance by the choir only), his *Kirchengesäng, Psalmen und geistliche Lieder auf die gemeinen Melodien mit vier Stimmen simpliciter gesetzt*, which, according to the preface, were so constructed that the ordinary man could sing them in the Christian assembly to figurate music.*

It would be wrong, however, to suppose that all the masters of church music who, in the sixteenth and seventeenth centuries, removed the melody to the soprano part, were imitators of Osiander, and that it was for purely practical reasons that they abandoned the earlier system. The real reason is quite different, and must be sought in the fact that in the meantime German church music had shaken off the influence of the purely contrapuntal music of the Netherlands school, and had fallen under that of the Italians, in which the melodic style began to dominate the contrapuntal. Melchior Vulpius,** Seth Calvisius,*** Michael

---

* Hans Leo Hassler was born in Nuremberg in 1564. The Fugger family sent him, when he was twenty, to Venice, to study music with the masters living there. From 1601—1608 he was organist and choir-master in his native town; in 1608 he was called by the Electoral Prince to Dresden. His constitution, however, was already almost ruined by consumption. He died the 8th June 1612 in Frankfort, whither he had accompanied his master to the assembly of princes.

** Melchior Vulpius was born in 1560. In 1600 he became Cantor at Weimar; his death in 1616 was a great loss to art. *Pars prima cantionum sacrarum cum VI, VII, VIII, et pluribus vocibus;* Jena, 1602. *Kirchengesäng und geistliche Lieder;* Erfurt, 1603. A *St. Matthew Passion* of his was also published at Erfurt.

*** Seth Calvisius, born in 1556, was equally famous in his day as philologist, mathematician and musician. He was one of the predecessors of Bach at St. Thomas's church in Leipzig. He died in 1615. *Kirchengesänge und geistliche Lieder Dr. Lutheri und anderer frommer Christen* ..... *mit vier Stimmen contrapunktweis richtig gesetzt;* Leipzig 1597.

Praetorius,* and Johann Eccard** thus follow in their admirable music not so much the lead of the Würtemberg Court preacher as the trend of the art itself.

It was a pure accident that through this change in polyphonic art the possibility was opened to the congregation to join in the *cantus firmus* with the choir. How far it availed itself of it we do not know, for in the history of art, as a rule, we never get to know the things that would be of practical interest to us, for these, being looked upon as matters of daily custom, are not recorded. The fact that at this epoch the term "chorale" begins to be applied to the melodies sung by the congregation throws no light on the question,*** unless we regard it as proving that by this time the melodies of the church song had ceased to be congregational property and had become the property of the choir.

In any case the composers themselves, in spite of the fine practical suggestions as to congregational singing that they put forward in their prefaces, thought only of the choir when composing, as is shown by their counterpoint, which, with all its simplicity, becomes richer and more and more in the style of the motet.† For us these chorale pieces,

---

* Michael Praetorius (1571—1621) was Kapellmeister to the Duke of Brunswick. *Musae Sionae: Geistliche Concertgesänge über die fürnembsten Teutsche Psalmen und Lieder, wie sie in der christlichen Kirche gesungen werden mit VIII und XII Stimmen gesetzt:* (1605—1610, 9 vols., containing 1244 hymns).

** Johannes Eccard, born in 1553, studied at Munich with Orlando Lasso. After he had been for some time Kapellmeister to the Fugger family at Augsburg, he entered in 1585 the service of the Duke of Prussia at Königsberg, where he at once began the collection and harmonisation of the melodies in vogue in Prussia. His great work, *Geistliche Lieder auf den Choral, oder die gebräuchliche Kirchenmelodie gerichtet und fünfstimmig gesetzt* (Königsberg 1597 & 1598) is the result of these labours. In 1608 the Electoral Prince Joachim Friedrich summoned him to Berlin. He died in 1612.

*** Until then the only term in use had been "sacred song".

† Reference may be made to the preface of Eccard to the hymns he published in 1597, and to that of Michael Praetorius to the *Musae Sionae*. Only one thing is clear from their remarks, — that so far as they are concerned they are merely experimenting. See also Rietschel, pp. 54 ff.

with their singularly beautiful blending of Italian and
German art, are choral works pure and simple, and the
idea of trying again the experiment of letting the congregation join in them would not occur to us. But if only
we could hear them even as choral works! When will the
time come when these treasures are exhibited each Sunday
in our church services?

The attempts to have the singing of the congregation
led by the choir were made about the end of the sixteenth
century and in the first decade of the seventeenth. By
the middle of the seventeenth century the question is
settled by the organ assuming this rôle. In 1650 appears
the *Tablature-book* of Samuel Scheidt, with a hundred
chorale harmonisations intended for the accompaniment of
the congregational singing.*

This was no thought-out experiment, but a solution
arising out of the facts, i. e. the progress of organ-building.
The sacred instrument had in the meantime been made
more practically fitted for polyphonic playing, and endowed
with such fulness of tone that it overwhelmed the small
and weak choirs of that time. Whereas hitherto it had
accompanied the choir, which supported the singing of
the congregation, its powerful tone now made it possible
for it to assume the lead. But again we cannot be sure of
the date at which the organ began to support the choir
in the chorale, or when it began to coöperate with the
choir in general. This was certainly not the case before
the beginning of the seventeenth century. Vulpius,
Praetorius, Eccard and the others appear to know nothing
of it. But as early as 1627 Johann Hermann Schein,
Cantor of St. Thomas's church in Leipzig, adds a figured

---

* *Tablaturbuch* 100 *geistlicher Lieder und Psalmen Doctoris
Martini Lutheri und anderer gottseliger Männer, für die Herren
Organisten, mit der christlichen Kirchen und Gemeine auf der Orgel,
desgleichen auch zu Hause, zu spielen und zu singen. Auf alle Feste
und Sonntage durchs gantze Jahr. Mit vier Stimmen componiert
von Samuel Scheidt.* (Görlitz, 1650). Scheidt (1587—1654) was
organist at Halle. He is the real father of German organ music.

bass, — intended for "organists, instrumentalists, and lutenists" — to the four, five, and six-part chorale pieces for the choir in his *Cantionale* of that year; and this most probably points to a joint performance by choir and organ.*

We must not, however, conceive the organ accompaniment to the chorale, as it was practised in the second half of the seventeenth century, as a supplanting of the choir by the organ in the chorale. The choir, even in Bach's time, coöperated in the chorale as in earlier times, — polyphonically indeed — although the organ took the lead, as it were a kind of second and stronger choir without words.

This transference of vocal polyphony to the organ by means of chorale accompaniment was of cardinal significance to the art of organ music. The chorale was the teacher of the organists, leading them from the false and fruitless virtuosity of the keyboard to the true, simple organ style. From this moment German organ music severs itself from that of Italy, France, and the Netherlands, and, always under the control of the chorale, pursues the path along which, in the course of two generations, it was to arrive at perfection. Scheidt, already in possession of the true organ style derived from the chorale, sees that his life-work consists in combating the "colored" organ style of the school of the Dutchman Sweelinck.**

It is an illustration of how an idea is, in the end, always stronger than circumstances. Organ music did not come

---

* Rietschel, pp. 57 and 53. In 1637 Theophilus Stade, organist of St. Lorenz's in Nuremberg, brought out a new edition of Hassler's hymns, with a preface in which he dedicates them to his "dear and faithful colleagues who, by means of the organ, maintain the congregation in the right tune, height and depth." This shows that at that time, in Nuremberg, the organ participated to some extent in the chorale. How it did so, however, cannot be gathered either from the preface or from the book itself. But the mere employment of the organ with the choir is an interesting fact.

** Jan Pieters Sweelinck (1540—1621) was organist at Amsterdam. All the North German organists came under his influence.

to perfection in Paris or in Venice, where everything seemed to be in its favour, but among the poor cantors and schoolmasters of an impoverished country, as the Germany of the two generations after the Thirty Years' War was. How small Frescobaldi, the organist of St. Peter's in Rome, whose fame among his contemporaries was so great, seems beside a Samuel Scheidt, whose name was unknown on the other side of the Alps! *

From the moment when organ, choir and congregation together gave out the chorale, it was inevitable that the antiphonal method, under which the organ alone performed certain of the verses, should sooner or later fall into disuse. But of the perfection of these independent organ renderings at that time we may judge from Scheidt's *Tablatura nova*, published in 1624. It consists for the most part of a species of variations upon the chorales most generally used, — the number of variations corresponding to the number of verses of the song, — and upon the hymns of the various seasons of the church year, which at that time were still sung in Halle in Latin, and not, as in other places, in German. In addition there are liturgical pieces, such as the *Kyrie, Gloria, Magnificat,* and the *Psalmus sub communione* "Jesus Christus unser Heiland", which are all treated in the same way.**

---

* At the same time the technical powers of the Roman organists were in some respects really extraordinary. It is only lately, when the works as well as the names of these men have become known to us, that we have been able to estimate these powers. Special reference may be made to Alex. Guilmant's *Archives des Maîtres de l'orgue,* which up to the present have contained the compositions of Titelouze, A. Raison, Roberday, L. Marchand, Clérambault, du Mage, d'Aquin Gigault, Grigny, F. Couperin, Boyvin and Dandrieu. A study of these works gives one the impression that Bach knew more of them, and was more influenced by these composers, than is generally supposed. These publications, that supply one of the most important chapters in the history of organ music, should be available in every library. Very many of these old pieces are still suitable for performance.

** Scheidt's *Tablatura nova* is in three parts. The first two contain the chorales, in which each verse is made the subject of a

The Celli Tablature that appeared twenty-three years earlier is on the same lines, except that it also contains the complete "catechism songs".

How long the custom, testified to in all contemporary tablatures, of rendering vocal pieces on the organ alone, still lasted after the process of decay had once set in, can no longer be ascertained. When we consider the extremely numerous arrangements by Bach of the chorale "Allein Gott in der Höh sei Ehr", we are inclined to think that even down to his day there persisted, under certain circumstances, the practice testified to by Scheidt, of the organ responding to the *Gloria* intoned by the priest at the altar.   ·

As to the position of the congregational singing in Bach's time, we have only conjecture to go upon. One thing at any rate had been achieved, — the number of the hymns affiliated to the service had considerably increased. Each Gospel had one or more of these allotted to it, so that the same ones were always sung on a particular Sunday. They were called the *Cantica de tempore;* in the hymn-books they formed the first class and were arranged according to the Sundays of the ecclesiastical year. The cantor selected them himself without consulting anyone else. In our day, on the contrary, the hymns are always selected by the clergyman, to tally with the spirit of his sermon.

---

separate musical treatment, together with variations of the same kind upon secular songs, such as the *cantio Belgica* "Wehe, Windgen, wehe" (twelve verses) the *cantio Gallica* "Est-ce Mars" (ten verses), and the German song "Also geht's, also steht's" (seven verses). The third part, with the *Kyries, Glorias, Magnificats* in the various tones, and hymns, is meant to serve as a liturgical annual for organists. The hymns are: —

    Hymnus de adventu: Veni redemptor.
    Hymnus de nativitate: A Solus ortus cardine.
    Hymnus tempore quadragesimali: Christe qui lux es et dies.
    Hymnus de resurrectione: Vita sanctorum, decus angelorum.
    Hymnus de sancto spiritu: Veni creator spiritus.
    Hymnus de sancta Trinitate: O Lux, beata Trinitas. Credo (Choralis in Basso).
    Psalmus sub communione: "Jesus Christus unser Heiland".

This use of the *Cantica de tempore* helps us to understand how the organists of the time of Pachelbel and Bach came to write cycles of chorale preludes for each Sunday of the ecclesiastical year.

Whether the congregation took possession of all these hymns and took an active and hearty part in the singing of them is, however, another question. It is well known that Mattheson and the famous Hamburg musicians thought nothing at all of the congregational chorale, and in general refused to recognise singing of this kind as music. From this we may conclude that it did not occupy a prominent place in their churches, and that they, for their part, did nothing to encourage it. It must have been the same in other towns that had celebrated choirs. The cantata — that sacred concert intercalated in the service — absorbed all the interest, and the art-song, as at the beginning of the Reformation, had once more triumphed.

We do not know whether things were better in this respect in Leipzig than in other towns. The truth is that no remark of Bach's has come down to us to show that, in contradistinction to his contemporaries, he felt any particular interest in congregational singing. In his Passions, at any rate, he does not desire its co-operation, in spite of the splendid rôle that he assigns to the chorale in those works. It is highly probable that in Bach's time the singing of the Leipzig congregations was not so good as is commonly supposed.

Not until the concert style of music was banished from the service, in the generation after Bach, and the town choirs that had been allotted to the churches ceased to exist, did congregational singing become the characteristic and sole service-music of the Protestant church. In the epoch of rationalism and pietism the ideal was realised which the Reformation had indeed perceived, but, for conservative and artistic reasons, had not pursued. However barbarously rationalism behaved towards the old hymn, it did good work for congregational singing. Its ultimate aim, of course, was to substitute a new kind of hymn for the old, the diction and the ideas of which had by then become so antiquated as to unfit it for use as a real congregational hymn.

Whether the problem has been really solved by allowing the organ to support the congregational singing is doubtful. The method has established itself, because it is practical. But the ideal is not congregational singing of this kind, directed by, and dependent on, the organ; the true ideal is free and confident unaccompanied singing, as in the congregational singing of the Middle Ages and of the first Reformation period. Perhaps that complete and unfettered cooperation of organ, choir and worshippers was, in its way, an ideal, towards which we shall some day aspire more than we do now.

CHAPTER V.

THE CHORALE PRELUDES BEFORE BACH.

BIBLIOGRAPHY.

PHILIPP SPITTA: *J. S. Bach.* I. 96 etc.

A. G. RITTER: *Zur Geschichte des Orgelspiels, vornehmlich des deutschen, im XIV. bis zum Anfang des XVIII. Jahrhunderts;* Leipzig, 1884; 2 vols.

CARL VON WINTERFELD: *Der evangelische Kirchengesang;* vol. II, 1845.

FRANZ COMMER: *Musica sacra.* Bote and Bock, Berlin.

M. STRAUBE: *Alte Meister des Orgelspiels;* Peters, Leipzig 1904.

In proportion as the independent performance of the verses of the songs and hymns on the organ fell into disuse through the logic of events, preludising on the chorale became of importance. How this preludising was carried out until the time of Scheidt we do not know, since no compositions of this kind have been preserved. None even of Scheidt's have come down to us. But from his time to that of Bach the most notable German masters of the organ dedicate their powers not to free composition but to the chorale prelude, or, as they said in those days, to "preambling to the chorales".

The three great masters in this field are Pachelbel, Böhm and Buxtehude. We cannot, indeed, say that in technique they created anything new beyond Scheidt. In this respect, indeed, organ music has on the whole not gone beyond the Halle master even to the present day; nor can we imagine how it is ever to be done. Scheidt was one of those men whose penetrating intelligence, when a new world opens out before them, darts through it at once from end to end, with the clearness and swiftness of light. In his polyphonic chorale verses for the organ he saw himself faced by the problem of making the melody stand out clearly in performance, with a special tone-colour, not only in the soprano but also in the alto, tenor and bass; and at a glance he surveyed all possible solutions, and embodied his knowledge in those famous pieces which, speaking generally, contain everything that we can imagine in the way of employing the manuals and pedals in conformity with their special qualities.*

---

* See the well-known remarks at the end of the third part of the *Tablatura nova* (1624): "If it is a *Bicinium*" [i. e. in two parts] "and the chorale a discant, the chorale is to be played with the right hand on the upper manual or 'work', while the left hand plays the two parts on the *Rückpositiv*. If the chorale is a discant with four parts, the chorale is played on the *Rückpositiv* with the right hand, the alto and tenor on the upper manual or 'work' with the left hand, and the bass with the pedal. If the chorale is a tenor, the chorale is played on the *Rückpositiv* with the left hand, the other parts on the upper manual or 'work' with the right hand, and the bass with the pedal. The alto can also, in special circumstances, be played with four parts on the *Rückpositiv*, but the discant must be taken on the upper manual with the right hand, and the tenor and the bass on the pedal in two parts at the same time, but it must be particularly arranged so that the tenor does not go higher than $\bar{c}$, since the d is seldom found on the pedals, and they must also not be set widely apart from each other, only an octave, or fifth, or third, for otherwise we cannot fully span such intervals with the feet.

"NB. But this is the finest and most suitable style of all, to play the alto on the pedal; the knack and dexterity however are in

In the third decade of the seventeenth century he speaks of the playing of two obbligato parts on the pedal as quite a matter of course, and thinks that every organ should have a four-feet pedal stop, so that the organist may be able, under any circumstances, to play a middle part with the feet!

The path was now traced out for the organ players, and, — what in the first place was almost more important, — for the organ builders.* They had only to go forward. Middle German and North German organ music outdistanced that of the Romans and the Southern Germans almost at a bound. Spitta rightly says that what was regarded in the south as a test of the highest virtuosity looks almost like an elementary exercise in comparison with the compositions of the northern organists.**

Thus as regards technique there were no new conquests for Pachelbel, Böhm, Buxtehude and their epoch to strive after. It was reserved for them, however, to create the various forms of the chorale prelude.

Pachelbel's conception of it is almost the grandest;*** he conceives the chorale prelude as a chorale fugue. Each

---

the registering and the colouring in the organ, and knowing how to make good use of four or eight-feet tones. An eight-feet tone must always be on the positive, and a four-feet tone on the pedal."

* On the development of the art of organ building see Otto Wangemann, *Geschichte der Orgel und der Orgelbaukunst*, Demmin 1880; and *Die Orgel, ihre Geschichte und ihr Bau*, 3rd ed., Leipzig 1895.

** *Über J. S. Bach* (*Sammlung musikalischer Vorträge;* Leipzig, 1879).

*** Johann Pachelbel was born in 1653. From 1674 to 1677 he was assistant organist at St. Stephen's in Vienna. Later on we find him in Eisenach, Erfurt — where he remained twelve years — Stuttgart and Gotha. In 1695 he became organist at St. Sebald's, in his native town of Nuremberg. He died in 1706. His works are:

Acht Choräle zum Präambulieren, published by Christian Weigel, Nuremberg, 1693.

Tabulaturbuch geistlicher Gesänge D. Martini Lutheri und anderer gottseliger Männer sambt beygefügten Choral-Fugen durchs gantze Jahr. Allen Liebhabern des Claviers componieret von Johann Pachelben, Organisten zu St. Sebald in Nürnberg, 1704; containing

separate phrase of the melody is worked out in a fughetta-like prelude, at the conclusion of which it appears as a *cantus firmus.* The chorale prelude as a whole thus consists simply of separate fugues, which are held together by the fact that their themes, taken in succession, form the melody of the chorale. It is the form of the chorale prelude as we have it, for example, in the two great arrangements by Bach of *Aus tiefer Not* (VI. Nos. 13 and 14).

This style was very largely cultivated at that time. Pachelbel exercised an influence upon central Germany that cannot easily be over-estimated. He was not a genius; he was not even always clever, and his art is not free from a certain stiffness and formality. He had, however, a real sense of the dignity of the organ, and communicated it to his pupils. That was his greatest service. We must remember that in Scheidt, as in Frescobaldi, a secular conception of organ music as an art exists side by side with the religious conception of it. Even the *Tablatura nova* bears traces of this dualism, for it impartially gives variations upon secular songs and upon chorales. With Pachelbel this impartiality disappears for ever from German organ music.

If the average level of German organ playing in Bach's time was higher than any that has been attained since, it was entirely owing to Pachelbel. As a type of that generation of organists we may mention Johann Gottfried Walther, Bach's colleague at Weimar, whom Mattheson, the Hamburg author, called "Pachelbel the second".* He

---

160 harmonisations of melodies, and 80 small chorale preludes. (The manuscript is in the Grand-ducal Library at Weimar.)

Examples of Pachelbel's chorales will be found in Ritter and Commer. A portion of his work has appeared in the *Denkmäler der Tonkunst in Oesterreich,* VIII. Jahrg. Bd. II.

* Johann Gottfried Walther, born in 1684, was intended for the study of law, but at an early age showed such rich musical gifts that in 1702 he was made organist at Weimar. In 1707 he became organist at the Town Church at Weimar — Bach being at that time at the Court — in which post he remained until his death (1748). He is best known as the author of the *Musikalische Lexikon* (Leipzig,

composed, as Mattheson tells us in his *Critica musica* (1725), a complete year of chorale preludes of the Pachelbel type. Two of them, by an error of transmission, were included among Bach's works.* This is a testimony to the art of them. They are, indeed, written in a correct organ-style, that at times shows considerable richness of invention. The chorale preludes of Johann Christoph Bach (1642—1703, organist at Eisenach, and Johann Michael Bach (1648—1694), organist at Gehren, (the uncles of John Sebastian), also give us an idea of the thorough capabilities of the organists of Pachelbel's generation.**

With all its excellencies, however, the Pachelbel form of the chorale prelude labours under the grave artistic defect of incoherence. The chorale melody — the bond that should hold together the separate fughettas, — cannot really give them intrinsic unity. In the last resort they amount to no more than a string of fragments.

The chorale prelude of the Pachelbel type is, indeed, really conceived on choral lines. When the words are added to the melody, the two together weld together the separate fugal movements into an effective whole. In the chorale choruses in Bach's cantatas that are constructed on the model of Pachelbel's chorale preludes, — in the cantata *Ein Feste Burg* for example, — the impression of homogeneity is very strong. In Pachelbel's chorale preludes, where the melody is deprived of the words, this is not

---

1732), which contains very valuable articles upon the music and musicians of his day. His great collection of chorale preludes by all kinds of composers is also important. More than thirty chorale preludes of Buxtehude's have been preserved for us solely in Walther's transcriptions.

* Bach VI. Nos. 24 and 28. (See Spitta I, 382, II, 37.)

** Forty-four of Johann Christoph Bach's chorale preludes, and seventy-two of Johann Michael's, have come down to us. We may also mention Friedrich Wilhelm Zachau (died 1714), of the Liebfrauenkirche in Halle, — the teacher of Handel, and Johann Kuhnau (1667—1722), Bach's predecessor in the cantorship of St. Thomas's Church, Leipzig. Tunder, Buxtehude's predecessor in Lübeck, appears also to have done important work in this field, but unfortunately little of his organ work has been preserved.

the case; each fughetta has an independent existence. This was perceived by the composers of the time, who consequently felt themselves justified in elevating the fughettas upon the first lines of the chorale to the status of independent compositions. It may be taken as certain that a number of the surviving chorale fughettas of Pachelbel upon the first lines of the chorale originally belonged to complete chorale preludes, and were first separated from the whole by the copyist, for reasons of a practical nature.*

Böhm,** the Lüneburg master, has an entirely different conception of the chorale prelude. He is under the influence of the "coloristic" style of the school of Sweelinck. His favorite method is to break the chorale melody up into luxuriant coloratura, and to keep this rich and flowing paraphrase moving about over a simple harmonic accompaniment of a more or less free nature. He has nothing of Pachelbel's formal dignity; his works are all life and movement. He makes use of the *basso ostinato*, i. e., the continual repetition of a characteristic motive in the pedal, a means with which Bach, in his chorale preludes, afterwards attained such striking effects. Bach's arrangement of *Nun kommt der Heiden Heiland* (VII. No. 45) will give some idea of the style of Böhm.

Only parenthetic mention can be made of the Hamburg organist Johann Adam Reinken, who has attained a certain fame in the history of the chorale prelude by means of two works of appalling length. Heinrich Scheidemann, a pupil of Sweelinck, organist at St Catharine's church in Hamburg, had been his teacher. Reinken succeeded to

---

* This is certainly the case with a number of the small chorale preludes from the Tablature Book of 1704. See Eitner, *Monatshefte für Musikgeschichte*, 1874, and Ritter, *Geschichte des Orgelspiels* I, 151.

** Georg Böhm, born in 1661, became organist in 1698 of St. John's Church in Lüneburg, which post he filled until his death in 1733. Eighteen of his chorales have been preserved. Examples will be found in Commer, Ritter, A. W. Gottschalg's collection, and Straube's *Alte Meister des Orgelspiels* (Peters, 1904).

the latter's post in 1664, and occupied it fifty-eight years,
until his death in 1722. He was very proud of his two
lengthy chorales. The first, on "Es ist gewisslich an der
Zeit", contained two hundred and thirty-two bars; the
other, on "An Wasserflüssen Babylons", ran to three hundred and thirty-five. He had the latter engraved on copper.
The melody, as in Böhm, moves about in colorature of all
kinds, while the accompaniment, which is more in Pachelbel's
style, is constructed out of the motives of the separate
lines of the melody. He uses the double pedal a good
deal.

Great as is the technique and the virtuosic ability shewn
in these two works, from the musical point of view they
are unsatisfactory. Everything is calculated merely for
outward effect. The melody is tormented to death, and
the hearer feasts on the dexterity of the torture.*

Incomparably higher stands the Lübeck organist Dietrich
Buxtehude (1637—1707), who in 1668 succeeded the famous
Franz Tunder at St. Mary's Church. He is the greatest
organist between Scheidt and Bach, and may, indeed, be
regarded as the real creator of the German organ toccata.**
His chorale preludes are chorale fantasias of the most
varied kinds, from the simplest to the most ingenious.
In the simple ones the melody goes its way quietly, just
embellished here and there with a few ornaments, and
accompanied by interesting and always ingenious harmonies.
Bach's chorale preludes upon *Herzlich thut mich verlangen*
(V. No. 27) and *Liebster Jesu wir sind hier* (V. No. 36), are
written in the style of these simple fantasias of Buxtehude,

---

* An analysis of the chorale prelude "An Wasserflüssen Babylons" is given by Ritter. All the same, Reinken is a notable
artist.

** The organ toccata derives ultimately from Claudio Merulo
(1532—1604), the great master of the Venetian organ school, which
in turn developed out of the school of the Netherlands. The toccata was afterwards brought by Frescobaldi to the highest perfection it ever reached in Italy. In Georg Muffat's celebrated
Apparatus musico-organisticus (1690) we see the art of which he
is the last great representative coming to a standstill.

and give a good idea of his work, except that the copy
rather idealises the original, since the fervour with which
Bach fills these little fantasias, is not, as a rule, found in
those of Buxtehude in anything like the same degree.* In
the large chorale preludes Buxtehude tears the melody in
pieces, throws the fragments into the flood of a brilliant,
animated fantasia, and sends them scudding along, one
in the soprano, another in the alto, another in the tenor,
another in the bass, according as his fancy suggests. Bach's
chorale prelude on *Ein feste Burg* (VI. No. 22) is wholly
conceived in the spirit of this virtuosic style — using the
term in its good sense — of Buxtehude.**

Such are the forms of the chorale prelude created by the
masters of the end of the seventeenth century. From the
formal standpoint they performed their task to the full,
since they worked out rigorously all the possible types
of the species. There are three of these. In the first, the
whole prelude is constructed out of the motives of the
melody, in which case the latter is not altered in any way,
but runs through the whole as a *cantus firmus*. This is
the "motivistic" method of Pachelbel. In the second, the
melody is broken up into arabesques, that climb and
wind like a flowering creeper about a simple harmonic
stem. This is the "coloristic" method of Böhm. In the
third the melody forms the core of a free fantasia, as in
the chorale fantasias of Buxtehude.

All other imaginable kinds of chorale prelude are only
intermediate forms between these three main types; we
may, for example, in a Pachelbel chorale-fugue, lightly

---

* Buxtehude's organ works were edited by Philipp Spitta in
two volumes (Breitkopf and Härtel, 1876—1877). The first contains the miscellaneous compositions, the second the chorale preludes.
A new edition has been prepared by Seiffert. The small chorale
fantasias number thirty-two.

** Together with Buxtehude may be mentioned the Husum
organist Nicolaus Bruhns (1665—1697) a richly endowed artist
who died young. His chorale prelude on "Nun komm der Heiden
Heiland" is given in Commer.

colour and ornament the *cantus firmus*, or weave motives
of the melody into the harmonies that support the chorale
arabesque in the Böhm style, or, lastly, derive the themes
of the Buxtehude fantasia more or less freely from the
melody of the chorale.

Bach found these main types and the intermediate forms
already in existence. He created no new ones; even
Brahms and Reger, modern as they are, have not done so,
for it is quite impossible. The only difference between
Bach and his predecessors is that he did what they could
not — made something more than form of them.

The more we try to see into the development of things,
in any field whatever, the more we become conscious that
to each epoch there are set certain limits of knowledge,
before which it has to come to a halt, and always at the
very moment when it was apparently bound to advance
to a higher and definitive knowledge that seemed just
within its grasp. The real history of progress in physics,
philosophy, and religion, and more especially in psychology,
is the history of incomprehensible cessations, of conceptions
that were unattainable by a given epoch, in spite of all
that happened to lead it up to them, — of the thoughts it
did not think, not because it could not, but because there
was some mysterious command upon it not to. In the
same way, the true history of art is the history of invisible,
insuperable barriers, which only fall when the due time
comes, without anyone understanding why this happens
exactly when it does, and not just as well earlier or later.
Thus it is incomprehensible that the masters who created
the types of the chorale prelude did not recognise that
they were no more than forms, and felt no necessity to
give life to the form by breathing into it the poetic spirit
that was associated with the melody. They could not see
that the chorale prelude, really to answer to its title, must
be born not only out of the melody but out of the text.
As the pre-Bachian masters of the chorale movement
harmonised only the melody, not the text, the inspiration

of their chorale preludes is a purely musical one, owing nothing to poetry. No matter how ingenious their ideas may be, they never flow from the text.

In Buxtehude everything is interesting. Many chorale preludes are full of real feeling; in one or two of them, indeed, the text is to some extent reflected in the music, — in the prelude upon "Durch Adams Fall ist ganz verderbt", for example, where he more than once suggests the "fall" by figures in the bass. On closer investigation, however, we discover that these reminiscences of the text are more or less accidental, and that he was as little concerned as the others deliberately to take the poetry as his starting-point.

Thus all they did was really only pioneer work. Perhaps we should not know that it was only such, if the greater spirit had not come after them, who, almost before he had ceased to be their apprentice, comprehended, with the intuition of genius, that the true chorale prelude must bring out the poetry that gives the melody its name, and prepare the hearer not only for the melody but also for the contents, — a spirit, too, who had the secret of making tones speak.

In no other art does the perfect consign the imperfect to oblivion so thoroughly as it does in music. Early painting retains its own artistic charm for all time. It deals with nature, with reality, and renders it, no matter how awkwardly, with a primitive truth that makes so direct an appeal to the spectator of all epochs that he himself looks at the scene with the child-like eyes of those early artists. Music, however, does not depict the external universe, but is the image of an invisible world, which can only be expressed in eternal tones by those who see it in its whole perfection and can reproduce it as they have seen it. Anything less than this pales and fades in the course of time, even to unrecognisability. It may indeed be of historical interest, as the record of an aspiration towards a goal; but it has lost the power of giving direct artistic satisfaction.

This is the experience of everyone who has been affected
by the chorale preludes of Buxtehude and the other old
masters. At first he is amazed at the artistic treasures he
has discovered; when, however, he goes further into them,
a more sober mood comes over him. He realises that he
has been looking at them comparatively, — i. e., with the
historical understanding — and has appraised them with
that acquired, idealising justice which is indeed appropriate
to the investigator, but must be wholly foreign to the
artist, the criterion of art being absolute and immediate.

Thus the chorale preludes of the composers before Bach
are finally, for the modern admirer who wishes to do them
justice, and even more than justice, no more than what
they are in themselves, — forms that they created for
the greater master who was to come after them, so that
he might find them when he needed them, and make living
things of them.

CHAPTER VI.

THE CANTATA AND THE PASSION BEFORE BACH.

BIBLIOGRAPHY.

PHILIPP SPITTA: *J. S. Bach.* Vol. I. 1873.
C. VON WINTERFELD: *Der evangelische Kirchengesang im XVIII.
   Jahrhundert;* Vol. 3. Leipzig, 1847.
R. FREIHERR VON LILIENCRON: *Liturgisch-musikalische Geschichte
   der evangelischen Gottesdienste von 1523—1700;* Schleswig, 1893.
OTTO KADE: *Die älteste Passionskomposition bis zum Jahr 1631;*
   Gütersloh, 1893.
C. H. BITTER: *Beiträge zur Geschichte des Oratoriums;* Berlin, 1892.
JOSEPH SITTARD: *Kompendium der Geschichte der Kirchenmusik;*
   Stuttgart, 1881.
FRANZ M. BÖHME: *Die Geschichte des Oratoriums für Musikfreunde
   kurz und fasslich dargestellt;* 2nd ed. Gütersloh, 1887.
OTTO WANGEMANN: *Geschichte des Oratoriums;* Demmin, 1881.
PHILIPP SPITTA: *Heinrich Schütz' Leben und Werke (Musikgeschicht-
   liche Aufsätze);* Berlin, 1894, pp. 1—60.
PHILIPP SPITTA: *Die Passionen nach den vier Evangelien von Hein-
   rich Schütz;* Leipzig, 1886.

PHILIPP SPITTA: *Die Anfänge madrigalischer Dichtkunst in Deutsch-land (Musikgeschichtliche Aufsätze);* Berlin, 1894, pp. 63—76.
C. STIEHL: *Die Organisten an der St. Marienkirche und die Abend-musiken zu Lübeck;* Leipzig, 1886.
ARREY VON DOMMER: *Elemente der Musik;* 1862.
WILHELM LANGHANS: *Die Geschichte der Musik des XVII., XVIII. und XIX. Jahrhunderts;* Leipzig, 1882. Vol. I.
(The works of the composers mentioned in this chapter have almost all been published in the *Denkmäler der Tonkunst.*)

In the history of the cantata there are two questions to be considered, — a liturgical one and a musical one.

How did it come about that in the evangelical church service a sacred concert should be inserted between the reading of the Gospel and the sermon, that is to say, precisely in the place where one would least expect a musical interruption of this kind? This is the liturgical question. The musical question is concerned with the evolution of the old purely vocal motet into the cantata of Bach's time, with its arias, recitatives, and rich instrumental accompaniment.

In order to understand how the cantata won its place in the church service we must begin at the new arrangement of worship in the Reformation epoch. Luther did not banish the Mass from the service, but retained it, cutting out only the offertorium, — the essentially Catholic act of sacrifice, — and substituting the sermon for it.*

This alteration did not in any way affect the musical structure of the church service, since the great choral portions of the Mass, — the *Kyrie, Gloria, Credo, Sanctus* with *Benedictus*, and *Agnus Dei*, — still figured in the Protestant worship in the same place as in the Catholic.

---

* See the three famous documents, *Von der Ordnung des Gottes-dienstes in der Gemeine* (1523), *Formula Missae et Communionis pro ecclesia Wittenbergensi* (1523), and *Deutsche Mess und Ordnung des Gottesdienstes* (1526). On the German Masses before Luther see Julius Smend, *Die Evangelischen deutschen Messen bis zu Luthers Deutscher Messe*, Göttingen, 1896. The present account relies largely on the exhaustive study of Liliencron, *Liturgisch-musi-kalische Geschichte der evangelischen Gottesdienste von 1523—1700* (Schleswig, 1893).

It is true that they could be replaced by German hymns: the *Kyrie* by "Kyrie Gott Vater in Ewigkeit", * the *Gloria* by "Allein Gott in der Höh sei Ehr", the *Credo* by "Wir glauben all an einen Gott", the *Sanctus* by Luther's "Jesaia dem Propheten das geschah", the *Agnus Dei* by "O Lamm Gottes unschuldig". But in the churches that had choirs this did not happen, since Luther himself had thought it desirable to retain the Latin choral song, at all events at first. In this he was partly influenced by the consideration that the Latin song would be a salutary exercise in that language for the young.

From the time of Luther to that of Bach, these great musical pieces were common to both Protestant and Catholic services. The Protestant cantors composed Masses exactly like the Catholics, and the Mass-movements of the Italian masters were performed in the Protestant churches without anyone thinking it strange. Collections of Masses were published, in which both Protestant and Catholic composers were represented. Bach himself copied out a number of Italian church-compositions, — the copies have come down to us — not because he had no better way of employing his time, but because they were to be performed on Sundays at St. Thomas's Church. Thus the distinction between Protestant and Catholic church-music, of which we hear so much, had not made its appearance at that epoch.

The service in the churches that followed the Lutheran observance was accordingly constituted in this fashion: *Introit: Kyrie: Gloria:* Epistle; *Gradual:* Gospel: *Credo* (Nicene Creed); Sermon; Communion with *Sanctus, Benedictus* and *Agnus Dei.* This sequence was in the main observed everywhere, however much the arrangements of the service — for Luther had thought the time was unripe for imposing a definitive uniformity on it, — might deviate in detail. The *Kyrie, Gloria, Credo, Sanctus, Benedictus* and *Agnus Dei* were always the same for every Sunday.

---

* Bach VII, No. 39 (a, b, c) and No. 40 (a, b, c).

The *Introit* and the *Gradual*, however, changed each week, since the words of these had to be appropriate to each particular Sunday. The *Offertorium*, which again has to be in keeping with the day, had fallen into disuse and been supplanted by the German sermon.

What was inevitable under the circumstances now happened: the German hymns, in keeping with the German sermon, aimed at expressing the character of each Sunday. In the *Introit*, that Latin antiphonal song between the priest and the choir, the hymns could find no place of entry. In the *Gradual*, however, between the Epistle and the Gospel, where from the earliest time the verses of a German hymn suited to the time of the year alternated with the Latin hymn, they could now be sung by the choir or by the congregation. How strong the tendency was to give the German hymns the imprint of the ecclesiastical season is shewn by the fact that in the course of the second half of the sixteenth century each Sunday had allotted to it once for all its two or three hymns. A hymn-book published in 1566 is entitled *Geistliche Lieder nach Ordnung der Jahreszeit ausgeteilt* ("Spiritual Songs distributed according to the Order of the Season").*

A still greater significance than that of these German *Gradual* hymns, which led from the Epistle into the Gospel, became attached to the hymns which were inserted between the reading of the Gospel and the *Credo* on the one side and the sermon on the other. They naturally had the closest bearing on the Gospel, and were thus specially in keeping with the particular Sunday. And since these hymns were given to the choir, — the congregation singing, between the Gospel and the sermon, the hymn "Wir glauben all' an einen Gott" — nothing stood in the way of writing more

---

* See also page 38. The earliest hymn-books shew no distributive plan at all; while this arrangement of the hymns according to the "order of the season" corresponds to that of the Missal, which, as we know, falls into two parts, — *Ordinarium* and *Proprium de Tempore et de Sanctis.*

and more new hymns touching on the Gospel for the day, for performance at this point.

Thus by the side of the German sermon on the Gospel for a given Sunday there sprang up a kind of parhelion, in the form of a sermon in music. Whatever does not come within the range of its rays is lost in shadow. Musicians suddenly became conscious of a greater task before them than for ever writing fresh music to the statutory hymns of the Mass; there were new poems on the Gospel to be set to music year by year. The effect of this freer church music on them was to make them practically indifferent to the statutory musical portion of the service. The same *Kyrie* or *Gloria* could be sung every Sunday, so long as the motets bearing on the sermon were new and expressive. So it came about that even in the churches where the art had its due place, the Mass was given wholly in figurate music only in rare cases, on high Feast-days. Ordinarily they were satisfied with "musicising" the *Kyrie* and the *Gloria*. The remainder was indeed retained in the service, but was musically starved, the whole strength of the artistic feeling being poured into the sermon-motets. Thus the Protestant artists turned away from the old god to serve the new one, who was more interesting and promised them more reward. They took more pleasure in composing new motet-texts than in turning into tone again and again, with deadly contempt, the woefully unmusical Nicene Creed. They would rather write a whole year's sermon-music than one complete Mass. Bach, in fact, composed five yearly series and only one complete Mass; and when he needed the music for a Mass, he borrowed it from the Italians, or from his own cantatas.* He did not borrow his cantatas from other composers, although, as a matter of fact he could just as well have made use of material of this kind as of the Mass-fragments that he borrowed. He preferred to compose his own cantatas, —

---

* See Bach's four short Masses (B. G., Year VIII).

which was new and therefore always interesting work —
and to borrow the Mass-movements that he needed; for
the composition of Latin texts had little interest for him.
In this he was only following the instinct of Protestant
church-music since the middle of the sixteenth century.

The first important cycle of Gospel settings appeared
in 1542. It was Martin Agricola's *Sangbüchlein aller
Sonntagsevangelien; eine kurtze deutsche Segen-Music mit
sampt den Evangelien durchs gantze Jahr auf alle Sonntage.*
Afterwards Nicolaus Hermann* and Homerus Herpol**
did valuable work in this field. Texts were provided by
the preachers Bartholomäus Ringwalt*** and Johann
Heermann† the poet of "O Gott, du frommer Gott" and
"Herzliebster Jesu, was hast du verbrochen". The latter
entitled his work: *Andächtige Kirchseuffzer, oder Evangelische Schliessglöcklein, in den Safft und Kern aller gewöhnlichen Sonntags- und vornehmsten Fest Evangelien
Reimweis gegossen und damit seine Predigten beschlossen hat
Johannes Heermann.*

This ecclesiastical art was free, bound by no tradition
and cramped by no convention. The task it had set itself,
of expounding the Gospel in music, was so great and so
admirable that all the progress in music the whole world
over seemed appointed only to bring German evangelical
music nearer to its goal. So Protestant church music
from the beginning of the seventeenth century to that of

---

* Nicolaus Hermann was cantor in Joachimsthal. *Die Sonntagsevangelien über das gantze Jahr, in Gesange verfasset,* 1560.

** Homerus Herpol: *Novum et insigne opus musicum, in quo
textus evangeliorum totius anni, vero ritui ecclesiae correspondens,
quinque vocum modulamine singulari industria et gravitate expri-
mitur;* Freiburg i. B., 1555.

*** Bartholomäus Ringwalt: *The Gospels for each Sunday and
Feast day,* "durchs gantze Jahr neben etzlichen Busspsalmen in
Reim und Gesangweise vertieret". 2nd ed. 1581.

† Johann Heermann was a poet of suffering. In his whole
life he could not recollect having had one completely healthy day.
As a pastor in Silesia he saw the desolation wrought by the Thirty
Years' War there.

the eighteenth consciously and deliberately gave itself up to all the influences of both religious and secular music, from whatever source, without shrinking from or fearing anything new, animated only by a holy impulse to creation.

The Landgrave Moritz of Hesse-Cassel must have been moved by a singular presentiment when he came to Marburg, in 1609, to urge his former chapel-boy, now a law student, Heinrich Schütz, to go to Venice with a stipend of a hundred thalers for two years, to study with the masters living there. In the person of this youth, German art itself crossed the Alps. Instead of two years he remained four. His teacher was Giovanni Gabrieli, who had such an affection for him that on his dying bed he bequeathed a ring to him. Gabrieli died in 1613; Schütz accompanied him to the grave before returning home. His other teacher was Monteverde, the creator of the old Italian opera, by whose instruction he benefited again in 1628 when he spent another year in Venice. These two masters between them gave German art, which was now sitting at their feet in the person of Schütz, just what it needed for its renaissance. From Giovanni Gabrieli it learned a new polyphony. While Germany was still under the influence of the animated but slender counterpoint of the Netherlands school, and lacked the power to develop it further unaided, the three great Venetian masters Andrea Gabrieli (1510—1586), his nephew Giovanni Gabrieli (1557—1613), and Claudio Merulo (1532—1604) had evolved a style which was at once bolder and more singable than that of the northern school.* The polyphony is transfigured by its melodic quality. Each separate voice really sings, is a musical personality. This new style was developed simultaneously in organ music and choral music. At the same time instrumental music entered upon a quite new stage;

---

* The founder of the Venetian School was Adrian Willaert (1480—1562), a pupil of Josquin. His successors at St. Mark's were Cyprian de Rore from Mechlin (1516—1565), and Giuseppe Zarlino (1517—1590), who was especially eminent as a theorist.

it began to be independent. Giovanni Gabrieli not only used his small orchestra to support the choir, but gave it short independent preludes to play. The gift of Monteverde,* the first great opera composer, to German art was even more precious; he implanted the dramatic sense in it.

This oldest Italian opera must be absolved from the censure that Wagner pronounced upon the later one. It was not a loose collection of arias, but really what it claimed to be — a *dramma per musica*. Monteverde, of all composers, perhaps has the closest affinity with Wagner; there is some truth in Guido Adler's remark that the creator of *The Ring* should really be regarded as a representative of the Renaissance, and more particularly of the Renaissance opera.** The creators of the *stilo rappresentativo*, as the new kind of music was called, had the same ideals as Wagner. For them, as for him, music was not an end-in-itself, but served only to express the drama, and it was their desire that the orchestra should be invisible.*** Their melody, however, took the form of dramatic declamation, the inherent expressiveness of which can still move the modern hearer most profoundly . Monteverde's lament of Ariadne (*Lamento d'Arrianna*) may be cited as an example.

---

* Claudio Monteverde (1567—1643) lived from 1590 at the court of the Duke of Mantua; in 1613 he became Giovanni Gabrieli's successor at St. Mark's, Venice, which post he retained until his death. His first opera, *Orfeo*, was produced in 1607. The Venice opera house was not founded until 1637. The creators of the Italian opera were the Florentines Giulio Caccini and Jacopo Peri. They jointly wrote, for the wedding-feast of Henry IV. and Marie de Medicis, a *dramma per musica* entitled *Euridice*; it was produced on 6th October 1600, which date may reasonably be regarded as the official birthday of the opera.

** Guido Adler, *Richard Wagner: Vorlesungen, gehalten an der Universität Wien;* Leipzig, 1904.

*** The score of *Orfeo* has survived in its entirety. Monteverde's orchestra consisted of two clavicembali, two organi de legno, two contrabassi da viola, ten viole di brazzo, one arpia doppia, two violini piccioli alla francese, two chitarroni, three bassi da gamba, four tromboni, two cornetti, one flautino, one clarino, and three trombe sordine. See Wilhelm Langhans, *Geschichte der Musik des XVII., XVIII., and XIX. Jahrhunderts;* Leipzig, 1882, I, 92.

This mighty Renaissance art made its entry through Schütz into the German church. We can scarcely realise the enthusiasm with which it was greeted on this side of the Alps. What questions and answers there must have been when Schütz and Michael Praetorius — who, without having himself studied in Italy, looked to that country for the regeneration of German art, — met in Dresden in the latter part of the summer of 1614, where they had to provide the music for a christening in the family of the Electoral Prince!

It was Schütz's destiny, during years of restless wandering, to carry the new art from court to court, even as far as Copenhagen. It is true that in 1617 he was appointed Kapellmeister to the Electoral Prince at Dresden, which post he occupied for fifty-five years, until his death. But from the beginning of the thirties the Kapelle existed mostly only in name, the miseries of the Thirty Years' War having compelled the court to retrench to the utmost. In 1639 the number of the musicians had fallen from thirty-six to ten.* Salaries were paid when there happened to be any money; in the meanwhile Schütz and his subordinates had to shift as best they could. More than once we find him resident for a considerable time at the court of Copenhagen, in the service of the Danish Crown Prince, the son-in-law of the Electoral Prince of Saxony. Other princely courts also offered him temporary shelter. It was in these sad times that he wrote his finest works, for which, however, it was often years before he could find an engraver. Probably much of it that only existed in manuscript has been lost to us.** We owe the preservation

---

* Philipp Spitta, *Heinrich Schütz' Leben und Werke*, in *Musikgeschichtliche Aufsätze*. Berlin, 1894, p. 24.

** Spitta (*Schütz*, p. 37) says: "A quantity of valuable music perished by fire in Dresden in 1760 and in Copenhagen in 1794; in Gera too, the great fire of 1780, which reduced all the churches to ashes, probably destroyed the numerous compositions of Schütz which were preserved there." Perhaps it is only because of this accident of destruction that we possess no organ works by Schütz.

of the *Seven Last Words* to the Cassel library; other works were preserved at Wolfenbüttel.

Even when the war was over and Schütz settled down again definitively in Dresden, he could not succeed in re-organising the Kapelle. All the personal sacrifices he had made, in order to keep together through the period of misery at least a nucleus of young musicians, in expectation of a better time, seemed to have been in vain. When the new Electoral Prince, George II., who took a greater interest in music than his father had done, came to the throne in 1656, the Italians whom he favoured threw the old man of seventy into the shade. In deep dejection he cursed the day when he devoted himself to music and entered the service of princes. He would willingly have gone to some other large art-loving town — he thought indeed of Hamburg — if the distress of the Prince's musicians and the infirmities of age had not retained him in Dresden. But the art that he cursed, as Jeremiah did his prophetic calling, sustained him. The old man wrote four great Biblical "Histories", — a Christmas History (1664) which has been almost entirely lost, a St. John Passion (1665), a St. Matthew Passion (1666) and a St. Luke Passion. He passed away gently in the afternoon of the 6th November 1673, during the singing of the friends who surrounded his couch. His pupil Christoph Bernhard, cantor at St. Jacobi's in Hamburg, had, at his request, — his own strength being insufficient for the work, — sent him his funeral text, — the passage from the Psalms "Deine Rechte sind mein Lied in meinem Hause", — arranged as a five-part motet, for which Schütz had thanked him.*

The music to his *Daphne*, the first German opera, is also lost. Only the text has been preserved; it is a poem by Opitz, founded on the Italian text of Ottavio Rinuccini. The opera was produced in Torgau in 1627, on the occasion of the marriage of the eldest daughter of the Electoral Prince to the Landgrave George II. of Hesse-Darmstadt.

* The chief works of Schütz are: *Psalmen Davids samt etlichen Motetten und Concerten* (1619); *Historia der fröhlichen und siegreichen Auferstehung unseres einzigen Erlösers und Seligmachers*

To our surprise we do not find among Schütz's works just what we should have most expected to find — complete yearly series of compositions on the Gospels for each Sunday. If he did not write any it was because the only kind of text which, as an Italian of the new school, he could use for this kind of work, did not appear in Germany until he was an old man. The texts for the Gospel music were strophic hymns, and were in no way distinguishable from the texts of the congregational hymns. The only way they could be composed was as sacred songs or motets with a chorale-like *cantus firmus*. Italian music, on the other hand, demanded a poem of much freer construction — the madrigal.*

The music of a Monteverde had been a re-birth from musical declamation. Being in essence the negation of song, it could not employ any song-text that was compressed into an artificial or monotonous verse-metre; what it demanded was a free rhymed prose, in which rhyme and metre existed only as servants of the music. With this aversion to rhyming lines of the same length, that broke up the musical tissue in an obviously unnatural way, music entered the path that was to lead it, after a couple of centuries of wandering, to the style of Wagner.

A fundamental problem now presents itself which, in the last resort, runs through the whole history of music.

Jesu Christi (1623); *Cantiones sacrae* (1625); *Beckers gereimte Psalmen* (1628); *Symphoniae sacrae*, Part I (1629); *Kleine geistliche Concerte*, Part II (1639); *Die sieben Worte unseres Erlösers und Seligmachers Jesu Christi, so Er am Stamm des heiligen Kreutzes gesprochen, gantz beweglich gesetzt* (1645); *Symphoniae sacrae*, Part II (1647); *Geistliche Chormusik* (1648); *Symphoniae sacrae*, Part III (1650); *Zwölf geistliche Gesänge* (1657); *Johannespassion* (1665); *Matthäuspassion* (1666); *Lukaspassion* (1666?). According to Spitta the St. Mark Passion is not by Schütz. See Spitta's complete edition of his works (Breitkopf and Härtel).

* On this point see Spitta, *Bach*, Vol. I; also his *Die Anfänge madrigalischer Dichtung in Deutschland* (*Musikgeschichtliche Aufsätze*, Berlin, 1894), pp. 62 ff. The madrigal is Italian in origin and denotes originally a pastoral poem, the name being obviously connected with *mandra*, a flock. (Spitta, p. 63.)

If the opera begins to decline immediately after Monteverde, ultimately to degenerate into a loosely-knit, undramatic string of arias, the fault lay not with music but with poetry, which offered it neither an adequate matter nor an adequate form, but went on its own way, merely dropping now and then something towards which the languishing art could stoop as St. Peter did towards the cherries. *

The history of sacred music until Bach is likewise exclusively a history of the musical texts, and so it forms the true pendant to the history of the opera, — which is equivalent to saying that the history is a tragic one.

The madrigal, says Caspar Ziegler ** in his treatise of 1653 upon this text-form, is a short, epigrammatic poem, in which the culminating effect ("Konklusion") resides in the last two rhymes or even in the last line alone. The preceding lines may be of any number, and each may be just as long as the poet likes to make it, but usually of seven or eleven syllables, some rhymed, some unrhymed. "A madrigal must not be constrained in form; it will often be more like ordinary speech than a poem . . . . . I must however mention in conclusion that no single *Genus carminis* in the German tongue suits music better than a madrigal. For the union of the two gives the best possible results; and since the words can be set so finely in their natural construction, the harmony also is so much better and more agreeable." ***

According to Ziegler, these madrigals were sung in the *stylo recitativo*. When a great many of them are strung together, it is desirable, he thinks, to let an arietta or an aria of several stanzas "run between", so as to get the

---

* The reference is to Goethe's poem *Legende vom Hufeisen* [Tr.].

** Caspar Ziegler, born at Leipzig in 1621, was a theologian and jurist; he was professor in Wittenberg at the time of his death (1690). The title of his treatise runs thus — *Von den Madrigalen, einer schönen und zur Musik bequemsten Art Verse, wie sie nach der Italiener Manier in unserer deutschen Sprache auszuarbeiten, nebenst etlichen Exempeln* (Leipzig, 1653; 2nd edition 1685).

*** See the complete citation in Spitta, pp. 65 and 66.

needful variety. With Ziegler, however, recitative does not mean the bare *recitativo secco** of the later Italian opera or of the Bach Passions, but the dramatic melodic recitative of Monteverde, resembling our arioso. In the same way his arietta or aria is far removed from the later formal *da capo* aria, also used by Bach; it denotes simply a melodic piece of a more pronounced song-like structure than the arioso. **

Thus for Caspar Ziegler the ideal text is one that permits the musician to pass by means of a continuous "affektvoll" (passionate) — as the term then was — declamation from melodic recitative to pure melody and back again. He thus lays down the whole ideal of declamatory music. There was lacking only the poet to realise the ideal and to give the musicians texts of this kind for their Gospel music. In that critical moment, however, German literature was not sufficiently advanced, and later, when it perhaps might have found it possible, music and poetry had drifted so far away from each other that each had lost sight of the ideal of co-operation.

How admirably suited the madrigal style is to music may be seen from Bach's *St. Matthew Passion*. The texts of the ariosos that precede the great arias are in the madrigal manner. They consist of a succession of freely arranged verses which are only preliminaries leading up to the ultimate "Konklusion". For example:

> "Mein Jesus schweigt zu falschen Lügen stille,
> Um uns damit zu zeigen,
> Dass sein erbarmungsvoller Wille
> Für uns zum Leiden sei geneigt,
> Und dass wir in der gleichen Pein
> Ihm sollen ähnlich sein
>   . . . . . und in Verfolgung stille schweigen."

---

* *Secco* really means "dry", in contradiction to *accompagnato*, the animated melodic declamation of Monteverde with instrumental accompaniment.

** The *da capo* aria consists of a main section and a subordinate section, after which the main section is repeated.

or again:

"Er hat uns allen wohlgetan.
Den Blinden gab er das Gesicht;
Die Lahmen macht er gehend;
Er sagt uns seines Vaters Wort;
Er trieb die Teufel fort;
Betrübte hat er aufgericht;
Er nahm die Sünder auf und an...
..... Sonst hat mein Jesus nichts getan." *

These are the attempts at a musical-poetic style that we
meet with here and there in Bach's work. But where else
has the master's art such freedom of speech, where else is
it so incomparable?

The most characteristic German madrigal of the seventeenth century is the "Hirtenlust" of the poet-musician
Johann Hermann Schein, a friend of Schütz. This work
appeared in 1624; curiously enough Ziegler does not
mention it, although it represents the ideal of the declamatory song for which he is pleading. Schein also left a
collection of sacred madrigals with the title *Israels Brünn-
lein* (1623).**

Schütz received Ziegler's treatise immediately after its
publication, and he sent a friendly letter to the author,
who was a relation of his. In this he heartily wishes him,
in the name of music, good luck in his exertions for the
German "madrigal". "The German composers", he says,
"who until now have repeatedly tried to set to music in
good style the beautiful inventions of the new poetry of

---

* Of the same type are the ariosos "Du lieber Heiland du,
wenn deine Jünger thöricht streiten" (No. 9), "Wiewohl mein Herz
in Tränen schwimmt, dass Jesus von uns Abschied nimmt" (No. 18),
"Der Heiland fällt vor seinem Vater nieder (No. 28), "Erbarm
es Gott! Hier steht der Heiland angebunden!" (No. 60), "Ja frei-
lich, will unser Fleisch und Blut zum Kreuz gezwungen sein (No. 65),
"Ach Golgatha, unsel'ges Golgatha!" (No. 69), and "Am Abend,
da es kühle war, ward Adams Fallen offenbar" (No. 74).
** Professor A. Prüfer of Leipzig has opened my eyes to the
significance of Schein. See his collected edition of Schein's works
(Breitkopf and Härtel, vol. 3, 1907).

to-day, have yet always lamented that the *genus Poëseos* which best suits the making of a skilful composition, — namely the madrigal — has hitherto not been seized upon by them, but neglected".*

Schütz thus did not feel himself to be in a position to devote himself to the strophic form of text.** With him begins the estrangement between the art-song and the chorale, which hitherto had been harmoniously united in the chorale motet. For Schütz, in contrast with the composers of his time, the harmonisation of the chorale has no interest whatever. Nor was he greatly concerned about congregational singing. It is quite a mistake to intersperse his Passions, when we perform them nowadays, with chorale verses, or even with congregational hymns. Schütz himself never thought of doing so.

In the course of time, this estrangement developed into a bitter war. Mattheson, the famous Hamburg contemporary of Bach, wears his pen to the stump*** in proving again and again that the true church music must get rid of the chorale in particular and the strophic song in general, since the strophe interrupts the musical development, and in general is to be regarded as the "maladie de la mélodie", — the French play upon words being Mattheson's own.

---

* See Spitta, p. 73. In the original the citation forms a subordinate sentence.

** This does not mean that he did not occasionally compose strophic songs. He did so, for example, in the *Aria de vitae fugacitate*, written on the death of his sister-in-law (1625), in which he treated the chorale "Ich hab mein Sach Gott heimgestellt". (See the two arrangements in his Collected Works, XII, No. 3 and VI, No. 24.) He also set to music in 1628 the rhymed Psalms of Cornelius Becker, in the form of sacred songs for chorus. (Collected Works, XVI.) We meet with strophic texts here and there in other works of his. Professor Prüfer of Leipzig, the highest authority on the German song of that epoch, has shewn me the significance of the German secular madrigals of Schütz (vol. XV of the complete edition of his works). They are in the concerto style, independent instrumental parts being added to the figured bass.

*** *Critica musica*, 1722.

The problem, then, that gave such trouble to all the composers of German church music before Bach, and indeed to him as well, already faced Schütz in its acutest form. The new music cannot work with the old-style strophic songs upon the Gospels, for these are quite undramatic. On the other hand, the poetry of the time is unable to give music the dramatic texts in madrigal form into which it could throw itself and gratify its new-born dramatic instincts. The dramatic-musical representation of the Gospel for the day remained an ideal of the future, which Bach and his contemporaries tried to realise in their cantatas. Schütz, therefore, disregarding the Gospel cycle and contemporary Gospel poems, has direct recourse to the Bible itself, plunging into its treasures in the hope of finding the dramatic texts which he cannot get from the poetasters of his time. He composes Psalms, detached verses from the Bible, whole dramatic fragments. Where the Bible does not of itself provide him with something musically dramatic, he makes it by arranging the finest passages in dialogue form. The Pharisee and the publican go into the temple; a prophet exhorts his people; King David laments over his son Absalom; above the prostrate Paul is heard the voice calling from above, until the questions die away in the sky; the Saviour on the cross speaks the Seven Last Words. Where is there, indeed, such a German requiem as the funerary music woven by Schütz out of Biblical texts and songs? * Thus his texts have escaped the doom that has overtaken the poetry of his time. The music has not, as with Bach, to cover with its own splendour the nakedness of the words; here it is only the artistic setting that brings out more fully the brilliance of the precious stones of the text.

---

* This music was composed at the death of Prince Heinrich Postumus von Reuss, Schütz's sovereign, and performed at his funeral on 4th February 1636. When the Prince felt himself to be near his end, he had a coffin made, the lid and sides of which he ordered to be covered with his favorite Biblical hymns. Schütz compiled his work from these. See Spitta, p. 17.

If Schütz, in so far as he goes back for his texts almost exclusively to the words of the Bible, is anything but an innovator, on the other hand, from the musical point of view he must really be regarded as a revolutionary. In German church music, Gabrieli's manner of employing several choruses in order to get massive dramatic effects was a revolution, upon which Schütz discourses in the preface to his *Psalmen Davids* (1619). So too was the independent employment of the orchestra in the works Schütz wrote after his second Italian sojourn, when he became acquainted with Monteverde's music. Another revolution was the introduction of recitative-like solo songs. In order to grasp the significance of this innovation, we must realise that hitherto, in Protestant church music, the Biblical words had always been rendered by a single voice in the psalmody, or as it was then called, the "collect tone" i. e. the monotonous recitation, not yet divided into bars, which had been customary in the Catholic church, and which Luther and Walther had taken over for their own church service with a few trifling modifications. It was in this old style that the Evangelist still recited in the *Historie von der fröhlichen und siegreichen Auferstehung* of 1623.* But from the moment when Schütz became acquainted with Monteverde's recitative-like arioso, he employs this, and does not shrink from setting in this manner even the Seven Words of Jesus on the Cross.

All this is revolutionary. In the last resort, however, it is merely the visible expression of the essentially revolutionary thing in Schütz's art, — the ideal he had set himself of making music characteristic and pathetic. He may renounce choral effects, instrumental accompaniment, even dramatic recitative, as he does in his last works, — the Passions, — where the choir sings unaccompanied and the

---

* In the preface to this work, Schütz tells us the manner in which he wishes this recitative to be accompanied on the organ or other instruments.

story of the Passion is recited to the "collect" tone; but his art remains the same.*

The new form, startling as it is, and great as was the transformation it wrought, is only the servant of the new spirit. And Schütz's art is primitive art, but of such a kind that it cannot be surpassed by any later art, precisely because it is not form but spirit. As we find it hard to part from the first spring days and pass into the season of full unfolding and ripening, so we tear ourselves almost regretfully away from this primitive art, with its buds full of the coming wealth of ideas and forms, in order to see what ultimately became of it. In art, as in everything else, is not all unfolding and ripening a kind of withering, since in the full bloom we no longer have truth and reality appealing to us with that mysterious directness that is more magically eloquent than even perfection itself? For primitive art of this kind, the later product, perfect though it be, is not a heightening of something less perfect, but merely the revelation of all that was latent in the primitive organism.

Bach did not know Schütz 's music, or if he did, he did not greatly value it. He copied out the works of all kinds of previous and contemporary masters; of Schütz not a line has come down to us in Bach's handwriting. As Spitta says, Schütz's relation to him can only be conceived as an ideal one.** He does not stand on Schütz's shoulders, but is unconsciously nourished by his work, just as in nature a new vegetation draws its sustenance from the invisible but still active forces of its buried predecessor.***

---

* Spitta well says, that Schütz in the "collect" tones of his Passions, "has written the most expressive recitative of his time" (p. 52).

** Spitta, *Schütz*, p. 59.

*** See also Spitta's admirable lecture on *Handel, Bach and Schütz*, delivered in 1885, and published in 1892, in Breitkopf and Härtel's *Sammlung musikalischer Vorträge*. The article on Schütz in Walther's *Musiklexikon* of 1732 (p. 559) is very interesting. It shows that Schütz was indeed a celebrity in the eyes of Bach's contemporaries,

With Schütz, "concert-music" made its way into the church, and transformed the motet into the cantata. The new form is met with under various names; it is called indifferently Motetta, Concerto, Symphonia, or Dialogue. The term "cantata", in the usual meaning of the word, does not come till later; even in Bach's time this term was almost exclusively employed to designate the solo cantata. He himself entitles one of his first cantatas, the "Ratswechsel" cantata for Mühlhausen (1708, No. 71), a "motetta". In the church ordinances, the place for the performance of the cantata is indicated simply by the words "Hernach wird musiziert" ("here follows music").*

---

but that they had no idea of his quality and importance. Schütz remained a long time forgotten. Attention was first drawn to his work, and the significance of it shewn, by Winterfeld in his *Geschichte des evangelischen Kirchengesangs* (1845), although he did the work much less than justice, estimating the past by the narrow ideal he had before him of Protestant church-music, which he found in Eccard and the masters of that time, — i. e., in the representatives of the pure undramatic vocal style, — more fully than in Schütz. In Winterfeld's opinion Schütz begins the epoch of decline, which continues to Bach. This theory of Winterfeld, however, is not quite so narrow and false as it is generally represented to be. There is a good deal of truth in it, for Italian art in the end did indeed lead German church music into the wrong path. There is nothing of this, however, in Schütz. At a later date, Philipp Spitta became the advocate of Schütz, and erected a living monument to him in his edition of his works.

Karl Riedel, of Leipzig, was one of the first to perform Schütz's works, with the famous choir that he founded in 1854. He did not do the best thing possible, however, by compiling a new Passion out of those of Schütz, instead of producing each of these in its original form.

* A definite study of the musical history of the cantata is still lacking. It cannot be written until the numerous compositions that bear upon the question are sifted out and the most valuable published. Whether we shall then be able to shew a connected evolution is as yet doubtful.

The question of the continual Italian influence on the German cantata is also a difficult one to settle. Ludovico Grossi da Viadana (1564—1645), Schütz's older contemporary, influenced him and the German masters very strongly. He was the first to lay down the principle that vocal writing should be built on the foundation of the figured bass. His celebrated *Canto Concerti ecclesiastici*

But if the name varies, the fact is indisputable; in place of the sermon motet it was now permissible to perform choral works with soli and orchestra. This innovation had come about without a single voice being raised in opposition. This was possible because it was an epoch of living ideals. In the German towns of that time, large and small, we find ideals such as have animated no other citizen communities since the time of the ancient Greeks. Fatal as it was from the political standpoint that religion had become an affair of states and communes, yet by this very means those ancient conditions were renewed in which the citizen community regarded it as its highest civic duty to look to the artistic form of its own religious service. The service is the concern not of the church but of the town. It is not the consistory that engages the cantor and appoints the singers and the instrumentalists for the church, but the town council and the citizens. The reputation and the credit of the town are involved in having an artistic

---

were published at Venice in 1602 ff. In Germany, Michael Prae-torius in particular cultivated and developed the style of Viadana. Praetorius demands the harmonic figuring of the bass, which Viadana had not yet supplied in his compositions. On the path thus indicated by the organ harmonies, the voices could now move much more freely than before. From that time the pure *a capella* style passed more and more out of use. Even in Bach's time, no choral work is performed without the organ.

At the same time, however, composers necessarily began to lose more and more the feeling for the pure vocal style. Even with Gabrieli, Viadana, Schütz and Praetorius the vocal writing has already an instrumental tinge; later on it became quite instrumental. The pure vocal style did not exist for Bach and his contemporaries.

The cantatas and oratorios of Giacomo Carissimi (1604—1674, Maestro di capella at Rome) had no particular influence on German church music, which at that time was developing wholly under the stimulus it had received from Schütz and Praetorius. To Carissimi's pupil Agostino Steffani, who was Kapellmeister in Hanover from 1685, Handel owed some valuable stimuli. Some of Carissimi's oratorios — *Jephthah, Belshazzar, The Judgment of Solomon,* and *Jonah,* — were edited in 1869 by Handel's biographer, Chrysander. The manuscripts of other oratorios of his are in the Bibliothèque Nationale at Paris.

cultus. When Christoph Bernhard, Schütz's favorite pupil, went to Hamburg in 1663, to be cantor and musical director at the Johanneum, "the leading people of the town", so Mattheson tells us, "went as far as Bergedorf to meet him with six coaches, — a distance of two miles". Johann Rudolf Ahle (1625—1673) was both cantor and burgomaster at Mühlhausen in Thuringia.

The town musicians were chiefly intended to assist in the church music. The educational institutions of the town had also to lend their aid to the art. The Latin schools furnished the choirs. Every boy with a good voice entered the school, and was maintained by the town during the whole period of his education. If he lost his voice at puberty, he had meanwhile learned an instrument and could now play in the orchestra. If he had any artistic talent, he could safely continue his studies at the university, with the certainty of being able to live by his art. Telemann, the Hamburg master, secured an important position for himself in Leipzig even when a student.

One result of this close connection between the educational system and music was that the level of culture among the musicians of that time was higher than it has ever been since*. If we examine the careers of the artists of that time we see that almost all of them decided to take up music during or after their university course. German jurisprudence may be proud of having provided

---

* We very often find them holding the highest positions as teachers. The Landgrave of Cassel had settled upon Schütz as tutor to his children, and unwillingly parted with him to Saxony. In 1674 the Electoral Prince of Saxony asked the Hamburg town council to let him have Christoph Bernhard back to be preceptor to his beloved grand-child, as well as Vice-Kapellmeister. Mattheson, in Hamburg, was the tutor of the children of Johann von Wichs and those of the English ambassador, whose legation secretary he afterwards became. The employment of the musician of that epoch in all kinds of offices requiring a sound general and university education can be proved by many other interesting examples.

almost all the best musicians of the seventeenth century and the early part of the eighteenth. It can claim Schütz, Walther, Mattheson, Handel, Kuhnau, Emmanuel Bach, and many other distinguished names.

"Whether a composer *necessario* must have studied" is the question put by one Johann Beerens in an essay published in 1719; he answered it with a decisive affirmative. The real quality of their culture is seen when we examine their literary productions, from the *Syntagma Musicum* of Michael Praetorius * to the works of Emmanuel Bach, Gerber, Adlung, Marpurg and the rest. On the other hand, this close connection between art and education resulted in every educated person having some knowledge of music, and those who owed their schooling to it remained true to it, to whatever position of dignity they rose. This general diffusion of artistic culture explains the interest, — quite incomprehensible from the standpoint of the present day, — that was taken in the music of the church. To the Protestant towns of that time the artistic church service was what the theatre was to the Greek community — the centre of art and religion.

For the rulers, again, great and small, the religious service was a concern of state. Many of them, indeed, when they were looking out for a good Kapellmeister or cantor, disregarded the injunction as to "unyoking, extorting, or alienating" — as Luther puts it in his explanation of the tenth commandment, — and did anything but admonish the person on whom they had cast covetous eyes to remain where he was and do his duty. A good musician in those days had his value as a political commodity. The desire to stand well with the Elector of Saxony was certainly not the least consideration that induced the Landgrave of Hesse-Cassel to yield to the

---

* Michael Praetorius (1571—1620), was Kapellmeister at Wolfenbüttel. His *Syntagma Musicum* (Part I, History of Music; Part II, History of Instruments; Part III, Practical Instruction) appeared 1615—1619.

continual solicitations of Johann George of Saxony, and let him have the young Schütz.

The misery of the Thirty Years' War broke up many of these unions of souls. The princes who had fostered art in obedience to an ideal made the greatest sacrifices and did all they possibly could to make the service the last to feel the retrenchments necessitated by the events of the time. The Prince of Liegnitz was one of these. Johann George of Saxony, however, who had ostentatiously carried his Kapelle about with him everywhere, practised his first economies in connection with his musicians.

Unfortunately it is for the most part only in account papers, yellow with age, and the dreary protocols of town councils, that we can read the story of the efforts made by the German communities of that epoch for religious music; and most of the documents still slumber in the archives.* It thus happens that we have more information upon the material side of the case than upon the artistic. From the transactions of the Mühlhausen "Society" we may learn all that happened at the annual banquet, the *Convivium musicale,* — what was served at table and what it cost. From the council records one would think that this formal, solid feasting was the main feature of the affair.

Surveying the situation as a whole, we must acknowledge that the conditions were singularly favourable for the coming of great church music. Yet this epoch created nothing great and durable. Not that it was lacking in creative force or the joy of creation. Never was so much

---

* See Otto Taubert, *Die Pflege der Musik in Torgau* (Torgau, 1868); Philipp Spitta, *Die musikalische Sozietät und das "Convivium Musicale" zu Mühlhausen im XVII. Jahrhundert (Musikgeschichtliche Aufsätze,* Berlin, 1894, pp. 77—85); Joseph Sittard, *Geschichte des Musik- und Konzertwesens in Hamburg vom XIV. Jahrhundert bis auf die Gegenwart* (Altona-Leipzig, 1890).

The registers give us a good idea of the relations of the Hamburg town-musicians to the upper pastry-cook under whose orders they were at weddings and banquets.

music composed as then. Every cantor made it his pride to supply a cantata of his own for each Sunday and feast-day. No one was looked upon as a musician unless he could compose. Men of the most mediocre talent had a complete mastery of the technique of composition. They laid the foundation of it by copying out voice-parts, and afterwards a thorough practical education made them capable of producing serviceable music at quite an early age. The system of instruction in that epoch cannot at all be compared with ours, which is almost wholly directed to making performers; it was at once more practical and had a far loftier ideal. From the standpoint of education, printed music is a Danaus-gift, since it enables students to escape the elementary instruction given by copying music.

Although the conditions were so favourable, that epoch created nothing durable. Imagine what a corresponding epoch would have produced in painting under similar circumstances! In music we have merely names deserving of reverence and respect, but not immortal works. And even if all the cantatas of that time that are still sleeping in sacristies and church vaults, awaiting their discoverer, should be brought into the light of day, we should be no richer in really great art. The way from Schütz to Bach goes over hills, not over mountains.

The problem of the text is still unsolved. To some extent the form of the strophic song holds its ground; some composers experiment with the madrigal form; others go back to the Bible and the old church hymn. But no definitive form is evolved.

The most important representative of the transitional cantata is Andreas Hammerschmidt (1611—1675), organist of St. John's Church in Zittau, whose *Musikalische Andachten* and *Musikalische Gespräche* were universally admired *.

---

* *Musikalische Andachten*, in five Parts, 1638—1653. I. *Geistliche Konzerte*, Freiberg, 1638. II. *Geistliche Madrigalien*, Freiberg, 1641. III. *Geistliche Symphonien*, Freiberg, 1642. IV. *Geistliche*

Johann Rudolf Ahle* (1625—1673) of Mühlhausen, and Wolfgang Karl Briegel (1626—1712) of Darmstadt, were also held in high esteem. In comparison with Schütz, their music may be called almost conservative.

The art of Johann Christoph Bach, the court and town organist at Eisenach (1642—1703) is much bolder. Johann Sebastian, his nephew, thought a great deal of him, and produced his Michaelmas cantata "Es erhub sich ein Streit" (Rev. XII, 7—12) in Leipzig. This has come down to us. The work of the uncle foreshadows the art of the nephew. The cantata is written in twenty-two real parts, and contains some astonishing harmonic audacities. Johann Christoph's mastery of polyphony was so great that he never played on the organ or the clavier in fewer than five real parts. Philipp Emmanuel Bach inherited from his father, along with the copies of his great-uncle's works, his father's admiration for him. When Forkel, the first biographer of Bach, visited Philipp Emmanuel in Hamburg, the latter played him some of the compositions of his ancestor. "I still have a very lively recollection", writes the biographer later, "how pleasantly the old man smiled at me during the most remarkable and boldest passages, when he gave me the pleasure of letting me hear some of these old works in Hamburg" **.

Johann Michael, the brother of Johann Christoph, organist and town-clerk of Gehren, was less important.

Motetten und Konzerte, Freiberg, 1646. V. *Geistliche Chormusik auf Madrigalmanier*, Freiberg, 1653. *Dialogi oder Gespräche zwischen Gott und einer gläubigen Seele*, in two Parts, Dresden, 1645 and 1646. *Musikalische Gespräche über die Evangelia*, in two Parts, Dresden, 1655 and 1656.

* *Geistliche Dialoge mit zwei, drei, vier und mehr Stimmen*, Erfurt, 1648. Also collections of Sacred Songs, "Konzerte", Motets, "Andachten", &c. His son and successor, Johann George Ahle, was of less importance.

** Forkel, *Über Johann Sebastian Bachs Leben, Kunst und Kunstwerke*, Leipzig, 1802, p. 2. Max Schneider, in the *Bachjahrbuch* for 1907, pp. 101—177, gives a full thematic index to the compositions of the older generations of the Bach family.

Nevertheless Johann Sebastian copied out several of his motets, one of which was for a long time erroneously regarded as his own work.

In the north, where the church music at first did not ally itself with contemporary poetry, it mostly followed the lines of Schütz, deriving its texts simply from the Bible and the hymn-books, and throwing the whole weight of the dramatic expression upon the music alone. As the north had suffered least during the Thirty Years' War, it was able to do much more for art than was possible elsewhere. Nuremberg, in the south, ceased to be an artistic centre. For the next two generations Dresden and Leipzig allowed Hamburg and Lübeck to take the lead of them. Hamburg in particular was regarded as the land of promise for musicians. The old Schütz would have liked to settle there. When Bach was looking round for a definitive post he set his hopes on Hamburg; and it is practically by an accident that he did not go there, — if indeed we can call by that term what was really the successful intrigue of a mediocrity, backed by money, against a man of ability.

In Hamburg we find the two most important pupils of Schütz, — Matthias Weckmann (1621—1674) and Christoph Bernhard (1627—1692)*. In Lübeck was Franz Tunder (1614—1667), a pupil of Frescobaldi and the predecessor of Buxtehude, who, in accordance with the custom of the time, married the organist's office in the person of the daughter of its previous occupier. His successor Schiefferdecker did the same thing**.

---

* Max Seiffert, *Matthias Weckmann und das "Collegium Musicum" in Hamburg* (*Sammelbände der Internationalen Musikgesellschaft*, 1900—1901, pp. 76—132). This article gives one of the best pictures of the artistic life of that epoch.

** On 4th May 1706 Buxtehude, at that time sixty-nine years old, petitioned the authorities that after his death his post might be given to one of his daughters, for whom he had a good "subjectum" in view. His request was granted. See C. Stiehl, *Die Organisten an der St. Marienkirche und die Abendmusiken zu Lübeck*, Leipzig, 1886.

When and how the celebrated *Abendmusiken* (evening performances of music) originated in the Lübeck Marienkirche seems to be no longer ascertainable with certainty. Mention is first made of them in the protocol book of the Marienkirche for 1673, according to which "any one who henceforth shall be appointed and engaged as musician to the council" must assist at the organ at the five *Abendmusiken* gratis *. The organist himself had to pay the assistant musicians, whom he engaged out of the musicians' guild. For this he received his *douceur* from the leading citizens.

In Buxtehude's time it was customary for the organist to present to the "high patrons" the printed text-books of the *Abendmusiken*, as we learn from a copy inscribed by him in 1700 to a certain Herr "Dietr. Wulfrath" **. If the collection did not cover the expenses, the town council helped. It also looked after the maintenance of order. At the performances in commemoration of the Emperor Leopold I., on 2nd December 1705 — Bach was staying in Lübeck at the time and was present — the pressure of the crowd was so great that "two corporals and eighteen privates" were necessary. As a rule the "council house guard" sufficed ***.

---

* For further particulars see the above cited work of Stiehl.

** The custom of having printed programme-books appears to have existed in Lübeck since at least 1677. When an enquiry was made, in the fifties of the eighteenth century, for a complete collection of the text-books of the *Abendmusiken* for the Lübeck public library, some one offered the whole collection from 1677—1757. As it is not in the town library now, it is doubtful whether it was acquired. See Stiehl, p. 7. On the whole it appears to have been a fairly common custom at that time to give the audience the printed text of a cantata. Johann Daniel Gumprecht, in the preface to his *Sabbatsgedanken* (1695) speaks of it as a recognized demand of the time.

*** Stiehl, p. 8. In the weekly record of the Marienkirche of 1700 we read: "Also on this day, by the grace of God, the *Abendmusiken* customary in the church from old time; but further, at the desire of the council, a congratulatory poem on the well-being of the town of Lübeck was printed and was by me publicly presented in a populous

When the Lübeck cantor Ruetz, a contemporary of Bach, enquired in 1753 among the old people how the *Abendmusiken* were begun, he was told that in old times the organist at St. Mary's used to play something on the organ for the citizens before they went to the bourse, and that the *Abendmusiken* developed gradually out of these performances. This conjecture, which has been repeated in all the histories of music, flattering as it is for the old Lübeck speculators, has no claim to authenticity. It does not explain why the performances took place on Sunday, and in the cold season of the year *. The music was given, that is, between four and five o'clock on the Sundays between Martinmas and Christmas, at the conclusion of the afternoon service, with the exception of the first Sunday in Advent; thus five concerts were given each season. It is much more probable that the performances originated in an Advent festival, — although it must be set against this view that in conformity with the Gospel selection in the old church, which dealt with the last judgment, Advent was regarded as a time of penitence and mourning, during which all music, even the organ, had to cease. In Leipzig and most other places no cantatas were given on these Sundays.

The five cantatas constituted a single whole. The titles have come down to us of three cycles of the kind composed by Buxtehude. One was called "The Wedding of the Lamb"; the second "Heavenly Delight of the Soul

---

assembly in a complete *Musica*; and in order to prevent any tumult, in and about the church, the council house guard had to be in attendance, for which they received as usual 6 marks."

* In Bach's time Ruetz complains that "the *Abendmusiken* were given in such an inclement and raw season, namely in the middle of winter, that after one had passed three hours (i. e. at the afternoon service) in the cold, one had also to freeze for a fourth. The horrid noise of mischievous youths, and the unruly running, racing and brawling behind the choir, destroy almost all the charm the music might have had; not to mention the iniquities and ungodlinesses that are committed under cover of the obscurity and the low lights".

upon Earth over the Birth of our Saviour Jesus Christ
and His becoming Man"; the third "The most Terrible
and most Joyful of all Things, namely the End of Time
and the Beginning of Eternity, exhibited in Dialogue".
All three titles indicate Advent. Unhappily both texts
and music are lost.

When Stiehl, in 1885, was writing upon Tunder in Eitner's
Monatshefte für Musikgeschichte, and, in the following year,
upon the organists of the Marienkirche, he lamented the
fact that we possess hardly any of the choral works of
the northern masters of that time, those of Lübeck or
those of Hamburg, except some twenty church cantatas
of Buxtehude*. But when travelling in Sweden, in 1889,
he discovered that the famous library at Upsala had preserved a great number of these church compositions. It
possesses the musical collection of the Düben family, in
which, at that time, the office of Hofkapellmeister at
Stockholm had been hereditary for three generations, up
to Karl Gustaf Düben, who occupied it from 1719. The
Dübens kept up a brisk correspondence with the two
North German musical centres, often visited their friends
among the composers, and copied out whatever particularly pleased them. From their cantatas we first learn
what Tunder, Weckmann and Bernhard could do**;
Buxtehude also we now know better***.

One feature that is common to all of them is the frequently brilliant treatment of the orchestra. They aim
at colour effects, especially Weckmann and Buxtehude.
The latter employs, in the cantata *Ihr lieben Christen*

---

* There are twenty church cantatas in manuscript in the Lübeck
library, and two in the Berlin library. The latter two, — *Dixit
Dominus* and *Nun freut euch ihr Frommen* appeared in the *Monatshefte für Musikgeschichte*.

** See Stiehl, *Die Familie Düben und die Buxtehudeschen Manu-
skripte auf der Bibliothek zu Upsala* (Eitner's *Monatshefte für Musikgeschichte*, 1889).

*** There are a hundred manuscripts of Buxtehude at Upsala,
and eighteen of Tunder.

freuet euch, three violins, two violas, three cornets, three
trombones, two trumpets, bassoon, contrabass and organ
continuo. The wind predominate, and are combined with
the organ in all kinds of ways*. A composition of the
year 1697, for the consecration of the new altar at the
Marienkirche, requires three choruses, kettle-drums and
trumpets. Tunder is almost more important than Buxtehude. His cantata on *Ein' feste Burg* is a powerful and
spirited work.

Already, however, the influence of the instrumental
style on vocal works begins to be visible. We feel that
we are coming to the epoch when the pure vocal style is
no longer the concern of any German composer. With Weckmann we often fancy we are reading Bach, so instrumental
is his writing for the voices**.

At the same time we must not form an exaggerated
idea of the means that these instrumentally-minded composers had at their disposal. At Lübeck, difficulties arose
from the character of the church. Under the most favourable circumstances Buxtehude could accommodate
forty choristers on the six rows of seats running by the
side of the great organ. Since it was hardly possible for
him to get each voice doubled, the chorus, according to
our views, must have been completely smothered by the
instrumental mass. In Hamburg it was no better. The
cantor at St. Peter's, for example, had at his disposal in
1730 seven singers, against whom there were seventeen

---

* In this respect the northern composers do not follow the lead
of Schütz, who had made some steps towards emancipating himself from the old preference for the wind, and giving more promin-
ence to the strings.

** In the Marienkirche there seems to have always been a strong
preference for instrumental effects. It was the duty of the violinists
and lutenists to "assist" with music (i. e. solo numbers) on the
organ when the consuls, the members of the council, or the prin-
cipals of the church took communion. In 1659 the lutenist was
enjoined to "let himself be heard on the organ several times per
month in addition to the Feast Days". These orders were still in
force in 1737. See Stiehl, p. 12.

instrumentalists, without counting the three trumpets and the kettle-drum *.

In their method of employing the chorale, these composers hark back to the epoch before Schütz. It plays a great part in their works, whereas he had been disposed to put it aside. They write whole cantatas upon chorales, and so create the type of the chorale cantata, which, later on, alternately attracts and repels Bach again and again. Strictly speaking, this form of cantata is a mere medley, since a strophic song is not in place in the text of a work with solo pieces. The whole species invites the criticism that a new patch does not suit an old garment. But the chorale is put to marvellous uses in the cantatas constructed out of passages from the Bible. Buxtehude's texts are often quite impressive in their harmony of Biblical passages and chorale strophes, especially when the chorale threads its way through the whole like a central idea. The symbolism of the wordless, purely instrumental chorale melody, with which Bach was afterwards to express his deepest thoughts, is also already perfected.

Thus the problem of the text seems to be settled at last. Contemporary poetry abandons the attempt to create a free form, and the musician constructs the cantata for himself out of verses from the Bible and strophes from the hymn-books, which he contrasts with each other or builds up in a dramatic sequence. One could wish that the artists of that time had realised that this was the only solution, — that the treasures of the Bible and of the German hymn-books were inexhaustible and will last out as long as music and the world themselves; and that music therefore had everything it needed within its own hands, and had no need of poets for its texts.

But just at this moment there springs up again the antique ideal of the co-operation of poetry and music in

---

* Joseph Sittard, *Geschichte der Musik und des Konzertwesens in Hamburg* (Altona-Leipzig, 1890), p. 40. Sittard gives also the equipment of the other churches.

a dramatic representation of religious ideas. It bewitches Protestant church music, luring it onward with the charm of a great ideal, helped by the insufficiency of the German poetry of the time; and the course of music became an uncertain wandering. The fatal thing is that Bach, as the child of his time, had to take part in this wandering, and kept groping after the true form of the cantata his whole life long. Inspired by the idea of the religious drama, the poorest poetry was blind to its own incompetence.

The new cantata differs from the old both textually and musically, — textually, for the most part, in that it dispenses with Bible passages and chorale verses, and trusts entirely to free poetry. This free text, however, is laid out on the plan of the contemporary Italian opera, which has nothing in common with Monteverde's music-drama, but consists of *da capo* arias and recitatives that come near to speech. In this new art, which is under the Neapolitan influence, the melodic and the declamatory are no longer blended as they were in Monteverde's arioso, but separate into unmelodic recitative and undeclamatory song*. Nothing is left of that strong musical-dramatic feeling that we find in the *dramma per musica* of the Renaissance.

The dramatic is now wholly transformed into the reflective, — i. e. into the aria. As this has no longer to consist of music that conforms with the action, it becomes purely formal, while the recitative, the carrier of the action, renounces all melodic form. Thus the new recitative and the new aria only resulted from the inability of the operatic art of that time to create real dramatic music. As soon as a mind appears that can conceive and express music and action in one artistic idea, it revolts against this divorce of song and declamation. This was the case with Gluck and with Wagner, who both, like Monteverde, had in view the true *dramma per musica*.

---

* This change becomes evident in the operas and cantatas of Alessandro Scarlatti (1659—1725).

At the end of the eighteenth century, however, the two new forms that had sprung out of the decline of the Italian musical stage were received with royal honours by the German composers of evangelical church music. Anyone who did not welcome them was regarded as a scorner of the true musical gospel. They pushed choral music into the background; and church music came to consist almost exclusively of solo songs.

This time the Passion music, which hitherto had gone on its way unmolested, also became embroiled in the revolution; henceforward its venerable antiquity was to be no protection against innovation. Till then it had really had no history. As far back as the fourth century, according to tradition, the story of the Passion according to St. Matthew was recited on Palm Sunday, and that according to St. Luke on the Wednesday of Passion Week. In the eighth and ninth centuries the Passion according to St. Mark was allotted to Tuesday in the Holy Week, and the Passion according to St. John to Good Friday*. Already in the thirteenth century Durandus desires the recital to be in dramatic form. Only the words of the Evangelist are to be delivered in the Gospel-tone, i. e., as psalmody, while the gentle words of Jesus and the cries of the unbelieving people are to be rendered characteristically**. The psalmody method of delivery lasts until the end of the fifteenth century. The Passion is recited like every other passage from the Gospel. At the beginning of the sixteenth century the composers of the Netherlands undertake, for the first time, to set the story

---

* See, on the whole subject, Otto Kade's thorough and interesting work *Die älteste Passions-Komposition bis zum Jahr 1631*. Gütersloh, 1893.

** *Non legitur tota passio sub tono Evangelii, sed cantus verborum Christi dulcius moderatur. Evangelistae verba in tono Evangelii proferantur, verba vero impiissimorum Judaeorum clamose et cum asperitate vocantur.* Whether by this is meant a kind of recitation with the rôles distributed, as Kade thinks, cannot be decided. We only know what Durandus wants, but not how it was done.

of the Passion to music. The first musical Passion is by Jacobus Obrecht (born 1450), and dates from 1505; Luther's friend, Johann Walther, copied it out twice. When it was published by Georg Rhaw, in 1538, Melanchthon contributed a preface to it. In the epoch that followed, Passion music was written by both Catholic and Protestant composers, as in the case of the various portions of the Mass; nor is any distinction made between German and Latin Passions.

The numerous Passions of that time fall, according to their form, into two groups, — motet Passions and dramatic Passions. In the former, the whole text, including the words of Jesus, is rendered by the choir; in the latter, the words of the Evangelist and the speeches of Jesus are recited by one person in the old Gospel-tone, and only the cries of the people are set polyphonically, — though the chorus renders also the words of Pilate, of the false witnesses, and of the malefactors.

The dramatic Passion naturally triumphed over the undramatic motet Passion*. The *St. Matthew Passion* of Johann Walther is the first German composition in this style; according to tradition, it was performed on Palm Sunday in 1530. His *St. John Passion*, which was given on Good Friday, has survived to our day. It was sung yearly in Zittau from 1609 to 1816, in a Czech translation.

Schütz retains the dramatic Passion as he had received it. He dispenses with instrumental means of every kind, making the Evangelist psalmodise in the old collect tone, and makes no use, in the Passions, of the declamatory arioso that he elsewhere employs for the solo renderings of Bible passages. No aria, no chorale interrupts the action.

The severe beauty of this old Passion form, transfigured by Schütz's art, is unique of its kind. It reminds

---

* Among the most prominent of the composers of Latin Passions are Claudin von Sermisy (1534), Orlandus Lassus — with four Passions dating from 1575 ff., — and William Byrd (1607). Their works belong to the dramatic species.

us of the affecting representations of the Passion by the realistic painters of the Netherlands. Its profound effect — when the singer taking the part of the Evangelist knows how to enter into the old style* — can almost make us believe that we are listening to one of Bach's Passions.

The lack of the pathetic and the contemplative, however, necessarily discredited the old dramatic Passion and the older church music in general, in an epoch that took rhetorical reflection for the essence of drama.

The new movement begins with the founding of the Hamburg opera. When, in 1678**, Gerhard Schott, the Licentiate Lütjens and the organist Reinken coöperated in the building of a theatre, they had in their minds not so much a secular as a religious opera. Theile's *Adam und Eva* was the first opera (Singspiel) to be given on the stage***; then came *Michael und David* (1679), *Die Makkabäische Mutter und ihre sieben Söhne* (1679), *Esther* (1680), *Christi Geburt* (1681), and *Kain und Abel, oder der verzweifelte Brudermörder* (1682).

It is, as a matter of fact, hard to find anything religious in the trivial and absurd texts of these operas; that age, however, thought otherwise. The clergy took a prominent part in supporting the undertaking. One clergyman, Heinrich Elmenhorst, wrote the texts of several Singspiele, and from the pulpit recommended the faithful to go to the opera.

---

* Only those who have heard Friedrich Spitta as the Evangelist in a Schütz Passion can appreciate fully the beauty of the Collect tone in its dramatic transfiguration.

** The Dresden opera was founded in 1662 by Carlo Pallavicini.

*** The opening took place on 2nd January 1678. The full title of the first opera runs thus: *Adam und Eva. Der erschaffene, gefallene und aufgerichtete Mensch. In einem Singspiel dargestellt.* Theile was a pupil of Schütz and the teacher of Buxtehude. The opera is lost. On the beginning of the opera in Germany see Hermann Kretzschmar, *Das erste Jahrhundert der deutschen Oper* (*Sammelbände der Internationalen Musikgesellschaft*, 1901—1902, pp. 270—293).

When, in course of time, the theatre had forfeited the good opinion of many serious-minded citizens* by reason of the coarseness and tastelessness that had flaunted themselves on the stage, Elmenhorst, in his *Dramatologia antiqua-hodierna*, tried to rehabilitate the institution. He argues that this theatre is simply the ancient Greek drama applied to Christian ends. As the Greeks represented on the stage, for religious edification, the stories of their gods and heroes, so it is a necessity to Christendom to see the Biblical stories unfolded before the eye in animated action. The theological faculties of Rostock and Wittenberg, being consulted on the matter, declared themselves in principle for the religious opera.

All this, however, could not arrest its decline**; and in the course of time the religious drama disappeared from the stage. But the ideal that is upheld in Elmenhorst's work still lived and dominated the artistic life of Hamburg in the epoch — the most brilliant for Hamburg — that followed, when Keiser, Mattheson, Handel and Telemann lived and worked there. Reinhard Keiser came to Hamburg in 1694. Handel lived there from 1703 to 1705. Mattheson, a Hamburger by birth, belonged to the opera from childhood; his true work, however, did not begin until 1705, when he abandoned the career of singer and actor. Telemann was invited to Hamburg in 1721***.

---

* In his *Theatromachia, oder die Werke der Finsternis* (1682) Anton Reiser, the pastor of St. Jacob's, numbers the opera among the works of the devil. In the same year Magister Rauch replied to him in his *Theatrophonia zur Verteidigung der christlichen, vornehmlich aber der musikalischen Opera.*

** From about 1730 the opera fell into deeper and deeper decay. In 1740 an Italian troupe took possession of it; in 1750 the opera-house, with the whole of its fittings, was sold by public auction to the highest bidder.

*** Reinhard Keiser (or Kaiser) was born in 1673; he received his general education at the St. Thomas school in Leipzig, and later at the university of that town. From 1697 onwards he devoted his energies to the Hamburg opera house, writing for it also religious operas, among which may be mentioned *Die über die Liebe triumphierende Weisheit, oder Salom, in einem Singspiel auf dem*

What position these artists occupied, whether they
held office in the theatre or in the church, mattered nothing, since they all wrote impartially for both church and
opera. From 1715 to 1728 Mattheson was cantor of the
cathedral, in which post he was able to do a good deal
for the new church music. When his increasing deafness
forced him to resign, Keiser, who until then had officiated

---

grossen hamburgischen Schauplatze dargestellt (1703), and *Der ge-
stürzte und wieder erhöhte Nebukadnezar, König von Babylon unter
dem grossen Propheten Daniel* (1704). Keiser really had talent
and a rich and lively imagination. His frivolous way of living
prevented him from exercising the influence he might have done.
He died in Hamburg in 1739.

Johann Mattheson was born in Hamburg in 1681. He is of importance not so much for his purely musical work as for his books.
He is the first literary champion of "modern music". His eighty-
four works are most valuable documents for the musical history
of the time. Without the *Syntagma musicum* (1614—1620) of
Michael Praetorius, Walther's *Musiklexikon* (1732) and Mattheson's
works we should know very little about the music of the seventeenth and early eighteenth centuries.

When Handel went to Hamburg, Mattheson constituted himself his instructor and protector, and in this capacity seems to have
made himself a bit of a burden.

Mattheson particularly champions the new form of church
music in his *Der musikalische Patriot* (1728). His *Grosse Generalbassschule* (1731) and *Der vollkommene Kapellmeister* (1739) were
also of great importance. The *Grundlage einer Ehrenpforte* (1740)
contains a very valuable collection of autobiographical articles
on all the notable musicians of the time.

His main calling was that of secretary to the English embassy
in Hamburg. He died in 1764.

Georg Philipp Telemann, although less talented than Keiser and
Mattheson, was more highly regarded than they by his German
contemporaries. Born at Magdeburg in 1681, he went to Leipzig
in 1701 to study law, and remained there three years. He became
organist at the New Church. His foundation of the *Collegium
Musicum* was of great importance for the musical life of Leipzig.
This society was chiefly recruited from student circles. After having
been successively Kapellmeister at Sorau, Eisenach, and at the
Church of St. Francis and St. Catharine at Frankfort-on-the-Main,
he went to Hamburg in 1721 as cantor at the Johanneum. He
also wrote a good deal for the opera. His models were the French.
Telemann's works — he enumerates them in Mattheson's *Ehrenpforte* — are legion. He died in 1767.

only at the opera, became his successor. Telemann had been called to Hamburg to be choir-master and cantor at the Johanneum; but he was also engaged by the theatre to provide operas at a yearly salary of three hundred thalers. Handel, who had gone to Hamburg mainly for the opera, also wrote music for the church*.

These composers gave up the effort to consider the Hamburg theatre, in accordance with the intentions of its founders, as primarily a home of religious art, and to maintain it on that level; but in exchange they tried to import the religious opera into the church service, not troubling themselves as to whether it had any appropriateness to the ecclesiastical season or to the Gospel for the day. To what Gospel are the" Theatrical Soliloquies" of Telemann appropriate, — such as *Der verkaufte Joseph, Der von Zedekia geschlagene Micha, Der von seinem Volke verfolgte David, Der sterbende Simson*, or *Der versenkte Jonas?* They even wrote oratorios in two parts, intended for performance before and after the sermon, choosing for them any dramatic scene that took their fancy. Not that they were any less pious or less in sympathy with the church than their predecessors had been. On the contrary, they believed that this free, self-existent church music was the only true music, and that credit was due to them for having set it free from its Babylonian bondage. They aimed at creating a Protestant, i. e., a subjective and dramatic art. All they really achieved, however, was the introduction into church music of the emotional theatrical style with its orchestral painting of situations. It finally became a question whether the operatic *secco recitative* and

---

* The first of his operas to be performed was *Almira* (1704); *Nero* followed in 1705. *Florindo* and *Daphne* were already finished when he left Hamburg, but were not given until 1708. Of his church compositions of this time may be mentioned a cantata on the chorale "Ach Herr, mich armen Sünder", an oratorio in two parts, for St. John's Day, *Die Erlösung des Volkes Gottes aus Aegypten*", and a Passion written in 1704, to a text by the Hamburg opera-librettist Postel.

the formal three-section *da capo* aria should not also be
admitted into the music of the church.

Naturally these composers could do nothing with the
choir-boys whom they had at their disposal in the churches.
To the choir, indeed, they attached little importance, as
their music mainly consisted of solo numbers. For their
arias, however, they needed accomplished singers, male
and female. Until then, women had not been allowed to
sing either in the Protestant or the Catholic church, except with the rest of the congregation in the chorale. The
treble and alto parts in the choruses and in the soli were
taken by boys. Mattheson pours his scorn on the church
choristers of that epoch who had to do duty as soloists.
He describes the treble "with a feeble falsetto, singing
like a toothless old woman;" the alto, "with a voice like
a calf"; the tenor, "who brays like a hoarse jackass"; the
bass, "who rumbles out the eight-feet G in the depths,
like a cock-chafer in an empty boot, in a way that would
waken a sleeping hare hardly thirty paces off, while he
howls the four-feet G like an Indian lion". Is it possible
— so runs his perpetual refrain upon this question — to
make music at all with the singers provided by the church?
Before condemning the new church music, people should
provide the composers with the performers necessary for
its adequate rendering.

Nor was he satisfied with mere platonic discussion.
Soon after he became cantor of the cathedral, he succeeded
in introducing female singers; and in 1716 some ladies
named Rischmüller, Schwarz and Schober made the
church resound with their runs and trills to the glory
of God.

Mattheson plumed himself upon this achievement all
his life. "I was the very first", he wrote in his *Generalbassschule*, "to employ three or four female singers in the
ordinary church music, before and after the sermon; though
with what difficulty and vexatiousness, and against what
opposition, cannot be described. At first I was implored

not to bring any women into the choir; in the end they could not have enough of them."

After the death of Telemann, in 1767, the female singers seem to have disappeared again from the churches. The example of the Hamburgers had not found many imitators. We know that at Lübeck, which modelled its church music upon that of Hamburg immediately after Buxtehude's death, no female singers took place in the *Abendmusiken* until 1733 at the earliest. In Leipzig they never did so*.

The new style of church music did not triumph without a struggle. In 1726 there appeared an attack on it by a certain Joachim Meyer of Göttingen, who was both a musician and *Doctor juris***. Mattheson made a very clever reply. He brings forward in defence of theatrical church music the same argument that Elmenhorst had used to vindicate the religious theatre. For him, too, the church art for which he is fighting is the antique tragedy transplanted into Christendom. Every religious festival, he says, is theatrical, since the Biblical stories and the religious ideas they contain are represented in some way or other. The most perfect representation, however, is art***.

---

* Buxtehude's son-in-law and successor, Schiefferdecker, had previously been at the Hamburg opera. During his twenty-five years of office (1707—1732) he did not give a single work of his father-in-law at the *Abendmusiken*, but wrote each year an oratorio in five parts in the Hamburg style. The texts have survived. His successor Johann Paul Kuntzen also came from Hamburg. He too employed female singers in the *Abendmusiken*.

** *Unvorgreifliche Gedanken über die neulich eingerissene theatralische Kirchenmusik und von den darin bisher üblichen Kantaten, mit Vergleichung der Musik voriger Zeiten zur Verbesserung der unsrigen vorgestellet*, 1726.

*** *Der neue Göttingische, aber viel schlechter als die alten Lacedämonischen urteilende Ephorus, wegen der Kirchenmusik eines andern belehrt* (1727). Joachim Meyer replied in his *Der anmassliche Hamburger 'criticus sine crisi'* (1728). See also Mattheson's *Der musikalische Patriot* (1728). The Berlin cantor Freudenberg, under the pseudonym of Innocentius Frankenberg, took the side of the innovators in his *Gerechte Wagschal* (1729).

The most important and stubborn opponent of the
new style was Johann Kuhnau (1660—1722), Bach's predecessor at St. Thomas's, Leipzig, whose talents and
capabilities were everywhere recognised, and whose famous
dramatic clavier sonatas on Biblical histories made it
impossible to call him a reactionary*. He threw himself into the fight just when the new tendency began to
attract attention. When he printed his cantata texts for
the ecclesiastical year 1709—1710, he accompanied them
with a preface, in which he laid down his own ideas of the
true style for church music, in contrast with the theatrical
style**.

His views did not suit the taste of all the Leipzigers,
particularly of the circle that had formed round Telemann. In his last years he had to yield to the pressure
of the time, and write a Passion in the new style, which
was performed in 1721. After his death it was proposed
to make Telemann, who was the antipodes of Kuhnau,
his successor.

From about 1700, all opposition to the new church
music was in vain. The educated people, clerical as well
as lay, had before their eyes the antique ideal of the religious
drama, which Elmenhorst and Mattheson had advocated
so cleverly and with such real enthusiasm. Neither they
nor the musicians themselves were conscious how far poetry
and music were from attaining this ideal.

We, for our part, cannot place ourselves at the point
of view of an epoch which revelled in the confident joy
of creation, and went on its way without being crushed

---

* Kuhnau had written an opera, which, however, had been a
failure. See Richard Münnich's careful study *Kuhnaus Leben*, in
the *Sammelbände der Internationalen Musikgesellschaft*, 1901—1902,
pp. 473—527.

** See Richter, *Eine Abhandlung Johann Kuhnaus*, in Eitner's
Monatshefte für Musikgeschichte, 1902. At the beginning of each
ecclesiastical year, Kuhnau issued in printed form the texts of the
cantata cycle that was to be produced. Upon the fragments of
these publications that have come down to us from the years
1707—1721, see Richter, *loc. cit.*

or made self-reflective by any great tradition either of
classical dramatic poetry or classical music, but in un-
moved simplicity prized its own imperfect work as being
the realisation of the ideal it was aiming at, and thought
that all it needed to produce classical art was to pursue
an antique ideal.

From our standpoint we must always judge that age
unjustly, for we lack the self-confident creative force that
was at once its strength and its weakness. We feel ourselves to be epigones. The tribute paid by these men to
antiquity, however, was merely a rhetorical one; they
were convinced that with them the last great artistic epoch
had arrived. Feeling themselves thus free of the jurisdiction of antiquity, they fell victims to every deception
and illusion, and finally obeyed the voice that counselled
them, if they would make church music wholly new, to
cease taking their texts from the Bible and the old
congregational hymn.

The fate of the cantata was decided by the appearance
of the first yearly cycle of Erdmann Neumeister's *Kirchen-
andachten**. This first cycle was composed for the court
church in Weissenfels, and was set to music by Philipp
Krieger (1649—1725), the court-Kapellmeister there. Neumeister's "madrigal cantatas" have nothing in common
with the earlier attempts at the madrigal in German
religious poetry, but are imitations of the Italian opera
texts, the author himself declaring, in his preface, that
for him a cantata is only a fragment of an opera. He
makes each of them consist of four arias and four recitatives. He discards altogether Biblical passages and verses
from the hymn-books, nor are there any choruses.

In the succeeding cycles he makes some concessions.
The second (1708) again gives the chorus its due; in the
third (1711) a modest place is again granted to Biblical

---

* Erdmann Neumeister, born in 1671, was court deacon at
Weissenfels and afterwards at Sorau. In 1715 he became the minister
of St. Jacob's, Hamburg.

passages and hymn verses by the side of arias and recitatives. The "modern" cantata was henceforth cultivated
in this infelicitous compromise. In 1716 Tilgner issued
in one volume all the texts of Neumeister that had appeared
during the five previous years. The composers at once
seized upon them. Telemann, who at that time was not
yet in Hamburg but in Eisenach, had set the third and
fourth cycles to music on their first appearance in 1711 and
1714 respectively. Bach also composed music to Neumeister's texts. He knew the author personally, and admired
him as a genuine poet. Neumeister, on his side, valued Bach
very highly and would gladly have had him in Hamburg.

Neumeister had a rival in Salomo Franck (born in 1659)
of Weimar, who was secretary to the Consistory in Arnstadt from 1691 to 1697, where he published his *Madri-
galische Seelen-Lust über das heilige Leiden unseres Erlösers* (1697). Bach's Passions show traces of the influence
of this poem. At a later date Franck became personally
acquainted with Bach, — when the latter was stationed
at Weimar — and supplied him with some cantata texts.
The poems of Franck that appeared after 1711 are influenced by Neumeister. He harks back, however, much
more than the latter to the old madrigalesque religious
poetry, and, if not so clever, is more profound than the
man he had taken for his model.

In the future it became a recognised part of the business of a poet to write cantata texts. To do so it was not
necessary for him to have any personal connection with
sacred poetry; he could insert a yearly cycle of texts for
church pieces in the middle of some gallant or satirical
publication. Thus for a long time the sources of a number
of cantatas by Bach, that are connected textually, musically, and chronologically, were unknown until Philipp
Spitta found them in the collected poems of Marianne
von Ziegler, a contemporary Leipzig poetess*.

---

* Spitta, *Marianne von Ziegler und Joh. Seb. Bach,* in *Zur
Musik.* Berlin, 1892.

The new cantata brought with it the new Passion. The first theatrical Passion was produced in Hamburg in 1704, during the Monday and Wednesday vespers of Holy Week. The text was by Christian Friedrich Hunold, a writer of opera libretti living in Hamburg from 1700 to 1706, who did not enjoy the best of reputations. In the literary world he was known by the name of Menantes*. Keiser supplied the music.

The whole Passion was now represented as a dramatic action. The place of the Biblical story of the Passion was taken by a versified text that connected the separate scenes. It is noteworthy that in this Passion we already have the "Daughter of Zion", whom we shall meet with again in Bach.

The indignation was universal, not so much on account of the new departure itself as on account of the extremely wretched theatrical style. In the same year Handel also wrote a Passion to a text by Postel, another Hamburg opera poet, which was performed without winning any success.

In 1712 appeared the Passion poem of the Hamburg town councillor Barthold Heinrich Brockes. In the main he retains the plan and the constituents of Keiser's Passion. He makes use of free recitative and *da capo* arias, admits the Daughter of Zion, and replaces the Gospel narrative by a versified recital of the Passion, keeping more closely, however, to the Biblical wording than Hunold-Menantes. The only really new feature was the insertion of chorale strophes**; for the rest he did nothing more than discard

---

* Spitta, *Bach und Christian Friedrich Hunold*, in *Musikalische Aufsätze*, Berlin, 1904, pp. 89 ff. In Hamburg, Hunold was known as an obscene littérateur; in 1706 he had to leave the town on account of a licentious novel. He went in 1708 to Halle, where he gave lectures on poetry and jurisprudence. He knew Bach, and supplied him with texts for secular cantatas.

** The Passions of Schütz contain no chorale strophes. So far as we know, the Brandenburg-Prussian Kapellmeister Johann Sebastiani was the first to use chorale verses in his Passions. *Das*

some of the theatrical elements of Hunold's Passion, and to purge the diction of its worst impurities.

And this text became the classical one for the Passion! Keiser set it to music in 1712, Handel and Telemann in 1716, and Mattheson in 1718. The last-named's Passion was performed during the service on Palm Sunday in 1718. Telemann produced his in Frankfort. "It was excellently performed", he himself tells us, "in the chief church on several special week-days, in the presence of various great people and an indescribable throng of hearers, for the good of the orphan institution. I may record the singular fact that guards were posted at the church doors, who allowed no one to enter who had not a printed copy of the Passion, and that most of the members of the ministry were at the altar in their robes of office. Moreover, this Passion has been heard in many German churches and concert-halls." *

When Handel set Brockes's text to music, he had developed far beyond the other Hamburg composers. Later on he made use of this music in other works. We possess the work, however, only in a copy made by Bach and his wife. The manuscript comprises sixty pages; the first twenty-three are by Bach, the remainder by Anna Magdalena, his second wife. It is thus probable that Bach gave a performance of Handel's Passion in Leipzig.

How are we to explain the enthusiasm of composers for Brockes's Passion poem? It was certainly not the distinction of its language that attracted them, for the verse is positively vulgar. The scourging is described in the following recitative:

Leyden und Sterben unsers Herrn und Heylandes Jesu Christi, in eine recitierende Harmonie von fünf singenden und sechs spielenden Stimmen, nebst dem Basso continuo gesetzet, worinnen zur Erweckung mehrerer Devotion unterschiedliche Verse aus denen gewöhnlichen Kirchen-Liedern mit eingeführet und dem Texte accomodiret worden; Königsberg, 1672.

* Wilhelm Langhans, *Geschichte der Musik im XVII., XVIII. und XIX. Jahrhundert*, 1882, p. 430 ff.

"Drauf zerrten die Kriegknecht' ihn herein
Und riefen ihre Wut mehr anzuflammen
Die ganze Schar zusammen.
Die banden ihn an einen Stein
Und geißelten den zarten Rücken
Mit nägelvollen Stricken."

After Peter's denial there follows this aria: —

"Heul, du Scham der Menschenkinder,
Winsle, wilder Sündenknecht!
Tränenwasser ist zu schlecht;
Weine Blut, verstockter Sünder!"

At the same time the text had some dramatic vitality, and it was extremely rich in opportunities for musical painting. The inflated diction did not at all repel the composers, who took it to be the characteristic of a poetic sensibility that was akin to music. Compared with Hunold-Menantes's Passion poem and the libretti of the Hamburg operas, the style must indeed have seemed positively pure.

Literary Germany before the time of Gottsched and Lessing possessed nothing of our modern sense of verbal values. The connection with music was really pernicious to the poetry of the time, for it was being perpetually worked up into an over-exuberance of feeling, in which it aimed at drastic images and pathetic expression without any other thought than that of making its ideas as strong and flowery as possible. Not until it parted company from music, and was placed on a footing of its own by Gottsched and Lessing, did it find itself again.

Bach, however, lived in the decadent epoch when music and poetry led each other astray, an epoch of excessive scribbling, of superficial art, in which even men of real talent like Keiser went to ruin, an epoch which seemed fated to be impotent to create anything of durable value*. Whereas at other times and in other places the great artist has been only one star among others, whose light, if less brilliant

---

* The verdict of Eitner, the best judge of that epoch, upon it is equally severe. See his *Kantaten aus dem Ende des XVII. und Anfang des XVIII. Jahrhunderts* (*Monatshefte für Musikgeschichte*, 1884).

than his, he nevertheless did not extinguish, Bach is surrounded by mere will-of-the-wisps, which his epoch — and
he with it — mistook for stars. Of the innumerable cantatas that were written and admired at that time, his alone
have survived their own day, and even these exhibit,
both in their form and in their texts, traces of the dead
world from which they have come. There is no stronger
testimony to the greatness of Bach than the fact that in
an epoch of error, and sharing its errors, he nevertheless
wrote imperishable works. We have finally, however, the
sad consciousness that he was only great enough to save
himself, but not his epoch as well — that he did not hurl
himself against it and strive to lead it back from this
stilted poetry and the empty forms of Italian recitative
and the *da capo* aria, to the true, simple, and really dramatic church music.

To this clear perception, which was to a certain degree
attainable by a Kuhnau, Bach never arrived. He was in
fact not the beginning of a new epoch, but the end of an
old one, in which the knowledge and the errors of successive centuries found expression for the last time, as if
seeking salvation together by genius. Since Bach held his
peace, and, though inwardly opposed to his epoch, nevertheless went its way with it, it was inevitable that his works
should be thrown into the general grave with those of
his contemporaries, there to await their resurrection.

If the talents succumb to the errors of their time,
what matters? But when the men of genius are ensnared
in them, centuries have to suffer for it. The very greatness of Aristotle held Greek natural philosophy back
when it was already on the path that would have led it
to the discoveries of Galileo and Copernicus. Bach, with
an easy consciousness of his own strength, burdened himself with the Italian forms and formulas, and so retarded
the progress of German religious music along the path that
would have led it, even at that time, to an art such as
Wagner was afterwards to realise in drama.

CHAPTER VII.

FROM EISENACH TO LEIPZIG.

The Bach family can be traced back in Thuringia as
far as the beginning of the Reformation.   In the family
chronicle begun by Johann Sebastian and continued by his
son Philipp Emmanuel, the baker Veit Bach is named as
the progenitor of the line to which the composer belonged*.
Forkel, in his biography of Bach (1802), expressed the
opinion that this Veit Bach came from Hungary.   The
truth is, however, that he had emigrated there from Thuringia, returning when the Germans in Hungary began to
suffer during the counter-Reformation.   He settled in
Wechmar, near Gotha.   When he went into the mill to
grind his corn, he would take his guitar with him and
play, regardless of the racket around him.

One of his grand-children, Heinrich, settled at Arnstadt**.   His sons Johann Christoph (died 1703) and Johann Michael (died 1694) were especially prominent members of the race.   Johann Christoph was organist in Eisenach***; Johann Michael was organist and town clerk at
Gehren.

The members of this huge family of musicians had, as
Forkel says, "a very great attachment to each other".
"Since it was impossible to live all together in one place,
they made a point of seeing each other at least once a year,

---

   * This family chronicle is in fifty-three sections; each gives
a short biographical notice of a male member of the family.   The
important document passed from Philipp Emanuel to Forkel, the
first biographer of Bach, from him to the Hamburg music-teacher
Pölchau, and from him to the Berlin Royal Library.   The genealog-
ical tree which Forkel received from Bach's son along with the
family chronicle has been lost.   See Spitta's *Bach*, preface.
   ** The history of Bach's ancestors has been told in masterly
fashion by Spitta in the first volume of his biography.   For confused tradition he has substituted facts based on documents.
   *** See p. 74 as to his Michaelmas cantata *Es erhub sich ein
Streit.*

and appointed a certain day at which they were all to be present at a chosen place. Even when the family had greatly increased, and had spread itself abroad beyond Thuringia, in various parts of Upper and Lower Saxony and in France, they continued their yearly foregatherings. The rendezvous was generally Erfurt, Eisenach, or Arnstadt. The manner in which they passed the time during the meeting was wholly musical. As the company consisted of cantors, organists and town musicians, all connected in some way with the church, and as it was the general custom at that time to commence all things with religion, the first thing they did when they met together was to sing a chorale. From this devout beginning they passed to jests, which often contrasted very strongly with the chorale. That is to say, they improvised folk-songs together, (some of which were comic, some even indecent), in such a way that the various impromptu parts made a kind of harmony, though the words were different in each voice. They called this kind of extempore counterpoint *quodlibet*, and could not only laugh heartily at it themselves, but it aroused also an equally hearty and uncontrollable laughter in every one who heard them" *.

Bach's grandfather, Christoph Bach (died 1661), was a son of Hans Caspar Bach and a grandchild of Veit Bach; Bach's father, Johann Ambrosius, lived first in Erfurt and afterwards, from about 1671, in Eisenach. He had a twin brother, Johann Christoph, court and town musician at Arnstadt, who was so like him that even their respective wives could only distinguish them by their clothes. They had the most tender affection for each other; speech, sentiments, the style of their music, their methods of performance, — all were alike. When one was ill, so was the other. They died within a short time of each other. They were the admiration of all who saw them **.

---

* Forkel, pp. 3 and 4.
** Forkel, p. 4.

Bach's mother, Elisabeth, was a Lämmerhirt by birth. Her father was a furrier at Erfurt.

Johann Sebastian was born on the 21st March 1685, at Eisenach. His mother died nine years later, leaving her husband with four children, of whom Johann Sebastian was the youngest. Not long afterwards, at the beginning of 1695, the father also died; he had married for the second time a little while before. Bach was thus left an orphan at the age of ten. The eldest of the brothers, Johann Christoph (born in 1671), took the two youngest, Johann Jakob and Johann Sebastian, with him to Ohrdruf, where he was organist. They attended the gymnasium there, and their brother instructed them in music. Johann Sebastian was too zealous for his teacher. He asked the latter for a volume containing clavier pieces by Froberger, Kerl, Pachelbel and others. Being refused it, he dragged it with his tiny hands through the latticed door of the cupboard in which it was kept, and copied it out on moon-lit nights. In six months the copy was complete. The brother heard of it, however, and took the copy from him*.

In 1700, as Johann Christoph's family was always increasing, Bach had to think of finding a shelter elsewhere. His good soprano voice secured him a place in the school of the convent of St. Michael in Lüneburg, with his friend Erdmann. He soon lost his voice, but was retained because he was useful as a violinist in the orchestra. We do not know whether he received lessons from the organ virtuoso Böhm. He at any rate heard him play, though Böhm was not at St. Michael's church but at St. John's. It is a fact of great consequence that in the choir to which he belonged he had opportunities of becoming acquainted with the best specimens of German church music. The catalogue of the well-stocked musical library of the gymnasium has

---

* These anecdotes appear in the *Nekrolog* (obituary notice) of Bach written by his pupil Agricola and Philipp Emmanuel, that appeared in Mizler's *Musikalische Bibliothek* in 1754.

been preserved; it includes works by Italian as well as German composers *.

From Lüneburg Bach went more than once to Hamburg to hear the famous Reinken, and, no doubt, to see the opera**. He also went to Celle. The court band there consisted largely of French players. Duke Georg Wilhelm of Brunswick, having married a Huguenot lady, Desmier d'Olbreuse, surrounded himself with a French court; even the Court organist, Charles Gaudou, was a Frenchman***. We do not know who procured for Bach the entrée to the court concerts. It is possible that he was employed as assistant violinist, for after leaving the gymnasium in 1703, at the age of eighteen, he procured an engagement in the band of Duke Johann Ernst at Weimar†. He stayed there only a few months, however, going to Arnstadt in 1704 as organist at the New Church. The instrument had just been built ††. At the Franciscan church the organist

---

* W. Junghans, *Johann Sebastian Bach als Schüler der Partikularschule zu St. Michaelis in Lüneburg* (*Gymnasialprogramm*, Lüneburg, 1870). Here are given also the wages of the choristers, derived from the old accounts. Their earnings were considerable for that time. This explains the strong attraction that the institution had for the youth of the surrounding country. Whoever joined it was at any rate sure of a living, and could even lay a little by. On the career of Georg Böhm, and his relations with the Bach family, see the thorough and interesting article of Richard Buchmayer in the *Bachjahrbuch* for 1908, pp. 105—122.

** Once on the way back from Hamburg to Lüneburg, Bach, hungry and penniless, was standing in front of an inn. The windows opened, and some herring-heads were thrown into the street. He picked them up and found in each of them a Danish ducat. This anecdote, without which no biography of Bach is complete, is told by Marpurg in his *Legenden einiger Musikheiligen*, Cologne, 1786.

*** Interesting details on the musical conditions at the Celle court are given by André Pirro in his *J. S. Bach* (Alcan, Paris, 1906), p. 26 ff.

† This was not the Court band. Johann Ernst was the younger brother of the reigning Duke. See Spitta I, 220 ff.

†† Spitta (I, 224, 225) gives the specification as follows: — Oberwerk (Upper Manual): 1. Principal (i. e., diapason) 8 ft., 2. Viola da gamba 8 ft., 3. Quintatön 16 ft., 4. Gedackt 8 ft., 5. Quint 6 ft., 6. Octave 4 ft., 7. Mixture 4 ranks; 8. Gemshorn 8 ft., 9. Cymbal

was Christoph Herthum.   He had married a woman of
the Bach family, and besides being an organist was a
Count's clerk of the kitchen.

In Arnstadt Bach laid the foundation of his mastery
of the organ.   As his office claimed him only three times
a week, he had a good deal of time to himself.   In October
1705 he was granted leave of absence for four weeks, in
order to go to Lübeck and hear the great organist Buxtehude.   He was thus present at the great memorial performance on 2nd December 1705, on the occasion of the
death of Leopold I.   We do not know whether he learned
from Buxtehude only by hearing him play, or whether he
had lessons from him.   In any case the attraction of the
master was so strong for him that he quite forgot the
necessity of returning to Arnstadt.   He stayed over Christmas and the New Year in Lübeck, and did not get back
to Arnstadt until the middle of February, 1706.

On the 21st of that month he was summoned before the
Consistory, to justify his having exceeded his holiday.   The
proceedings of the meeting are still preserved*.   Bach
did not condescend to make any excuses, but said he
thought that his deputy would have filled the office in
such a way that no complaint would have been possible.
The Consistory availed itself of the opportunity to remon-
strate with him on his extravagant way of accompanying
the chorales; and further reproached him with not attending to the choir of scholars, and with having performed
so little figurate music.

---

1 ft. 2 ranks; 10. Trumpet 8 ft., 11. Tremulant; 12. Cymbelstern.
Brust-positiv (Choir): 1. Principal 4 ft., 2. Lieblich gedackt 8 ft.,
3. Spitz flute 4 ft., Quint 3 ft., 5. Sesqualtera; 6. Nachthorn 4 ft.,
7. Mixture 1 ft. 2 ranks.   Pedal Organ: 1. Principal 8 ft., 2. Sub-
bass 16 ft., 3. Posaune 16 ft., 4. Flute 4 ft., 5. Cornet 2 ft.

The church itself had been finished in 1683.   It was intended
to replace the church of St. Boniface, that was destroyed during
the great Arnstadt fire of 1581.   See Weissgerber, *Johann Sebastian
Bach in Arnstadt* (*Gymnasialprogramm*, Arnstadt, 1904).

    * They are in the archives of the Principality of Sondershausen.
See Spitta I, 315 ff.

We must not regard the church authorities as being lacking in a sense of the genius of the young organist. Their complaints were wholly justified. Bach had been unable to do anything with the choir, thus already revealing that lack of talent for organisation that later on was to make his situation in Leipzig so difficult. In this he differed radically from Schütz, who always knew how to get the best results out of the material at his disposal, and to train his forces gradually up to the highest possible efficiency. Bach, on the contrary, was no pedagogue; he could not even maintain discipline. If things did not go as he wanted, he flew into a temper, — thereby only making the matter worse — lost heart, and let things go as they chose. He was on very bad terms with the singers, and with the scholar who led the choir. Before his Lübeck journey there had been a fracas between himself and one of the scholars, Geyersbach. The latter, having had an injurious epithet applied to him by Bach, had set upon him with a stick in the street. Bach had drawn his sword. Fortunately other scholars had thrown themselves between them and separated them*. The affair had gone before the Consistory, where it was proved that Bach had really used the offensive epithet in question.

At the February sitting he was required to say definitely whether he would attend to the choir or not; eight days were given him for reflection. In November he had not yet replied. He was again summoned to a sitting, on the eleventh, when he promised to give his reply in writing. Whether he ever did so we do not know.

At this last sitting he was reproached with having recently "made music" in the church with a "stranger maiden", without having received permission to do so. He made the excuse that he had spoken about it to the clergyman, Magister Uthe. It need hardly be said that this "music-making" was a private and week-day matter,

---

* André Pirro, *J. S. Bach*, p. 38.

and that the "stranger maiden" did not take part in the
Sunday service. This was not permitted under any circumstances; at that time women were not allowed to sing
in church even in Hamburg.

His position had become untenable. Just then, on 2nd
December 1706, the organist of the church of St. Blasius
in Mühlhausen, Johann Georg Ahle, died. In the spring
of 1707 Bach received an invitation to give a trial performance on the organ of this free imperial town, which
was artistic in its sympathies. On the 15th June he
received the appointment; on the 29th he gave up the keys
of the Arnstadt organ at the council house, and left to his
cousin Ernst, son of Johann Christoph Bach, his father's
twin brother, the five gulden of his salary which were
still unpaid*. His emoluments in Mühlhausen consisted
of 85 gulden, 3 coombs of corn, 2 cords of wood and
6 trusses of brushwood, — both to be delivered at his door
— and 3 pounds of fish per annum**.

On the 17th October of the same year Bach married
his cousin Maria Barbara Bach, daughter of Johann Michael
Bach, the organist and clerk at Gehren. They were
married at Dornheim, near Arnstadt, by Johann Lorenz
Stauber, who was connected with the Bach family by
ties of friendship and kinship. This Maria Barbara Bach
was presumably the "stranger maiden" with whom Bach
had "made music" in the church at Arnstadt. Her mother,
the daughter of Wedermann, the town-clerk at Arnstadt,
had an unmarried sister in that town, — Regina, — whom
she may have been visiting. Soon afterwards, in 1708,
this aunt married Stauber, the clergyman at Dornheim,
who had lost his wife a year before.

When Bach entered upon his post at Mühlhausen, the
musical conditions of the town were in a woeful state of
decay. The town was living on its past reputation. The

---

* This cousin had probably acted as his deputy during his absence in Lübeck.

** Spitta I, 337.

congregation was split in two by a disagreement between
the orthodox party and the pietists, by which art did not
profit much. A fortnight before the appointment of the
new organist, a fire had reduced to ashes a great part of
the town, and that the richest and most beautiful. It
can easily be understood that just then the burghers had
something else to think about than the reorganisation of
the church music. They thought they had done their
part when they had engaged an artist at an exceptionally
good salary. He, however, had no capacity for reorganisation. A year after his appointment he applied for his
release. In his petition he frankly acknowledges that he
is going because he does not see any immediate improvement in the musical conditions*. They parted, however,
on good terms with each other. Bach was still to super-
intend the work on the organ, the renovation of which
had been undertaken according to his plans.

In his new post Bach had nothing to do with a choir;
he went to Weimar as Court organist and chamber musician
to the reigning Duke Wilhelm Ernst**, one of the most
distinguished and cultured princes of his time, and thoroughly devoted to art. When Bach entered his service
the Duke was in his forty-sixth year***. In the religious
struggles he was on the side of orthodoxy, and took care
that his people had the pure doctrine. He had married
a Princess of Jena, but they soon separated.

The court band numbered about twenty members.
Many of them — as was usual at that time, — also acted
as footmen, cooks or huntsmen. On special occasions
they waited on their master in Hungarian costume; so
that Bach also must have donned this dress†. The organ
in the castle church was not large, but it is evident from

---

* Spitta I, 373, 374.
** On the Weimar epoch see Paul von Bojanowski, *Das Weimar
J. S. Bachs*, Weimar, 1903.
*** See Spitta's sympathetic portrait of him (I, 375 ff.).
† Spitta, I, 378.

the specification of it that has been preserved that it must have had a uniformly fine tone *. Bach must occasionally have been incommoded by the fact that the pitch of the organ was the cornet-tone, i. e., a minor third above the ordinary pitch (Kammerton).

In the town church there was a considerably larger organ. It was played by Johann Gottfried Walther, the subsequent author of the first German musical lexicon **. On his mother's side — she was a Lämmerhirt by birth, — he was related to Bach. The two men seem to have formed a sincere friendship with each other, though we do not know whether they still had much intercourse after Bach had left Weimar. Spitta is of opinion that later on a certain estrangement sprang up between them, since Walther in his *Musiklexikon* (1732) devotes only a moderately short article to Bach. The inference is not conclusive. Walther's articles are confined to an enumeration of printed works. The section on Handel is still shorter than that on Bach.

Bach's salary to begin with was 156 gulden; it increased until in 1713 it was 225 gulden. In the following year it was probably again increased, Bach having been then advanced to the position of Konzertmeister. From this time he had to provide cantatas for the church service. The Kapellmeister was Johann Samuel Drese, who was already well on in his sixties; his son Johann Wilhelm acted as his deputy.

We do not know whether Bach had any close personal relations with the prince his master. Probably not, for

---

* It had two manuals and a well-equipped pedal. Upper Manual: 1. Principal 8 ft., 2. Quintatön 16 ft., 3. Gemshorn 8 ft., 4. Gedackt 8 ft., 5. Quintatön 4 ft., 6. Octave 4 ft., 7. Mixture 6 ft., 8. Cymbel 3 ranks; 9. Glockenspiel. Lower Manual: 1. Principal 8 ft., 2. Viola di gamba 8 ft., 3. Gedackt 8 ft., 4. Trumpet 8 ft., 5. Small Gedackt 4 ft., 6. Octave 4 ft., 7. Waldflöte 2 ft., 8. Sesquialtera. Pedal Organ: 1. Great "Untersatz" (support) 32 ft., 2. Sub-Bass 16 ft., 3. Bass-Trombone 16 ft., 4. Violin-Bass 16 ft., 5. Principal-Bass 8 ft., 6. Trumpet-Bass 8 ft., 7. Cornet-Bass 4 ft. Spitta I, 380. The organ was placed under a cupola in the third gallery. See the picture of the church in von Bojanowski.

** On Walther see p. 43 of the present volume.

in that case it would be inexplicable how he came to be passed over when, in 1716, a successor had to be appointed to the deceased Kapellmeister. At first an attempt was made to secure Telemann, who was at that time in Frankfort. When he declined the offer, the post was given to Drese's son. He was a musician of little account, his sole claim being that he had always acted for his father during his last years.

After this event, Bach's only thought was how to get away from Weimar as quickly as possible. When Prince Leopold of Anhalt-Cöthen offered him the post of Kapellmeister at his Court he snatched at it eagerly, which he certainly would not have done had it not been a case of finding another situation at any cost. The office, indeed, had little that was attractive for a man with the objects that Bach had in view. The Cöthen Court belonged to the reformed church; there was consequently no church music. The church of the castle contained a small organ of inferior quality; that of the reformed town-church was rather larger. Bach was merely the director of his master's chamber music.

In his haste to leave Weimar he seems to have demanded his immediate release in a rather peremptory way. The Duke, who did not approve of behaviour of this kind, had the refractory Court organist arrested on the 2nd November, and kept under arrest until the 2nd December*.

He took up his new position at Christmas 1717**. If it was not wholly satisfactory from the artistic stand-

---

* See von Bojanowski, p. 63. He quotes from Bormann's records: "On 6th November the late concertmeister and organist Bach was arrested in the justice's room on account of his obstinately insisting upon his resignation being accepted at once, and was finally set free on the 2nd December and notified that he had been ungraciously allowed to resign."

** For information about Bach in Cöthen see Rudolf Bunge, *Bachjahrbuch*, 1905, pp. 14—47. One is shocked at the history of the band and the penury of the poor musicians after the death of Prince Leopold. See Bunge, p. 34.

point, in another respect it was extremely agreeable. The
Prince was young — he was not yet twenty-five — and
had had a sound musical education. He had travelled in
Italy, taking with him Johann David Heinichen (1683
—1729) one of the most notable musical theoreticians of
the time, to initiate him into Italian art. In the orchestra,
which was not very large, the Prince himself seems to have
played the violin. He also possessed a well-trained bass
voice. He was well qualified to appreciate the worth of
his new Kapellmeister. He was proud of him, and took
him with him on all his journeys. In time a cordial friendship grew up between the two men, which lasted even after
Bach had left Cöthen.

The six years that he passed in this small capital were
the most pleasant in Bach's whole career. He had time
for composition, and there was no unpleasantness of any
kind to mar his joy in his work. During the Cöthen
epoch, however, there befel the most serious misfortune
he had yet known. Returning with the Prince from Carls-
bad in July 1720, he found that his wife had died suddenly
in his absence, and had been buried on the 7th July. All
her husband could do was to make a pious pilgrimage to
the grave of her who for thirteen years had been the faithful and devoted sharer of his lot. Of the seven children
that Maria Barbara had born to him, four were living at
the time of her death; the eldest, a daughter named Katha-
rina Dorothea, was twelve years old; Wilhelm Friedemann
was ten; then came Philipp Emmanuel and his brother
Johann Gottfried Bernhard, who was about a year younger
than he*.

A year and a half later Bach found a new life-partner
in Anna Magdalena Wülken, the daughter of Johann
Caspar Wülken, Court and field trumpeter at Weissenfels.

---

* In 1703 the parents had lost two twins shortly after their
birth; another son, born 15th November 1718 in Weimar, and
named after his godfather Prince Leopold August, died on 28th
September 1719. See Spitta II, 8.

The marriage was solemnised on 3rd December 1721; the bridegroom was thirty-six, the bride twenty-one. This marriage was a thoroughly happy one in every respect. Anna Magdalena was not only a careful housewife, who behaved with the utmost kindness to Bach's motherless children; she was also an artist, who could enter intelligently into her husband's work. She had a good and well-trained soprano voice. Her husband made it his care to develop her musical faculties. We still possess two *Klavierbüchlein* [Little Books for the Clavier] *von Anna Magdalena Bach*, the first belonging to 1722, the second, — which is in a fine green leather binding — bearing the date 1725. The first contains twenty-four easy pieces for the clavier; the second consists of preludes, suites, chorales, and sacred and secular songs. Bach also instructed his wife in the art of playing from figured basses. At the end of the *Klavierbüchlein* of 1725 we find "some highly important rules of General Basso" recorded in his handwriting. His scholar richly repaid him for the pains he took with her, for she was useful to him in copying music. A number of the finest works of Bach have come down to us in her writing. In the course of years her script became so much like that of her husband that it is difficult to distinguish one from the other. For a long time, for instance, the score of the cantata *O heil'ges Geist- und Wasserbad* (No. 165) was regarded as an autograph of Bach's, until Spitta proved it to be a copy made by Anna Magdalena*. How many hours must she have had to steal from her household duties when the week was drawing to a close, and the parts of the new cantata were not yet copied!

She also taught the children to do this kind of work. In the second oboe part in the cantata *Ihr, die ihr euch von Christo nennet* (No. 164), the headings, the key-signa-

---

* Spitta II, 690. In the *Bachjahrbuch* for 1906, pp. 134, 135, Johannes Schreyer questions the theory that the two note-books were written for Anna Magdalena.

tures and the bar-lines are in her writing, but not the notes, which are clumsy and awkwardly connected. A small monogram at the end of the part, in which an attempt is made to intertwine the three initials W. F. B., shows the copyist to have been Wilhelm Friedemann Bach. The cantata probably belongs to the year 1724; the boy at that time was fourteen years old; it was his first fair copy. We can see him sitting at the table: the sunlight plays on the floor; the mother, busily flitting to and fro, supervises his work. He has just written *Il Fine* at the end. But it is not done well enough for her; she writes the words again in her large, easy characters. There is a footstep on the stairs; the door opens; the father has come home.

His growing boys now made it imperative for Bach to think of looking out for another post. In Cöthen he could not procure for them the education that they needed. He himself longed to be back at his organ, and lamented his virtual severance from church music. Hamburg attracted him. Although the opera there had for some time now lost a good deal of its earlier glory, the town was still one of the musical centres of Germany. Here Mattheson sat in judgment upon artists and their works; here raged the war between the new and the old church music; here were the most splendid organs; here lived Erdmann Neumeister, the celebrated librettist of church cantatas.

It so happened that the organist's post at St. Jacob's church became vacant in September 1720, by the death of its quondam occupier Heinrich Friese. A few weeks afterwards, Bach went to Hamburg and performed on the organ of St. Catharine's church before Reinken, — who was then nearly a hundred years old — and a select company*. The story is well known of how the old master of the organ went up to the younger one, who had just improvised for half an hour on the chorale "An Wasserflüssen Babylon", and complimented him with the words:

* Forkel (p. 8) gives the date of the journey wrongly as 1722.

"I thought this art had perished, but I see that it still lives on in you." The praise was all the more flattering inasmuch as Reinken himself had treated the same melody at length in a chorale prelude, of which he was not a little proud*.

Bach was exempted from giving a trial exhibition for the post at St. Jacob's. We may be sure that Neumeister, who was the clergyman of the church, strenuously urged his election. His candidature failed, however. The choice, which was made on the 19th December, fell on a certain Johann Joachim Heitmann. The church accounts let us see wherein consisted his superiority over Bach in the eyes of the authorities of St. Jacob's. On 6th January 1721 he paid into the church treasury the sum of 4000 marks in acknowledgment of his election. The fact that he expended so much to secure the post leads us to surmise that it must have had some very lucrative perquisites attached to it.

Neumeister was indignant, and gave vent to his vexation in a sermon. Speaking at Christmas of the angels who made music at the birth of Christ, he added that their art would certainly have availed them nothing in Hamburg; he really believed, he said, that if one of the angels of Bethlehem, who could play divinely, were to come down from heaven and try to become organist at St. Jacob's, but had no money, he would simply have to fly back again**.

Whether Mattheson exerted himself on behalf of Bach in this affair is not known. That Bach did not settle at Hamburg can only be regarded as a misfortune. The position offered much fewer difficulties and occasions for mortification than the one he afterwards accepted in Leipzig. On the other hand we must not forget that in Hamburg he would have had to dispense almost entirely with the chorus in his church music, since there was no choir

---

* Ante, pp. 45, 46.
** For further details as to the election see Spitta II, 19 ff. We owe the passage from Neumeister's sermon to Mattheson, who refers to the episode in 1728 in his *Musikalische Patriot* (p. 316), without, however, mentioning Bach directly by name.

there. And what encouragement for his creative work would he have found among a committee that set finance above art?

A year and a half later, in June 1722, the post of cantor at St. Thomas's church in Leipzig became vacant. The council was looking for a worthy successor to Kuhnau. It did not, however, think of Bach in the first place, but entered into negociations with Telemann, who was at that time regarded as the leading German composer, and was favorably remembered by the Leipzigers from his student days (1701—1704)*. The negociations were broken off because Telemann could not obtain his release from Hamburg, where he had but recently (1721) been appointed director of the town music. After him, the Darmstadt Kapellmeister Graupner, a capable pupil of Kuhnau, was most thought of in connection with the post. Bach did not apply until towards the end of the year. He delayed it so long because he found it hard to leave his agreeable situation with his cultivated prince, and to surrender the position of Kapellmeister for that of a simple cantor, to be under the orders of a school rector and to teach choir boys. He finally succeeded in making the resolution to sacrifice his leisure and his pride to his children. "At first it was not altogether agreeable to me", he writes some years later to his friend Erdmann, "to change the position of Kapellmeister for that of cantor. Consequently I delayed my resolution for a quarter of a year; nevertheless this post was so favorably described to me that finally, especially as my sons appeared to be inclined to study, I ventured upon it in the name of the Most High and went to Leipzig, passed my trial, and at once set about the removal."

---

* See p. 86. The story of the election is told by Richter in his interesting essay *Die Wahl J. S. Bachs zum Kantor der Thomasschule im Jahre 1723*, in the *Bachjahrbuch* for 1905, pp. 48—67. See also Kleefeld, *Bach und Graupner als Bewerber um das Leipziger Thomaskantorat*, in *Peters Jahrbuch*, p. 70.

He was not exempted from the trial, which had not been waived even in the case of Telemann. He produced the cantata *Jesus nahm zu sich die Zwölfe* on Quinquagesima Sunday, 7th February 1723. As Graupner could not get his discharge from the Darmstadt court, and the other competitors could not measure themselves against Bach, he was elected unanimously.

It has recently become the fashion to reproach the Leipzig council with having only taken up with Bach after it had vainly tried to secure the "shallow" Telemann and the insignificant Graupner. The reproach is unjustified. Both the other men were well known in Leipzig, and had a reputation with their contemporaries that Bach did not yet possess. It is too much to expect of a committee that it should anticipate the judgment of posterity. The town council's business was to find a musician of recognised ability to succeed Kuhnau, and not to be influenced by any other consideration. It therefore finally selected Bach. The choice honoured both the judges and the competitor; for Bach certainly felt it an honour to become the successor of Kuhnau.

His nomination was notified to him on 5th May 1723; and on Monday, the 31st of the same month, he was installed in his new office. He took up his quarters in the cantor's house in the left wing of the St. Thomas's school buildings. His wanderings were at an end.

CHAPTER VIII.

BACH IN LEIPZIG.

One cannot help feeling a little sadness when one reads the agreement that Bach had to sign upon his nomination*. He was not to leave Leipzig without the permission of the burgomaster, and he undertook, for the sake of

---

* See Spitta II, 185 ff.

1. Die St Thomas Kirche, 2. Die Thomas Schule.
3. Der Steinerne Wasser-Kasten.

Krügner fe. Lipsiæ

St. Thomas's Church and School in 1723

The illustration shows the old school (erected in 1553), in which Bach worked; it was extended and heightened in 1732

(1) St. Thomas's Church. (2) St. Thomas's School. (3) The Stone Cistern

economy, to instruct the boys not only in singing but in instrumental playing, so that they might also be available in the church orchestra. It was further part of his duty to accompany the choir of school boys who sang the motet or chorale at funerals. At the less important burials, in which only a portion of the St. Thomas's choir took part, one of the senior scholars would often act as his deputy. But how often must he have walked abstractedly with his scholars at the head of the procession, in wind and rain, turning over his next cantata in his mind!

Before his definite installation he had to undergo, as was the custom of the time, an examination of his religious belief, out of which he came satisfactorily. He also had to sign the Concordia Formula, for without signing this no one could hold an appointment in Saxony*.

It was not the best of omens that at this formal induction into his office, on Monday, the 31st May, the representatives of the consistory and those of the council almost came to blows, the delegates of the council being of the opinion that some remarks that Licentiat Weisse, — who had come in lieu of Superintendent Deyling, — had addressed to Bach in the name of the consistory, claimed for the church committee a right at the ceremony that did not belong to it. The affair afterwards led to a long discussion between the council and the consistory. Thus on the very first day there broke out that rivalry between the two bodies that controlled the cantor, which was

---

* The Concordia Formula is the last symbolical document of Lutheranism. It was drawn up at the end of the eighth decade of the 16th century at the instance of the Electoral Prince of Saxony, and was meant to unite the whole of the Lutheran established churches of Germany. The majority accepted it. This confession put an end to the theological controversies that had agitated the church of the time, and condemned not only Calvinism, but also the milder tendency in Lutheranism that came from Melanchthon. In a later day, pietism and the "Aufklärung" lowered the authority of the Concordia Formula. Its political and juristic authority broke down, with the rest of the old Germany, during the Napoleonic wars.

afterwards to re-appear so frequently. We cannot say that Bach suffered from this tension. It ministered admirably to his own need for independence, for he played the consistory off against the council and the council against the consistory, and meanwhile did what he liked.

His work at St. Thomas's school was not vexatious. Besides the rector there were seven teachers. The cantor came immediately after the subrector, thus being third in rank, and, like the rector, he had to teach only three hours a day. Besides taking the upper classes in singing, the cantor had to instruct the third class in Latin. Bach had expressly declared his willingness to take these classes, and he appears to have felt a certain pride in doing so, while Telemann had asked to be absolved from non-musical teaching. Afterwards, however, this work did not please him, and he asked his colleague Magister Petzold to act as his deputy in return for a renumeration of fifty thalers per annum. The council gave its consent to this.

Singing classes were held on the three first days of the week, at nine o'clock and twelve o'clock. On Thursday the cantor was quite free; on Friday he taught a singing class at twelve o'clock. On Saturday afternoon, after vespers, while private confession was going on below, the rehearsals for the cantatas took place. Bach seems not to have taken the instruction in singing very seriously. The reproach is always being made against him that he left it almost entirely to the older scholars, instead of attending to it himself. To what extent he was really lax in his views of his duties we cannot now judge; but the charges that were made against him can hardly have been without some justification.

But even if he fulfilled all his duties most scrupulously he would be occupied in the school no more than two or three hours each day. Every four weeks he had to inspect the school. This was the duty of the four principal teachers, who during this week had to submit to the general regulations of the school, and perhaps even sleep in it.

We know that in his later years, when it was his turn to do the inspection, Bach was exceedingly irregular in his attendance at devotions and at grace. In any case he was not overworked, and had plenty of leisure for composition.

He gives his salary, in the letter to Erdmann, as about seven hundred thalers*. Of these, indeed, only something over a hundred thalers was fixed; this was augmented by school-fees and receipts from legacies, of which he received a share. The main part of his income, however, came from the wedding and funeral ceremonies, from which he always received something according to the "class". The highest payment for weddings was two thalers, for funerals one thaler fifteen groschen.

The income of the cantor was thus rather variable. Kuhnau had complained that many wealthy people, in order to avoid expense, were married in a neighbouring village church, or dispensed with music of any kind, vocal or instrumental, at their funeral. Occasionally even the weather had something to do with it. In 1729, as Bach himself says in the letter to Erdmann, the air was so healthy that he was a hundred thalers to the bad on the ordinary funeral receipts. That year — which was a happy one for posterity, for it gave us the *St. Matthew Passion*, — left a bad memory with the creator of that work, for during it the people of Leipzig would not die in sufficiently large numbers!

Another part of the emoluments consisted of the share the cantor received of the monies which the alumni collected by singing at the houses at Michaelmas and the New Year. Compositions for special occasions appear to have been fairly well paid for. Leipzig was certainly not an Eldorado for musicians. The burghers, like the council, thought a good deal of art, but spent nothing on it. Marianne von Ziegler, the intelligent widow of an officer, and

---

* The letter will be given in full later on.

a crowned poetess, at whose house a good deal of music was performed, says in a letter of this date: "The remuneration that the musicians get for their trouble here is as a rule poor, and they often have to be thankful if, in return for several hours of musical service, they get a lean bone to pick. How then can such people live, since no one has any care for them or gives them any help?"* The foreign musicians in Dresden and at other princely courts were differently situated.

On the whole, however, Bach's income, if we take into consideration the value of money at that time, cannot have been a poor one. He brought up his large family honestly, gave his children a good education, was profuse and cordial in his hospitality, and at his death left not only a rich collection of first-rate musical instruments, but also a not insignificant sum of money. His household property, judging from the inventory that was drawn up when it came to be divided, was that of a well-to-do burgher**. Anna Magdalena was certainly an excellent housewife. Bach himself was a good man of business, and did not treat money matters as an unimportant part of life. One even has the impression that he frequently put them very decidedly in the foreground.

The position of the cantor would thus have been from every point of view desirable if better conditions had prevailed in St. Thomas's school at the time. When Bach joined the institution, however, it was in an advanced state of decline. This had not come about all in a day. For years previously the rector and the council had seen clearly what was going on, and they had exchanged many documents on the subject, enacting new ordinances and reviving old ones. No effectual remedy, however, had been

---

* See Philipp Spitta, *Marianne von Ziegler und Joh. Seb. Bach*, in *Zur Musik*, Berlin, 1892, pp. 93—119. The composer used the works of this poetess, (who was closely connected with the Gottsched circle) for the texts of eight of his finest cantatas.

** The inventory of the property Bach left is in the district court at Leipzig. It is given in Spitta, III, 351 ff.

found. Kuhnau in his latter days had suffered a good deal from the bad state of affairs, which were the result of several causes. The rooms in which the scholars were lodged were far too few in number, and left a good deal to be desired from the point of view of health. The school was therefore a centre of contagion. The scholars lived almost in dirt; Kuhnau, in one of his memorials, speaks of certain scholars as scabious. It was consequently not surprising that the burghers sent their children elsewhere. In the three lower classes, that had formerly contained a hundred and twenty scholars, there were in 1717 only fifty-three *. The charitable portion was always completely occupied, for the free admissions were in much request. These young people, however, were hard to keep in order. Discipline had quite disappeared. The rector at that time, Heinrich Ernesti, who had presided over the institution since 1684, was a man without any energy.

If the place was to be reformed, the singing in the streets would first have to be abolished. This was impossible, however, since the rector and the two head teachers made a not inconsiderable profit out of the collections, and the scholars themselves were dependent upon these earnings.

How art fared in such an establishment can easily be imagined. Kuhnau's memorials to the town council paint a truly wretched picture **. The voices of the young scholars were ruined by their going about singing in storm and rain before they had had proper training. As these rounds were mostly made at the New Year, it was impossible to rehearse with any thoroughness the cantatas for that season. Formerly boys with good voices had been engaged as supernumerary alumni. From false considerations of economy this practice had been in the course of time given up, to the great detriment of the music. Previously, also, the cantor had had at his disposal certain small allowances by means of which he could ensure the coöperation

---

* Spitta II, 199 ff.
** See Spitta III, 303—305; Five Memorials of Kuhnau.

of musical students for the orchestra and male voices for the choir. These also had been gradually taken from him. The majority of the students consequently stayed away, and the cantor had to do the best he could with the eight town-pipers and his own boys. Seeing no way out of the difficulty, Kuhnau begs that something from the receipts of the alms-bag may be devoted to the choir, so that he may provide the voluntary helpers with some entertainment, and give them a dinner once a year. "This" he observes at the end of the memorial, "since it concerns the advancement of church music and the glory of God, would be as much, perhaps even more, a *causa pia* than if the money were given to beggars, who would not do the same good with it."

The town council turned a deaf ear to these appeals. Speaking generally, the cantor had not control of so much as a pfennig. To get a board with nails in it fixed in the church, on which the violins could be hung, he had to address a petition to the council. He also had to beg for some violin cases, in order that the instruments might not receive more damage than was necessary when being taken from one church to another. The impression given us by all these petitions is that Kuhnau had no standing at all as regards the council.

The situation was particularly critical from the fact that Kuhnau was quite uninterested in the newer musical life in Leipzig. The new art was antipathetic to him; he hated everything connected with the opera or operatic music*. Moreover he not only saw his best choristers and soloists enticed from the school by the opera before they had fin-

---

* He had composed an opera, which, however, had been a complete failure. No doubt this was the origin of his violent hatred of the newer music. See Richard Münnich's able article, *Kuhnaus Leben*, in the *Sammelbände der Internationalen Musikgesellschaft*, 1901—1902, pp. 473—527. Kuhnau's rough satire on the Italian musicians and their German imitators, *Der musikalische Quacksalber* (1700), has recently been re-issued by Benndorf (Behr, Berlin, 1900).

ished their time, but found that the more music-loving of
the students — even those who did not ask for remuneration — turned their backs on the official church music
and hankered after an art that offered more satisfaction
to the children of the epoch.   The foundation of Telemann's singing union at the beginning of the eighteenth
century had been a severe blow for the cantor of St. Thomas's. Still worse was to come. Though he was the director
of the services at all the churches in Leipzig, one of them
made arrangements to dispense with him, and to supplant
the other churches in the favour of the citizens and the
council by admitting the modern style of music.   This
was the New Church, at which Telemann was organist in
1704. His successors continued the singing union he had
founded, and so drew the students to them.

Telemann's performances on feast days and at fair times
had caused some sensation. The council had been generous
with its help. In vain did Kuhnau assert his rights as
director of the church music in Leipzig. He did not succeed in bringing the New Church under his jurisdiction
again, in spite of his warnings to the council as to the
dangers of theatrical music in the church service. When
on one occasion he refused to place the St. Thomas
singers at the disposal of the New Church for a performance of the Passion, he was compelled to do so by his
superiors.

He almost, indeed, lost another church.   Until 1710 the
university church of St. Paul had been used only for the
academic services at the three great feasts, at the commemoration services for the Reformation, and once a
quarter. The cantor of St. Thomas's had been in charge
of the music, for which he had been paid by the university.
In 1710 the university arranged a service in this church
for each Sunday, and the question arose as to who should
have the musical direction of this. A law student, Joh.
Friedr. Fasch, who later on became Kapellmeister in
Zerbst, who had founded a second *Collegium musicum* by

the side of that of Telemann, applied for the post*. Kuhnau
could only save this "new service", as it was called, for
the cantor of St. Thomas's by declaring his readiness to
attend to the music for it gratis, and to be content with
the payment he already received for the academic festival
services.

This was the condition of things when Bach entered
upon his office. There was no hope of any improvement
in the state of the school so long as the old rector, — with
whom, for the rest, he was on very good terms, — was
still alive. To accomplish anything at all he had to set
his hope on the university, and try to interest the academic
world in his artistic undertakings. The prime essential
was to get the university service in his hands, and to restore
the full authority of the cantor of St. Thomas's as supreme
director of the whole of the Leipzig church music. During
the long interregnum a certain Görner, — an arrogant but
insignificant musician, who had formerly been organist at
St. Paul's, and now held that office at St. Nicholas's —
had offered to look after the music for the university church.
If Telemann had succeeded Kuhnau in Leipzig, he would
have received the post of director of the academic church
music, since he had done the university the honour to
ask expressly for it, as if he were not aware that the post belonged by prescriptive right to the cantor of St. Thomas's.
Bach appears to have omitted to do this; and the university authorities now definitively assigned the old and the
new service to Görner, just to show "that the academy is
not bound to accept the town cantor every time"**. This
was on the 3rd April 1723, — three weeks before Bach
was appointed by the council.

------

* The son of this Fasch, Karl Friedrich Christian (1736—1800)
founded in 1792 the Berlin Singakademie, which in course of time
revived Bach's *St. Matthew Passion.*
** Spitta II, 210 ff. B. F. Richter published the results of some
new research into this matter in the *Monatshefte für Musikgeschichte*
for 1901, p. 100 ff.

Scarcely was the new cantor settled when he plunged into the fight over his position. On 28th September 1723 he petitioned the university for the twelve thalers that had always been allowed for the "old service" — they were paid out of endowments — and that Kuhnau had regularly received. He met with a refusal, but appears to have provided some festival compositions for which he received payment. The affair went on for two years. On 3rd November 1725 Bach addressed a written appeal direct to the King, who had the matter looked into at once, and demanded a report from the university, to which Bach afterwards replied. The end of all this discussion was that the university was ordered to pay the cantor the twelve thalers, both for the past and in the future, since they were provided by old endowments; Görner retained the "new service", for which he was specially paid; Bach provided the compositions for the feast days; for academic festival functions the university appointed now one, now the other. Bach had thus won only half a victory. Görner was the director of the university music, though as organist of St. Nicholas's he was Bach's subordinate*.

This energetic action did not win much sympathy for the master in the academic world. Even the members of the council were perhaps not altogether pleased to find that they had a cantor who dared, at the first opportunity, to make a direct appeal to the sovereign, trusting to his good connections in Court circles. It is certain that the university gave the preference to Görner when commissioning compositions for academic festival occasions. When a certain Herr von Kirchbach, acting on instructions from the Court, commissioned Bach to write the funeral ode for Queen Christiane Eberhardine, who had died on 7th September, the university tried to get the bearer of the order

---

* Johann Gottlieb Görner was born in 1697, at Penig in Saxony. In May 1712 he entered the St. Thomas school as an alumnus, became organist of St. Paul's in 1716, organist of St. Nicholas's in 1721, and of St. Thomas's in 1729. He died 15th February 1778.

from the Court for the "ovation" — which was to take
place at St. Paul's — to countermand the commission that
had been given to Bach, and transfer it to Görner, and
sent word to von Kirchbach that "Bach would not be admitted". .When von Kirchbach offered twelve thalers to
the university music director as compensation for not
getting the commission, the university authorities gave
way, but demanded that Bach should sign a declaration
admitting that the permission to produce his music at this
ceremony in St. Paul's was to be regarded as a favour for
one occasion only, carrying with it no similar rights for the
future, and that he should not undertake such commissions
again without the permission of the university*. Bach
naturally would not sign this document. The university
registrar, who called on him at eleven in the morning of the
11th October to get his signature, had to go away at mid-
day without having effected his purpose.

In 1729 Görner was promoted to the organistship at
St. Thomas's, but still retained his post as university musical director. Bach must have been more than once
nettled by this presumptuous person. It is related that
once, at the rehearsal of a cantata, he flew into such a
passion with the organist, who was always going wrong
in the accompaniments, that he tore off his wig and threw
it at the man's head, telling him that he would have done
better to have been a cobbler. If the anecdote is true,
it is most likely to have been Görner who was the object
of this singular missile.

In time the relations of the two men seem to have improved. When Bach's property was divided after his
death, Görner was appointed guardian of the four children
who were under age**, which would hardly be explicable

---

* The document is still preserved; it is couched in terms that
are truly humiliating for Bach. See Richter, *Joh. Seb. Bach und
die Universität zu Leipzig*, in the *Monatshefte für Musikgeschichte*,
1901, pp. 150 ff.
** Spitta III, 357.

unless his latter relations with Bach had been fairly good.

Until the year 1729 nothing unusual occured between the composer and the council. Bach accommodated himself to the situation as well as he could, and did his duty in the school and in the church. As the New Church and St. Paul's had by now become almost independent, he had for the most part only St. Thomas's and St. Nicholas's to attend to.

The forces at his disposal were slight. St. Thomas's had a total of fifty-five alumni. Out of these, four choirs had to be formed: one for St. Thomas's, one for St. Nicholas's, one for the New Church, and one for St. Peter's. Bach naturally left to the last two the choirs composed of the indifferent and bad singers; at a pinch they could be used in the chorales and motets, but were no use in solo music, which, indeed, was not essential in these two churches.

Even in the best circumstances he could not get more than three voices to a part in his choirs. As a rule he had to be thankful if he could get the two principal choirs at this strength, that is, composed of twelve singers each. And small as his vocal forces were, there had to be deducted from them the singers whom he needed in the orchestra. The council gave him only eight town-musicians. No more students could be found to help; the gaps therefore had to be filled with scholars. In ordinary cases he had an orchestra of about eighteen to twenty, — two or three first violins, as many seconds*, two violas, two violoncellos, one "violon" or contrabass, two or three oboes, according to requirements, and one or two bassoons, flutes and trumpets.

---

* Kuhnau, in one of his memorials, asked for four to each string part. Copious details of the musical conditions at St. Thomas's school during Bach's time are given by B. F. Richter in his article on *Stadtpfeifer und Alumnen der Thomasschule in Leipzig zu Bachs Zeit*, in the *Bachjahrbuch* for 1907, pp. 32—78. He gives the names of the singers and instrumentalists whom Bach had at his disposal during his cantorate.

Deductions of course had to be made for those who were sick or hoarse, those whose musical education was not sufficiently advanced to permit of their entering the choir, and those who were generally good for nothing. At the end of the school year, when the scholars had had a whole year's training, he would be able to bring together the sixteen singers and twenty instrumentalists, and even perform the Passion with a double chorus and a double orchestra, as in the case of the *St. Matthew Passion*, for example, — though it is still doubtful whether, at the first performance of this work, he had three or four voices to each part. But how he managed after Easter, at the beginning of the new school year, remains a mystery. Certainly many a cantata is orchestrated as it is simply because at that particular time Bach had only those instruments at his disposal.

The chorus and the orchestra were divided into solo and ripieno groups*. The soloists sang the arias and recitatives, and also sang with the choir. Special soloists were not employed. Kuhnau had urged the council to engage two extra soloists, who should be exempt from all other duties, especially that of singing in the streets. His request, however, was not granted. The arias and recitatives of the *St. Matthew Passion* were thus sung by schoolboys. We must not rate their performances either too high or too low. The technique of singing was at that time a more general possession than it is now. Colorature and trills were practised even in the elementary stage of instruction, and anyone who possessed the least natural aptitude for singing could soon acquire a certain, though may be a superficial, facility. Unfortunately we have no means whatever of learning how Bach taught singing. Possibly his scholars sang the arias better, from a technical point of view, than we might expect; into the spirit of them, however, they could hardly penetrate. They had

---

* Ripieno (Italian for "full"), is the antithesis of solo.

not the necessary time for this. We must remember that they had to perform a new aria and a new recitative each Sunday, to say nothing of the Feast days.

The orchestral ripieno played only in the choruses and in the tutti passages of the arias; the solo singers were accompanied by the solo group of instruments alone. This consisted chiefly of strings, there being very few of the wind to each part. Here again we can form no conception of how the musical mechanics — for the town-musicians were nothing else — or the scholars, — who, in addition to their other occupations, had to learn an instrument from an older scholar in a few months — managed with the oboe, flute and trumpet parts, that offer such great difficulties even to the expert wind players of the present day. We can only suppose that the art of wind-instrument playing stood on a higher general level then than we can now imagine. It is always difficult to form even relatively accurate ideas upon the state of executive art in a particular period of the past. These are purely practical matters upon which we possess no documents, and upon which documents in any case could tell us nothing. Certain arts and aptitudes assuredly die with particular generations, and never again re-appear in quite the same way.

At the head of each of the four choirs was a prefect. These posts were much sought after, the prefects taking a special share of the receipts from the street singing and the other odd sources, so that they could lay by, while at school, something substantial for their later student period. The cantor conducted the choir that performed the cantata on a given Sunday; the duty was shared on alternate Sundays by St. Thomas's and St. Nicholas's. If the cantor conducted the cantata at St. Thomas's, the prefect of the other choir conducted the motet at St. Nicholas's, and *vice versâ*.

This rotation could on no account be deviated from as regards either the cantatas or the Passions. It happened once that Bach wished to produce the Passion at

St. Thomas's, — where the space was more adequate —
though for that year it was the turn of St. Nicholas's. The
printed programmes, in which St. Thomas's was mentioned
as the place of performance, were actually in the hands
of the public. It mattered nothing. The town council
would not permit the cantor to do as he chose, and the
latter had to yield.

Of Bach as a conductor nothing is known. At that
time it seems to have been customary to conduct church
music with a sheet of music rolled up like a baton. On
the title page of Walther's musical lexicon, the conductor,
a roll of music in each hand, stands behind the organist
and by the side of the contrabassist. Many, again, conducted from the clavicembalo; others led with the violin.
There was no question of conducting in the modern sense,
i. e., a communication and translation of musical intentions; it was simply a matter of keeping the players and
singers in correct time. Later on Bach had the Rückpositiv of the instrument at St. Thomas's arranged so that
he could play on this independently of the great organ.
He undoubtedly had the manual fitted up in this way for
convenience in conducting. Sitting there, he could survey
both choir and orchestra, and in the more difficult solo
numbers could himself play from the figured basses.

Cantatas were sung each Sunday, with the exception of
the last three in Advent and the six of Lent; in addition
there were the three Feasts of the Virgin, the New Year,
Epiphany, Ascension, the Feast of St. John, Michaelmas,
and the Reformation Feast, — in all, fifty-nine cantatas
every year. If Bach really wrote five complete yearly
cycles of cantatas, as the obituary notice says and Forkel
also affirms, then the total number comes to two hundred
and ninety-five. About one hundred, then, must be regarded as lost, since we possess only a hundred and ninety.

The service in both the principal churches began at
seven o'clock. The organ prelude was followed by the
motet; then came the *Introit*; after this the *Kyrie*, that

was sung once in German — in the hymn "Kyrie Gott Vater in Ewigkeit" — and once in Latin. The *Gloria* was intoned from the altar, and answered either by the choir with *et in terra pax*, or by the congregation with "Allein Gott in der Höh' sei Ehr" (To God alone on high be praise), the German version of the *Gloria*. After the collect, the Epistle was read, or rather sung in the old psalmody. This was followed by a congregational hymn, whereupon the Gospel was chanted by the priest, who also intoned the *Credo*. Then the organist began to preludise, keeping mainly in the keys which the instruments needed for tuning. At a sign from the cantor he ceased, and the cantata began, at the end of which the hymn "Wir glauben all an einen Gott" (We all believe in one God) was sung.

The cantata lasted on an average about twenty minutes. In the summer the cantor did not need to keep to this time so precisely as in the winter, when the cold made them take care that the already long service was not made too long. It was no light matter to stay in the cold church three or four hours, which was the time the service lasted. In St. Nicholas's Church the choristers maintained a coal fire; at St. Thomas's they went out during the sermon and warmed themselves in the school. They did not, however, escape the sermon, for while there they had to read one, the rector usually being present, — as Kuhnau, to whom we owe this interesting information, says in one of his memorials to the council. There was no fear of their miscalculating the time, since the sermon, according to rule, had to last exactly an hour, from eight to nine o'clock.

The sermon was followed by a prayer and the blessing, and then a congregational hymn led into the second part of the service, the communion celebration. German hymns were usually sung during the communion. The choir at St. Thomas's was as a rule no longer at its full strength at this stage, as the alumni had to prepare the table in the school for the meal at eleven o'clock. Kuhnau even found it sufficient for the prefect alone to remain behind in the church to lead the communion hymns*. The cantor usually left immediately after the cantata. Thus Kuhnau had been able to offer to take charge of the music at the university service, since he could get there from St. Thomas's in time for the cantata. Bach must often have remained to play the organ during the communion, there being plenty of scope here for preludising and improvising, as is proved by his chorale preludes upon communion hymns. In the first part of the service the organist mostly had his opportunity during the opening prelude, and afterwards before the congregational hymn that came between the Epistle and the Gospel. The chorale "Allein Gott in der Höh' sei Ehr" seems also to have been prefaced by a performance on the organ, for otherwise it is hard to explain why Bach wrote more preludes upon this melody than upon any other.

At a quarter to twelve there was a short service with a sermon, at which the choir had not to assist. Vespers began at a quarter past one with a motet. After various prayers and congregational hymns came a sermon, as a rule upon the Epistle; this was followed by the German Magnificat. At the end "Nun danket alle Gott" (Now thank we all our God) was sung.

On the three last Sundays in Advent, and in Lent, no cantatas were given, the organ was silenced**, and the motets were discontinued. Instead of these, the Nicene

---

* See Kuhnau's memorial of 18th Dec. 1717: "The scholars have a coal fire in the St. Nicholas's church. At St. Thomas's they go out and read the sermon, the Herr Rector generally being with them. Ours, however, cannot have this or indeed endure it. Thus during communion the choir is not intact, many of them having to go out to attend to the arrangements for eating. Nor are they necessary; for it has always been found to be better that the prefect alone should start the hymns and verses and sing them with the congregation."

** This means that even the congregational hymns were not accompanied by the organ, but were led by the choir alone. On ordinary Sundays, too, the sermon hymn was sung without organ accompaniment.

Creed was sung by the choir in Latin; and after the Epistle
the Litany, the hymn of intercession of the ancient church,
was sung, the congregation joining in. On these Sundays
the *Kyrie* seems to have been rendered in the concerted
musical form. We know this to have been the case on the
first Sunday in Advent.

The services on Feast days were quite overloaded with
figurate music. On the first two days — the three great
Feasts were each celebrated for three days — cantatas
were given at vespers as well*. The St. Thomas choir
gave the cantata it had performed at its own church in
the morning at St. Nicholas's in the afternoon, the choir
of the latter church singing at St. Thomas's, in the afternoon, the cantata that had been given at St. Nicholas's
in the morning. On the morning of the first day of the
Feast, Bach always conducted in St. Nicholas's, that church
deriving a certain pre-eminence from the fact that the
superintendent, Salomo Deyling, was minister there. On the
third day, music was given in one of the churches only.

Further, on Feast days the old hymns were sung at the
commencement, before the organ prelude. During the
communion service the *Sanctus* was sung, and at vespers,
after the sermon, the Magnificat. The first Sunday in
Advent and the Annunciation, even though they came
during Lent, were celebrated as Feast Sundays, with organ
and figurate music.

As is generally known, Bach has noted down the order
of the service for a certain first Sunday in Advent on the
cover of the cantata *Nun komm der Heiden Heiland* (No.61).
It is headed, "Order of divine service in Leipzig on the
morning of the first Sunday in Advent", and runs thus: —

"The Prelude. Motet. Prelude to the *Kyrie*, which
is accompanied throughout. Intoning at the altar. Reading of the Epistle. The Litany sung. Prelude to the

---

* Also at New Year, Epiphany, Ascension, Trinity and Annunciation.

chorale. Reading of the Gospel. Prelude to the principal music*. The Creed to be sung. The sermon. After the sermon, as usual, some verses of a hymn to be sung. *Verba institutionis.* Then preludes and singing of chorales alternately until the end of the communion *et sic porro.*"

At the evening service on Good Friday the Passion was performed. If it were in two parts, the first was sung before, the second after, the sermon; if in one part only, it came before the sermon. This was the more rational, as the sermon was preached on the burial of Christ; while the two-part Passion took up the story again, *after* the sermon, with the trial and condemnation. When Bach came to Leipzig, the Passion performances at vespers were still quite new, dating only from 1721. In that year Kuhnau had had to bow to the taste of the times by writing a Passion in the modern concert style, so that St. Thomas's should not lag too far behind the New Church. Previously Leipzig had known only the old motet Passion in the *a capella* style, which took the place of the reading of the Gospel at the principal service. As the first vesper Passion was produced at St. Thomas's in 1721, and the services were held in alternate years at each of the two principal churches, it is easy to discover in which church Bach's Passions were given in any particular year. The first, the *St. John Passion* of 1724, would necessarily be performed at St. Nicholas's.

From 1766 onwards the Passions were transferred to the morning service; at a later date they were abolished altogether.

Latin still prevailed in the Leipzig service in Bach's day, the Feast hymns being sung and the Epistle and Gospel read in that language. We cannot exactly determine, however, the proportions of Latin and German in the service at that time. From 1702 onward, the council fought for a purely German service; at first it seems to

---

* I. e. the cantata.

have little support, though it was able to effect a few changes at once*.

There was no specific Leipzig hymn-book; the congregation was supposed to know the hymns allotted to each Sunday. Any one who wanted to refer to them made use of the Dresden hymn-book**, which was what the choristers used. We know from the inventory of Bach's effects that he himself possessed the collection, in eight volumes, of *Andächtiger Seelen geistliches Brand- und Gantz-Opfer* (Leipzig 1697), to which he must have turned when looking for good chorale verses for his cantatas.

It was the ancient custom for the cantor to choose the sermon hymns. Bach had to decide upon the hymns for the whole of the Leipzig churches. The choice offered was not large; tradition had allotted certain hymns to each Gospel, and the hymn-books were arranged accordingly. In Leipzig the churches followed in this matter the Dresden hymn-book.

Now it happened that in 1727 the afternoon preacher at St. Nicholas's, Magister Gaudlitz, desired to choose the hymns for his own sermons. He asked the permission of the Consistory and of the cantor to do this, and obtained it from both. This arrangement lasted a year. Then Bach took it into his head to ignore entirely the wishes of the preacher, and to select the hymns again from the Dresden hymn-book. Gaudlitz complained to the Consistory, who requested the cantor to keep to the previous arrangement. Bach, however, although the matter was one that concerned the church service alone, saw fit to call up

---

* Thus the *Te Deum*, which at matins at St. Nicholas's was given out alternately by the organist and the choir, was replaced by the German version, "Herr Gott, dich loben wir." The wonderful harmonisation of this chorale verse by verse, (included in the Peters Edition among the chorale preludes, VI, 26), was therefore written by Bach for matins. This arrangement would also be used at the Reformation Feast, where it was customary to sing the *Te Deum*. It has come down to us in a copy made by Forkel.

** First issued in 1694.

the Council against the Consistory and the poor Magister. He made a written report to the Council on the matter, and enlarged upon all the possible dangers of the innovation. How far this helped him again to "his rights" against the Consistory we cannot discover. The affair does not show Bach in a particularly favourable light. If he had wanted to guard his rights he should have done so at the beginning; if afterwards he desired to annul the agreement, he should have taken another course than the one he did*.

In 1729 a serious conflict broke out between Bach and the Council**. In Easter of this year, some foundation scholars were received into the school whom Bach had found, on examination, to be quite unmusical; several who, he said, were particularly competent, had been rejected; while some of the candidates appear not to have presented themselves to him for examination at all. In the same year Bach assumed the direction of the Telemann Society. This brought about once more the old and desirable situation which the Council had so long wished for, — the students were again at the disposal of the cantor of St. Thomas's for his church performances. But the members of the Council, on their part, should now have restored to the cantor the old stipends for the students who were regularly employed in the choir and the orchestra. This they omitted to do; nor did they offer to fill up the foundation scholarships still unallotted.

Naturally there was now no hope for good music in the churches for the year 1730. The poor condition of the choir must indeed have been noticeable in 1729, at the first performance of the *St. Matthew Passion*; while at the celebration of the two-hundredth anniversary of the Augsburg Confession, on 25th, 26th, and 27th June 1730, it appears to have been unmistakeable.

---

* On this matter see Spitta II, 231 ff.
** For full details see Spitta II, 239 ff.

The Council laid the blame on Bach; he laid it on the Council. When, in the summer of 1730, the Council was electing a new rector — Ernesti having died on the 16th October 1729, — one of the members expressed the hope that they would fare better in this selection than they had done in that of the cantor. The reproach was general that Bach did not take enough trouble with the choir and with the singing lessons.

There may have been some truth in this; Bach had really lost heart. He was no organiser; whatever he undertook to do, he did it with the impetuosity of genius. But if those around him were not carried away by his enthusiasm, he was powerless. He knew nothing of the means by which a slower and more methodical mind would have gained its ends bit by bit. He could not even maintain discipline; such authority as he could count upon was merely that of genius and of the man in pursuit of an ideal. This, however, made no impression on the scholars. Of the pedagogue's authority, which alone could have kept them in order, he had nothing; and the passionate wrath by which he let himself be carried away, every now and then, made it still harder for him to get discipline. Disorder was therefore rife in the choir. More than once he had to call in the aid of the rector to procure obedience. Ernesti was very well disposed towards him, and supported him so far as his ill-health permitted; but his second successor, — also named Ernesti — in the end deserted Bach altogether.

Other matters were discussed at the Council meeting on the 2nd August 1730, where the rancour against the cantor broke out*. Magister Petzold, who acted as his deputy in the teaching of Latin, had done his work badly. Bach, without the knowledge of the Council, had sent a scholar from the choir into the country — probably to assist at some musical festivities; he himself had gone away with-

---

* See Spitta II, 243 ff.

out permission. "Not only does the cantor do nothing, but he will not give any explanation . . . . We must therefore stop it once for all" said one of the councillors. Another, the syndic Job, declared the cantor to be "incorrigible".

As a matter of fact they were not so angry with him for his errors or omissions in the performance of his duties, as for the disrespect he showed for the authority of the Council. He was, in fact, no cantor, but the Herr Kapellmeister of the courts of Cöthen and Weissenfels, who had taken service with the Leipzig Council, but wanted to make his subordinate position something different from what it really was. The indifference he exhibited towards the Council in great things and in small provoked them to an attempt to break the pride of this man, who too often ignored, — generally without reason — the deference appropriate to his position.

Bach, for his part, was in the right when he energetically repelled the reproach that he was answerable for the bad state of the church music. In a memorial dated 23rd August 1730 he details the constitution of the choir, and states that of the total number of alumni "seventeen are competent, twenty not yet fully capable, and seventeen incapable". Discretion forbids him to say anything as to the quality or the musical attainments of the eight town musicians. Nevertheless it should be considered that some are *emeriti*, and some in no such *exercitio* as they should be. For example, he always has to recruit the second violins, the violas, the violoncelli and the violon (i. e., the contrabass) from among the scholars. Had the councillors really asked themselves how he was to manage on Feast days, when cantatas had to be produced simultaneously in the two churches? The new art demands much better performers than "the old style of music, which no longer sounds well in our ears". Therefore they ought to increase, rather than diminish, the money allotted to the students who assisted. Everywhere it is the custom to underpay German artists, and to "abandon them to the cares of getting a livelihood", which cares prevent many of them from going on with their musical training*. The conclusion is "therefore simple"; if the subventions are to be continually withheld, he does not know "how he is to improve the music".

The language of the memorial is that of an indictment. It is signed "Joh. Seb. Bach, Director Musices", without any of the usual submissive formulae.   It was something different from the memorials that the Council was accustomed to receive from its cantor.   Bach's predecessor, in similar circumstances, used to sign himself "Your Magnificence's, Right Noble's and Most Wise's dutiful and most obedient Johann Kuhnau, cantor at St. Thomas's school".

While Bach was thus justifying himself to the Council, the latter had already taken action against him.   It was at first proposed to remove him to a lower class in the school, where, instead of teaching Latin, he would have had to give elementary instruction, for which he would not have been allowed a deputy.   On reconsideration, however, they appointed on their own account a capable deputy for the Latin lessons, whom Bach, of course had to pay as he had done the other.   But it was resolved to reduce his emoluments so far as that was practicable.   His salary and perquisites of course could not be touched. But there were legacies and endowments which the Council

---

* The passage in the memorial runs: "It is moreover somewhat strange that it is expected of German musicians that they should be capable ..... of at once performing *ex tempore* every kind of music, whether Italian or French, English or Polish, as those virtuosi can before whom it may be placed and who have studied it a long time previously, and, indeed, almost learned it by heart, and who *quod notandum* are very well paid, so that their trouble and industry are richly rewarded; but all this is not considered, and these people are left to take care of themselves, so that many a one, in the need of finding a livelihood, cannot think of attaining proficiency, much less of distinguishing himself.   To show this by one example, we need only go to Dresden, and see how the musicians are paid by the King ...."

could distribute among the teachers as it thought fit. Little
as he had had from these in the past, he was to receive
nothing at all in the future. In 1730 there were two hundred
and seventy thalers to distribute; the subrector received
a hundred and thirty thalers, the third teacher a hundred,
and Bach nothing.

The bitterness of his soul may be seen from a letter he
wrote on the 28th October of this year to Erdmann, his
former fellow-student at Lüneburg, begging him to help
him to find a new appointment. This letter, one of the
few by Bach that we possess, was packed with other old
papers in an old chest after the death of its addressee,
sealed, and sent to Moscow. There it wandered into the
State archives, whence it was rescued by Spitta's friend
O. von Riesemann, of Reval, who had been entrusted by
Bach's biographer with the search for whatever might be
left of Erdmann's papers*.

The letter runs thus: —

"Honoured Sir,
"Your Excellency will excuse an old and faithful servant for
taking the liberty to trouble you with this letter. Nearly four years
have now flown by since your Excellency honoured me with a gracious answer to the letter I sent you, but as I remember that you
graciously wished me to give you some news of my vicissitudes,
I shall now most obediently proceed to do so. From my youth up
my history has been well known to you, until the change which took
me as Kapellmeister to Cöthen. There lived there a gracious Prince,
who both loved and understood music, and with whom I thought
to live the rest of my days. It so happened, however, that his Serene Highness married a Princess of Berenburg, and then it seemed
as if the musical inclination of the said Prince had grown a little
lukewarm, while at the same time the new Princess appeared to be
an amusement to him; so God willed it that I should be called to
this place as Director Musices and cantor at St. Thomas's school.
At first it was not wholly agreeable to me to become a cantor after
having been a Kapellmeister, on which account I delayed making
a decision for a quarter of a year; however, this post was described
to me in such favourable terms that finally — especially as my sons
seemed inclined towards study, — I ventured upon it in the name of

---

* Erdmann had become the Russian agent in Dantzig. Spitta
gives further details of the lucky discovery in the preface to the
first volume of his biography, p. V ff.

the Most High, and betook myself to Leipzig, passed my examination, and then made the move. Here, by God's will, I am to this day. But now, since I find (1) that the appointment here is not nearly so considerable as I was led to understand, (2) that it has been deprived of many perquisites, (3) that the town is very dear to live in, and (4) that the authorities are strange people, with little devotion to music, so that I have to endure almost constant vexation, envy, and persecution, I feel compelled to seek, with the Almighty's aid, my fortune elsewhere. Should your Excellency know of, or be able to find, a suitable appointment in your town for an old and faithful servant, I humbly beg you to give me your gracious recommendation thereto; on my part I will not fail, by using my best diligence, to give satisfaction and justify your kind recommendation and intercession. My position here is worth about 700 thalers, and when there are rather more funerals than usual the perquisites increase proportionately; but if the air is healthy the fees decrease, last year, for example, being more than 100 thalers below the average from funerals. In Thuringia I can make 400 thalers go further than twice as many here, on account of the excessive cost of living. And now I must tell you a little about my domestic circumstances. I am married for the second time, my first wife having died in Cöthen. Of the first marriage, three sons and a daughter are still living, whom your Excellency saw in Weimar, as you may be graciously pleased to remember. Of the second marriage, one son and two daughters are living. My eldest son is *Studiosus Juris*, the other two are one in the first and the other in the second class, and the eldest daughter is still unmarried. The children of the other marriage are still little, the eldest, a boy, being six years old. They are one and all born musicians, and I can assure you that I can already form a concert, vocal and instrumental, with my family, especially as my wife sings a good soprano, and my eldest daughter joins in quite well. I should almost overstep the bounds of politeness by troubling your Excellency with any more, so I hasten to conclude with all devoted respects, and remain your Excellency's life-long most obedient and humble servant,

Joh. Seb. Bach.*

Leipzig, 28th October 1730.

For a letter to an old comrade of the Lüneburg days, the epistle is, according to our notions, couched in too submissive a tone. Perhaps the two were no longer on terms of friendship — Erdmann had been in Saxony in 1725 without visiting Bach — so that the letter was really one from the musician to the great gentleman, asking for his kind protection. This he probably found bitter enough.

---

* Spitta II, 253, 254.

Happily his condition was not so bad as he imagined it to be. He was known to the new rector, Johann Matthias Gesner, who had been subrector of the Weimar Gymnasium at the time when Bach was stationed at the Court there. Moreover he was warmly interested in music. As he was a capable teacher and an excellent organiser, he soon succeeded in bringing some degree of order into the school. The Council prized him very highly, and when he interested himself in Bach, the Council abandoned the measures it had taken against the cantor. In 1732 Bach was again admitted to a share in any money that was to be distributed. Gesner had previously had him definitely released from the necessity of teaching Latin.

It has recently become the habit to paint the malignity of the Leipzig Council in the blackest colours; Bach is spoken of as being "degraded" by his superiors. The author of a recent biography goes to the length of saying that "so far as it was possible for the Council to paralyse the creative faculty of the genius, it honestly tried to do so"*. That is not the question. On the contrary, never did the Council spend more on music than at the very time when it was most at loggerheads with Bach**. The way in which the members of the Council tried to impress on him the inferiority of his position was of course unhandsome; but we must not forget that Bach had done what he could to irritate them.

He did not regard the friendship of the rector as a sufficient guarantee against future measures. In spite of his titles as Kapellmeister at Cöthen and at Weissenfels, for the members of the Council and for the university he was merely the cantor. Of what avail was it for him to sign himself not cantor but *Director Musices*? Only one thing could win for him the respect of the Leipzig authorities, —

---

* Wolfrum, *Joh. Seb. Bach*, Berlin, 1905.
** On the expenditure at that time for church music see Spitta II, 252. Spitta does full justice to the Council.

to become attached in some way to the Court of the so-vereign. He therefore conceived the plan of petitioning in Dresden for the title of Court composer. It was not the mania for a title that urged him to this, but the struggle for dignity. This is clear from the document in which he solicits the grant. As every one knows, the document took the form of a dedicatory epistle accompanying the parts of the *Kyrie* and *Gloria* of the B minor mass, which he presented to the young Electoral Prince*. It is dated 27th July 1733, and runs thus:

"In the deepest devotion I lay before your Kingly Majesty the accompanying trifling work [proof] of the science I have attained in music, with the very humble petition that you will graciously regard it not according to the poorness of the composition, but according to your world-renowned clemency, and deign to take me under your most powerful protection. For some years now, and up to the present time, I have had the direction of the music in the two chief churches in Leipzig; but I have innocently had to suffer at different times, from one vexatious cause and another, a diminu-tion of the fees attached to this office, which might be withheld altogether unless your Kingly Majesty would be gracious enough to confer on me a Praedicate of your Court Kapelle, and would issue a command in the proper quarter for the granting of a patent to that effect. Such a gracious granting of my humble petition will bind me in infinite veneration, and I offer myself in the most dutiful obedience, whenever your Kingly Majesty may graciously desire it, for the composition of church music or music for the orchestra, to show my indefatigable diligence, and to dedicate my whole powers to your services, remaining in constant fidelity your Kingly Majesty's most humble and obedient servant,

Johann Sebastian Bach."**

He had to wait three years for the desired distinction. Not that he was regarded in any but a favourable light; but the Prince had other cares. The troubles that had broken out in Poland demanded his presence in his other kingdom, where he remained from November 1734 to August 1736. After his return, Bach's well-wishers seem to

---

* He appears to have gone to Dresden himself for the purpose. The dedication is addressed from there.

** See Spitta III, 38.

have reminded him of the matter;* and Bach received his nomination as Court composer on 19th November 1736. It came just at the right time to help him in a new struggle with his superiors.

In 1734 Gesner accepted a professorship at Göttingen. The Council itself was to blame for losing so soon this strong and capable man; it had refused him permission to accept, in addition to his rectorship, a professorship at the Leipzig university, though his immediate predecessor had been allowed to do so.

Ernesti, the subrector, was appointed in his place. He tried to carry the reforms of Gesner still further, without, however, possessing the fine humanity of his predecessor. At first he and Bach got on excellently together; the rector twice acted as godfather to children of the cantor. In 1736, however, Ernesti ordered the head prefect Gottlieb Theodor Krause, — who, in a fit of anger, had punished some choristers for behaving unbecomingly at a wedding ceremony — to be dismissed and degraded by a public castigation. Bach interceded for his prefect, and wanted to take the whole responsibility on himself, but in vain. To escape the punishment, Krause, who would shortly have gone to the university, absconded from the school. His place was given to the second prefect — another Krause, Johann Gottlob. Bach did not think very highly of him. The question of making him a prefect had arisen a year before, and Bach had then told the rector that Krause was "a dissolute dog". Being in a good humour, however, — Ernesti and he were discussing the matter on their way home from a good wedding-feast — he declared himself agreeable to Ernesti's nomination, nor had he any objection to make when Krause was promoted from fourth to third prefect, and later to second. He even accepted him for a time as first prefect, although he was angry with

---

* On 27th September 1736 Bach had drawn up a second petition, which he seems to have delivered to the Prince during his visit to Leipzig. Spitta III, 8.

the rector for his severity towards the other Krause. Some weeks after, however, he removed him to the second prefect-ship and promoted the third prefect to the first place. He notified this to the rector, who made no objection. When Krause complained to Ernesti, the latter referred him to Bach, who allowed himself to be carried away into telling Krause that he had put him back into the second prefect-ship because the rector had advanced him to the first on his own authority, and he would now show the rector who was master there. Krause immediately reported this to Ernesti; and when the latter asked Bach for an explana-tion, he repeated it to his face. Thus, for a matter quite insignificant in itself, he imprudently raised the question of the right of appointment of the prefects, upon which the school laws threw no clear light.

The rector demanded categorically the re-instatement of Krause as first prefect. Bach appears at first to have re-gretted his foolish impetuosity, and to have complied. But on one of the following Sundays, when Krause was preparing to conduct the motet, he turned him out in the middle of the hymn. At vespers the prefect again appeared in his place in obedience to the orders of the rector, who had at the same time forbidden the scholars to obey any prefect whatever appointed by Bach. The latter again turned Krause away. On the following Sunday, the 19th August, the same scenes were enacted. The scholars did not know whether they were to obey the rector or the cantor. The second prefect, Küttler, was sent away by Bach on the Sunday evening from the school meal, for having obeyed Ernesti instead of him.

The offended master addressed himself to the Council, after having first tried, but without success, his old tactics of taking shelter behind the Consistory. This time he managed it badly, and the Consistory would not take his part. The memorials in which the cantor and the rector fought each other are preserved for us in the archives of the Council. The miserable business dragged on for two

years. Bach's memorials show him to have been blinded
by the fury of his wrath. Ernesti keeps cool and behaves
as m asterof the situation; too adroit always to act honour-
ably, he turns the mistakes of his antagonist to his own advantage*. He does not stop at the vilest slander. It is
not difficult to imagine what the state of discipline of the
choir was all this time.

The church authorities, even those who had always
been favourably disposed towards Bach, were angry with
him for having tried to drag them into the dispute. Even
his protector, Superintendent Deyling, was offended with
him, and made him aware of it.

The Council avoided taking energetic measures. Krause
was to leave the school at Easter 1737, and the conflict
would thus come to a natural end. For Bach, however, this
did not at all settle the matter. He wanted to have the
question of right decided — whether the rector was entitled
to interfere in matters concerning the prefects, — and to
force Ernesti to make public amends to him, so as to restore
his authority among the scholars. As in the meantime
he had become a Court composer, he made a direct appeal
to the King, who immediately demanded a report. In
February 1738 the affair was still unsettled; at Easter the
King and Queen came to Leipzig, and Bach performed an
Abend-Musik in the open air in honour of the royal couple.
This is lost; but we learn from contemporary accounts
that it made a very good impression. It would appear
that the King then settled the dispute in Bach's favour,
since from this time the records of the Council are silent
upon it. Bach, however, had won nothing. Ernesti remained rector and created difficulties for him whenever
he could. The other teachers sided with the head of the
school.

This affair of St. Thomas's was typical of what went
on everywhere in the schools of that time. It was an

---

* The documents relating to the affair are given in Spitta III,
307 ff.

epoch in which the constitutions of schools were being reorganised. People were beginning to prosecute studies for study's sake, with the result that music was no longer allowed to occupy so much space and time in the work of the school. It was being squeezed out; the choirs of boarders had outlived their time, like the old choirs of scholars in general. A new epoch was beginning.

It was a misfortune that Bach's cantorate came during this time of transition. Henceforth the alumni of St. Thomas's fell into two categories — those who were there for study, and those who were there to render the music. The cantor had a grudge against the first, the rector against the second. Ernesti was an enemy of music. When he met a student practising an instrument, he would ask him sarcastically: "Are you also going to be an ale-house fiddler?" Bach, on his part, abhorred the pupils who were bent merely on acquiring general knowledge and only casually took up music, as the pastor Joh. Friedr. Köhler, himself at one time a student at St. Thomas's, tells us in his history of the Leipzig school system*.

The Krause affair had deprived Bach of his authority over both teachers and pupils. Henceforth he did his work at St. Thomas's as a stranger. Whether his relations with Superintendent Deyling ever resumed their early cordiality we do not know. The Council embarrassed him no more. Once it even confirmed some expenditure that the cantor had made without previously asking the permission of the Council. This indicates a friendly disposition towards him. The prompt interference of the monarch on behalf of his Court composer had instilled respect into his employers; and henceforth they avoided conflict.

At the end of the thirties or the beginning of the forties, — the date cannot be accurately determined — Bach gave

---

* Spitta III, 11, 12. The work exists only in manuscript in the Royal Library at Dresden: *Historia Scholarum Lipsiensium collecta a Joh. Friedr. Köhlero, pastore Tauchensi*, 1776 ff.

up the direction of the Telemann singing society, and so withdrew from public musical life. About that time, in 1741, a concert society was founded, with a wealthy merchant named Zehmisch at its head, out of which the Gewandhaus concerts afterwards grew. Bach was not connected with it, — at his own wish, not that of the founders of the society. He had no desire to come out of his retreat, feeling that the new generation and he no longer understood each other.

Speaking generally, he does not seem to have been closely connected with any Leipzig circle. He did not belong to that of the poetess Marianne von Ziegler, who received many musicians at her house; at any rate he is never mentioned in her letters. He came into contact with Gottsched in the autumn of 1727, when the latter was commissioned by Herr von Kirchbach to write the text for the funeral ode in commemoration of Queen Christiane Eberhardine. But later on, in 1736, when Frau Gottsched wished to study musical composition, he did not offer to teach her himself, but recommended his pupil Johann Ludwig Krebs, who became sincerely enthusiastic over the talent and the charm of his pupil.

Bach was very intimate with the librettist Christian Friedrich Henrici, who wrote under the pseudonym of Picander. He was a post-office official, who wrote satires and humorous verses in order to attract attention and to find a patron who would help him to a better appointment. Later on, indeed, he was promoted to a collectorship of land and drink taxes. Every one was astounded when, in 1724, he turned to religious poetry, and published a yearly cycle of cantata texts. He continued, however, with the utmost unconcern, to print the most vulgar and unpleasant effusions. People wondered how Bach could feel attracted to so coarse and unsympathetic a man.

He had many domestic troubles to bear in Leipzig. Of the thirteen children that Anna Magdalena bore to him, seven died; at his own death, of his twenty children only

nine were living — five sons and four daughters*. The
eldest son of Anna Magdalena, Gottfried Heinrich, was
of weak intellect. At the division of the estate he was
represented by a guardian. After the death of his father,
his brother-in-law Altnikol took him with him to Naumburg, where he lived until 1763. Emmanuel was of opinion
that he had some musical genius, which, however, remained undeveloped. Legends gathered at an early date
about this son. Rochlitz, an admirer of Bach, tells us in
his *Für Freunde der Tonkunst* (1832)** that the master
had a son named David, who, when he improvised at the
piano in his own way, often moved the father to tears.
No son of this name is mentioned in any of the genealogies
that have come down to us.

Bach's happiest time, in spite of all external discomforts,
was that of the years just before and after the *St. Matthew
Passion*, when he still had all his children round him.
Friedemann and Emmanuel were already capable musicians and a source of delight to him. It was at this time
that he could hold the domestic concerts of which he speaks
in the letter of 1730 to Erdmann***. In the same letter
he says that Friedemann is studying law. Emmanuel,
after leaving school, took up the same pursuit. This does

---

* Two sons, (Wilhelm Friedemann and Carl Philipp Emmanuel)
and one daughter, (Catharina Dorothea), were of the first marriage;
the third son of Maria Barbara, named Bernhard, died at Jena in
1738. Of Anna Magdalena's children there survived him: Gottfried Heinrich (1724—1763), Elisabeth Juliane Friederike (born
1726, year of death not known), Johann Christoph Friedrich
(1732—1795), Johann Christian (1735—1782), Johanna Caroline
(1737—1781), and Regine Susanna (1742—1809).
The following children of Anna Magdalena all died at Leipzig:
Christiane Sophie Henriette (born 1723, died 29th June 1726);
Christian Gottlieb (born 1725, died 21st September 1728); Ernestus
Andreas (died 1st November 1727, soon after birth); Regine Johanna (born 1728, died 25th April 1733); Christiane Benedicta
(died 4th January 1730, soon after birth); Christiane Dorothea
(born 1731, died 31st August 1732); Johann August Abraham
(died 6th November 1733, shortly after birth).
** IV, 278 ff.
*** See p. 136.

not imply, however, that Bach intended his sons to be anything else but professional musicians. A university course of some kind was at that time part of the complete education of the artist. Other pupils of Bach also went in for an academic course of study, though firmly resolved to adopt music as their profession. In many musical positions, in fact, an education of this kind was essential.

Wilhelm Friedemann studied three years; then he applied for the post of organist at St. Sophia's Church in Dresden, to which he was appointed in 1733, having come out the best at the examination performance on the 22nd June. He remained there thirteen years. In 1746 he went to St. Mary's Church at Halle, where Handel's old teacher, Zachau, had at one time been organist. The appointment of his favorite son to this famous post must have been very gratifying to Bach. Even at that time Wilhelm Friedemann shewed signs of the disorderly temperament that later on quite mastered him and brought him to adversity. The father could have had no presentiment of the tragic finish of this musical career that had so ideal a beginning, though in his last years he certainly had some anxiety about his son, who had begun to be addicted to drink, and quite neglected his art. Bach may have learned of the misuse his favorite son had made of one of his own Passions. Being commissioned to write some music for a university festival at Halle, at a fee of one hundred thalers, Friedemann, being too indolent to compose music of his own, simply adapted to his text the music of one of his father's Passions. The work was actually performed, but the fraud was exposed by a cantor from the neighbourhood of Leipzig who chanced to be present. The indignation was so great that Friedemann was not paid the fee that had been agreed upon*.

---

* On Bach's sons see C. H. Bitter's *Carl Philipp Emmanuel und Wilhelm Friedemann Bach und deren Brüder*, Berlin, 1868. The story of Friedemann's plagiarism from his father is told by the famous musical theorist Marpurg (1718—1795), an admirer of

Emmanuel caused his father nothing but joy.   He sent him to study at Frankfort- on- the-Oder, where the young artist founded a *Collegium musicum* among his fellow-students.   In 1738, as he was preparing to accompany a young and distinguished Livonian on his travels, Frederick the Great, at that time Crown Prince, called him to him at Ruppin, and in 1740 appointed him his clavier accompanist.   In his autobiography, Bach's son boasts that "he had the honour of accompanying on the piano, quite alone, at Charlottenburg, the first flute solo that Frederick played after becoming King".   Soon after his appointment he married the daughter of a Berlin wine dealer, and Johann Sebastian Bach became a grandfather.   "My son in Berlin has already two male heirs; the first was born about the time when, unhappily, the Prussians invaded us; the other is about fourteen days old", he says in 1748 in the postscript to a letter to his cousin Elias Bach of Schweinfurt*.

In the Kapelle of Frederick the Great there were many admirers and pupils of Sebastian Bach.   The royal virtuoso greatly prized his accompanist, though there was no such close relation between them as there was between himself

Bach, in his *Legenden einiger Musikheiligen* (1786), pp. 60—63. He mentions no names, but relates the story in such a way that every one can guess whom he means.

In 1764 Friedemann gave up his post in Halle, left his wife and his little daughter, and became a vagabond.   For some time (1771—1774) he stayed in Brunswick; later on he went to Berlin, where he procured some pupils.   Mendelssohn's grandmother was taught by him.   His ever-increasing asperity made it hard for people to interest themselves in him.   One of his acquaintances wrote at a later time: "Friends of art and of the name of Bach have literally raised him more than once out of the very dust, lodged him decently, and provided him with the necessaries of life.   They could never keep him in order, however, for any length of time.   His wilfulness, his vulgar pride and his strong passion for drink caused him always to relapse into misery".   He died 1st July 1784, at the age of seventy-four.   In the following year, Handel's *Messiah* was given in Berlin.   The widow of Bach's favorite son received a grant from the receipts of the concert.   See Bitter, p. 267.

* The eldest grandson was born on the 30th November 1745.

and Quantz. According to Zelter, Emmanuel was of too independent a nature as an artist to agree with all the musical opinions of the King, who would brook no contradiction in these matters. All the same he stayed twenty-seven years in the King's service. When Telemann, the musical director at the Johanneum in Hamburg, died in 1767, after having held the office for forty-six years, Emmanuel succeeded him. This event, of course, the father did not live to see*.

J. G. Bernhard, the third son of Bach's first marriage, became organist at Mühlhausen in 1735, when scarcely twenty years old, — not at St. Blasius's, however, where his father had once officiated, but at St. Mary's. In the spring of 1737 he became organist at St. Jacob's Church in Sangershausen. He quitted that town in a year, leaving behind him considerable debts, and died soon afterwards at Jena**.

Johann Christoph Friedrich, born in 1732, a man of a quiet, pleasant disposition, became during the life-time of his father chamber musician to the Count von der Lippe at Bückeburg***.

---

* In Hamburg, Emmanuel became acquainted with Klopstock and Reimarus. Every artist passing through the town visited his house. He died in 1788. It was proposed to erect a memorial to him in St. Michael's Church, with an inscription by the author of *Der Messias*. It got no further, however, than the inscription, which we still have. His youngest son, Sebastian, was a painter, — to his father's horror, so Forkel tells us. He died at Rome, barely twenty-six years old, during the life-time of his father.

** We still have the two letters that Bach wrote in recommendation of his son to Sangershausen; also the two he sent to Herr and Frau Klemm (with whom J. G. Bernhard had lodged), in response to their request for a payment of his debts. In one of these we can see the deeply-stricken father; the other is short and business-like. See S. Schmidt, *Vier aufgefundene Originalbriefe von J. S. Bach*, in the *Zeitschrift der Internationalen Musikgesellschaft* III, 1901 —1902, pp. 351 ff.

*** He remained in this post until his death, in 1795. His son, Wilhelm Friedrich Ernst, born in 1759, later on became cembalist

The delight of Bach as he grew old was his youngest son, Johann Christian, whom he was able to teach up to his fifteenth year. His affection for him was so great that during his life-time he gave him three of his finest claviers, which so angered the sons of the first marriage that they tried to dispute the gift.

Bach certainly could not have anticipated that the fame of this youngest born of his would at first completely overshadow his own. There is something fabulous about the life of Johann Christian; it has the charm of some bright romance. At the age of fifteen, after the division of the estate, he went to Berlin, to Emmanuel. He was soon seized, however, by a longing for Italy. He went there in 1754 — the first of the Bachs who went to the home of art beyond the Alps for his musical culture — and at once found rich patrons in Milan. To perfect his musical education he became a pupil of Padre Martini. For a time he lived in Naples, where he soon became one of the most celebrated of opera composers. After his conversion to the Roman Catholic faith, about the end of the fifties, he was appointed organist of Milan cathedral. The document relating to "Signor Giovanni Bacchi" is still in existence. In 1762 he went to London, where he had been commissioned to write an opera. It was produced at the King's Theatre in the Haymarket in the presence of the whole court, with extraordinary success. The composer was appointed master of music to the queen, and soon became one of the favorite music teachers of the higher aristocracy; they used to charge half-a-guinea a lesson, and kept a horse and carriage in order to get to all their pupils in good time. In 1767 he married a London operatic star, Cecilia Grassi. The Electoral Prince of the Palatinate sent for him to Mannheim for the production of an opera there. In 1779 he was living in Paris, where again he had

---

to Queen Louise of Prussia and music teacher to her children. He was the sole direct descendant of the great cantor who was present at the unveiling of the Leipzig monument in 1843. He died in 1845.

been commissioned to write an opera, for the manuscript of which he was to receive ten thousand francs*.

Would the embittered cantor, when he taught his youngest son in the school house at Leipzig, have dared to cherish such lofty dreams for him? Did he ever imagine that life would pour into the lap of this child of fortune all the good things it had denied to himself?

On 20th January 1749, Elisabeth Juliane Friederike Bach (born 1726), became the wife of Altnikol, the devoted pupil who, a little while before, on the master's recommendation, had received the appointment of organist in Naumburg. Bach rejoiced greatly at this marriage.

Two little girls were playing in the room while he sat correcting and making clear copies of his fugues — Johanna Karoline, aged twelve, and the six-year-old Regine Susanna. The mother went to and fro and tended her husband, who took no care of his failing eyes, but obstinately made them serve him as long as there was a gleam of light. He did not know that he had only a few more months to live; the wife and the two children did not know what misery was in store for them.

---

* The "London Bach" died 1st January 1782. Opinions upon him were sharply divided from the beginning. Rochlitz regarded him merely as a musician who sacrificed his artistic ambition to the applause of fine ladies. His numberless works are, in truth, merely fashionable compositions. On the other hand we must not forget that the man with whom Mozart, during his residence in London in 1764 and 1765, studied for a year and a quarter, and of whom he thought highly all his life, was at any rate an artist. His melodic invention is not always banal. Whether he was really the man of pleasure he was depicted as being by many of his contemporaries and by his first biographer Bitter, is an open question. Max Schwarz, in an exhaustive and singularly able study, has recently attempted a vindication of him artistically and morally. (*Johann Christian Bach*, in the *Sammelbände der Internationalen Musikgesellschaft* II, 1900—1901; pp. 401—454) It is to be wished that the other sons of Bach could find modern biographers of the same kind. The details given above are derived from this study.

CHAPTER IX.

APPEARANCE, NATURE, AND CHARACTER.

In the conflicts that agitated his life and embittered his soul, Bach does not always appear in a sympathetic light. His irritability and his stubborn belief that he was always in the right can neither be excused nor glozed over. Least of all can we find excuse for the fact that at first he would be too easy-going, would always remember too late what he called his rights, and then, in his blind rage, would make a great affair out of what was merely a trifle.

Such was Bach in his relations with people whom he suspected of a desire to encroach upon his freedom. The real Bach, however, was quite another being; all testimonies agree that in ordinary intercourse he was the most amiable and modest of men. He was, above all, upright and incapable of any injustice. His impartiality was well known. It was particularly evident in the judgments he was so often asked to give upon organ matters. In these affairs he was dreaded for his strictness, for nothing escaped his sharp eye. Whether it was an examination of candidates for an organist's post, or the scrutiny of a newly-erected organ, in either case he was so conscientious and impartial that, as Forkel says, the number of his friends was seldom increased by it*. It even made enemies for him. When, for example, the young Scheibe was a candidate with Görner and others, in 1729, for the post of organist at St. Thomas's, it availed him nothing that his father, the organ builder, was a friend of Bach. The latter declared for Görner, with whom he had had so many tussles, and whose arrogant nature could not be sympathetic to him. Scheibe bore them both a life-long grudge for it. To his indignation we owe a highly interesting

---

* Forkel, p. 22.

criticism of Bach in the Hamburg *Critische Musikus* of 1737. The master was hurt by it, but his relations with the elder Scheibe remained unaffected; he still expressed himself very favourably upon his work after the article, as he had done before.

Bach was more than impartial: he was benevolent. If, when trying an organ, he found that the sum agreed on was too small in comparison with the good work that had been done, so that the builder would make only a little profit or perhaps an actual loss, he did not hesitate to recommend the congregation in question to make an additional payment, his suggestion being often adopted*. The organ examiners of our own day would do well to follow his example in this regard, and to impress upon congregations the necessity for paying prices for organs on which art and the builders can subsist, instead of accepting only the lowest tender.

If Bach could do any one a service, he never refused. When his pupils were trying for a situation, he exerted himself most warmly on their behalf. In circumstances like these he did not mind writing to the church authorities in the most submissive terms**.

Along with this kindness there went an agreeable modesty. The man who faced his superiors with a pride that must necessarily have offended them, let no one else feel his superiority. His modesty was not the hypocritical and conceited thing in which celebrities often love to drape themselves in order to bulk still larger in the eyes of the world, but the sane and healthy modesty that

---

* Forkel, p. 23.
** See the four letters he wrote in 1726 to the Council at Plauen recommending as cantor Georg Gottfried Wagner, a former student of theology and philosophy at St Thomas's who had studied music with him. He describes him as "well versed *in humanioribus* and *in musicis*", "free and unmarried", and of quite "honest" way of life. We owe these letters to Wilhelm Fischer, who discovered them in the archives of the Council of Plauen. They will be found in the *Neue Zeitschrift für Musik*, 1901, pp. 484 and 485.

comes from the simple consciousness of one's own worth. He always preserved his dignity even when writing to kings. The petitions he addressed to his sovereign are couched in the submissive formulae of the epoch; but behind these formulae, prescribed by custom, a resolute pride is evident. We can read between the lines: "I, J. S. Bach, have the right to demand this of my prince". The document he sent to Frederick the Great with the *Musikalisches Opfer* is in a somewhat different tone. He writes to him as his equal, in spite of the respect that he pays to his royal dignity. Divested of its fine courtliness, the letter runs: "Johann Sebastian Bach regards it as the greatest honour to add something to the fame of Frederick the Great by publishing a work based on a theme of his invention."

He criticised the work of his pupils severely, but gave praise wherever he could; upon other musicians he never passed an opinion. Even his triumphs over others he was unwilling to hear discussed. Forkel tells us that he never mentioned voluntarily his musical contest with Marchand*. The full details of that victory are well known. Marchand, (1669—1732), court organist to the King at Versailles, and titular organist at several churches in Paris, had fallen into disfavour with his royal master in 1717, and had betaken himself to Germany**. At the Dresden court his elegant style of playing made so good an impression that the King promised him an appointment. The idea of measuring the Frenchman and Bach against each other in artistic rivalry came from Volumier, the leader of the Court band. According to Forkel, Bach was summoned expressly for this purpose to Dresden by a message from the King. It is more probable, however, that he had gone to the Court to hear the famous artist and to learn from him, and that, being there, it occurred

---

* Forkel, p. 45.
** Later on he returned to Paris.

to his friends among the Dresden musicians to give Marchand — whose overbearing and vain-glorious character must have made him unpopular — a dangerous antagonist in the person of the simple Weimar conductor. Bach informed Marchand by letter that he was prepared to perform any musical task that he chose to set him, if he, on his side, would accept the same obligation. The whole company took the liveliest interest in the contest, which was to take place in the house of the minister, Count Flemming. The invited audience, the referees, and Bach were there at the appointed time, but not Marchand. When they sent for him, they learned that he had left early in the morning in post haste. Bach accordingly had to play alone, which he did to the admiration of all. It is a curious fact that he received from the Court neither a gift nor an order for this affair. Forkel affirms that the King had intended him to receive a hundred louis d'or, but that they never reached him. They were probably intercepted by Court officials*.

When asked how he had managed to bring his art to such perfection, Bach usually answered: "I have had to work hard; anyone who will work equally hard will be able to do as much"**.

Even in his dealings with pretentious artists he did not lose his amiability, and did not let it appear that he had seen through their vanity. One day, seemingly about 1730, the Brunswick organist Heinrich Lorenz Hurlebusch visited him, not to hear Bach, but for Bach to hear him play the clavichord. Bach, says Forkel***, received

---

* Forkel, p, 8. The Necrology also says that Bach was cheated out of the money intended for him (p. 164).

** Forkel, p. 45.

*** Forkel, p. 46. Hurlebusch was organist at three churches in Brunswick at the same time, and had his son as assistant. Walther's verdict on him in the *Musikalische Lexikon* (1732) is interesting: "He handles the organ very charmingly, excels in French suites, has an excellent *judicium* and *ingenium*, and is very popular in society and a paragon of politeness." Hurlebusch appeared

him in a friendly and courteous way, and listened with patience to his playing, which was quite ordinary. When Hurlebusch was leaving, he gave to Bach's eldest sons a printed collection of his sonatas, exhorting them to study them diligently (they who had already studied such very different things!); whereupon Bach only smiled, and did not behave any the less graciously to his visitor. Forkel dwells especially on Bach's modesty. The composer's sons, from whom Forkel got his information, took care that this trait in the character of their father was properly emphasised. They wanted to give a *démenti* to the wild stories that were current about him, as he himself had tried to do when living. Forkel expressly contradicts the legend that Bach would sometimes go into a church disguised as a poor village schoolmaster and ask the organist to be allowed to play a chorale, merely to enjoy the astonishment his playing created among the company, or to hear the organist say it must either be Bach or the devil*.

The friendly modesty of Bach's attitude towards all artists was a matter of common knowledge to his contemporaries. We find a corroboration of it in a dedication addressed to him. Georg Andreas Sorge, "court and town organist to the Count of Reuss and Plau at Lobenstein", was impelled, although he was not Bach's pupil, to dedicate to the "prince of all clavichord and organ players" some quite insignificant clavier pieces of his own; and in the dedication he commends him for the fact that "the great musical virtue that your Excellency possesses is embellished with the excellent virtue of affability and unfeigned love of your neighbour." **

---

several times in Hamburg. He performed there on 5th February 1722, 18th December 1727, and 11th February 1728. See Sittard, *Geschichte des Musik- und Konzertwesens in Hamburg*, pp. 69, 70.

* Forkel, pp. 45 and 46. The story of Bach and the village organist is to be found in Marpurg's *Legenden einiger Musikheiligen* (1786), pp. 98—100).

** Schletterer, *Eine Widmung an Joh. Seb. Bach*, in Eitner's *Monatshefte für Musikgeschichte*, 1879.

His attitude towards Handel, indeed, shews how Bach admired whatever he thought great, without a touch of personal vanity. It was not his fault that he and his great contemporary never met. Handel came from England three times to visit his native town of Halle. The first time was in 1719, when Bach was living in Cöthen, only four miles from Halle. Bach set out at once to visit the famous artist; but when he arrived Handel had just left. When the latter came a second time to his native town, in 1729, Bach was in Leipzig, but ill. He sent his eldest son Wilhelm Friedemann with a most courteous invitation to Handel to visit him in Leipzig. Handel regretted that he could not come. At the time of Handel's third stay in Halle, Bach was dead. He regretted all his life not having known Handel. His longing to meet him certainly did not come from the desire to pit himself against him. In Germany such a contest was indeed desired, for comparisons between the two men were always being made. It was universally admitted that Bach would be the victor on the organ. Bach's wish, however, was not to compete with him for pre-eminence, but to learn from him. How highly he valued him is seen from the fact that, assisted by Anna Magdalena, he made a manuscript copy of a Passion by Handel, which points to the fact that he also performed it.

The copies that he made of other men's music are, on the whole, the finest testimony to his modesty. Long after the time when he could regard himself as any one's pupil, he made copies of Palestrina, Frescobaldi, Lotti, Caldara, Ludwig and Bernhard Bach, Telemann, Keiser, Grigny, Dieupart and many others. Sometimes we ask ourselves how it was that his critical sense did not stop him every now and then in his copying. It seems incomprehensible to us that he could bring himself to copy out whole cantatas by Telemann. But these men were acknowledged masters: he respected them and was desirous of spreading their works. Which of the contemporary composers troubled to make a copy of the *St. Matthew Passion*, with the view of preserving that work for posterity?

Bach took thoroughly to heart the injunction to be always hospitable. "Any lover of art, stranger or fellow-countryman", says Forkel, "could visit his house and be sure of meeting with a friendly reception. These sociable virtues, together with his great artistic fame, caused his house to be rarely free from visitors"*. The members of the numerous and wide-branching Bach family who happened to be in Leipzig for their studies were always heartily welcomed by him**. His cousin Johann Elias Bach, cantor at Schweinfurt, who in 1739 had stayed a long time in Leipzig, still remembered gratefully in 1748 the sociable friendliness shown him in the house adjoining St. Thomas's Church, and felt himself bound to send his famous relation a small cask of new wine. When it arrived it was two-thirds empty, and contained no more than six quarts. Bach tells the sender this on the 2nd November 1748, gives him an account showing how much the present has cost him, and adds the request not to let his kindness put him to such expense again. The conclusion of the letter runs: — "Although my worthy cousin is good enough to offer to send me some more of the same liquor, I must decline on account of the excessive expenses here; for the freight was 16 gr., the delivery 2 gr., the inspector 2 gr., the town excise 5 gr. 3 pf. and the general excise 3 gr., so that my good cousin can calculate for himself that it cost me nearly 5 gr. a measure, which is much too expensive for a present".***

This letter is at the same time a testimony to Bach's sense of economy in household affairs, that is so strongly noticeable in other things. He was very particular in money matters. During his struggle with Görner over the university church, he put the financial question in the

---

* Forkel, p. 45.
** Spitta III, 273.
*** See the letter in Spitta III, 272, 273.

forefront. In the letter to Erdmann he cannot help showing his indignation over the healthy year 1729, when the
Leipzigers took so little pleasure in dying that the burial
fees brought the cantor a hundred thalers less than usual.
He tells his cousin Elias Bach, of Schweinfurt, who had
asked him for a copy of the "Prussian Fugue", that it is
out of print at the moment, but that he may inquire
again in a few months, — and remit the necessary thaler
at the same time*.

In all these cases there is indeed nothing more than a
certain frankness in the treatment of money matters,
which in the case of a man with so large a family is partly
natural. That Bach was not avaricious is proved by the
hospitality he dispensed.

His business sense, however, seems not to have been unknown to his fellow-townsmen. Rector Ernesti the younger
takes advantage of this in his fight with the cantor, and
ventures to assert, in a document addressed to the Council,
that Bach is not insusceptible to money when making recommendation for admission among the alumni, and that
many times an old specie thaler had made a soloist of one
who was no soloist before**. The responsibility for this
slander must be borne by the man who dared to utter it.

The economical sense of the father came out very strongly
in Emmanuel, — so strongly as to throw a certain shadow
over his artistic nature. As early as 1756 the way in which
he announces that he is prepared to sell the plates of the
Art of Fugue at any decent price, makes an unpleasant
impression on us***. When, in 1785, G. F. G. Schwencke,
a pupil of Emmanuel Bach and of Kirnberger, was trying
for the post of organist at St. Nicholas's in Hamburg, he
was unsuccessful in spite of his splendid playing at the

---

* See the letter in Spitta III, 271, 272.
** Ernesti's memorial of 13th September 1736. See Spitta II,
904 (German edition only).
*** The announcement is given by Bitter, *Carl Philipp Emmanuel
Bach und Wilhelm Friedemann Bach* (1868), pp. 171 and 172.

examination; the appointment went to the son of the deceased organist, Lambo. Schwencke thus refers to the matter in a letter: "If Herr Lambo, who for the most part played miserably, worked his theme out well, it was probably because he had previously studied it, and therefore probable that Bach had been bribed. He was avaricious enough for this." * Here again the responsibility for the calumny must lie with the man who uttered it. It is certain, however, that Emmanuel had the reputation of being avaricious. One of his friends, Reichardt, writing on him, after his death, in the *Musikalmanach* for 1796, said that" Even towards young artists who came to him full of the desire of learning, he was in the highest degree mercenary" **. A letter of his written in June 1777, while his son was hovering between life and death in Rome, is characteristic of him. "My poor son in Rome", he says, "has been down for five months with a very painful illness, and is not yet quite out of danger. O God, how my heart suffers! Three months ago I sent him fifty ducats, and in another fortnight I shall have to pay another two hundred thalers for doctors and surgeons." *** On the other hand this man, who in the midst of his anguish over his son still has an eye to his money, was as hospitable as his father had been. He had also inherited the family feeling. As we have seen, at the division of the property he was greatly irritated with the fifteen-year-old Johann Christian because the boy maintained that the father had made him a present of three pedal claviers†; nevertheless he afterwards took charge of him and brought him up.

In one thing only did the family spirit forsake him: he did not take his stepmother in her hour of poverty, and allowed her, two years after the death of her husband

---

* Joseph Sittard, *Geschichte des Musik- und Konzertwesens in Hamburg*, 1890, p. 52.
** Bitter, *E. und Fr. Bach* I, 173.
*** Bitter, I, 346.
† See Spitta III, 351—360.

(1752) to beg for alms from the Council that he had so proudly withstood, and finally let her die in receipt of poor relief, on 27th February 1760. Even if he felt no special sympathy for her, and was himself not in flourishing circumstances, he owed it to the honour of his father to save Magdalena Bach from want. Thus Bach's economical sense became meanness in his second son. Friedemann, the firstborn, inherited his father's obstinacy of spirit, and was ruined by it.

In the portraits in which Bach's physiognomy has been preserved for us we can read a good deal about the nature and the bearing of the man. Until about twelve years ago, virtually only two original portraits of the master were known. One was in the possession of the firm of Peters, the musical publishers; it had been the property of Philipp Emmanuel, whose daughter sold it in 1828 to Greuter, a flute virtuoso and Conservatoire Inspector at Leipzig; the other belongs to the St. Thomas's school, to which it was presented in 1809 by August Eberhard Müller, the successor of Hiller in the cantorate. To hang it up in one of the school-rooms was no doubt natural, but not the best thing for the picture, for Bach had to submit *in effigie* to the humours of the later Thomaners, and more than once served as target for missiles of all kinds. Both pictures are signed with the same name — Hausmann — which is a little astonishing, since they show notable differences in execution; both have suffered not a little from being painted over at a later date*.

---

* On the question of the portraits, see Professor Wilhelm His's *Anatomische Forschungen über Johann Sebastian Bachs Gebeine und Antlitz nebst Bemerkungen über dessen Bilder*, Leipzig, 1895. He thinks it not impossible that the Peters portrait may be a free and not very capable copy of that in the Thomas school. Professor His discusses the non-authentic Bach portraits and the *provenance* of the various engravings. See also the brief and lucid essay of the respected librarian of the Peters Musikbibliothek, Dr. Emil Vogel, on the portraits of Bach (*Jahrbuch der Musikbibliothek Peters*, No. 3, 1897, p. 13—18.)

The portrait in the St. Thomas school is perhaps the one that Bach had painted when he joined the Mizler Society, the statutes of which ordained that a new member must contribute "his portrait well painted on canvas" to the library of the society; for in this portrait Bach holds in his hand the "Canon triplex à 6 voc." which he submitted to the society as his qualifying work. As Bach joined the society in the summer of 1747, this portrait would depict him in his latest years.

A third authentic portrait of Bach used to be at Erfurt in possession of the organist Kittel, the last pupil of Bach; it probably belonged at one time to the ducal family of Weissenfels. After Kittel's death, in 1809, it was, in accordance with his wishes, hung up on the organ. During the Napoleonic wars, when the church was used as a hospital, it disappeared from the edifice with other valuable paintings. The French soldiers no doubt sold old Bach to the marine-store dealer for a few glasses of brandy.

The well-known Bach portrait by C. F. Rr. Liszewski in the Joachimsthal Gymnasium in Berlin was not painted until 1772, twenty-two years after Bach's death. It is interesting because it is clearly not derived from either the Peters or the St. Thomas school portrait, and so presupposes another original. It shows Bach *de face*, sitting at a table with some music paper, as if about to run through, on the adjacent piano, some composition that he has just finished.

An entertaining story of a Bach portrait is thus told by Zelter in a letter to Goethe:

"Kirnberger had in his room a portrait of his master Sebastian Bach, that I have always admired, hanging over the piano, between two windows. A wealthy Leipzig linen merchant, who had of old seen Kirnberger, when he was a Thomaner, singing at his father's door, comes to Berlin, and resolves to honour the now famous Kirnberger with a visit. Scarcely has the Leipziger sat down when he cries out: 'Eh! Good Lord! I see you have our cantor Bach hanging there; we have him also in Leipzig, in the St. Thomas school. He was a rough fellow; if the vain fool hasn't had himself painted in a splendid velvet coat!' Kirnberger quietly gets up, goes behind the man's chair, and, taking hold of his visitor with both hands, calls out, first softly, then crescendo, 'Out, dog! out, dog!' My Leipziger, in a mortal fright, runs for his hat and stick, opens the door as fast as he can, and bolts into the street. Kirnberger now has the picture taken down and cleaned, the chair of the Philistine washed, and the picture, covered with a cloth, again put back into its place. When anyone asked him what the cloth was for, he answered, 'Never mind! there's something behind it!' This was the origin of the report that Kirnberger had lost his reason*."

It was always a matter of regret that, having neither a death-mask nor a skull of Bach, it was impossible to model a reasonably true bust of him. His grave was unknown. It was only known that he was buried in St. John's churchyard, and, as the sexton's receipt shows, in an oaken coffin. There was a tradition that the grave was on the south side of the church, six paces from the door. The churchyard had long been converted into a public place when, in 1894, after the dismantling of the old church, excavations for the extension of the foundations of the new church were begun at the spot where Bach's bones should be resting. Here there were discovered, on 22nd October 1894, three oaken coffins**. One contained the bones of a young woman, another a skeleton with the skull in pieces, the third the bones of an "elderly man, not very large, but well-built". The skull exhibited at the first glance the characteristic features that one would have ex-

---

* The letter is dated 24th January 1829. *Briefwechsel zwischen Goethe und Zelter*, ed. Reclam III, 107.

** Dr. G. Wustmann's researches into the written and verbal traditions as to Bach's burial-place revealed the great importance of the information that he had been placed in an oaken coffin. In the year of his death, out of 1400 persons who were buried outside the enclosed burial ground, only twelve were interred in oaken coffins. Professor Wilhelm His acted as anatomical expert. See his report to the Leipzig Town Council, *Johann Sebastian Bach: Forschungen über dessen Grabstätte, Gebeine und Antlitz*, (F. C. W. Vogel, Leipzig). An extract from this report is given in the *Musikalische Wochenblatt* (Jahrgang XXVI, 1895), pp. 339 and 340. See also the *Allgemeine Musikzeitung* for 1895, pp. 384 ff. The detailed results of the anatomical inquiry are given by His in the brochure mentioned on page 160.

pected from the pictures of Bach's head — prominent lower jaw, high forehead, deep-set eye-sockets, and marked nasal angle. The identity of the skull with that of the cantor of St. Thomas's is thus as good as certain, — more certain than in the case of the Schiller skull, for example.

Among the interesting peculiarities of Bach's skull may be mentioned the extraordinary toughness of the bone of the temple that encloses the inner organ of hearing, and the quite remarkable largeness of the fenestra rotunda*. The plaster cast shows that the two upper flexures of the temple, in which the musical faculty has of late been supposed to be located, were not extraordinarily developed in him**.

A Leipzig sculptor, Seffner, then tried to model the features upon a cast of the skull, after copious researches had been made into the relation of the fleshy parts of the face to the bony parts in elderly people, in order to settle the course of the line of the skin over the line of the bones***. The bust thus obtained shewed not only a surprising similarity to both of the Bach portraits, but even surpassed them in vivacious and characteristic expression.

Recently Professor Fritz Volbach, of Mainz, has discovered yet another portrait of Bach. It is a realistic

---

* The bones in which the ear of Beethoven was embedded could not be compared with it, as they had been sawn out of the skull, the intention being to preserve them in the Vienna Museum of Pathological Anatomy, whence, however, they have disappeared. It is supposed that one of the attendants sold them to an English doctor.

** See the article of the Strassburg anatomist Prof. Schwalbe, *Über alte und neue Phrenologie (Korrespondenzblatt der deutschen Gesellschaft für Antropologie, Ethnologie und Urgeschichte*, XXXVII. Jahrgang, Nos. 9—11, 1906). According to this theory, Schubert must be counted among the unmusical musicians, since the two upper flexures of his temple are even smaller than those of Kant, who had so great a contempt for music. The capacity of Bach's skull was 1479.5 ccm.; the height of the body, judging from the length of the bones, would be 166.8 cm.

*** On the method of these measurements, and on earlier attempts of the same kind, see His's *Anatomische Forschungen über J. S. Bachs Gebeine, usw.*, pp. 24—32.

piece of work, showing the face of a man who has tasted of the bitterness of life. There is something fascinating in the harsh expression of these features, which are painted full face. Round the tightly compressed lips run the hard lines of an inflexible obstinacy. It is thus that the cantor of St. Thomas's may have looked in his last years as he entered the school where some new vexation or another was awaiting him *. In the two other portraits the severity is softened by a touch of easy good nature. Even the short-sighted eyes look out upon the world from their half-closed lids with a certain friendliness, that is not even negated by the heavy eyebrows arched above them. The face cannot be called beautiful; the nose is too massive for that, and the underjaw too prominent. How sharply this projected may be estimated from the fact that the front teeth of the lower jaw are level with those of the upper, instead of closing within these. In the attempt to mitigate this peculiarity somewhat, the Hausmann portraits cease to be characteristic.

The longer we contemplate it, the more enigmatic becomes the expression of the master's face. How did this ordinary visage become transformed into that of the artist? What was it like when Bach was absorbed in the world of music? Was there reflected in it then the wonderful serenity that shines through his art?

In the last resort the whole man is for the most part an enigma, for to our eyes the outer man differs so much from the inner that neither seems to have any part in the other. In the case of Bach, more than in that of any other genius, the man as he looked and behaved was only the opaque envelope destined to lodge the artistic soul within. In Beethoven, the inner man seizes upon the outer man, uproots him from his normal life, agitates him and inflames him, until the inner light pierces through him and finally consumes him. Not so with Bach. His is rather a case

---

* The discoverer of the painting thinks, with some reason, that this is the Erfurt picture. (In a letter to the present writer.)

JOH. SEB. BACH

From the portrait recently discovered by Dr. Fritz Volbach

of dualism; his artistic vicissitudes and creations go on side by side with the normal and almost commonplace tenor of his work-a-day existence, without mixing with or making any impression on this.

Bach fought for his everyday life, but not for the recognition of his art and of his works. In this respect he is very different from Beethoven and Wagner, and in general from what we understand by an "artist".

The recognition that the world gave to the master of the organ and the clavier, — really only the external and contemporary side of his artistic activity, — he took as a matter of course. He did not ask the world for the recognition of that part of his work that was not of his own age, and in which his deepest emotions found expression. It did not even occur to him that he should or could expect this from his epoch. He did nothing to make his cantatas and Passions known, and nothing to preserve them. It is not his fault if they have survived to our day.

A modern student of Bach has said, *à propos* of some of the later chorale cantatas, in which the expert in Bach's scores notices a certain weakening of invention, that his whole work can be understood only as a mighty struggle for recognition, in which fight he was finally crippled*. Bach was certainly crippled at that time, not however in the struggle for recognition, but in the struggle for good cantata texts, in which he was finally thrown back again upon the chorale cantata, and, in a kind of fit of desperation, distorted chorale strophes into arias **. But this phenomenon has nothing to do with Bach's artistic life.

The unique thing about him is precisely the fact that he made no effort to win recognition for his greatest works, and did not summon the world to make acquaintance

---

* See Bernhard Friedrich Richter's interesting essay: *Die Wahl J. S. Bachs zum Kantor der Thomasschule im Jahr 1723*, in the *Bachjahrbuch* for 1905, pp. 48—67. See especially pp. 49 and 67 — "Bach wanted to compel the world to recognise him."

** For a more detailed examination of the later chorale cantatas, see the analysis of them in chapter XXXIV.

with them.   Hence the kind of consecration that rests upon his works.   We feel an unaffected charm in his cantatas such as we do not meet with in other art-works. The grey volumes of the old Bachgesellschaft speak a moving language.   They discourse to us of something that will be imperishable simply because it is big and true, something that was written not in the hope of recognition but because it had to come out of him.   Bach's cantatas and Passions are not only children of the muse, but also children of leisure*, in the honourable and profound sense that this word had in the old days, when it signified the hours of a man's life that he employed for himself and himself alone.

Bach himself was not conscious of the extraordinary greatness of his work.   He was aware only of his admitted mastery of the organ and clavier and counterpoint.   But he never dreamt that his works alone, not those of the men all round him, would remain visible to the coming generations.   If it is one of the signs of the great creative artist, born before his time, that he waits for "his day", and wears himself out in the waiting, then was Bach neither great nor born before his time.   No one was less conscious than he that his work was ahead of his epoch.   In this respect he stands, perhaps, highest among all creative artists; his immense strength functioned without self-consciousness, like the forces of nature; and for this reason it is as cosmic and copious as these.

Nor did Bach reflect whether the Thomaners could perform his works properly, or whether the congregation understood them.   He had put all his devotion into them, and God at any rate certainly understood them.   The S. D. G. (*Soli Deo Gloria*, "to God alone be praise") and the J. J. (*Jesu juva*, "Help me, Jesus!") with which he garnishes his scores, are for him no formulas, but the Credo that

---

* The play upon words in the German cannot be reproduced in English, — "sind nicht nur Kinder der Muse, sondern auch Kinder der Musse".   [Tr.]

runs through all his work. Music is an act of worship with Bach. His artistic activity and his personality are both based on his piety. If he is to be understood from any standpoint at all, it is from this. For him, art was religion, and so had no concern with the world or with wordly success. It was an end in itself. Bach includes religion in the definition of art in general. All great art, even secular, is in itself religious in his eyes; for him the tones do not perish, but ascend to God like praise too deep for utterance.

"Figured bass", he says in the rules and principles of accompaniment that he gave his pupils*, "is the most perfect foundation of music. It is executed with both hands in such a manner that the left hand plays the notes that are written, while the right adds consonances and dissonances thereto, making an agreeable harmony for the glory of God and the justifiable gratification of the soul. Like all music, the figured bass should have no other end and aim than the glory of God and the recreation of the soul; where this is not kept in mind there is no true music, but only an infernal clamour and ranting."

The *Orgelbüchlein* (Little Organ Book) — the collection of small chorale preludes that Bach put together in Cöthen, — is adorned with the following dictum:

> Dem höchsten Gott allein zu Ehren,
> Dem Nächsten draus sich zu belehren.

("For the glory of the most high God, and for the instruction of my neighbour.")

Lastly, musical education also belonged to the sphere of religion; and so Bach wrote in Friedemann's *Klavierbüchlein* (Little Clavier Book), over the first piano pieces he gave to his eldest son, "In Nomine Jesu".

At the same time he recognised that there was a species of art whose only purpose was entertainment. He did

---

* They are preserved in a copy dating from 1738. See Spitta III, 317 ff.

not rank it highly, as we see from his somewhat satirical reference to the little songs of the Dresden opera when he asked Friedemann to accompany him there. All the same, when he was in the mood he could shake "little songs" that bordered on the burlesque out of his sleeve, as if he had to give himself up to heartfelt laughter now and then in order to get back again to proper seriousness.

His culture was not merely serious but religious. In the inventory of the property he left we find a large number of theological works, among them a complete edition of Luther's writings, Tauler's sermons, and Arnd's *Wahres Christentum*. Polemical literature is well represented, and it enables us to see that Bach's views were strictly Lutheran. In Cöthen he would not permit his children to attend the reformed school, but had them taught in the newly founded Lutheran school*.

To pietism also he was sharply opposed**. When he was in Mühlhausen there was a struggle between an orthodox and a pietist divine there; he took the part of the representative of rigid Lutheranism, Georg Christian Eilmar, who appears to us in anything but a sympathetic light in his controversy with his older colleague Frohne. He must have had close personal relations with Eilmar, for he asked him to be godfather to his first child***.

---

* See R. Bunge, *J. S. Bach in Cöthen*, in the *Bachjahrbuch* for 1905, p. 28.

** Pietism derives from the Alsatian Philipp Jakob Spener (born in Rappoltsweiler in 1635), who successively filled high clerical positions in Frankfort-on-the-Main, Dresden, and Berlin. New paths were opened by his *Pia desideria, oder herzliches Verlangen nach gottgefälliger Besserung der wahren evangelischen Kirche* (1675), in which he insisted on subjective devotion and a thorough absorption in the Bible. When Spener died, in 1705, Germany was in conflict on these points. Pietism did not, indeed, wish to attack the established dogmas of the church; but through the significance that it attaches to personal conviction it did, as a matter of fact depreciate these. It was essentially a Reformation within the Reformation. The Protestantism of today is in part the product of pietism.

*** Upon the religious troubles in Mühlhausen, and Bach's attitude towards Eilmar, see Spitta I, 358 ff.

As for the real points at issue in that epoch, Bach was as little conscious of these as his contemporaries were. Pietism was unsympathetic to him as a disintegrating innovation. He was dogmatically opposed to the representatives of orthodoxy. The submissive humility which the disciples of Spener affected was antipathetic to him. In addition, pietism was fundamentally inimical to art of any kind in worship, and was especially set against the concert style of the church music. The musical performances of the Passion were a particular abomination to it; it wished the service to be adorned only with simple congregational hymns. So every cantor necessarily hated the pietists, and Bach took it particularly ill of them that they dragged his religious and artistic ideals in the dust. Nevertheless we possess no utterance of his, written or verbal, against the new sect.

For all that, his own works exhibit visible traces of pietism; the texts of the cantatas and Passions are strongly influenced by it, as indeed the whole of the religious poetry of the early eighteenth century is. It can be seen in the reflections and the sentimental attitude with which Bach's librettists were so conversant. Thus the opponent of pietism invested with his music poetry filled with the breath of pietism, and so made it immortal.

In the last resort, however, Bach's real religion was not orthodox Lutheranism, but mysticism. In his innermost essence he belongs to the history of German mysticism. This robust man, who seems to be in the thick of life with his family and his work, and whose mouth seems to express something like comfortable joy in life, was inwardly dead to the world. His whole thought was transfigured by a wonderful, serene longing for death. Again and again, whenever the text affords the least pretext for it, he gives voice to this longing in his music; and nowhere is his speech so moving as in the cantatas in which he discourses on the release from the body of this death. The Epiphany and certain bass cantatas are the revelation of his most intimate religious feelings. Sometimes it is a sorrowful and weary longing that the music expresses; at others, a glad, serene desire, finding voice in one of those lulling cradle-songs that only he could write; then again a passionate, ecstatic longing, that calls death to it jubilantly, and goes forth in rapture to meet it. As we listen to arias like "Schlummert ein ihr müden Augen"*, "Ach schlage doch bald, sel'ge Stunde"**, or the simple melody "Komm, süsser Tod", we feel that we are in the presence of a musician who is not merely bent on rendering into tone the thoughts of his text, but has seized upon the words and made them his own, breathing into them something of himself that was yearning for expression.

This is Bach's religion as it appears in the cantatas. It transfigured his life. The existence that, considered from the outside, seems all conflict and struggle and bitterness, was in truth tranquil and serene.

CHAPTER X.

ARTISTIC JOURNEYS, CRITICS AND FRIENDS.

Bach loved travelling. As a young man it attracted him because of his desire to learn from every master. Later, when he himself was a master, he felt the necessity from time to time of getting away from the narrowness of his environment, and realising himself in freedom elsewhere. It appears that he undertook these artistic journeys early, as a rule in the autumn; though unfortunately our information about his travels is very scanty.

Bach's first master, the Prince of Weimar, appears to have been generous in the matter of furlough. In 1709 Bach, with his friend Walther, opened the organ at Mühlhausen, performing for that purpose the chorale prelude

---

* From the cantata *Ich habe genug* (No. 82).
** From the cantata *Christus, der ist mein Leben* (No. 95).

upon "Ein feste Burg" (Peters VI, 22), — if indeed he did not compose it expressly for this occasion — in order to show the Council the full wealth of tone of the renovated instrument.

Of the artistic journeys of the following years we know nothing. In 1713 or 1714 he performed before the Court at Cassel, at the invitation of the Hereditary Prince, the future King of Sweden. When the Prince heard Bach play a pedal solo, he was so enraptured at the dexterity of it that he drew a ring from his finger and placed it on that of Bach. The anecdote is told by Constantin Bellermann, Rector of Minden, in a pamphlet issued in 1743. He does not give the date of the journey, and thinks that at that time Bach was already in Leipzig. As a matter of fact he did go on one occasion from Leipzig to Cassel to examine a renovated organ; but this was about 1732. By that time the Hereditary Prince was King of Sweden, and we know positively that he was not in Cassel. The journey during which Bach played before the Hereditary Prince must be dated about 1713 or 1714. In those years the Prince spent some time at home, while before then he was almost constantly in camp, being commander in the Spanish War of Succession. At the end of 1714 he went to Sweden, where he married, in 1715, Ulrike Elenore, the sister of Charles XII*.

To the same period belongs a journey in which Bach touched upon Halle. By the death of Zachau (14th August 1712), the post of organist at the Liebfrauenkirche there had become vacant. It was left unfilled for a time, a new organ, with thirty-six stops, being in course of construction. After Bach had tested so much of the instrument as was already playable, he presented himself to the church authorities and said he would have no objection to becoming Zachau's successor. He was asked to write at once a

* Bellermann thus confuses the two journeys to Cassel; Spitta does the same (Spitta I, 515, 634, 635). The matter was cleared up by Scherer, in his *Joh. Seb. Bachs Aufenthalt in Kassel,* in Eitner's *Monatshefte für Musikgeschichte,* 1893.

cantata as a test piece, which he did. When he returned to Weimar, he made closer enquiries as to the emoluments of the post, and finding that they were lower than what he already had he broke off the negociations at the last moment. The Halle people, who thought they had already secured him, were very displeased. They took it ill of him that he had kept them in suspense in this way, and maintained that he had only begun negociations with them in order to extort an increase in salary from the Duke. Bach did not allow this to pass; he refuted the imputations in a courteous but firm letter of 14th March 1714. Later on the Halle people were reconciled to him, and in 1716 they invited him, with Kuhnau and Rolle of Quedlinburg, to the testing of the now completed organ. We still possess a letter in which Bach answered this invitation. It is addressed to his friend Herr August Becker, *Lizentiat Juris*, who had acted also as negociator between him and the Council in the affair of the appointment*. It runs thus: —

"Most Noble
            and Particularly Highly Honoured Sir, —
    I am greatly obliged by your honour's very particular and most gracious confidence, and by that of the whole of the most honoured *Collegium*; and as it is always the greatest pleasure to me to give your worship my most willing service, I shall now more than ever strive to serve your worship well, and according to my best ability give satisfaction in the *examine* you ask of me. I beg you therefore to communicate this my resolution without delay to the most honoured *Collegium*, and at the same time to give them my most humble compliments and assure them of my dutiful respects for their special confidence.
    I also acknowledge with humble gratitude all the trouble your honour has taken for me both now and formerly, and I assure you that I shall always feel the greatest pleasure, as long as I live, in subscribing myself, most honoured Sir,

                    Your most obedient servant
                        Joh. Seb. Bach
                                Concertmeister."

---

* On the Halle affair see Spitta I, 515 ff., and M. Seiffert's *J. S. Bach 1716 in Halle*, in the *Sammelbände der Internationalen Musikgesellschaft*, VI, 1905. Zachau had been Handel's teacher.

The opening of the organ took place on the 3rd May. In conjunction with it the Council gave the "deputies" a dinner, the menu of which we can reconstruct from the receipts. It included: "Bäffallamote" (i. e. *bœuf à la mode*), pike, gammon of bacon, peas, potatoes, spinach with little sausages, boiled pumpkins, fritters, preserved lemon-peel, preserved cherries, warm asparagus salad, cabbage salad, radishes, fresh butter and roast veal. The cost of the whole was eleven thalers twelve groschen; the drink came to fifteen thalers twelve groschen. Servants were also placed at the disposal of the "deputies" *.

Bach seems to have visited Leipzig for the first time in 1714. On the inner cover of the cantate *Nun komm der Heiden Heiland* (No. 61), which certainly belongs to the year 1714, he has noted down the "Order of the morning service in Leipzig for the first Sunday in Advent". The most natural assumption is that he performed this work in Leipzig on the first Sunday in Advent in 1714, also officiating at the organ during the service. We must not forget, however, that this is a pure hypothesis, for it is also possible that Bach wrote this cantata in 1714 for Weimar, but did not produce it until later, perhaps on the first Sunday in Advent 1722, when applying in person for the cantorate of St. Thomas's **.

In the autumn of 1717 he went to Dresden, where the Marchand incident happened; he also appears to have been about this time in Meiningen, where his distant and considerably older cousin Johann Ludwig Bach was Kapellmeister. Bach must have thought very highly of his compositions, for he made copies of many of them ***.

We know positively that Bach was in Leipzig on the

---

* See Seiffert's article already referred to.

** This explanation is thought the more probable one by Bernhard Friedrich Richter, in his interesting essay *Die Wahl Joh. Seb. Bachs zum Kantor der Thomasschule im Jahr 1723*, in the *Bachjahrbuch* for 1905, p. 48 ff.

*** An appreciation of Johann Ludwig Bach's compositions will be found in Spitta I, 574 ff.

16th December 1717, on which day he had been invited by the University to test the new organ in St. Paul's church. His verdict was extremely laudatory; and from that time Scheibe, the builder of the instrument, had a reputation everywhere as one of the best organ builders, whereas previously he was hardly known.

When Bach undertook this journey, he had not long been released from his Weimar captivity, and had just settled in Cöthen. In his new position he had more opportunities for travelling than in the old one, since it was part of his duties to accompany Duke Leopold everywhere. These duties he would probably not be unwilling to fulfil. He spent, for instance, part of the summer of 1720 with his master in Karlsbad. It was on his return from this journey that he found in his home, instead of his beloved wife, only his motherless children. In the autumn of the same year he undertook the journey to Hamburg that gained him the admiration of Reinken and the art-lovers there.

Even when he was cantor at St. Thomas's he made a point of escaping every year from the narrow circle of Leipzig and its artistic conditions. According to agreement, he should have applied for leave to the Burgomaster each time. This, however, he frequently did not do, contenting himself with providing a reliable deputy and telling the rector. If he had not a capable first prefect at the time, the cantata would be conducted by the organist of the New Church, who, as soon as it was over, would get back to his own organ in time to fulfil his duties there*.

So long as Duke Leopold was alive — he died the 19th November 1728 — Bach often went to Cöthen, to produce one or other of his compositions on festival occasions. At the entombment of his former master, in 1729, he con-

---

* Ernesti mentioned this in one of his memorials to the council on the subject of the Krause case. See Spitta II, 904 (German ed.), and English ed. III, 230.

tributed a large piece of funerary music for two choirs, which he appears to have taken from the *St. Matthew Passion,* upon which he was then engaged.

As shortly before his Leipzig appointment he received the *praedicate* of Weissenfels Court composer, he also had duties towards this Court, that from time to time called for his presence there.

He went to Dresden frequently. He appears to have been summoned to the Court there shortly before 1725 for some occasion or other*; he also went there now and then to hear the opera. He was accompanied on these occasions by his favorite Friedemann. Some days previously he would say to him "Friedemann, shall we go again to hear the pretty little Dresden songs?"** He was present at the first performance, on 13th September 1731, of Hasse's opera *Cleofide,* in which the composer's wife Faustina appeared. On the following day he performed on the organ in St. Sophia's Church before the whole Kapelle and many connoisseurs. The Dresden musicians thought very highly of him. Hasse and his wife were much attached to him, and more than once visited him in Leipzig***.

Bach probably visited Dresden still more frequently after Friedemann's appointment as organist there in 1733. Moreover, his appointment as Court composer made it his duty to keep in touch with the musical life of Dresden. He received the decree in the last days of November 1736; on the first December he performed from two till four o'clock on the new Silbermann organ in the Frauenkirche at Dresden†.

While the reigning Duke Wilhelm Ernst was still alive he did not return to Weimar, as we can readily understand. When, however, in 1728, Ernest August, the younger Duke, succeeded to power, he certainly went there

---

* Spitta III, 223.
** Forkel, p. 48.
*** Forkel, p. 48.
† Spitta III, 226.

now and then, for he was on terms of cordial friendship with this artistic and intelligent prince.

In 1727 he performed for the second time in Hamburg, perhaps at the invitation of Telemann, who thought a very great deal of him. About the same time he seems to have visited Erfurt.

Probably most of his journeys were for the purpose of testing new organs. Interesting information upon a trip of this nature is given in a document in the municipal Board of Works in Cassel. Bach had been invited there in 1732 to try the renovated organ at St. Martin's, which had been in the repairers' hands for two years. For this he received fifty thalers remuneration and twenty-six thalers for travelling expenses. In addition the Council paid the expenses of the Herr Kapellmeister and his wife at their lodgings, two thalers for the "porters" who carried Herr Bach twenty-five paces, and a thaler for the man-servant who waited on him during the eight days of his sojourn*. These things were evidently done more splendidly in those days than they are now.

At the end of July and the beginning of August 1736, during the conflict with Ernesti over the appointment of the first prefect, Bach was absent from Leipzig for a fort-night. We do not know where he went. His last journey may be described in Forkel's words, who narrates it approximately in the terms in which he had it from Friede-mann:

"The fame of Johann Sebastian's all-surpassing art was so wide-spread that even the King very often heard it spoken of and extolled. He was consequently desirous to hear for himself so great an artist, and make his acquaintance. At first he quietly hinted to Bach's son his desire that his father should some day come to Potsdam; then he began to ask definitely why the father did not come. The son could not but communicate these expressions of the King to his father, who, however, was mostly overwhelmed with too many occupations to attend to them at once. But as the King's remarks were repeated by the son in several letters, he at length, in 1747,

---

* Scherer, *J. S. Bachs Aufenthalt in Cassel*, in Eitner's *Monats-hefte für Musikgeschichte*, 1893.

arranged to make the journey, accompanied by his eldest son, Wilhelm Friedemann. At this time the King had a chamber concert every evening, at which he himself played some concerto on the flute. One evening, just as he had got his flute ready, and his musicians were assembled, an officer brought him the list of strangers who had arrived. He looked over the paper with his flute in his hand, immediately turned round to the musicians, and said with some agitation, "Gentlemen, old Bach has come!" The flute was thereupon laid aside, and old Bach, who had gone to his son's quarters, was at once commanded to come to the castle. I had the story from Wilhelm Friedemann, who accompanied his father, and I must say that to this very day I recall with delight the way in which he told it to me. In those days it was still customary to make rather long-winded compliments. The first appearance of Johann Sebastian Bach before so great a king, who did not even allow him time to exchange his travelling clothes for the black coat of the cantor, must thus necessarily have led to many excuses being made. I will not here give specimens of these excuses, but merely remark that Wilhelm Friedemann gave them in the style of formal dialogue between the King and his self-excusing father.

But more interesting than all this is the fact that for this evening the King gave up his flute concerto, and invited the so-called "old Bach" to try his Silbermann forte-pianos, of which he had several in different rooms of the castle. The musicians accompanied them from room to room, and Bach had to try all the pianos and improvise upon them. After he had done this for some time, he asked the King to give him a fugue subject, for him to work out impromptu. The King was astonished at the erudite way in which his theme was developed extempore, and, apparently in order to see how far such an art could be carried, expressed a wish to hear also a fugue in six parts. As, however, it is not every theme that is suited for this kind of polyphony, Bach chose one himself, and developed it immediately, to the great admiration of all present, in the same brilliant and learned way as he had formerly done the theme of the King. Then the King wanted to hear him on the organ. He accordingly took him on the following days to all the organs to be found in Potsdam, as he had taken him previously to all the Silbermann forte-pianos. After his return to Leipzig he worked out in three and six parts the theme the King had given him, added various clever canonic manipulations of it, had it engraved on copper with the title of *Musikalisches Opfer* (Musical Offering) and dedicated it to its inventor. This was Bach's last journey."*

Bach's artistic journeys made him, at an early date, famous throughout Germany. After his victory over Marchand in 1717 he was one of the celebrities of the fatherland. The German musicians were proud to be able

---

* Forkel, pp. 9, 10.

to oppose a master of their own race to the French and Italian virtuosi. Let German musicians affect Italian ways if they would, in order to win a cheap renown*, let the very existence of a German art be denied; the fact remained that there was such a thing, and that it had publicly triumphed over the other.

Bach thus had no need to fight for recognition. Only the virtuoso, it is true, won fame; the composer of the cantatas and Passions had small share in this recognition. No one, not even his enemies, ventured to deny that he was the prince of clavichord players and the king of organists; but no one, even among his best friends, had a suspicion of the real greatness of the composer.

As a composer he was actually censured by the two leading critics of the time, Mattheson and Scheibe. Mattheson** examines the cantata *Ich hatte viel Bekümmernis* (No. 21), which Bach probably had performed during his visit to Hamburg in 1720, and finds the declamation imperfect, in that Bach at the commencement makes the chorus repeat three times the detached words "Ich, ich, ich", before it gives out the whole phrase, while in other places he has split up the phrases in a way that contradicts the sense. So far as the threefold repetition of the "I" is concerned the criticism is not wholly unjustified. It is curious that the great Hamburg art-oracle should have taken just this cantata, which is not impeccable in its declamation, as the basis for his verdict on the most perfect master of musical declamation! Had he taken the trouble to acquaint himself with other vocal compositions of Bach he would have been undeceived, and would certainly have enlisted him as an ally in his justifiable war against the careless musical declamation of the epoch.

---

* Kuhnau's *Der musikalische Quacksalber* (1700), shows us the feeling of the German musicans towards foreigners and those who assumed foreign manners. The work has recently been issued in a new edition (Behr, Berlin 1900).
** *Critica musica*, II, 368.

In truth, however, Mattheson had no particular desire to become acquainted with Bach's works. He had hailed him in 1717, in his *Das beschützte Orchester*, as a rising star*, and had asked him for an autobiographical contribution to the *Ehrenpforte*, which he was then planning; Bach did not send it to him, having no liking for things of that kind. During his sojourn in Hamburg, Bach probably did not think it necessary to court the protection of the famous critic, which would hardly increase Mattheson's good will towards him, for he could not endure independent characters, and only felt sympathetic towards people who sought and glorified his authority. So on the few occasions on which he mentions Bach, his tone is one of recognition but at the same time of indifference.

Scheibe's criticism of Bach is much more interesting. It is true that he also was not unbiassed, for he bore Bach a grudge for having rejected him when he applied for the organist's post at St. Thomas's in 1729. His criticism appeared in the *Kritische Musikus* for 1737, a journal that Scheibe edited from 1737 to 1740 in Hamburg, where he had taken up his abode. An anonymous "Friend", who is instructed by him in the art of criticising according to the true rules of reason, sends him in a travel-letter a miscellany of good and bad upon the musicians of several towns that he has just visited. The people concerned are indeed not mentioned by name, but they are so clearly indicated that they are easily recognised. The passage in which Bach recognised himself runs thus:

"Herr . . . is the most eminent musician in . . . He is a wonderful artist on the clavichord and the organ, and so far he has met with only one with whom he can contend for superiority. I have several times heard this great man play. His dexterity is astonishing, and one can hardly comprehend how it is possible for him to cross his fingers and his feet so remarkably and so nimbly, or to make

---

* "I have seen some pieces by the celebrated Weimar organist, Herr Johann Sebastian Bach, both for the church and instrumental, that are certainly written in such a way as to make us esteem the man highly." See Spitta II, 21, etc.

the widest leaps with them, without once striking a wrong note or distorting his body, no matter how quick his movements are.

"This great man would be the admiration of all nations if he had more amenity, and if his works were not made unnatural by their turgid and confused character, and their beauty obscured by too much art. As he judges by his own fingers, his pieces are extremely hard to play; he expects the singers and the instrumentalists to do with their throats and their instruments what he can play on the clavier. This, however, is impossible. All graces, all little embellishments, and everything that one understands by style in playing, he writes out in the exact notes, which not only deprives his pieces of the beauty of harmony, but makes the melody absolutely indistinct. All the parts work together and with the same difficulty, so that we cannot distinguish any leading voice. In short, he is in music what formerly Herr von Lohenstein was in poetry. Turgidity has led them both from the natural to the artificial, and from the lofty to the obscure; and in each of them one wonders at the painful labour of it all, that nevertheless comes to nothing, since it is at variance with reason."*

It would be a mistake to see in this criticism only an outburst of the personal resentment that Scheibe harboured against Bach. Scheibe regarded himself — and to a certain extent with justice — as the literary champion of a new music. He makes war on the contemporary art which, by its imitation of the Italian style and its deliberate artificiality, has departed from the true ideal, and has no longer any poetic value. As a pupil of Gottsched, he believes himself called to preach the return to simple nature in music, to declare war on the aria and all erudite formulae, to deride perpetually the unnaturalness of the Italian opera and especially its German imitation, and to uphold as the ideal that form of art in which the words are not a mere pretext for the music, but word and tone unite in perfect unity. The opera of the future is for him a real musical drama. Certain chapters in which he discusses stage music are really excellent; much of what he says might have been expressed in the same way, word

---

* *Der kritische Musikus*, No. 6; Tuesday, 14th May 1737, pp. 46 and 47. Scheibe himself was, of course, the author of the "Letter". In March 1738 the first year's numbers of the journal appeared in volume form with an index. The second volume, extending from March 1739 to March 1740, appeared in 1740.

for word, by Wagner. It is therefore not to be wondered
at that Scheibe's views exercised so deep an influence on
Gluck*.

It was precisely these theories of his, indeed, that made
it impossible for him to do justice to Bach. The latter's
astounding contrapuntal technique made him seem to
Scheibe the chief representative of artificial music. Perhaps, however, the critic of the Gottsched circle bore him
the worst grudge for showing no interest whatever in the
aspirations towards the art of the future, and was not
in the least particular as to the poetic quality of his texts.
Scheibe wanted his criticism to strike the most eminent
of the class of musicians who persisted in being musicians
and nothing more. Of the fact that this learned music
had within it a poetry of its own, Scheibe had as little
intuition as the sons and the friends of the master.

Bach was incensed to the highest degree by this criticism, and asked his friend Magister Birnbaum, a professor
of rhetoric at the Leipzig University, to take up the pen
for him. The latter gladly did so, and first of all published
in January 1738 an anonymous article, which, however,
was not very effective. Scheibe easily countered it by
shewing up the dilettante quality of the musical judgments
of the anonymous writer, whose name was not unknown
to him**. From this reply we learn that the "Herr

* See especially pp. 177—208 of the first volume, and pp. 1 ff. of
the second. On Scheibe see the interesting article of Eugen Reichel,
"Gottsched und Johann Adolf Scheibe", in the *Sammelbände der
Internationalen Musikgesellschaft*, 1900—1901, pp. 654—668.

Johann Adolf Scheibe was born in Leipzig in 1708. He went to
Hamburg in 1735; from there he went to Kulmbach as Kapell-
meister in 1740; from 1744 he conducted the Court orchestra at
Copenhagen. He lost this post in 1749, and thereafter held no per-
manent appointment. After a life of erratic wandering he died in
Copenhagen in 1776.

** Scheibe's reply is to be found in the *Kritische Musikus* of Tuesday, the 18th February 1738 (I, 203 ff.), and in a supplement to
this number: *Beantwortung der unparteiischen Anmerkungen über
eine bedenkliche Stelle in dem sechsten Hauptstück des kritischen
Musikus. Ausgefertigt von Johann Adolf Scheibe.* Hamburg, 1738

Hofcompositeur" himself distributed the vindication of himself to his friends and acquaintances, with no small gratification, on the 8th January of this year.

One unpleasant feature of the controversy is the way in which Scheibe always adverts to the fact that Bach is not in a position himself to take up the pen against him, and how, at every opportunity, he represents him as a musician who lacks the necessary general education. With exquisite humour he sketches an imaginary letter of Bach's, in which the master shows the philosophers and quill-drivers to the door of the temple of art. Scheibe probably inwove into the letter some authentic sayings of Bach that had remained in his memory from an earlier time, — as when he makes him say: "I have always been of the opinion that a musician has enough to do simply with his art, without wasting his time on long-winded books and learned philosophical discussions."*

Against the reproach that the master was lacking in the general artistic culture that is indispensable to musicians, Birnbaum vindicated the offended cantor in an article of March 1738, signed with his name. From this we learn something of Bach the aesthetician: "Bach knows so perfectly", the Magister says, "the analogies between the working-out of a musical piece and the art of rhetoric, that people not only listen to him with satisfaction and delight when he expounds lucidly the resemblances and correspondences of the two, but admire also the skilful application of them in his works." To this Scheibe has nothing that is very rational to say**.

---

* *Kritischer Musikus* of 2nd April 1739, II, 34—36. Bach's style seems to be not badly imitated in the letter.

** Birnbaum's article is entitled: *M. Johann Abraham Birn-baums Verteidigung seiner unparteiischen Anmerkungen, über eine bedenkliche Stelle in dem sechsten Stück des kritischen Musikus, wider Johann Adolf Scheibens Beantwortung derselben.* ("Magister Johann Abraham Birnbaum's vindication of his impartial remarks upon a questionable passage in the sixth number of the *Kritischer Musikus*, against Johann Adolf Scheibe's reply to the same.")

All the same, Bach's "prickly" critic — the adjective often occurs in the controversy — regards him as one of the greatest composers of pure music. In the number for 22nd December 1739 Scheibe is lavish in his praise of the Italian Concerto*. As a cantata composer, to be sure, he ranks him below Telemann and Graun**.

On the whole it may be said that Scheibe's criticism did harm to the author himself, but brought good to the object of his attack, since its offensive tone everywhere stimulated sympathy for Bach. Later on Scheibe also appears to have recognised that he had not gone about the affair in the right way. In the preface to the second edition of the *Kritischer Musikus* we can see the glimmerings of something like an apology.

In spite of its incivility, Scheibe's criticism is really the most interesting of contemporary criticism of Bach. The other deliverances upon him run on general lines of admiration and amazement and rhetorical analogies from ancient mythology. But we learn nothing from them of what we should most like to know, how the characteristic quality of Bach's art affected his contemporaries. We would gladly exchange all these panegyrics for a single sentence of some one who, at the first performance of the *St. Matthew Passion*, had an intuition of the real spirit of Bach's music.

Bach was probably most pleased with the monument that the friendship and affection of his former Rector, Gesner, erected to him under the cover of a Latin note to

Scheibe replied in the number of 30th June 1739 (II, pp. 141 to 144). In the second edition of the *Kritischer Musikus* (1745), he printed also both Birnbaum's articles. The above citation follows the first edition. On the whole affair see Spitta III, 252 ff.

* *Kritischer Musikus* II, 242, where the clavier pieces alone are discussed: "One of the best of published pieces is a clavier concerto of the famous Bach; it is in the key of F, and written in the best style of this *genre*. This clavier concerto is to be regarded as a perfect model of a well-worked-out concerto for one instrument."

** In the supplement to an article by Mattheson. See Spitta III, 252.

the *Institutiones variae* of Quintilian, an edition of which
he edited in 1738. At the end of a passage referring to
the artist who, while singing, accompanied himself on the
cithara and beat time with his feet, he adds this note: —

"All this, my Fabius, you would think quite trifling if you could
rise from the dead and see Bach — whom I mention because not
long ago he was my colleague at St. Thomas's school in Leipzig;
how with both hands, and using all his fingers, he plays the clavier,
that contains in itself the tones of many citharae, or that instrument of instruments, whose innumerable pipes are animated by
bellows; how he flies over the keys this way with both hands, and
that way with his nimble feet, and, unaided, calls forth a plurality
of quite different passages that yet harmonise with each other;
could you, I say, see how, while he achieves what a number of your
citharists and a thousand of your flute-players together could not
achieve, he not only sings one melody, like a man who has nothing
more to do but sing to the cithara, but attends to everything at
once, and keeps thirty or forty musicians in order, one by a nod,
another by stamping time with his foot, and a third with a warning
finger, and joins in with his own voice now in a high part, now in
a lower one, and again in a middle one; and how he alone, when
they are all working together at their loudest, — although he has
the hardest task of all — yet at once notices when and where something is wrong, and keeps them all together, and watches everything, and if there is any hesitation restores certainty; how rhythm
is in every limb of him; how his quick ear grasps every harmony,
and how he himself reproduces each voice within the small compass
of his own. In general I am a great admirer of antiquity, but I
believe that my friend Bach, and whoever may be at all like him,
comprises in himself many men like Orpheus and twenty singers
like Arion*."

The note probably achieved the purpose its author had
in view, — the mollifying of the cantor who had been so
nettled by Scheibe's sarcasms. If, by the way, the picture

---

* Quintilian, *Institutiones oratoriae* ad I, 12, 3: "Haec omnia,
Fabi, paucissima esse diceres, si videre ab inferis excitato contin-
geret Bachium, ut hoc potissimum utar, quod meus non ita pridem
in Thomano Lipsiensi collega fuit: manu utraque et digitis om-
nibus tractantem vel polycordum nostrum multas unum citharas
complexum, vel organum illud organorum, cujus infinitae numero
tibiae follibus animantur. . . . . Maximus alioquin antiquitatis fautor,
multos unum Orpheos et viginti Arionas complexum Bachium
meum, et si quis illi similis sit forte arbitror." A German translation is given by Spitta II, 89, 90 (German edition). The passage
is cited by J. A. Hiller in his biography of Bach (1784).

is not a purely rhetorical one, it points to the fact that Bach conducted his cantatas from the organ.

Bach was also celebrated in verse, although this honour fell to him less frequently than it afterwards did to his two eldest sons. He possessed at Hamburg a poetical acquaintance, Herr Friedrich Hudemann, Doctor of Law, whom he had distinguished in 1727 by dedicating a very learned canon to him. Hudemann, in return, addressed the following verses to Bach in a collection of poems, *Proben einiger Gedichte*, which he published at Hamburg in 1732:—

"Wenn vor gar langer Zeit des Orpheus Harfen-Klang
Wie er die Menschen traf, sich auch in Tiere drang,
So muß es, großer Bach, weit schöner dir gelingen:
Es kann nur deine Kunst vernünftge Seelen zwingen.
Und dieses trifft gewiß mit der Erfahrung ein:
Oft sieht man Sterbliche den Tieren ähnlich sein,
Wenn ihr zu blöder Geist nicht dein Verdienst erreichet,
Und in der Urteilskraft dem dummen Viehe gleichet,
Kaum treibst du deinen Schall an mein geschäftig Ohr,
So tönet, wie mich deucht, der ganze Musenchor.
Ein Orgelgriff von dir muß selbst der Neid beschämen,
Und jedem Lästerer die Schlangenzunge lähmen.
Apollo hat dich längst des Lorbeers wert geschätzt,
Und deines Namens Ruhm in Marmor eingeätzt.
Du aber kannst allein durch die beseelten Saiten
Dir die Unsterblichkeit, vollkommner Bach, bereiten." *

Contemporary works of musical biography tell us hardly anything about Bach. Since in spite of two requests he could not make up his mind to send Mattheson an autobiographical contribution for the *Ehrenpforte*, the latter was offended and passed him over in it without mention**.

---

* Quoted by Spitta II, 478 (German edition).
** The *Ehrenpforte* was to contain only autobiographical notices. Handel, who had also left Mattheson's enquiry unanswered, was nevertheless dealt with in the work in an article by the compiler himself. This honour probably fell to him because he had once been Mattheson's "pupil". Bach had not had that good fortune. The *Ehrenpforte* appeared in 1740.

Walther, in his musical lexicon of 1732, enumerates
only dates in Bach's career, and the work that had appeared
in print, — as he did in the case of every contemporary
musician. He cannot refrain from characterising the clavier
pieces — i. e. the six suites of the first part of the *Klavierübung* — as excellent. At the end he observes that even
the letters B A C H are melodic in their sequence — a
remark that owed its origin to the Leipzig Herr Bach*.

The enumeration of the names of all who felt friendship and respect for him would make a fairly long list.
The members of the Dresden Kapelle, and those of the
Berlin Kapelle, to which his son belonged, looked upon
him as one of themselves. Of the musicians, the two most
famous of that time, Hasse and Telemann, were most
cordially attached to him; all the Bachs honoured him as
the head of the great old family; his pupils were devoted
to him, and lost no opportunity of showing him their devotion, and of demonstrating their justifiable pride in their
teacher; the leading members of society in Dresden set up
for his patrons; the cultivated Livonian Freiherr von
Kayserling, who from 1733 to 1745 was Russian ambassador at the Dresden Court, befriended him whenever
he could **; princes — such as Duke Leopold of Cöthen,
Duke Ernst August of Weimar, and Duke Christian of
Weissenfels, — treated him as a friend.

When all is said, however, all these were only good acquaintances. Bach does not appear to have had a real
friend so closely bound up with him as to have a part in
his deepest thoughts and experiences. His intimates were
his wife and his two eldest sons; to others he did not reveal
the whole friendliness and joviality of his nature. He

---

* Walther's *Musikalisches Lexikon*, Leipzig, 1732. The article
on Bach commences on p. 64 and comprises 40 half-lines. The
whole volume contains 659 closely printed pages.
** It was probably he whom Bach had to thank for his appointment as Court composer. It was through him that he received the
patent of the 19th November 1736.

kept them all at a certain distance from him. For this reason we know nothing of Bach's real inner nature. No one has been able to hand down to us a remark in which he revealed anything of his inmost soul. Not even his sons could tell Forkel anything of this kind.

CHAPTER XI.

THE ARTIST AND TEACHER.

In his criticism of Bach, Scheibe in one place goes so far as to say that the Herr Hofcompositeur is lacking in the general culture that we ought to expect from a great composer*. What truth is there in this reproach?

As regards culture, Bach was not the inferior of any of the musicians of his epoch. The Latin schools at Ohrdruf and Lüneburg which he had attended enjoyed a first-rate reputation; and we now know that he went through the classes from the beginning. That he did not afterwards go to the university was entirely due to the prime necessity of earning his daily bread. He was well versed in Latin, or he would not have been able to offer to give the instruction in this language that it devolved upon him to give in

---

* In the *Beantwortung der unparteiischen Anmerkungen über eine bedenkliche Stelle in dem sechsten Stück des kritischen Musikus*, — Scheibe's reply to Birnbaum's first article, which appeared as a supplement to the first year's volume of the *Kritischer Musikus*, in 1738. On page 22 he says: "the prime cause of this defect (i. e. Bach's) deserves further consideration. This great man is not particularly well up in the sciences that are especially required of a learned composer. How can one be quite without blemishes in his musical work who has not, by knowledge of the world, qualified himself to investigate and understand the forces of nature and reason? How can one achieve all the benefits that come from the acquisition of good taste, who has barely concerned himself with critical observations, enquiries, and rules that are so necessary not only in rhetoric and poetry but in music that without them one cannot possibly be moving and expressive, principally because the attributes of good and bad style in writing, both in general and in particular, proceed almost entirely from these."

St. Thomas's school. The foreign words in his letters are always used in their correct sense. This shews that he also knew French, which is again clear from the dedication of the Brandenburg concertos, which is very elegantly expressed in that tongue. The addresses of his letters were usually written in French. He signed his name sometimes in German, sometimes in French, and sometimes in Italian. He was conversant with rhetoric as it was then taught, as Birnbaum expressly testifies in the second of his vindications. The fact, again, that men like Gesner and Birnbaum found his conversation interesting, speaks for his culture; so does the thorough, scholarly education that he gave his sons.

Unfortunately Emmanuel and Friedemann have made it impossible for us to know much about the reading of their father, since before the division of the property they placed on one side his collection of old mathematical and musical historical works, which therefore do not figure in the inventory. However, the list of Bach's theological books is alone enough to testify to the activity of his mind. It is interesting to know that he had a translation of Josephus's *History of the Jews*. We can imagine him, after the day's work, seeking recreation in the classical work of the favorite and friend of Vespasian!

Scheibe was thus mistaken. And yet, looked at from his own standpoint, a good deal of his reproach is not unfounded, only that he expressed it clumsily. Bach was self-taught, and as such had an aversion to all learned theories. Clavier-playing, organ-playing, harmony, composition, — he had learnt them all by himself; his sole teachers had been untiring work and incessant experiment.

To a man who had made the fundamental rules of art his own in this manner, many theories that were interesting or new for others were a matter of indifference, for he had been to the roots of things. Now Bach lived in the epoch when it was thought that the perfect art could be discovered by aesthetic reasoning, while others, again, thought that salvation for music lay in mathematical speculations upon the numbers that underlie intervals. To all these endeavours Bach opposed a robust indifference. "Our Bach", says the Necrology, "did not engage at all in deep theoretical considerations of music, but was all the stronger in the practice of it."*

Perhaps he let this indifference become too visible. It is certain that it was generally known how little he troubled about the mathematical basis of the fundamental laws of harmony. Not only Mattheson** but Scheibe testifies to this. "Let any one", says the latter, "ask a great Bach, who has perfect command of all artifices of art, and whose astounding works one cannot see or hear without surprise, whether, in the attainment of this great skill and dexterity, he even once thought of the mathematical relations of the tones, and whether he once consulted mathematics in the construction of so many musical artifices."***

"Two fifths and two octaves must not follow each other, since that is not only a *vitium*, but it sounds ill;" so ran the third rule of thorough-bass that Bach dictated to his pupils†. "It is not only a *vitium* but it sounds ill;" we imagine we can see him as he goes up and down listening to the scratching of the quill, and laughing merrily to himself!

He took so little interest in the activities of the scientific musical society that was constituted at Leipzig under his eyes, that at first he had no thought of becoming a member. The fact is all the more striking as Lorenz Christoph Mizler (1711—1778) the founder of the society, had been his pupil

---

* Mizler's *Musikalische Bibliothek*, 1754; vol.IV, Part I, p. 173.

** *Ehrenpforte*, p. 231, note, referring to the fact that Mizler claimed to be a pupil of Bach.

*** *Kritischer Musikus*, 1739, II, 355. Scheibe is here praising Bach.

† See Bach's rules for thorough-bass in the copy that has come to us from Peter Kellner (Spitta III, 315 ff.). Peter Kellner does not seem to have been a direct pupil of the master. See the preface to B. G. XXVII ¹.

for the clavier and composition, and had dedicated to him
in 1734, together with three other celebrities, his doctoral
dissertation "Quod musica ars sit pars eruditionis philo-
sophicae" — "Music is part of a philosophical education"*.
The "Sozietät der musikalischen Wissenschaften" was
founded by him in 1738. He was of opinion that as a result
of its inquiries a "new period in music" was going to open;
and he had a medal struck, on which, according to his
own description, "a naked child flies towards the dawn,
on its head a bright star, in its right hand a burning torch
inverted, beside which a swallow flies, denoting the dawn-
ing of day in music"**.

There was a good deal that was fantastic in the activities
of this Society. One cannot, however, but respect it
when one looks through Mizler's journal, the *Musikalische
Bibliothek*, the organ of the Society. It testifies to a solid
and learned spirit, and contains plenty of interesting matter.
The reader was kept admirably informed upon everything
that "happened in the sphere of music and of the adjoining sciences"***.

Telemann belonged to the Society from 1740; Handel
was made an honorary member in 1745; Bach, however,
in spite of all the importunities of Mizler, could not decide
to apply for admission. He finally did so in 1747, sub-
mitting as his specimen composition some canonic variations upon the Christmas hymn "Vom Himmel hoch da
komm ich her"†, and the "Canon triplex à 6 voc.", which
afterwards appeared in the *Musikalische Bibliothek*††.

---

* In 1736 Mizler gave lectures on mathematics, philosophy and
music at the Leipzig University. In 1743 he went to Warsaw,
where he later was made a Court counsellor. His journal, the *Musikalische Bibliothek*, appeared from 1736—1754.
** Mizler's *Musikalische Bibliothek*, Vol. IV, Part I. Leipzig,
1754, p. 105, 106.
*** See, for example, in Vol. IV, Part I (p. 48—68) the thorough
anatomical description of the ear for musicians. The articles on
general aesthetics are of less value.
† Peter's ed. of the organ chorale preludes, V, 92—102.
†† 1754, Vol. IV, Part I, Supplement.

Thereupon he was admitted as fourteenth member, in June 1747.

Among other things the Society occupied itself with the question of cantata texts, and cherished the design of issuing a pattern cycle*. It first contented itself with laying down fundamental principles for the writing of texts of this kind, and published the result of a conference upon this question, according to which the church cantatas should be shorter in winter than in summer, and consist of only three hundred and fifty bars, lasting about twenty-five minutes; in the good season eight to ten minutes could be added, and the "music" could extend to four hundred bars.

The normal cantata should be laid out as follows: — (1) chorale chorus or chorus upon a short passage from the Bible; (2) recitative of twelve or twenty lines in length; (3) an aria-arioso or a fugued chorale; (4) recitative; (5) aria; (6) chorale or fugue.

A warning is given against "too ardent and too emphatic poetry", since there is a risk, "if violent passions are expressed in church", of making a ridiculous effect. The librettist must not only have the gift of writing ably and edifyingly, but must also have some understanding of music. The *da capo* form is admitted for the arias; for the recitative, rhymes are desirable**.

Bach does not seem to have participated in these deliberations, for the cantata type that was put forward as the norm is quite different from his. The warning, indeed, that nothing passionate should be expressed in church seems rather to be directed against him than to emanate from him.

---

* 1754. Vol. IV, Part I, p. 104. "The Society is still working at the church cycle, and it will be some years yet before this can be finished." It was never issued.

** 1754, Vol. IV, Part I, p. 108—111; from the report of the proceedings of the Society in 1746 and the following years, 5th „Packet".

Posterity owes a debt of gratitude to the Mizler Society. In its journal for 1754 it gave a Necrology of Bach, that contains the earliest biographical material relating to him. Or should we rather say that the Society is indebted to Bach; for but for him who would remember this old association today?

The self-taught Bach thus belonged to no school. No preconceived opinions guided him in his studies. His authorities were all acknowledged masters, the old as well as the new. As often as the distances, his means and his leisure permitted, he went to hear contemporary celebrities and to learn what he could by observation of them. He copied out the works of others. In conformity with the old tradition of the Bachs, he did not extend his journeys beyond the German frontier. None the less was he thoroughly acquainted with Italian and French art. Among the French, Couperin chiefly attracted him. In Weimar he occupied himself especially with the Italians, — Frescobaldi (1583—1644), Legrenzi (Lotti's teacher), (1625—1690), Vivaldi (died 1743), Albinoni (1674—1745), and Corelli (1653—1713). Of the German clavecinists he had a particular regard for Froberger*. According to Forkel, he studied the contemporary French organ composers with the greatest assiduity**.

We have evidence of Bach's occupation with other masters in his transcriptions of their works, — sixteen clavier concertos, four organ concertos, and a violin concerto arranged for four claviers***. Misled by the inexact headings of the copies of these arrangements, musicians at one time thought they were all works by Vivaldi, whose violin concertos, at the time Bach was in Weimar, astonished the whole musical

---

* M. Jacob Adlung, *Anleitung zur musikalischen Gelahrtheit*, 1758, p. 711: "Froberger was highly thought of by the late Bach of Leipzig, although he was already somewhat old."

** Forkel, p. 24.

*** The clavier concertos are in B. G. XLII; the organ concertos in Vol. XXXVIII; the concerto for four claviers in Vol. XLIII.

world by the novelty of their style. Vivaldi was especially well known in Germany from his having been Concertmeister at the Darmstadt Court until 1713. Later research, assisted by the discovery of the originals of the Vivaldi concertos, has shewn that not all these transcriptions are based on works by Vivaldi*. From him are derived the clavier concertos Nos. 1, 2, 4, 5, 7, 9 and 14; the organ concertos Nos. 2 and 3, and the concerto for four claviers; clavier concerto No. 3 is an arrangement of an oboe concerto of the Venetian Benedetto Marcello (1686—1739); No. 14 is founded on a violin concerto by Telemann; Nos. 11 and 16 are derived from violin concertos of Duke Johann Ernst of Weimar, who was a pupil of Walther and a friend of Bach. This young prince, a nephew of the reigning Duke, died at Frankfort-on-the-Main in 1715, barely nineteen years old, after long and severe suffering. Bach's transcriptions are "like a greeting sent into eternity to the friend who had been torn from him".

Johann Ernst's concertos were until recently regarded as lost. It was only known that Telemann had edited six of them, and that Mattheson, in his great "General Bass School", had spoken of them in terms of high praise. "To find independent princes", he there says, "who compose music that can be performed, is indeed something that does not happen every day". In 1903 the Telemann edition was found by the active Bach investigator Schering in the Grand Ducal library. It has a preface in French by the editor, that bears the date of 1st February 1718. A second collection was to have followed, but it never appeared. The clavier concerto No. 13, the first movement of which re-appears in the first organ concerto, is also probably founded on a work by the young prince — as is shown by some remarks on the manuscript copy that we possess. The original, however, has not yet been discovered.

---

* In the B. G. edition (Vol. XLII) all sixteen clavier concertos still figure as transcriptions from Vivaldi.

The original of the clavier concertos Nos. 6, 8, 10, 12 and 15, and the organ concerto No. 4, are as yet unknown. They may come to light when the treasures of the old chamber music become better known*. When this happens, it is possible that this or that "original" work of Bach will prove to be a transcription. Spitta believed the three clavier sonatas to be especially characteristic of Bach's style, and even arranged them chronologically, placing the one in C major among the works of the composer's maturity: afterwards he had to recognise them as the work of Johann Adam Reinken, whom one was not exactly accustomed to regard as a striking composer. They were originally suites for three stringed instruments, published in the *Hortus musicus* of the Hamburg composer**.

What was Bach's object in making these transcriptions? It was formerly thought that he did this work simply for his own instruction. That may be so, to some degree, in the case of Vivaldi. The Prince of Weimar, however, was not an acknowledged master. Then did Bach wish to make

---

* Spitta (I, 411 ff.) is best acquainted with the Vivaldi concerto that forms the basis of Bach's clavichord concerto No. 2. For later research into the question of Bach's arrangements see: — (a) Paul Count Waldersee, *Antonio Vivaldis Violinkonzerte unter besonderer Berücksichtigung der von J. S. Bach bearbeiteten*, in the *Vierteljahrschrift für Musikwissenschaft*, 1885, p. 356—380. In this the editions are cited of the Vivaldi works concerned. Various collections of concertos for four, two and one solo violin, with accompaniment for string orchestra and cembalo, appeared in London and Amsterdam. It is interesting to note that of the twelve concertos that appeared as op. 8, the first six are pure programme music. The first four are accompanied by illustrative poems *(Sonetto dimostrativo)*, and bear the titles "La Primavera", "L'estate", "L'Automno", "L'Inverno"; the fifth and sixth are entitled "La Tempesta di Mare" and "Il Piacere" respectively. (b) Arnold Schering: *Zur Bach-Forschung*, in the *Sammelbände der Internationalen Musikgesellschaft*, 1902—1903, IV, 234—243, and 1903—1904, V, 565—570. The author shews that Bach transcribed Telemann, Duke Johann Ernst of Weimar, and Benedetto Marcello, and makes conjectures as to the derivation of the concertos the originals of which are still unknown.

** Spitta, *Bachiana*: No. 3, *Umarbeitung fremder Originale* in his *Musikgeschichtliche Aufsätze*, 1894, p. 111—120.

these chamber music works more generally known by arranging them for a single instrument? This was not the reason; for he did not concern himself in the least to transcribe them as they were in the original, but treated them all alike with the utmost freedom, no matter who the composer might be. Where he thinks the basses inexpressive, he substitutes others for them; he adds new or interesting middle parts almost throughout; he even transforms the upper voice completely when it occurs to him to do so. Not even the plan and the development of the works are respected. Sometimes he goes his own way immediately after the first bars, then follows the original for a little while, again branches off, returns once more, omits something here, inserts something there, without troubling himself whether his transcription becomes only half or twice as long as the original*. He does not learn from the originals, but, with his masterly corrections, rather sits in judgment on them — though this was certainly not his intention.

It is really quite inconceivable that Bach, now in the epoch of his first mastery, with a copious fund of themes and motives, should need to lean upon the ideas — often commonplace — of others. That his Weimar friend Johann Gottfried Walther should have delighted in making transcriptions, and cultivated the practice assiduously, is not astonishing; his was not at all a creative mind. But that Bach, whose inventive power is simply beyond comprehension, should have indulged in the practice, is merely part of the fact — incapable of psychological explanation — that whenever he could he went to external stimuli and examples for his own creations. This was the case not only in his youthful period, but also in his latest creative epoch. He liked other people's music in the most uncritical way, simply because it stimulated his own creative activity. In

---

* Detailed analyses of the method of the transcriptions are given in the above-cited essays of Waldersee, Schering, and Spitta.

certain cases it was an actual necessity to him. His contemporary Magister Pitschel, of Leipzig, tells us that before improvising he generally played, from the score, a
work by some other man, as if he first had to set the machine
of his invention going by artificial means. This fact was
a matter of common knowledge. "You know", writes
Magister Pitschel to his friend, "that the famous man who
in our town enjoys the greatest reputation for music and the
admiration of all connoisseurs, cannot, they say, ravish people
with his own combinations of tones, until he has played
something from a score to set his imagination in motion" *.

Forkel also tells us something of this suggestive action
of other men's music on Bach. He says that if a single
bass part, often badly figured, were set before him, he
would amuse himself by immediately playing a complete
trio or quartet from it; if he were in a gay humour and
fully conscious of his power, he would instantly extemporise to three obbligato voices a fourth of his own, thus
turning a trio into a quartet.

So that Bach transcribed the Vivaldi and other concertos not to make them more accessible to the public at
large, nor to learn from them, but simply because this
was his way and it gave him pleasure. Nevertheless it is
certain that he derived some profit from Vivaldi. He
learned from him clarity and design in the structure of a
work. Through the Italian he won freedom from the Northern masters and their ingenious, intricate style. There is
preparing that great synthesis of the North German art of
ideas and the Latin art of form that traverses Bach's work
in the most varied phases, till finally, in the organ works
of the later period, the art of Buxtehude and Pachelbel
again emerges, purified, transfigured, and more profound,
and closes the circle.

------

* Spitta III, 263. The passage occurs in the journal of the Gottsched party, *Belustigung des Verstandes und Witzes*, (Vol. I, Leipzig,
1741), in Pitschel's letter to a friend "on visiting public religious
service".

Bach further learned from Vivaldi the perfect violin technique, the art of writing "singably". The violin art of the North, which he had hitherto known, was in many respects more brilliant and splendid; but it had not the same knowledge of how to utilise the natural advantages of the instrument. It is interesting to observe that Bach transfers violin music to the clavier and the organ, and tries to get the effect of the strings on the keyed instruments. It shows, what we can also gather from his works, that for him there was really only one style, — that naturally suggested by the phrasing of the stringed instrument — and that all other styles are for him only modifications of this basic style.

At other times Bach borrows from his original only the theme, which he then works out quite independently. We know that the theme of the C minor organ fugue (Peters

IV, 6) is derived from Legrenzi (1625—1690), and that of the small one in B minor (Peters IV, 8) — from Corelli

(1653—1713). Albinoni (1674—1745) gave him the themes for two clavier fugues*.

We cannot say, of course, how many themes of his own owe their origin to the effect of other men's ideas. There are certainly more of these, however, than we should at first imagine. Who would think that the consummate theme of the great G minor organ fugue —

---

* Spitta I, 425, 426. One of the fugues is in A major (Peters' ed. of the Pianoforte Works I, Part 13, No. 10; B. G.XXXVI, p. 173), the other in B minor (Peter's ed. of the Pianoforte Works, Part 3, No. 5; B. G. XXXVI, p. 178).

was generated in Bach's imagination by another musician? We know, however, now that Reinken's *Hortus musicus* has been made accessible, that it was he who set Bach's invention on that path. The theme in question is found in the fifth Suite* —

Thus many a great idea, that in other men merely existed obscurely in an insignificant form, had to come to Bach to be endowed with the life that really belonged to it**.

In Leipzig, where he was mainly occupied with vocal compositions, he concerned himself more with the masters of Italian vocal music — Palestrina (1515—1594), Lotti (1667—1740), and Caldara (1670—1736). To the end of his days, he was, like all the great self-taught men, very receptive, and sure that he could always learn something from others. He showed the liveliest interest in everything that appeared in his own sphere. Kant was not more anxious to learn what was going on in European literature than Bach was to get hold of the works of contemporary composers.

He had also the open mind of the self-taught man for inventions. He was not interested in scientific and aesthetic theories upon music; whatever related to practice, however, seemed to him — even if it were concerned with the smallest detail — important enough to be worthy of his

---

* Spitta, *Bachiana*: No. 3, in *Musikgeschichtliche Aufsätze*, 1894, pp. 118, 119. A clavier fugue of Bach's in B flat major (Peters' supplement to the Pianoforte Works I, 11) is also derived from the *Hortus musicus*.

** The fundamental idea of the Italian Concerto is found in the final movement of a "symphony" in Georg Muffat's *Florilegium primum* (1695). See Arnold Schering's *Zur Bachforschung*, in the *Sammelbände der Internationalen Musikgesellschaft*, 1902—1903, p. 243.

serious attention. He was particularly interested in instru-
ment-making. As one of the leading experts of his epoch,
he witnessed the transition from the old to the modern
instruments, though he saw only the beginnings of the
new era, and still clung to the old with some tenacity.

What he thought upon the progress of organ and
clavier making we know from his pupil Agricola, who
in 1759 succeeded Graun as leader of the Royal Kapelle
in Berlin. Lorenz Albrecht showed him the manuscript
of the *Musica Mechanica Organoedi* of Jacob Adlung, with
the publication of which he had been entrusted after the
death of the author, and asked him to indicate, in the
notes, Bach's views upon clavier and organ-building, so
far as they differed from what was said there, — which
Agricola did. Where Agricola is silent, we may assume that
Adlung's opinions are in agreement with those of Bach*.

We also know from Forkel that Bach gave his special
attention to the improvement of the organ wind-chest and
bellows. "The first thing he did in examining an organ was
to draw all the sounding stops and then play the instrument, getting as much tone as was possible out of it. He
used to say, in jest, that he must first of all know whether
the instrument had good lungs"**. He liked good reed-
work, and an organ could hardly have too much of it to
please him; he did not object, for example, to the sixteen
reeds on the organ of St. Catharine's Church in Hamburg.

---

* Jacob Adlung was teacher of the Gymnasium at Erfurt, and
organist at the Rats- und Prediger-Kirche there. His first important
work, *Anleitung zur musikalischen Gelahrtheit* (1758) was published
by himself; the second, the famous *Musica Mechanica Organoedi*
was left by him at his death (1762) in manuscript, but ready for
printing. It appeared in 1768. Not only does it exhibit an admirable knowledge of physical science and great practical experience,
but also a fine aesthetic feeling, as shewn in his judgments. He
lost many valuable manuscripts in a fire. At the beginning of the
Musica Mechanica he gives the story of his own life. The index to
the *Musica Mechanica* is not a complete record of the passages in
which Bach is mentioned.

** Forkel, p. 23.

Reinken, who voiced it himself, also thought its disposition excellent*. On the same organ Bach was surprised by the clear and precise speaking of a 32-feet principal and the 16-feet pedal trombone**.

In order to move easily and surely from one manual to another, Bach liked them to be as close together as possible. The keys were to be short and narrow, so as to be spanned with ease; he liked the semitone keys — which were white on the old organs — to be narrow at the top and well rounded. He also appears, — so we gather from Agricola — to have favoured the old, narrow pedals, and to have insisted that the pedal-board should lie in a correct and natural position with regard to the manuals***.

In general it may be said that organ-building in Bach's time had attained to a beauty and richness of tone — particularly through the technical improvements of Andreas Silbermann of Strassburg (1678—1734) and Gottfried Silbermann of Freiberg (1683—1753), — which have not been surpassed since. A certain finality had been reached in this department. It was not so, however, in the sphere of clavier manufacture. Here three instruments, — two old and one new, — struggled with each other for predominance. The oldest was the clavichord, in which the strings were set in vibration by a rather primitive piece of mechanism, a "tangent" striking them from below. Nevertheless at the beginning of the eighteenth century some important improvements had been made in this instrument. Its advantage consisted in the fact that it permitted dynamic nuances, since the strength of the tone, as on our modern pianoforte, could be regulated by the touch; it had, however, the great disadvantage of not producing a very loud tone†.

---

* Adlung I, 66 and 187.
** Adlung I, 288.
*** Adlung II, 23, 24.
† The clavichord is described in Adlung II, 135 ff. As a rule it had two strings to each note (p. 144).

In the clavicembalo — also called clavecin, cembalo, or, in general, "Flügel", — the tone was made by the strings being plucked, or, as Adlung expresses it, "flipped", by a quill or metal pin*. It had a clear and penetrating tone, which, however, soon ceased. Nuances and a singing style were therefore both impossible upon it. In order to get at least two degrees of tone, in Bach's time clavicembali were built with two keyboards, one manual being for *forte*, the other for *piano*; further improvements were a pedal-board, also provided with strings, and a manual coupler by means of which the lower manual could be made to sound simultaneously a higher octave. It was for clavi-cembali of this kind that the Goldberg Variations, the Italian Concerto, and the so-called organ sonatas of Bach were written. Speaking generally, all organ works could be played on these instruments. This explains why Bach published a collection of long chorale preludes as the third part of the *Klavierübung***.

There also sprang up at this time the Hammerclavier — "piano e forte" — which was destined to combine the advantages of the clavichord and those of the clavicembalo, and to supplant them both. Our modern pianoforte is derived from it. The self-releasing hammer, by which the hammer-clavier first became possible, was invented about the same time in Italy by the Florentine ınstrument-maker Cristofori (before 1711), and in Germany by Gottlieb

---

* The clavicembalo is described in Adlung II, 102—115. The spinet was a small clavicembalo; the term "Epinette" comes from "épine", suggesting the "thorn" or quill that plucked the strings.

** In Bach's time the general name of "clavier" was given to all keyed instruments, including the organ. We still possess a cembalo that belonged to Bach. It passed from Friedemann to Count Voss in Berlin, and is now in the Royal collection of instruments there. Rust describes it in the preface to Vol. IX of the B. G. The tonal effect of the clavicembalo will be discussed in greater detail in the chapter on Bach's clavier works and the manner of performing them.

The best history of clavier construction is to be found in the supplement to Weitzmann's *Geschichte des Klavierspiels*.

Schröter, organist at the Hauptkirche in Nordhausen (1717). Gottfried Silbermann, the Freiberg organ builder, tried to improve upon the invention and to interest his friend Bach in it. The master's attitude towards the new instrument may be given in the words of Agricola, who is our sole testimony in the matter: —

"Herr Gottfried Silbermann," he says in a long note to Adlung's *Musica Mechanica**, "had at first made two of these instruments. The late Kapellmeister Joh. Sebastian Bach had seen and played upon one of these. He had praised the tone of it, indeed wondered at it, but had objected that it was too weak in the upper part, and that it was much too hard to play**. Herr Silbermann, who could not endure to have his work blamed, took this very ill. For a long time he was angry with Herr Bach for it. Nevertheless his conscience told him that Herr Bach was not altogether wrong. So he thought it best — to his great credit be it said — not to make any more instruments like these, but to try all the harder to correct the defects that Herr Jo. S. Bach had pointed out. He worked at this for many years. And that this was the true reason for this delay I doubt so much less, as I have heard it candidly confessed by Herr Silbermann himself. At last, when Herr Silbermann had really hit upon many improvements, especially with regard to the action, he again sold one to the Prince of Rudolstadt . . . . Shortly afterwards the King of Prussia ordered one of these instruments, and, as he was greatly pleased with it, he ordered several more of Herr Silbermann. In all these instruments, those who, like myself, had seen one of the two earlier ones, were especially able to see how industriously Herr Silbermann must have worked at improving them. Herr Silbermann had also had the praiseworthy ambition to show one of these new instruments to the late Herr Kapellmeister Bach, and to get him to try it, and he was warmly praised for it."

These were the Silbermann forte-pianos, on which Bach, according to Forkel, had to play before Frederick the Great at Potsdam. The King had acquired fifteen of them. "They now all lie about useless, in various corners of the royal castle", says Forkel in his biography of Bach (1802)***. This passage came into the mind of Robert Eitner, the able musical historian, when he was delayed

---

  * II, 116.
  ** According to a fairly probable calculation, Silbermann made both these hammer-claviers about 1733.
  *** p. 10.

in Potsdam by the rain one afternoon in 1873. He went into the castle, and found one of the Silbermann instruments in Frederick the Great's room*. We thus still possess one of the claviers upon which old Bach played to old Fritz.

At that time, however, he could not have found very much pleasure in the new instrument. At any rate he did not trouble to acquire one for himself. Five clavicembali are specified in the list of the property left at his death, among them the three with pedals which he had presented to his youngest son**.

He thus clung to the older, in fact to the very oldest instrument, — the clavichord. This was his favorite. The clavicembalo was too soulless for him, although he appreciated, and knew how to turn to account, the effect to be had by changing from one keyboard to the other. He played it in public. For himself, for private musical entertainment, and for practice, as Forkel says, he used only the clavichord. "He found it most apt for the expression of his finest thoughts, and did not believe that such variety of nuance in the tone could be got on any "Flügel" or pianoforte as on this instrument, that was indeed poor in tone, but extraordinarily flexible in detail."*** Mattheson also preferred the clavichord to the clavicembalo, on account of its "delicacy", as Adlung expresses it. The latter is also of opinion that "manieren" (embellishments) cannot be expressed on any other instrument so well as on the clavichord", and that "none sings so sweetly and so long".†

* See *Ein altes Pianoforte*, in Eitner's *Monatshefte für Musikgeschichte*, 1873. Eitner there gives an exact description of the instruments.

** Spitta III, 358, 359.

*** Forkel, p. 17.

† Adlung, *Musica mechanica* II, 144 and 152. It is curious that in the instruments left by Bach not a single clavichord is enumerated. Karl Nef, in his interesting essay *Klavizimbel und Klavichord*, thinks we must conclude from this that it is not certain that Bach preferred the clavichord, as Forkel would have us believe. See the *Jahrbuch der Musikbibliothek Peters*, 1903, p. 29.

In that epoch, every artist was still to some extent an instrument maker, and every instrument maker to some extent an artist. It was at least expected of every capable player that he should be able to keep his instrument in repair, including the tuning and, in the case of the clavicembalo, the renewing of defective quills. Bach was expert in both of these. "No one", says Forkel, "could ever quill his 'Flügel' to his satisfaction; he always did it himself. He also tuned both his 'Flügel' and his clavichord, and was so expert at this work that it never took him more than a quarter of an hour*." He was, indeed, not so expert as Adlung, who built claviers in his leisure hours, until he lost all his costly woods in a fire. He invented, however, a lute-clavier, which he got the organ builder Zacharias Hildebrand to make for him. Agricola gives a description of the instrument, which he himself had seen, in Adlung's work**. What Bach meant to do with this clavier is not quite clear. It could only be of use for playing his lute compositions on a keyed instrument.

The invention of the viola pomposa, on the other hand, which Bach had built by the Leipzig court instrument maker Hoffmann, had some practical value. It had five strings, tuned C', G, d, a, ē, thus occupying a middle place between the violas and the cellos; it was held like a violin.

---

* Forkel, p. 17.
** In Adlung's *Musica mechanica* II, 139. "The author of these remarks remembers to have seen and heard in Leipzig, about the year 1740, a lute-clavicembalo devised by Herr Johann Sebastian Bach and constructed by Herr Zacharias Hildebrand; it was slightly smaller than the ordinary clavicembalo, but in other respects was made like one. It had two catgut strings to each note and a so-called 'little octave' of brass strings. It is true that under ordinary circumstances (that is, when only one stop was drawn) it sounded more like the theorbo than the lute. But when the so-called lute stop (i. e. the damping of the metal strings) — was drawn with the cornet stop, then lutenists by profession might almost be deceived by it."
According to Rudolf Bunge (*Johann Sebastian Bachs Kapelle zu Cöthen*, in the *Bachjahrbuch* for 1905, p. 29), Bach had a lute-clavicembalo made for him by a master joiner when he was in Cöthen.

Bach had the difficult and hastily figured basses in the accompaniments of the arias played on it. Our information as to this instrument comes from Ernst Ludwig Gerber (1746—1819), who served under three ruling princes of Schwarzburg-Sondershausen as jurist and court organist, and occupied his spare time with the compilation of a historical-biographical dictionary of musicians, that was intended to complete Walther's work*. His father, who was also jurist and court organist to the princes of Schwarzburg-Sondershausen, had been Bach's pupil in Leipzig from 1724 to 1727, and had then heard the viola pomposa used as a substitute for the violoncello. How greatly Bach was pleased with this instrument may be guessed from the fact that to the five sonatas for violoncello he added another for viola pomposa. When he had this instrument constructed, whether earlier in Cöthen or later in Leipzig, we cannot now be sure. He also planned a pedal-glockenspiel, that was to have been added to the organ at St. Blasius's Church in Mühlhausen. Whether this happened is doubtful, as Bach left that town before the completion of the organ repairs which he was superintending**. In later times he set no value on trivialities of this kind in organs.

It was during his life-time, again, that the oboe d'amore was invented, and the flute traversière, which supplanted the old flute à bec, was improved. The story that at Cöthen he amused himself with inventing a musical clock is due to the imagination of one of his biographers***.

---

* *Historisch-biographisches Lexikon der Tonkünstler*, Part I, A—M, 1790; Part II, N—Z, 1792; Breitkopf, Leipzig. The accounts of the viola pomposa are in Vol. I, columns 90 and 491 ff. The second edition of the work appeared as *Neues historisch-biographisches Lexikon der Tonkünstler*, in four volumes, (I and II, 1812; III, 1813; IV, 1814; Kuhnel, Leipzig). For the musical history of the eighteenth century, Gerber's works are of priceless value. On the viola pomposa see also Spitta II, 69, III, 227, 250.
** Spitta II, 370.
*** Bitter, Joh. Seb. Bach I, 161. He thinks that a musical clock in the castle at Nienburg a. S. was at one time in the castle at Cöthen, and was made by Bach.

An innovation that Bach introduced in fingering was of permanent value. On the organ, as well as on the clavier, he desired an absolute and delicate legato style. Such a method of playing, however, was impossible without a reform of technique. At that time everyone placed his fingers just as it occurred to him to do; the thumb was not used at all, or only in cases of necessity. "My late father", says Emmanuel in his *Versuch über die wahre Art das Klavier zu spielen,* "told me that in his youth he had heard great men who never used the thumb except when it was necessary to make big stretches. As he lived in an epoch in which there came about gradually a most remarkable change in musical taste, he found it necessary to think out for himself a much more thorough use of the fingers, and especially of the thumb, which, besides performing other good services, is quite indispensable in the difficult keys, where it must be used as nature intends."*

About the same time as Bach, François Couperin (1668 to 1733) in Paris hit upon the new fingering, and published it in his book *L'art de toucher le clavecin* (1717). As Bach was deeply interested in Couperin's work, it was thought that he had got his fingering from him, — against which theory, however, Emmanuel rightly protested to Forkel. He points out how much more radical the reform of his father proved than that of Couperin**.

We must be careful, however, not to identify Bach's fingering with that of modern times. It was richer than ours, since it represents the transition from an old method to a new one, just as the richness of his harmonies is due to the fact that he writes in major and minor and yet keeps within the sphere of the old modes. Thus of the old fingering he retained the simple passing of one finger over another, while adopting the new method of employing the thumb.

---

* Section I, "On Fingering", p. 15.
** Forkel, p. 16. Examples of Bach's fingering are to be seen in Friedemann's *Klavierbüchlein.*

In time this free passing of one finger over another fell more and more into disuse, and fingering came to be based simply on the combinations made possible by the passing under of the thumb. Emmanuel occupies a middle position between his father and the modern method. He still retains, in principle, the crossing of the fingers, but discards the passing of the second over the third finger, the third over the second, and the fourth over the fifth. He regards the passing of the thumb under the fifth finger as an abomination. On the whole he cannot do much with the little finger; so that Bach evidently did not use this much*.

Every player of Bach's works, — unless he wishes to lose himself in complicated substitutions — has frequently to pass one finger over another, — especially the third over the fourth and the fourth over the fifth; so that Bach's music itself instructs us as to his fingering, and indeed compels us in some measure to adopt it.

Strongly incurved and loose fingers and loose wrists were also part of Bach's method of playing. The fingers rested directly on the keys. He himself played with so slight and easy a motion of the fingers that one could hardly notice it. Only the front joints of the fingers were in motion; the hand preserved its rounded form even in the most difficult passages; the fingers were only slightly raised above the keys.

His touch was very complex. He aimed chiefly at a singing tone. To this end he did not merely let the key, after pressing it down, come to rest and then ascend, but raised it by a gradual drawing-back of the finger-tips towards the inner flat of the hand, so as to give the string the proper time to vibrate and die away. By this means the tone was not only prolonged, but also made more beautiful, so that even on an instrument so poor in tone as the clavichord he could play cantabile and legato**.

---

* See Emmanuel's fingering of the scales in the *Versuch über die wahre Art das Klavier zu spielen* (1759) I, 21—31.

** Forkel (p. 12), discusses Bach's touch in detail.

This style of playing applies, of course, only to the clavichord, — where finger and string stood in intimate relation to each other, — and not to the clavicembalo. Bach's touch was therefore absolutely modern, for the latest theories upon the "singing tone" on the pianoforte agree in recognising it to depend not only on the striking of the keys, but also, to a great extent, on the regulation of their ascent. Bach is also modern in this respect, that he would have spoken not of a "touch" but only of a conscious transmission of strength and pressure to the keys. Sebastian Erard's invention of the double escapement (1823), which made possible endlessly varied gradations in the re-striking of a tone, would thus have been joyfully welcomed by Bach; the mechanism of the modern pianoforte is, in fact, mostly only the fulfilment of his boldest dreams. He would not have altogether agreed with the size of our keys and with the strength of pressure that they demand.

We have no definite information as to his organ pedalling. We may suppose that he did not use the heel much, the shortness of the pedals in those days not allowing this. On the other hand he would take advantage of the narrowness of the pedals of that time, which he himself favoured, to glide from one to the other with the toes.

What astonished his hearers, besides the plasticity and clearness of his playing, was his calmness during performance. Scheibe and Forkel refer to this as to something quite exceptional. Our pianists, and more especially our organists, would do well to take him as their model in this respect.

Of Bach as a violin player we unfortunately know little. This much is certain, that he had thoroughly studied the technique of the instrument, or he would not have written the sonatas for solo violin in the way he did. The ties that he indicates for the strings in his scores also reveal the master.

We do not exactly know how the violin was played in Bach's time*. It seems to be more and more certain that at that time the hairs of the violin bow were fastened without screws to the wood, and were stretched by the thumb of the right hand tighter or looser as one wanted. "Springing" bowing was thus out of the question, whereas double stopping was made possible to an extent which we today, with our bows stretched as they are, cannot form any idea. The chord sequences of the Chaconne, which we laboriously accomplish now by throwing the bow back on the lower strings, presented no difficulties in those days, when the player relaxed the bow for a moment so that it could curve over the strings. We can hardly imagine now the special tone-effects made possible by this technique. For echo effects the player suddenly loosened the hairs, thus obtaining a murmuring, ethereal tone.

In chamber music Bach played for preference the viola. "With this instrument he was as it were in the centre of the harmony, where he could hear and enjoy to the utmost what was going on on both sides of him **".

His mastery in improvisation was well known. He was often begged by friends to perform on the organ, and he generally complied with willingness. He probably preferred the organ of the University church for these performances, since it answered better to his wishes than that of St. Thomas's, although even it did not wholly satisfy him. He himself always regretted "not to have had a really large and really fine organ at hand for his regular use" ***.

If he improvised for as long as two hours together, the theme remained the same from the beginning to the end. First of all he made a prelude and a fugue out of it on the

---

* The following is based on Arnold Schering's article *Verschwundene Traditionen des Bachzeitalters*, in the *Bachjahrbuch* for 1904, p. 113.

** Forkel, p. 46.

*** See the Necrology in Mizler's *Musikalische Bibliothek*, IV, Part I, 1754, p. 172. It is nevertheless questionable whether he had the organ of the University church at his free disposal at any time, since the service there was not under his charge.

full organ. Then he showed his skill in registration in a
trio or a four-part movement; then, as a rule, came a chorale
prelude. Finally he developed a new fugue upon the old
theme. So at least we are told by Forkel, who also says
that, according to Emmanuel, the organ compositions that
we have give no adequate idea of the magnificence of
Bach's improvisation on the organ*.

Organ-builders and organists were appalled when they
saw him registering. "They thought that such a combination of stops could not possibly sound well together, but
wondered greatly when they perceived that the organ now
sounded at its best, the effect merely being a slightly strange
and unusual one, which could not be achieved by their
own style of registration"**. This refers, however, only to
the style of Bach's preliminary organ-registration for his
prelude or fugue, not to a constant change of registration
during the performance, after the manner that is today
thought best for his organ works. Bach was as ignorant
of this practice as of modern orchestration.

It gave him particular pleasure, when improvising, to go
into all possible keys, and to move about even in the most
distant ones in such a way that his hearers did not observe
it, but thought he had only modulated within the inner
circle of a single key***.

"In conducting", says the Necrology, "he was very
accurate, and extremely sure in the tempo, which he generally took very briskly." Forkel also lays stress on his
lively tempi. This however is to be understood relatively,
with reference to the way of taking tempi in those days.

It seems strange, at first sight, that Bach, when improvising, should have confined himself to a single theme.

---

* Forkel, pp. 18 and 22.
** Forkel, p. 20.
*** Forkel, p. 17. Nevertheless the "harmonic labyrinth" that
has come down to us with Bach's name attached to it is probably
not by him. See Spitta II, 43. This curious piece is given in the
B. G. XXXVIII, p. 225. In the preface the possibility is mentioned that it may be by Heinichen, the celebrated musical theorist.

One would have expected that this richly inventive genius would have been so overwhelmed by the weight of the ideas that thronged within him that he could not have kept to one theme alone, but would necessarily have given voice to them all. It was not so. Everything points to the fact that Bach did not invent easily, but slowly and with difficulty. We must not be misled by the fact that we possess hardly any sketches or draughts of his, and that the scores of his cantatas give the impression of having being thrown off in one breath, so quickly, in fact, that the flying pen could scarcely keep pace with the ideas. The working-out and elaboration of the themes may indeed not have cost him very much time, since it often happens with him that the whole piece, with all its developments, is already implicit in the theme, and evolves out of it with a certain aesthetic-mathematical necessity, quite irrespective of the formal element in the development of a chorale chorus, a fugue or a *da capo* aria.

We can, however, form only a faint idea of the long and arduous mental work that is presupposed in the development of a characteristic theme of this kind, according to its own mysterious inner laws, into a masterly piece of music. If Bach, as is generally supposed, had shaken themes out of his sleeve after the manner of genius, it would be incomprehensible how they all come to be so extraordinarily rich and charcteristic. In all his works there is not one that is banal. But neither do we get the impression in any one of these melodies, quivering as they are with inner life, of effortless invention; and the deeper we penetrate into Bach, the stronger does this feeling become*.

Bach thus worked like the mathematician, who sees the whole of a problem at once, and has only to realise it in definite values. His way of working, as Spitta says, was consequently quite different from that of Beethoven. The

---

* The judgment of the Necrology upon Bach's themes runs thus: "His melodies were indeed singular, but always diversely rich in invention and like those of no other composer". (p. 170).

latter experimented with his thoughts. In each case the explanation must be sought in the nature of the music itself. With Beethoven the work is developed by means of "episodes" that are independent of the theme. These do not occur in Bach; with him everything that "happens" is simply an emanation from the theme.

It was characteristic of his method of creation that he generally wrote in quick succession a string of works of the same kind, as if he wanted to pursue to its conclusion, in all its possible manifestations, some image that was floating before his eyes, and as if he had to exhaust the taste of this before he could pass on to something else. Those works of his that have an inner relationship to each other almost always originated about the same time.

He seldom took up a work a second time without fundamentally transforming it; to make a copy of anything was to improve upon it. Yet these corrections, however radical they might be, were as a rule only in the details, the plan of the piece being affected by them only in exceptional cases. Among the more thorough-going revisions may be mentioned that of the *St. John Passion*. Towards the end of his life he appears to have intended a revision of all his instrumental works. Death overtook him while he was revising the chorale preludes.

In Bach's documents we see the same mathematical habit of mind that we find in his compositions. Be it a petition to the Electoral Prince, or an estimate for the renovation of an organ, or a memorial to the Council, we are always struck by the same logical clearness and plasticity. Not a word too many, not a word too few. It is an aesthetic pleasure to read them. But wherever he wants to express something emotional, speech fails him completely. The passages in the texts which we are probably justified in attributing to him are so confused and awkward, so nonsensical, in fact, that we ask ourselves how he could pen such things, — to say nothing of the Saxon dialect which he uses in his verses. We must remember, however, that this curious change almost invariably occurs whenever the mathematical mind branches out into the domain of imaginative thought, whether in poetry or philosophical speculation.

Perhaps we can still better characterise Bach's mind as architectonic. The powerful aesthetic impression given by his works comes from the harmony of the whole structure, in which all the copious and animated details fit quite naturally. Bach's music is the perfected Gothic of the art. The further he advances in his fugues, the simpler and grander become the lines. The great organ fugue in G minor is among the most perfect in this respect. It is extremely rich in the most striking and most interesting evolutions of detail; but not one of them diverts the interest to itself; the only purpose of them all seems to be to throw into relief the fundamental simplicity, vitality, and lucidity of the structure.

In Bach's music, much more than in that of any other composer, the plastic outline of the whole is the result of the optical effect of the details; it requires, in order to become visible, a synthetic activity of the hearer's aesthetic imagination. Even to the best musician, at a first hearing, a Bach fugue seems chaos; while even to the ordinary musician this chaos becomes clear after repeated hearings, when the great lucid lines come out.

An anecdote that has survived shows that in practical architecture also Bach was gifted with unusual insight. "When he was in Berlin", says Forkel, "he was shown the new opera house. At the first glance he detected everything that was excellent or faulty in the non-musical portions of the building, which others had discovered only by experience. He was taken into the great dining room; he went into the gallery that runs round it, looked at the ceiling, and said, without more ado, that the architect had here accomplished, perhaps unconsciously, and without any one else being aware of it, a piece of jugglery. That is to say, when some one spoke quite softly against the wall in one corner of the gallery of the oblong room,

anyone who stood above the arch in the other corner, with
his face turned to the wall, could hear the words quite
distinctly, though they were not audible to any one else
in the whole room, either in the middle or at any other
spot. This effect came from the form and position of the
arches fixed to the ceiling, the peculiar quality of which
he detected at the first glance*."

A man with this open and lucid understanding of everything that concerned his art must have been a good teacher.
That he did not achieve anything with the pupils at St.
Thomas's was due to special external circumstances and
difficulties, and to his own inability to preserve discipline.
The member of the Council who declared, at the sitting
after his death, that "Herr Bach was certainly a great
musician, but no schoolmaster", was quite right. Kant,
looking back upon his own years as a private tutor, said of
himself that there had never been a worse teacher with
better intentions. Of Bach it could be said that no one
had ever been a worse schoolmaster with greater talent
for teaching. But to those who were willing to learn from
him he was an excellent guide.

We know the names of some of his pupils. In Weimar
and Cöthen there were Johann Martin Schubart, who succeeded him in the organist's post at Weimar in 1717; Johann Caspar Vogler, who in 1735 won a brilliant victory
over ten other candidates at an examination performance
in the Markt-Kirche at Hanover; Johann Tobias Krebs,
organist at Buttstedt, who left Walther in order to study
with Bach; Johann Caspar Ziegler, later at St. Ulrich's
Church in Halle; Bernhard Bach, his nephew from Ohrdruf, who afterwards succeeded his father, and to whom
we are indebted for many valuable copies of Bach's organ
works. Among those of the Leipzig period may be mentioned: Johann Nicolaus Gerber, afterwards organist and
jurist at Sondershausen; Samuel Anton Bach, the son of

---

* Forkel, pp. 20, 21.

Ludwig Bach of Meiningen, afterwards Court organist there; Johann Ernst Bach, the son of Johann Bernhard of Eisenach; Johann Elias Bach, cantor at Schweinfurt, who, though well on in years, came to study with his relative in 1739; Johann Ludwig Krebs, the son of the former Weimar pupil, who studied with Bach from 1726 to 1737, first as a foundation scholar at St. Thomas's, then as a student, and whom the master thought most highly of after his two sons, — he was afterwards organist at Zwickau, then at Zeitz, and finally at Altenburg, where he died in 1780; Johann Schneider, organist at St. Nicholas's in Leipzig, Bach's faithful assistant; Georg Friedrich Einicke, afterwards cantor at Frankenhausen; Johann Friedrich Agricola, (related on his mother's side to Handel), who in 1741 became organist at Berlin, and Royal Kapellmeister after Graun's death in 1759; Johann Friedrich Doles, Bach's second successor in the cantorate; Gottfried August Homilius, afterwards cantor at the Kreuzschule at Dresden; Johann Philipp Kirnberger, whom Gerber brought to Bach), who became Court musician to the Princess Amalia of Prussia and died in 1783; Rudolph Straube, who afterwards went to England; Christoph Transchel, afterwards an esteemed teacher of the pianoforte in Dresden (died 1800); Johann Theophilus Goldberg, the clavecinist of Count Kayserling, for whom Bach wrote the celebrated Variations; Johann Christoph Altnikol, who in 1749 became Bach's son-in-law; Johann Christian Kittel, who was eighteen years of age at Bach's death, and who, as organist at Erfurt, carried on the Bach tradition into the nineteenth century (he died in 1809); Johann Gottfried Müthel, afterwards organist at Riga, who came to Bach when the latter was already in his last illness*.

---

* For full information upon the labours and the fortunes of Bach's pupils, see Spitta I, 522 ff., II, 47 ff., III, 116 ff., 239 ff., 262. In the above list, those Thomaners are not included who, without having enjoyed Bach's special tuition, afterwards claimed him as their teacher. See Spitta III, 248 ff.

The chapter on Bach's work as a teacher is one of the most interesting in Forkel's book. Emmanuel and Friedemann must have given him copious information on the subject. "The first thing Bach did was to teach his pupils his own special style of touch. To this end, for several months they had to practise nothing but separate exercises for all the fingers of both hands, with constant regard to this clear and neat touch. These exercises were prescribed to everyone for several months; Bach's conviction was that they should be continued for at least six to twelve months. If it happened, however, that any one's patience was becoming exhausted after a few months, he was pleased to write little connected pieces, in which these exercises were embodied."* This was the origin of the *Little Preludes* for beginners, and of the *Inventions*, which Bach, according to Forkel, composed during the hours of instruction.

When the pupils had acquired the sense of touch, he gave them moderately difficult exercises. This is clear from the arrangement of Friedemann's *Klavierbüchlein*, in which, according to our ideas, the difficulties increase rather rapidly. He familiarised them from the beginning with the "manieren", i. e., the embellishments. In Friedemann's *Klavierbüchlein* they are all noted and explained on the first page, so that we would almost believe that the teacher had used them for the first finger exercises. This authentic information as to how Bach himself performed the embellishments is of the utmost practical significance for us.

Preludising on the part of the teacher played a great part in Bach's method of instruction. Gerber, who was his pupil from 1724—1727, had the first part of the *Well-tempered Clavichord* played for him by his master no less than three times, and reckoned those the happiest hours of his life when Bach, under the pretext of being unable to find any pleasure in "informing", sat down at one of his

---

* Forkel, p. 38.

excellent instruments and transformed the hours into minutes*.

After the pupils had made some progress in the technique of the instrument, the lessons in composition began. A musical education devoted merely to the technique of performance, such as is mostly the rule nowadays, unfortunately, was not usual then, and least of all with Bach. The pieces that he made his pupils play served at the same time as examples in composition, as the title-pages of the *Inventions* and of the *Orgelbüchlein* expressly declared**.

"Bach began teaching composition", says Forkel, "not with dry counterpoint that led nowhere, as was the way with other music teachers of his time; still less did he detain his pupils with calculation of the tone-relations, which in his opinion, did not concern composers so much as pure theorists and instrument makers. He went immediately to pure four-part thorough-bass, laying much stress on the setting-out of the voices, since in this way the conception of the pure progression of the harmony was made most

---

    * Gerber's son tells us this in his *Tonkünstlerlexikon* I, col. 490 ff.

    ** The title-page of the *Inventions* is as follows: — "Aufrichtige Anleitung, wormit denen Liebhabern des Claviers, besonders aber denen Lehrbegierigen, eine deutliche Art gezeiget wird nicht alleine mit zwei Stimmen reine spielen zu lernen, sondern auch bei weiteren Progressen mit dreien obligaten Partien richtig und wohl zu verfahren, anbei auch zugleich gute inventiones nicht allein zu bekommen, sondern auch selbige wohl durchzuführen, am allermeisten aber eine cantable Art im Spielen zu erlangen und darneben einen starken Vorschmack von der Composition zu bekommen." 1723. ("An honest guide, by which the lovers of the clavier, and especially those desirous of learning, are shewn a clear way not only to play neatly in two parts, but also, in further progress, to play correctly and well in three obbligato parts; and at the same time not only to acquire good ideas but also to work them out well, and above all to acquire a cantabile style of playing and withal a strong foretaste for composition.")

The twelve small preludes and fugues are for organ instruction what the *Inventions* were for the clavier. Then followed the chorale preludes of the *Orgelbüchlein*. The title-page of this runs as follows:—"Orgelbüchlein worinne einem anfahenden Organisten Anleitung gegeben wird auf allerhand Art einen Choral durchzuführen, anbei auch im Pedalstudio sich zu habilitieren; indem in solchen darinnen

intelligible. From there he went to the chorale. In these
exercises he himself set the original bass, and made his
pupils add only the alto and the tenor. Gradually he let
them make the bass also. Everywhere he insisted not
only on the utmost purity of the harmony in itself, but
also on naturalness of progression and a melodic flow of all
the separate voices."

He thus taught harmony and counterpoint simultaneously, and both practically. The filling-in of the figured
basses was to result in a genuine four-part piece, in which
every voice was to be interesting. We are in a position to
form a clear idea of his manner of teaching. The elements
of general-bass playing are described in his own hand in
the *Klavierbüchlein* of Anna Magdalena Bach (1725);* in
addition there is a manuscript that gives in full detail the
"Rules and principles for the four-part playing of thorough-
bass for his musical scholars"**; thirdly, we possess a
violin sonata by Albinoni, with the bass realised by Gerber,
and revised by Bach***.

---

befindlichen Chorälen das Pedal ganz obligat traktiret wird. Dem
höchsten Gott allein zu Ehren, dem Nächsten draus sich zu belehren."
("A Little Organ Book, wherein a guide is given to the beginning
organist for the working-out of a chorale in every kind of way, also
for perfecting himself in the study of the pedal, inasmuch as in the
chorales to be found in it the pedal is treated as quite obbligato. To
the honour of the Lord Most High, that my neighbour may be
taught thereby.") This work also belongs to the Cöthen period.

* They will be found in Spitta III, 347 ff.

** "Des Königlichen Hofcompositeurs etc. Herrn Johann Sebastian Bach zu Leipzig Vorschriften und Grundsätze zum vier-
stimmigen Spielen des Generalbass oder Accompagnement für seine
Scholaren in der Music. 1738." ("Rules and Principles for playing
thorough-bass or accompaniment in four parts, made for his musical
scholars by Herr Johann Sebastian Bach of Leipzig, Royal Court
Composer etc.") With many musical examples. This treatise was
dictated by Bach. It is given in Spitta III, 315 ff.

*** This sonata will be found in Spitta III, 388 ff. This is a most
valuable document, as it gives us a typical specimen of Bach's way
of realising the figured bass. No one should venture to accompany a cantata of Bach's without first having studied thoroughly
this exercise and his corrections. It cannot be denied that a detail
here and there in the accompaniment is somewhat odd.

One is astounded at the clearness and force of Bach's method of teaching, to judge from these evidences. "To avoid a succession of fifths or octaves", he says in one of the earliest lessons, "it is an old rule that the hands must always go against each other, so that when the left ascends, the right descends." *

His pupils were not allowed to bring him compositions of their own until they had fully mastered four-part writing. Instruction in free composition began with the two-part fugue. Composition at the clavier was strictly forbidden. Bach called this kind of composer a "clavier knight"; those who, when improvising, had to follow their fingers instead of their ideas, he called "clavier hussars"**.

A confused leading of the voices was forbidden; Bach permitted only obbligato, i. e., strictly independent, parts. He disputed the right of existence of harmonic inner parts "fallen from heaven". For a slovenly leading of the voices he had the expression "puddling".

Every piece of music, he told his pupils, is a conversation between the separate voices, that represent the characters. If one of them has nothing pertinent to say, it may keep silence for a while, until it can again enter quite naturally into the conversation. But none must break in with an interjection that is meaningless and has no reason to be there.

So long as they respected in this way the personalities of the voices and made the most of them, his pupils could permit themselves what liberties they liked. As regards intervals and melodic and harmonic sequences he let them do whatever they would or could, so long as it had some meaning and served to express an idea. Every modulation had to grow out of the preceding idea. Sudden audacities that were only meant to surprise the hearer were inadmissible.

---

* *Regula* 2 of the "Vorschriften und Grundsätze".
** Forkel, p. 23.

So long as they were with him his pupils were to learn, in addition to his own compositions, nothing but classical works. Bach knew only one way to get on in music, the way he himself had followed, — to go to school to every true master, and to learn from his works.

In spite of this excellent instruction, not one of his pupils became a great composer, — not even Friedemann or Emmanuel. It is difficult to form a just opinion upon the creative works of Bach's sons; there is a danger, now of underrating, now of overrating them. Emmanuel's great significance in the development of the pianoforte sonata is evident from the fact that Haydn, by his own confession, was impelled along a quite new path by the study of his works; many of Emmanuel's sonatas have even today lost nothing of their moving beauty. But at the same time there is so much in his works that is utterly insignificant that we can finally rank him only among the interesting talents. Friedemann had more genius; many things in his vocal works remind us of his father's style. His creative faculty, however, withered all too soon. His father shewed what he thought of his clever organ concerto in D minor by doing it the honour to copy it with his own hand. This interesting autograph is in the Berlin library. This, however, is practically all that Bach's sons achieved in organ composition. Emmanuel's seven organ sonatas, only one of which has an obbligato pedal part, are really a negation of the organ art of Johann Sebastian*.

---

* Analyses of the compositions of Emmanuel and Friedemann will be found in Bitter's work on Bach's sons (2 vols. 1868). Emmanuel's best-known church oratorio, *Die Israeliten in der Wüste*, dates from the year 1775. He also set to music Klopstock's *Morgengesang am Schöpfungsfeste* (1784) and Ramler's *Auferstehung und Himmelfahrt Jesu* (1787). Towards the end of his life he wrote two Passions, the first according to St. Matthew (1787), the second according to St. Luke (1788). He was most widely known by his melodies to the sacred songs of contemporary poets. He wrote a great many "characteristic pieces" for pianoforte — "La Buchholtz", "La Stahl", "La Complaisante", "Les langueurs tendres", "La Capricieuse", etc. We have nineteen orchestral symphonies

As executive artists they were unique in their epoch. Dr. Burney, who visited Emmanuel during his continental tour of 1772, tells us in his letters that he was greatly impressed by his piano playing. When improvising, he sat before the instrument motionless, as if absent-minded, and with a look of ecstacy on his face*. Friedemann was still able to astonish and transport his hearers when, at the age of sixty-four, and greatly weakened by an unsteady life and by drink, he gave an organ recital in Berlin.

They did not think very highly of each other's creative work. Friedemann used to say of Emmanuel that he "had done some pretty little things"**. Emmanuel did not express a particularly favorable opinion of Haydn.

The most important organ composer from Bach's school was Johann Ludwig Krebs, of whom the facetious dilettanti of the time said that "in a brook (Bach) there was only one crab (Krebs) caught"***. His organ chorales are worthy imitations of those of Bach.

The most important productions that have come down to us from the school of Bach are really two works of instruction, in which we have a reflection of his genius, — Philipp Emmanuel's *Versuch über die wahre Art das*

---

of his, and forty-seven piano concertos with orchestral accompaniment; sonatas he composed by the hundred. He published a great number of these in volumes of six at a time. He had, unlike his father, the satisfaction of seeing most of his works published. Hans von Bülow brought out a new edition of six of his sonatas (Peters); Leuckart issued six volumes. A complete catalogue of his works has been compiled by Alfred Wotquenne, the librarian of the Brussels Conservatoire (Breitkopf and Härtel, 1905). Little of Friedemann's music was printed. His organ concerto (published by Peters) should be known to every organist; suites and piano concertos, edited by Riemann, have been published by Steingräber.

* The same thing is said by J. F. Reichardt, in his *Briefe eines aufmerksamen Reisenden, die Musik treffend,* 1776, Part II, p. 15.

** There is an old anecdote of a meeting of the brothers at which Emmanuel recognised Friedemann by his playing (he was going about with a troupe of travelling musicians). *Leipziger Musikalische Zeitung,* 1799—1800, II. Jahrg. p. 830 ff.

*** Forkel, p. 43.

*Klavier zu spielen**, and Kirnberger's *Die Kunst des reinen Satzes in der Musik***.

But what, in the last resort, does it matter to a genius what his direct pupils do? He really becomes an instructor, in the true sense of the word, when his mouth has long been closed and his works begin to speak. When Bach referred his pupils again and again to the works of the masters, as containing the sole instruction that was of any use, he could not foresee that only to a later epoch would he himself be revealed as one of the true teachers.

It is said that Brahms awaited with impatience each new volume of the Bachgesellschaft. When once he had it in his hand, he put aside everything in order to read through it, "for", he said, "in old Bach there is always something astonishing, and, what is the main thing, there is always something to be learned from him." When a new volume of the Handel edition came, he placed it on the shelf, and said: "It is certainly interesting; as soon as I have time I will look through it."

CHAPTER XII.

DEATH AND RESURRECTION.

Bach enjoyed all his life the best of health. He seems never to have been seriously ill. In the summer of 1729 — we learn this accidentally — he had an indisposition that came at an inconvenient time for him, since it prevented him from visiting Handel, who was at that time in Halle.

Yet the state of his eyes was always rather unsatisfactory. Bach was extremely short-sighted. He never spared his eyes. In his youth he sat up, as we learn from the Necrol-

---

* Vol. I, Berlin, 1759; Vol. II, Berlin, 1762.
** Part I, 1774; Part II, sections 1—3, 1776—1779. The work is not complete; the conclusion of the chapters on fugue in particular is lacking.

ogy and from Forkel, whole nights through, copying music; the demands he made on his visual powers in later times were hardly less. They must thus have steadily deteriorated. This is probably one of the main reasons for the slackening in his productivity from about 1740 onwards.

At the end he was attacked by a painful malady of the eyes. "He was operated upon, partly from the desire to go on serving God and his neighbour with his still active mental and physical powers, partly on the advice of some of his friends, who placed much faith in an oculist lately arrived in Leipzig. Yet this operation, although it had to be repeated, turned out very badly. He not only lost his sight, but his otherwise exceedingly good bodily health was quite undermined by it, and by some mischievous medicines and other treatment, so that for a full half-year afterwards he was almost continually ailing*."

During his illness he went on with the revision of his great chorale fantasias, which had already occupied him for some time. The manuscript — part of the property left by Emmanuel — tells a story of suffering. In the second version of the chorale "Jesus Christus unser Heiland" appears the handwriting of Altnikol, who had become Bach's son-in-law in 1749**. Then we meet again with Bach's clear characters. He even found the strength to make a new and improved fair copy of the canonic variations on "Vom Himmel hoch da komm ich her", which he had had engraved and published in 1747, on joining the Mizler Society.

He appears to have passed his last days wholly in a darkened room. When he felt death drawing nigh, he dictated to Altnikol a chorale fantasia on the melody "Wenn

* Necrology, p. 167. In addition to this we have only Forkel's information as to Bach's illness and death (pp. 10 and 11.) According to this, the physician who performed the operation was an Englishman.
** B. G., XXV. Jahrg., 2. Lieferung, pp. 140 and 142. The collection at which Bach was working in his last days comprises eighteen chorales. See Rust's preface, pp. 20 and 21.

wir in höchsten Nöten sind", but told him to head it with
the beginning of the hymn "Vor deinen Thron tret' ich
allhier", that is sung to the same melody. In the manuscript we can see all the pauses that the sick man had to
permit himself; the drying ink becomes more watery from
day to day; the notes written in the twilight, with the
windows closely curtained, can hardly be deciphered*.

In the dark chamber, with the shades of death already
falling round him, the master made this work, that is
unique even among his creations. The contrapuntal art
that it reveals is so perfect that no description can give
any idea of it. Each segment of the melody is treated in
a fugue, in which the inversion of the subject figures each
time as the counter-subject. Moreover the flow of the
parts is so easy that after the second line we are no longer
conscious of the art, but are wholly enthralled by the spirit
that finds voice in these G major harmonies. The tumult
of the world no longer penetrated through the curtained
windows. The harmonies of the spheres were already
echoing round the dying master. So there is no sorrow
in the music; the tranquil quavers move along on the other
side of all human passion; over the whole thing gleams
the word "Transfiguration".

Bach's eyes all at once seemed to improve. On waking
one morning he could again see quite well, and could endure
the light. A few hours later he had a stroke. "This was
followed," says the Necrology, "by a violent fever, in
which, in spite of all possible care on the part of two of
the ablest physicians in Leipzig, he gently and blissfully
passed away, on the 28th July 1750, at a quarter to nine
in the evening, in the sixty-sixth year of his age."

The burial took place at St. John's cemetery on the
morning of Friday, the 31st, the second day of humiliation
in Saxony.

---

* The end of the manuscript is missing. It comprises in all
twenty-five and a half bars. Fortunately the chorale was included
in the first edition of the *Art of Fugue*, so that we possess it complete.

Bach was universally lamented. Magister Abraham Kriegel, his colleague at St. Thomas's school, eulogised him in an obituary notice*. Telemann, the famous musician, eulogised him in the following sonnet: —

"Lasst Welschland immer viel von Virtuosen sagen,
Die durch die Klingekunst sich dort berühmt gemacht:
Auf deutschem Boden sind sie gleichfalls zu erfragen,
Wo man des Beifalls sie nicht minder fähig acht't.
Erblichner Bach! Dir hat allein dein Orgelschlagen
Das edle Vorzugswort des "Großen" längst gebracht;
Und was für Kunst dein Kiel aufs Notenblatt getragen,
Das ward mit höchster Lust, auch oft mit Neid, betracht't.
So schlaf! Dein Name bleibt vom Untergange frei:
Die Schüler deiner Zucht, und ihrer Schüler Reih',
Bereiten für dein Haupt des Nachruhms Ehrenkrone;
Auch deiner Kinder Hand setzt ihren Schmuck daran;
Doch was insonderheit dich schätzbar machen kann,
Das zeiget uns Berlin in einem würdgen Sohne."**

Emmanuel and Agricola were commissioned to write the Necrology which the Mizler Society wished to devote to its member. It appeared in 1754.*** This Necrology contains the best-known anecdotes, — the fate of the music books in which the boy had copied out music at night, the contest with Marchand, the masterly organ performance before Reinken, the visit to Frederick the Great. It also gives the first list of the printed and unprinted works.

The deceased members of the Musical Society were, in addition, commemorated in a "Singgedicht". The com-

---

* *Nützliche Nachrichten von denen Bemühungen der Gelehrten und andern Begebenheiten in Leipzig*, 1750, p. 680. See Spitta III, 276.
** Quoted in Marpurg's *Historisch-kritische Beiträge zur Aufnahme der Musik*, Vol. I, 1754—1755, p. 561.
*** *Musikalische Bibliothek*, Vol. IV, Part I, p. 129 ff.: Memorial of three deceased members of the Society of Musical Sciences; 1, Georg Heinrich Bümler, Kapellmeister in Brandenburg-Anspach; 2, Gottfried Heinrich Stölzel, Kapellmeister at Saxe-Gotha; p. 158. "The third and last is the right noble Herr Joh. Seb. Bach, the world-famous organist, Court composer to the King of Poland and Elector of Saxony, and musical director in Leipzig."

position of the one for Bach was entrusted to a Dr. Georg Wenzky*. It is not exactly a masterpiece. First of all the Muses were invoked —

Chorus: "Dämpft, Musen, euer Saitenspiel!
           Brecht ab, brecht ab die Freudenlieder!
           Steckt dem Vergnügen itzt ein Ziel:
           Und singt zum Trost betrübter Brüder.
           Hört was für Klagen Leipzig singt.
               Es wird euch stören:
               Doch müßt ihrs hören."

Then "Leipzig" appears and announces in a recitative —

           "Der große Bach, der unsre Stadt,
           Ja der Europens weite Reiche
           Erhob, und wenig seiner Stärke hat,
           Ist ... leider! eine Leiche."

After the "composers" and "friends of music" have given vent to their grief in rhyme, the members of the Musical Society, as the true *initiés*, finally break out into a song of lamentation in the form of a two-part aria. At the end the "glorified one" speaks. He comforts the friends with the reflection that the musical conditions in heaven are better than those in Leipzig, whereupon the chorus brings the "Singgedicht" to an end.

Mattheson, the leading critic of that time, made an end, after Bach's death, of the secret envy he had cherished towards him all his life long, and wrote in warm praise of the *Art of Fugue*, which appeared in 1751. "Joh. Seb. Bach's so-called *Art of Fugue*", he writes in the same year, "a practical and splendid (praktisches und prächtiges) work of seventy folio copperplates, will astonish all the French and Italian fugue-writers, provided they can understand it, — I will not say, be able to play it. How would it be then if every German and every foreigner should venture his louis d'or on this treasure? Germany is and remains, without doubt, the true land of organ music and fugue**."

---

* It comes immediately after the Necrology, p. 173.
** Spitta, III, 204.

The same note had been struck by the celebrated Berlin musical theorist Friedrich Wilhelm Marpurg (1718—1795) in the preface that he wrote to the *Art of Fugue* at Emmanuel's request, although he had been a pupil not of Bach, but of Rameau in Paris*.

It would be a great mistake, however, to imagine that Bach was at that time regarded as one of the leading German composers. It was the organist who was famous; the theoretician of the fugue was admired; but the composer of the Passions and cantatas was only incidentally mentioned. In the same volume of the Mizler *Bibliothek* that contains the Necrology, there is a list of the artists who constituted the glory of German music; they come in the following order — Hasse, Handel, Telemann, the two Grauns, Stölzel, Bach, Pisendel, Quanz and Bümler**.

Bach's fame made hardly any advance during the eighteenth century. Johann Adam Hiller, in his *Lebensbeschreibung berühmter Musikgelehrter* (1784) allotted him only a few superficial pages, which, moreover, dealt only with the "coryphæus of all organists"; and Gerber, in his *Tonkünstlerlexikon*, does not take the slightest trouble to appreciate the composer as well as the virtuoso***.

For all that we must not be unjust to those who did not recognise his greatness at that time. They were not to blame; they could not do otherwise. In the first place we must take into consideration the artistic ideal of the men of that epoch; they were too simple to rank the art of the

---

* This preface is given in the B. G. edition of the *Art of Fugue*, XXV, 1, 1875, p. 15. Kirnberger and Marpurg could not endure each other.

** *Musikalische Bibliothek*, Vol. IV, Part I, 1754, p. 107. In the *Kritischer Musikus* of 5th May 1739 (page 80), Scheibe places Bach in the fifth place, after Fux, Hasse, Handel, and Telemann.

*** J. A. Hiller (1728—1804) was cantor at St. Thomas's from 1789 to 1801. His *Lebensbeschreibungen berühmter Musikgelehrter und Tonkünstler neuerer Zeit* appeared in Leipzig in 1784. Bach is discussed on pp. 9—23.

Ernst Ludwig Gerber's *Neues Tonkünstlerlexikon* appeared in 2 vols., in 1790—1792.

previous generation as highly as that of their own. They were convinced that music was always advancing, and as their own art was later than the old art, it must necessarily come nearer to the ideal. That epoch could not resign itself to regarding mere performers of other men's work as artists; if a man wished to appear before the public, it should be with works of his own. So implicitly was this principle accepted, that many people did not hesitate to perform the works of others under their own name. It was only when musicians began to recognise that other men's living thoughts were better than their own dead ones, and to be content with being purely executive artists, that the past ceased to be regarded as surpassed by the present. This however was not until the end of the eighteenth century and beginning of the nineteenth; but until it happened, Bach's day could not possibly come.

Nor must we forget that even during the master's lifetime art had taken a path that led it far away from cantatas and Passions. People were weary of fugues and of pieces constructed of obbligato parts, and longed for a music that should be spontaneous feeling and nothing else. The concept of Nature which, in the epoch of growing rationalism, transformed philosophy and poetry, asserted itself also in music. Answering as they did to the needs of the epoch, the emotional compositions of the day, with their "tender and pathetic expression", insignificant as they were in themselves, appealed to thoughtful artists as being nearer to truth than the music of the epoch of rigid rule.

That Bach's art in its own way was also true to nature, and that in his strict polyphony a volcanic emotion and thought were embedded, like substances petrified in lava — this the men of the expiring eighteenth century could not see. There has never been a movement so lacking in the historical sense as the rationalism of the eighteenth century. The art of the past, in every department, it regarded as mere affectation. Everything old was necessarily antiquated, at least in its form. If they were to appreciate its utterance, it must be expressed in a simpler and more natural way. In this spirit they restored so much of the ancient buildings as they allowed to remain; in this spirit did the Bach admirers of that epoch, — among them his own sons and Zelter, — undertake revisions of his works that are among the most barbarous things of their kind in the whole world.

Zelter, in particular, discovered French powder in Bach's pigtail. "Old Bach," he writes in one place, "is, with all his originality, a son of his country and of his epoch, and did not escape the influence of the French, especially of Couperin. People try to be agreeable, and so write what cannot last. This alien product, however, we can skim off him like a thin froth, bringing out the real worth of what lies immediately underneath. I have arranged in this way many of his church pieces for myself alone, and my heart tells me that old Bach nods approvingly at me, like the good Haydn: 'Yes, yes, that is just what I wanted'."*

"Bach's sons were the children of their epoch, and never understood their father; it was only from piety that they looked at him with child-like admiration." This remark of Eitner,** severe as it may be, is true. The London Bach was even lacking in piety. He spoke of his father as "the old perruque".

In the eyes of the public and the critics of the end of the eighteenth century the great composer of the Bach family was Emmanuel. No one stood so much in the way of his father's fame as he. Burney (1726—1814), the celebrated

---

* Zelter to Goethe, 5th April 1827. See *Goethes und Zelters Briefwechsel*, Reclam's ed., vol. II, pp. 467 and 468. On the 22nd April Goethe asks his musical friend to tell him more precisely what he means by French froth, and how he would skim it off from the German basic element (II, 472). He received no definite answer from Zelter on the point.

Karl Friedrich Zelter (1758—1832) was the conductor of the Berlin Singakademie.

** *Monatshefte für Musikgeschichte*, 1885: *Über Wilhelm Friedemann Bach*. Nevertheless Zelter tells us that Philipp Emmanuel said with regard to his father, "We are all children beside him". See the *Briefwechsel Goethes und Zelters*, Reclam ed. II, 517.

English critic, who visited him on his second continental tour, in 1772, extols him as one of the greatest composers for keyed instruments that ever lived, and is of opinion that he is not only more learned than his father, but "is far before him in variety of modulation". He makes only casual mention of the fact that Emmanuel had showed him the two volumes of the *Well-tempered Clavichord*; they were compositions that the deceased Herr Kapellmeister had written "on purpose for him when he was a boy". Burney was several days in Hamburg, and spent almost the whole time with Emmanuel; the latter, however, did not play him a single note of his father's music*.

In a conversation with his visitor, Emmanuel made merry over the composers who affected canons, and said "it was ever a certain proof to him of a total want of genius in any one that was fond of such wretched studies and unmeaning productions". On the other hand he praised Hasse, "the greatest cheat in the world", who, in his compositions, without considering the obbligato leading of the parts, made such divine effects "as one could never expect from a crowded score". This points to a quite new conception of orchestral composition, which was afterwards realised in the Beethovenian symphony; but at the same time it shows the son's complete lack of understanding of the character of his father's scores.

For Reichardt, the greatest critical authority of that epoch, old Bach ranks considerably below Handel, though both are reproached with clinging to old forms**. The only man who ventured to place Bach above Handel at that time was an enthusiastic anonymous author of an article

---

* Burney, *The Present State of Music in Germany, etc.*, 1773, II, 124 ff.

** Joh. Friedr. Reichardt (1752—1814), Kapellmeister to the Prussian Court, of which post he was deprived in 1792 on account of his sympathy with the French Revolution, had also a great name as a composer. He discusses Bach in the *Musikalisches Kunstmagazin* (2 vols. 1782—1791), Vol. I, p. 196. See also *Briefe eines aufmerksamen Reisenden*, 2 Parts, 1774—1776.

in the *Allgemeine deutsche Bibliothek* upon Bach's piano and organ works*.

Bach's case was greatly prejudiced by the German Handel-worship that dated from the first Berlin performance of the *Messiah* under Hiller (19th May 1786), especially as Hiller became cantor at St. Thomas's, Leipzig, in 1789, where for ten years he worked for Handel and his own teacher Hasse, as if a Johann Sebastian Bach had never existed. When he had completed his own collection of motets, and was desirous of doing still more to increase the supply of good church music, it did not occur to him to publish the few cantatas of Bach that lay in the musical library of the cantorate, but only to issue the finest pieces from Hasse's Italian operas, with a German church text added to them. The clergy of the town took the greatest interest in this undertaking**.

We learn from Zelter that Hiller tried "to inspire the Thomaners with abhorrence of the crudities" of Bach***.

The only cantor of St. Thomas's of the second half of the eighteenth century who did anything for Bach was Doles, and he only half-heartedly. Although he had actually been Bach's pupil, he made a rule for himself, when writing contrapuntally, "to observe its proper limits, and at the same time not to forget delicate and affecting melody", in which he took Hasse and Graun as his models†. Nevertheless,

----

* *Allgemeine deutsche Bibliothek*, edited by Nicolai, Vol. 81. This article is mentioned in Richard Hohenemser's interesting study, *Welche Einflüsse hatte die Wiederbelebung der älteren Musik im XIX. Jahrhundert auf die deutschen Komponisten?* Leipzig, 1900.

** The plan was not carried out, the hundred subscribers it received being insufficient. See Lampadius, *Die Kantoren der Thomasschule zu Leipzig*, 1902, p. 50.

*** *Briefwechsel zwischen Goethe und Zelter*, Reclam's ed., Vol. II, p. 507 (19th August 1827).

† See Richter's essay on Dole's autobiography, in the *Monatshefte für Musikgeschichte*, 1893. Bach's immediate successors were Gottlob Harrer (1750—1755), who had received his musical education in Italy, Johann Friedrich Doles (1756—1789), and Johann Adam Hiller (1789—1801).

as we know from Rochlitz, who was a Thomaner under him — from time to time he performed works by Bach, among them certain motets and Passions *. It was through Doles that Mozart, who revered and loved him, made the acquaintance of Bach's motet *Singet dem Herrn ein neues Lied*. Rochlitz, who was present at that performance, gives the following account of it: —

"Mozart knew Bach more by hearsay than from his works; at any rate he was quite ignorant of his motets, which had never been printed. Scarcely had the choir sung a few bars when he started up; a few bars more, and he called out: 'What is that?' And now his whole soul seemed to be in his ears. When the performance was over, he called out joyfully, 'That is indeed something from which we can learn!' He was told that this school, at which Sebastian Bach had been cantor, possessed a complete collection of his motets, and treasured them as sacred relics. 'That's right! that's fine!' he said. 'Let me see them.' As there were no scores of these works, he got them to bring him the separate parts; and now it was a joy to the silent observers to see how eagerly Mozart distributed the parts around him, in both hands, on his knees, on the nearest chairs, and, forgetting everything else, did not rise until he had carefully read through everything that was there of Bach's. He begged and obtained a copy for himself, which he valued very highly**."

The one who seemed in the best position to produce Bach's cantatas was Emmanuel, who was church music director at Hamburg. So far as we know, however, he performed only a few cantatas and sections of the B minor Mass. In any case he would not have been able to do much for his father's works, even if he had wished, for his chorus and orchestra were in a sorry state. Burney laments that a piece of church music which he heard in St. Catherine's — it was one of Emmanuel's own — should have been done so very badly, "and that the congregation should have listened to it so inattentively"***. Nothing remained in Hamburg at that time of the old enthusiasm for

---

* Rochlitz, *Für Freunde der Tonkunst*, II, 210 ff., III, 364.

** *Für Freunde der Tonkunst*, II, 212, 213 note. Rochlitz had already published this anecdote previously in the first volume of the Leipzig *Musikalische Zeitung*.

*** Burney, *The Present State of Music in Germany*, etc., II, 249.

church music. "You should have come here fifty years ago," said Emmanuel sadly to his visitor. It is evident, too, from the discussions upon the reform of church music after his death, that people had taken his productions of his father's works in ill part. At any rate the pastors were forced to defend him against the reproach that "many old compositions had been used, and with them also an old and often unedifying text". His apologists excused him on the ground "that it could not be otherwise with the excessive quantity of music"*. How little interest was felt in religious art is shown by the fact that the college of sexagenarians abolished the regular Sunday music from motives of economy, retaining only the music of the six feast days.

Conditions were no better in the other German towns. The regular music was abolished; the cantorate choirs were mostly extinct; voluntary mixed choirs scarcely existed as yet, and were not permitted in the church service**. Bach's cantatas were really impossible in the churches by reason not only of their music but of their old-orthodox texts. We must bear all this in mind before we speak of the lack of understanding of the musicians who let Bach's works fall into oblivion.

Religious music was possible only outside the church service, and even this had to be of the kind in which the effect depended more on the choral masses than on the text. For this reason Handel, the oratorio composer, triumphed over Bach, the master of the cantata. The reaction against rationalistic spiritual poetry had to be far

---

* On this and the following subject see Joseph Sittard's *Geschichte des Musik- und Konzertwesens in Hamburg*, 1890, p. 47 ff.

** The Berlin Singakademie was founded in 1791; the other singing societies did not originate till after 1800. The Frankfort Cäcilienverein, for example, which did so much for Bach, dates from 1818. At first, however, it occupied itself only with Handel, most of whose works it performed — *Alexander's Feast* in 1820, *Judas Maccabæus* in 1821, *Samson* in 1822, the *Hundredth Psalm* in 1823, *The Messiah* in 1824, and *Israel in Egypt* in 1827.

advanced before the public could again tolerate a Bach text*.

Even if anyone, in despite of the epoch, had wished to give Bach's works, he could hardly have done so, for the simple reason that they were nowhere to be had. The possessors of the five yearly series of cantatas were Emmanuel and Friedemann, who had divided the treasure among them. Those in Friedemann's hands were soon dispersed**. Emmanuel took more care of his. To publish them, however, was impossible, on account of the expense; nor would he have found many purchasers. His unfortunate experience with the *Art of Fugue*, — of which, by the autumn of 1756, only thirty copies had been sold — was not encouraging. So he confined himself to lending the scores of the cantatas to the few people who were interested in them, for inspection or for copying, — for which they had to pay him a fee, not even Forkel, his friend, being excepted. After his death his wife continued the business; when she died, in 1795, Anna Carolina, the sole surviving grand-daughter of Johann Sebastian Bach, appended to the obituary notice in the papers an announcement that she would continue with the utmost attentiveness the business hitherto carried on by her late mother with the music of her late father and grandfather***.

In Leipzig there were the parts of the motets — which belonged to the school—three Passions, and some cantatas. These were probably the works that Bach's widow offered to the Council in 1752, when she applied for relief†. The works of Bach in the possession of Amalie, the sister

---

* Even Zelter was repelled by the Bach texts; on the other hand he thought the libretto of *The Messiah* admirable. See the *Briefwechsel mit Goethe*, Reclam's ed. II, 259.

** Fortunately a great part of them came into the possession of Count Voss, of Berlin.

*** *Hamb. Korresp.* 1795, No. 122.

† According to Rochlitz, there were twenty-six chorale cantatas at the St. Thomas school in the time of Doles. *Für Freunde der Tonkunst*, III, 364.

of Frederick the Great and a pupil of Kirnberger, were temporarily withdrawn from publicity, and were known only to a few intimate friends. After her death, in 1787, her collection went to the Library of the Joachimsthal Gymnasium in Berlin *.

The piano and organ works were hardly more widely diffused. Of those that had been engraved, there had always been so few copies that they were scarcely better known than those which, in Bach's lifetime, circulated only in manuscript. It is hardly credible how little was known of Bach by those who spoke admiringly of him. It had always been so. Marpurg's celebrated "Treatise on fugue, according to the principles and examples of the best German and foreign masters" **, gives us the impression that, apart from the *Art of Fugue*, he had not seen many fugues of Bach; yet he refers enthusiastically to him in his preface. The chorale preludes, again, he scarcely knew, judging by the way in which he speaks of them ***. The *Well-tempered Clavichord* was perhaps the most widely known work. But at the end of the eighteenth century it seemed, on the whole, as if Bach were for ever dead.

At the very beginning of the nineteenth century, however, there was felt the breath of the spirit that was to wake him to immortal life in his works. In 1802 Forkel's biography appeared; this marks the turning of the tide.

Johann Nicolaus Forkel (1749—1818) was the University musical director at Göttingen. He was also a musical historian, engaged on a general history of music, that was to extend from the foundation of the world to his own time. As he feared that he might die before he got as far as Bach, and he thought it imperative that he should

---

* Robert Eitner, *Katalog der Musikaliensammlung des Joachimsthalschen Gymnasiums zu Berlin,* 1884.

** 2 vols., Berlin, 1753 and 1754. The first volume is dedicated to Telemann, the second to Friedemann and Emmanuel Bach.

*** Marpurg, *Hist.-krit. Beiträge zur Aufnahme der Musik,* 5 vols., 1754—1772. See the article on chorale accompaniment, Vol. IV, p. 192 ff.

preserve for the world what he had learned of the master from his two sons, he decided to anticipate and publish the chapters on Bach, especially as the "Bureau de Musique" of Hoffmeister and Kühnel in Leipzig was planning an edition of Bach's works*. His biography was to prepare for and justify that undertaking.

The significance of this work of sixty-nine pages does not lie in what it actually says, — although it contains plenty of interesting things, — nor chiefly in the fact that it made the world, for the first time, acquainted with Bach and his art, but in the conquering enthusiasm that animates it. Forkel appealed to the national sentiment. "The works that Johann Sebastian Bach has left us," he says at the beginning of his preface, "are a priceless national heritage, of a kind that no other race possesses." And again, "the preservation of the memory of this great man is not merely a concern of art; it is a concern of the nation". The book closes with the words: "and this man, the greatest musical poet and the greatest musical rhetorician that has ever existed, and probably that ever will exist, was a German. Be proud of him, oh Fatherland, be proud of him, but also be worthy of him!"

Zelter goes astray when he imagines that Forkel had written a life of Bach without knowing more about it than

---

* He did rightly: at his death the *Allgemeine Geschichte der Musik* had only arrived as far as the 16th century (2 vols., 1788 to 1801). Zelter, who could not endure him, writes to Goethe in 1825: "Forkel was both Doctor of Philosophy and Doctor of Music, but all his life came into immediate contact with neither the one nor the other, and made a bad end. He began a history of music, and ended just where a history is possible for us." *Briefwechsel Goethes und Zelters*, Reclam ed. II, 358. This verdict is unjust. The complete title of this first biography runs: *Über Johann Sebastian Bachs Leben, Kunst und Kunstwerke. Für patriotische Verehrer echter musikalischer Kunst.* Leipzig: Hoffmeister und Kühnel, Bureau de Musique 1802. The book is dedicated to Freiherr von Swieten (1734—1803) who, besides being an admirer of Bach, was a friend of Haydn and of Mozart and a patron of Beethoven. He was director of the Royal Library at Berlin, and also chairman of the Court Commission of Education there.

the whole world knew already*. No one before him had understood as he did the greatness of the Leipzig master. It is true that he treats of the creator of the cantatas and the Passions very briefly; but this was for the simple reason that Forkel had seen only a few of these works.

If Forkel was the first Bach biographer, Rochlitz was the first Bach æsthetician**. He tells in really thrilling style the story of how he came to Bach. The fact that as a boy he had sung in Bach's motets and Passions at St. Thomas's had merely made him "scared" of the master and his works. As a young man he feels himself attracted to him by a vague enthusiasm, and he studies the four-part chorale movements in the cantatas that Emmanuel had published. Light does not dawn on him, however, for in the absence of the text in this edition he does not understand what Bach is aiming at. From these he goes, not knowing of the existence of the *Inventions*, to the *Well-tempered Clavichord*. Against the pieces in this collection that please him he makes a mark. At first there are very few of these; with further acquaintance several more are added, then still more, till at last "in the first Part about half, and in the second Part perhaps two-thirds, have their mark in the margin". Then he ventures on the vocal compositions, and now Father Bach appears to him as "the Albrecht Dürer of German music", since he "chiefly

---

* *Briefwechsel Goethes und Zelters*, Reclam's ed. II, 358.

** Johann Friedrich Rochlitz (1769—1842) was editor of the *Allgemeine musikalische Zeitung*, founded by Breitkopf and Härtel in 1798. Everyone knows how he fought with his pen for Beethoven's symphonies in Germany. The various articles that he wrote upon Bach during the second and third decades of the nineteenth century are collected in his chief work *Für Freunde der Tonkunst*, 4 vols., Leipzig; Vols I and II, 1830 (2nd ed.); Vol. III, 1830 (1st ed.); Vol. IV, 1832 (1st ed.). See, in Vol. II, "*Geschmack an Sebastian Bach's Kompositionen, besonders für Klavier; Brief an einen Freund*" (pp. 203—229); in Vol. III, "*Joh. Seb. Kantate, 'Ein' feste Burg ist unser Gott*'" — written in 1822, to make known that work, which had just been published by Breitkopf (pp. 361—381); in Vol. IV, "*Über S. Bachs grosse Passionsmusik nach dem Evangelisten Johannes*" (pp. 397—448).

attains great expression by the profound development and
inexhaustible combination of simple ideas". In this he
contrasts Bach with the "moderns" of his own time, as one
of the old masters whom one discovers when one seeks the
way that leads from the art that "pleases" to that which
"contents". "But", he confesses, "we must, to be sure,
first of all get used to these old masters; it depends on them
as well as on us."

His analysis of the *St. John Passion* and the cantata
Ein' feste Burg are masterpieces of æsthetic criticism. The
finest thing about them is their immediate freshness. He
pronounces judgments towards which he has slowly and
painfully worked his way, and which he is almost afraid
to set forth, for even to himself they seem too astonishing.
He ventures to set Bach above Handel, for his parts always move so independently, and yet work together with
such marvellous unity as is hardly ever attained by other
composers. If Handel is more splendid, Bach is truer. If
the one is a Dürer, the other is a Rubens. It is rarely, he
goes on to say, that Bach pleases immediately, rarely that
he works directly on the emotions; he addresses himself to
the "active, inflammable, and penetrating" representative
reason. This gives the hearer the satisfaction that comes
from a perception of the truth. And the first Bach æsthetician says of the recitatives of the *St. John Passion*,
"This truth, this sincerity, this clear delineation of characters and events merely by tones and rhythms, this art
that is apparently simple and hidden, and yet is so rich,
deep and manifest, — who has ever exhibited this —
precisely this — more perfectly? Who can even imagine
it being exhibited more perfectly?"*

---

* Of the history of Protestant church music Rochlitz and his
contemporaries know nothing. They have no idea of what lies on
the other side of the rationalistic epoch. Rochlitz does not know
that there was a musical Passion in the church before Bach. He
thinks that Bach and his superintendent Deyling were the first to
invent the plan of a Passion of the type realised in the *St. John*. He
is ignorant, too, of the previous history of the cantata, for he re-

Bach's time is therefore bound to come. Rochlitz does not feel that it is now close; he rather believes that it will be delayed. He remarks that the first enthusiasm of 1800, "when the rolling wheel of fate for a brief moment brought the spoke of the revered Father Sebastian Bach to the highest point", is stifled. The projected edition of Bach's works did not come to anything, and many people no longer saw any practical object in publishing his complete works. However he recommended it, apart from any practical object, to the future, "since the revolution of things brings to the top again, after a shorter or longer interval, all the main manifestations of the greater human spirits".

This perception does honour to the artist Rochlitz; equally honorable to Rochlitz the man is his care of Bach's last child. When he learned that Regina Susanna, who had been eight years old at the death of her father, was in want, he published an appeal in the May number of the *Musikalische Zeitung* for 1800, which runs thus: —

"Rarely have I taken up the pen with so much alacrity as now; for scarcely ever could I, in confidence in the goodness of men, be so firmly convinced of doing something useful with it as now. The family of the Bachs has become extinct with the exception of one daughter of the great Sebastian. And this daughter, now very old, — this daughter is starving. Very few people know it; for she cannot, no, she must not, shall not, beg! She shall not do so; for surely people will listen to this appeal for her support; surely there are still good men who will consider, not me — how could I hope for that? — but a fitting occasion to see that the last twig of so fruitful a stem does not perish without care. If everyone who has learned something from the Bachs would give only the smallest trifle, how comfortably and free from care would the good woman be able to spend her last years!"

As one of the first who had learnt from Bach, Beethoven sent his contribution; a year later he gave Breitkopf and Härtel a work to publish for the same good object; there were also other donors, so that enough was got together

gards the chorale cantata as the most original creation of Bach, who based his cantatas upon chorale melodies in order that the congregation, who did not understand his music, might at least have some part in the well-known, all-pervasive tunes.

to set the remainder of the life of Bach's daughter free from galling care.

Beethoven had made the acquaintance of Bach through his Bonn teacher, Christian Gottlob Neefe (1748—1798). When still a boy he studied the *Well-tempered Clavichord*, which in after years he used to call his musical Bible. It was he who said. "Nicht Bach! Meer sollte er heissen"*. At the end of his life he planned an overture on the name of Bach**.

Zelter won two friends for Bach, — Goethe and the youthful Mendelssohn. He himself had had to struggle to understand Bach, and had only gradually comprehended that, as he writes to his friend on the 9th June 1827, Bach was "a poet of the first order". He closes this letter, which branches out into quite a dissertation on Bach, with the remark: "When everything has been weighed that can be said against him, this Leipzig cantor is a sign from God, clear, yet inexplicable"***; to which he does not forget to add proudly that he might say to him:

> "Du hast mir Arbeit gemacht,
> Ich habe dich wieder ans Licht gebracht,"

(Thou hast given me work; I have brought thee to the light)†.

Goethe listens willingly. Zelter sends him the *Well-tempered Clavichord*. Schütz, the organist at Berka, plays to him from it; whereupon something of the greatness of the old master dawns upon him. On 21st June 1827 he writes, "I expressed it to myself as if the eternal harmony were communing with itself, as might have happened in God's bosom shortly before the creation of the world. It was thus that my inner depth were stirred, and I seemed neither to possess nor to need ears, still less eyes, or any

---

* "He should be called Sea (Meer), not Brook (Bach)." [Tr.]
** See Arthur Prüfer, *Sebastian Bach und die Tonkunst des XIX. Jahrhunderts*. Leipzig, 1902, pp. 10 and 11.
*** "Klar, doch unerklärbar." [Tr.]
† *Goethes und Zelters Briefwechsel*, Reclam's ed. II, 481 ff.

other sense*." When the young Mendelssohn was staying
with him in May 1830, he had to play to Goethe a good
deal of Bach. He remarked of the overture to an orchestral
suite in D major, which his guest played on the piano
for him, "the opening is so pompous and important that
one can really see a file of trim people going down a great
staircase **."

Zelter always regretted that his friend could not attend
any of the performances of the motets in the Singakademie. "Could I," he writes on 7th September 1827, "let
you hear, some happy day, one of Sebastian Bach's
motets, you would feel yourself at the centre of the
world, as a man like you ought to be. I hear the works
for the many hundredth time, and am not finished with
them yet, and never will be***."

The best work that Zelter did for Bach was when he
prevailed upon himself to retire in favour of his pupil
Mendelssohn, and allow him to perform the *St. Matthew
Passion* with the chorus of the Singakademie†. This

---

* Ibid. II, 495.

** Mendelssohn quotes this saying in a letter of 22nd June 1830
from Munich to his teacher. He says that he has also played for
Goethe the *Inventions* and several things from the *Well-tempered
Clavichord*. See his *Reisebriefe aus den Jahren 1830—1832*, Leipzig,
1869, p. 17. Goethe, in his Diaries, records that Mendelssohn played
him works by old and new masters. He says nothing of the impression Bach made on him.

*** Ibid. II, 517. See also III, 457 and 458. Zelter seems also to
have performed some of the cantatas privately. He particularly
admired *Brich dem Hungrigen dein Brot, Ihr werdet weinen und
heulen, Jesus nahm zu sich die Zwölfe*, and *Unser Mund sei voll
Lachens*, in which he is astonished at Bach's "saintly simplicity"
and the "apostolical irony" of the musical interpretation of the
text, by reason of which "it often expresses something else than
what the words say." (II, 482). In general, however, Bach's texts
were an abomination to him. For this reason he did not contemplate a public performance of the cantatas and the Passions.

† Zelter had directed the Singakademie since 1800. It had
been founded in 1791 by Karl Friedrich Fasch, who in 1756 had
been appointed second clavicembalist at the court of Frederick the
Great. The father of this Fasch, Johann Friedrich (1688—1758),
Court Kapellmeister at Zerbst, had been Bach's competitor for the

had not been easy for him. He was on the point of dis-
missing with a surly reply the two "young people" —
Eduard Devrient accompanied Mendelssohn on the difficult
errand — who had disturbed him at his work on that January morning in 1829. Mendelssohn already had his hand
on the door to go; the old man growled something about
young cubs who thought themselves capable of everything;
but Devrient, from whom the whole plan had come, did
not lose heart, and at last brought him round.

The success of the work, so far as the singers were concerned, was decided after the first rehearsals. When
the two friends set out to engage the soloists, they remarked, in front of the opera-house, how wonderful it was
that the Passion should again come to light exactly a hundred years after its first performance under Bach, and
that "an actor and a young Jew" should be accountable
for it.

The performance took place on the 11th March. The
chorus numbered about four hundred; the orchestra was
mostly composed of dilettanti of the Philharmonic Society,
with leaders of the strings and the wind drawn from
the Royal band. Stürmer sang the Evangelist's music,
Devrient that of Jesus; Bader was the Peter, Busolt the
High Priest and Pilate, Weppler the Judas; the soprano
and alto soli were taken by ladies named Schätzel,
Milder, and Türrschmiedt. All gave their services free,
and relinquished their right to free tickets. The copying-
out of the parts had been undertaken by Rietz with his
brother and his brother-in-law; they too refused any

---

cantorship. He had previously, when a student, founded a choral
society in Leipzig.

The whole history of the memorable performance is given by
Eduard Devrient in his *Meine Erinnerungen an Felix Mendelssohn-
Bartholdy*, 2nd ed., Leipzig, 1872, pp. 48—68. See also a letter
from Fanny Mendelssohn of 22nd March 1829, given in Hensel's
Die Familie Mendelssohn, Berlin, 1879, I, 205—210.

It should also be mentioned that Thibaud had been performing
Bach with his Heidelberg choral society since 1825. See the preface
to Vol. XLVI of the B. G. edition, p. 301.

honorarium. Fanny Mendelssohn was angry with Spontini
for having accepted two free tickets.

Mendelssohn, who was then just twenty years old, conducted the whole excellently, although it was the first time
he had stood before a large orchestra and chorus*.   In
accordance with the tradition of the Singakademie he conducted from the piano, his face turned sideways to the
audience, so that he had the first choir at his back.   To
humour Devrient he beat time only in the intermezzi and
the difficult passages, for the rest letting his hand hang
quietly by the side.

The audience was transported, not only by the work
but also by the fine dynamics of the choir, which were
something unusual in those days. Not less powerful was
the religious impression made by Bach's music.   "The
crowded hall looked like a church," writes Fanny Mendelssohn. "Every one was filled with the most solemn devotion; one heard only an occasional involuntary ejacula-
tion that sprang from deep emotion."

On the 21st March, Bach's birthday, the work was re-
peated**. Spontini had wanted to prevent a further performance; but Mendelssohn and Devrient had gone direct
to the Crown Prince, whose orders the all-powerful ruler
of the Berlin opera had to obey. The enthusiasm was,

---

* The work had been severely "cut" for this performance. The
majority of the arias were omitted; of others, only the orchestral
introductions were given; in the part of the Evangelist everything
was left out that did not relate to the Passion. The recitative
"And the veil of the temple was rent" had been orchestrated by
Mendelssohn.

* The proceeds of both performances were devoted to the en-
dowment of two sewing-schools for poor children. A third performance was conducted by Zelter himself, Mendelssohn meanwhile
having gone to England. Thenceforth the *St. Matthew Passion*
was given almost every year in the Singakademie in Holy Week. By
its side, however, Graun's *Tod Jesu* maintained itself pertinaciously.
It was performed almost every year at the same time. Not until
about the middle of the century was it ousted by Bach's work.
See *Zur Geschichte der Singakademie in Berlin; am fünfzigsten
Jahrestag ihrer Stiftung,* Berlin, 1843.

if possible, even greater than before. Mendelssohn, however, was not quite satisfied with the performance; the chorus and the orchestra had indeed done excellently, but in the soli there had been errors made that put him out of humour.

On that evening a select company of admirers of Bach was invited to supper at Zelter's, who was now quite reconciled with the undertaking. Frau Eduard Devrient sat next to a man who seemed to her very affected, being continually anxious lest her wide lace-trimmed sleeve should touch the plate. "Do tell me who is the stupid fellow next to me," she said softly to Mendelssohn, who sat close by her. He held his serviette for a moment before his mouth, and whispered: "The stupid fellow next to you is the famous philosopher Hegel*."

Hegel took the warmest interest in Bach, and took the opportunity to refer in his *Aesthetic* to the master "whose grand, truly Protestant, pithy yet learned genius we have only lately learned to value again properly." Hegel saw in Bach's music the genuine Raphael-like beauty, in that it had progressed from the "merely melodic to the characteristic", though "the melodic remains justified as the sustaining and uniting soul**." In March 1829, while he was conducting the rehearsals for the *St. Matthew Passion*, Mendelssohn went to Hegel's lectures on æsthetics, which were then dealing with music***.

For Schopenhauer, who attributed so great a significance to music, Bach did not exist; he did not fit in with the philosopher's definition of the nature of music.

In the early years of the third decade the *St. Matthew Passion* was produced in a great number of German towns, among them Frankfort, Breslau, Königsberg, Dresden, and

---

* Therese Devrient, *Jugenderinnerungen*, Stuttgart, 1905, p. 309.
** Hegel, *Aesthetik*, Part 3; Vol. X of his collected works (1838). For Bach see p. 208.
*** See Zelter's letter of 22nd March 1829 to Goethe, in *Goethes und Zelters Briefwechsel*, III, 124 and 127.

Cassel. Leipzig did not hear it until 1841, when Mendelssohn was working there*.

The *St. John Passion*, which was performed for the first time on the 21st February 1833, in the Berlin Singakademie, had not the same rapid success.

The glory of having revived the B minor Mass belongs to Schelble (1789—1837), the founder of the Frankfort Caecilienverein. He had performed the *Credo* as early as 1828, but nobody had taken any notice of it. In 1831 he followed it up with the *Kyrie* and the *Gloria*. The Berlin Singakademie gave the first part in 1834, and the whole work, — much curtailed, however, — in 1835 **. Schelble did not live to hear the performance of the *Christmas Oratorio* that he had projected; it was not given until 1858.

Considered as a whole, Mendelssohn's victory hardly went further than the *St. Matthew Passion*. The fact that the piano and organ works now interested the public more was the bye-product of this victory; we must remember, in this connection, what Mendelssohn had done for Bach by public performances of these works. The programmes of his organ concerts were devoted almost exclusively to Bach. It was he who initiated Schumann into the beauty of the chorale fantasias.

Of their favorite chorale prelude, "Schmücke dich, o liebe Seele", Schumann writes; "Round the *cantus firmus* hung golden garlands of leaves, and it was full of such beatitude that you yourself" (i. e. Mendelssohn, who had played it to him) "confessed to me that if life were to deprive you of hope and faith, this one chorale would bring it all back again to you***."

---

* See the announcement of this performance in Schumann's *Neue Zeitschrift für Musik*, 1841, No. 25. On 23rd April 1843, on the occasion of the unveiling of the Bach monument at St. Thomas's school, Mendelssohn gave the Rathswahl cantata of 1723, *Preise Jerusalem*.

** *Zur Geschichte der Singakademie*, Berlin, 1843.

*** Schumann, *Musik und Musiker* I, 153. A letter of Mendelssohn of 14th November 1840, in which he describes to his sister

The cantatas still remained forgotten. Until 1843, the Singakademie had produced only one of them   Perhaps it would have been otherwise if Mendelssohn, as he had hoped, had become Zelter's successor. Things were rather better in Leipzig, where, since the cantorate of August Eberhard Müller (1801—1810), and more especially under his successor Johann Gottfried Schicht (1810—1823), Bach began to be honoured again at St. Thomas's. Mendelssohn, when in Leipzig, did a great deal to introduce Bach into the concert room. The real Bach epoch for the St. Thomas choir began during the cantorate of Moritz Hauptmann (1842—1868).

At Frankfort, Schelble produced the *Actus tragicus* (1833) and the cantata *Liebster Gott, wann werd ich sterben* (1843), as if he had a presentiment of the early death that was to call him away from his ideal work*.

In Breslau, Johann Theodor Mosewius (1788—1858) performed the cantatas *Ein' feste Burg* (1835), *Gottes Zeit* (1836), *Sei Lob und Ehr* (1837), *Wer nur den lieben Gott lässt walten* (1839), and the first two parts of the Christmas Oratorio, with the Singakademie founded by him in 1825. He also published at the same time, in order to make these works better known, an essay on *J. S. Bach in seinen Kirchenkantaten und Choralgesängen***. Mosewius is the

Fanny his method of playing the arpeggios in the *Chromatic Fantasia*, throws a characteristic light on his comprehension of Bach. In the upper part he accents and sustains a melodic note (*Briefe aus den Jahren 1833—1847*, 5th ed.   Leipzig, 1865, p. 241).   According to Kretzschmar (B. G. Vol. XLVI, Preface, p. 29) his most noteworthy remarks upon Bach are to be found in the still unpublished letters to Franz Hauser. He particularly liked the cantatas *Liebster Gott, wann werd' ich sterben, Christ unser Herr zum Jordan kam, Also hat Gott die Welt geliebt*, and *Jesu, der du meine Seele*.

* On Friday evenings, among friends, he performed a number of Bach's cantatas.   On his way to Paris, in the autumn of 1831, Mendelssohn heard him give the *Actus tragicus*, the Magnificat, and the B minor Mass; he writes to Zelter about them. See Hensel's *Die Familie Mendelssohn*, I, 333.

** Published in 1845; at the end of it there is a long list of Bach cantatas.   We also owe to Mosewius the first musical-æsthetic

first great Bach æsthetician after Rochlitz, whose ideas he resumes. He always dwells upon Bach's penetrating musical treatment of the text as the characteristic feature of his art. At the same time he recognises the pictorial elements in his style, and shows that Bach almost always gives a figurative turn to the spiritual meaning of the words. He thinks that the key to Bach's development is to be found in his passion for pictorial illustration. As he says — "Bach represents standing and moving, resting and hurrying, elevation and depression, with a naïveté almost characteristic of the first beginning of art. Without abandoning this minute detail-painting in his later works, his method now becomes, as it were, transfigured. His thought, vision, and emotion have remained unchanged, but in the later works the tone-painting is not so isolated; it is part and parcel of the melodic form that constitutes the basis of his movements, and his genius provided him with themes that contain, in their germ, all the possibilities of expression that the movement will afterwards require."*

In spite of its pictorial character, Mosewius regards Bach's music as genuine church music. "Precisely in Sebastian Bach," he says in one place, "we can clearly recognise that not this or that style alone can lay claim to the title of a church style, but that only a soul filled with the holiest and highest can speak the language that can bring the most exalted things home to us, and that discards the mean and the unworthy."** He therefore concludes that the cantatas are well suited for the church service, and would have them performed at the end of the sermon.

Mosewius was the last to criticise Bach impartially; after that the composer is drawn into a conflict of opinions

---

analysis of the *St. Matthew Passion* (Berlin, 1852). He gives an account of his first productions of Bach's works in his *Geschichte der Breslauischen Singakademie* (1850).

* P. 7.
** P. 10.

with which he had no concern, and more than a generation had to elapse before men could again contemplate
and criticise him purely as he was.

The discussion was mainly upon the question of true
and false church music. The reformation in church music,
which, in the middle of the nineteenth century, was everywhere victorious over the inartistic ideal of pietism and
rationalism, was not favorable to Bach. It harked back
to the epoch before him, and condemned his cantatas, in
common with the whole of the church music of the eighteenth century, as theatrical art, not calculated for the edification of the faithful. Carl von Winterfeldt undertook
the execution of the sentence in his work on *Der evangelische
Kirchengesang und sein Verhältnis zur Kunst des Ton-
satzes**. For him the true church style is that of an Eccard,
that aims at the objective, not the subjective, expression
of feeling. Bach, however, in spite of the ample piety
that is evident in his works, is not a church composer,
since his imagination always runs away with him, his art
is incomprehensible by the multitude, and he aims at
being dramatic. "Even the extraordinary impression he
makes on the souls of his hearers, and the means by which
he effects this, exclude the wonderful work of Bach from
the church, which is a place of worship."** Winterfeldt
did not say this without weighing his words, for he revered
Bach. He finally consoles himself with the thought that
he can at any rate exempt the organ works from the

---

* 3 vols, 1843—1847. For Bach, see III, 256—428. Carl von
Winterfeldt (1784—1852) was the pioneer of scientific research
into the history of church music. He has the great merit of having
depicted Bach, — who till then was regarded as an isolated phenomenon, — in his relation to the work and the ideals of his epoch,
and of having thrown some light on the history of the cantatas
and Passions. But it was a fairly long time before musicians got
rid of the old unhistorical ideas upon the church music of Bach's
time, as is abundantly clear from the remarks of Wagner, for example, upon Bach.
** Hegel, in his *Aesthetic*, repeatedly protests against this narrow
conception of church music.

condemnation, not seeing — as indeed Rochlitz and Mosewius before him had failed to see — that the chorale
fantasias are as pictorial in their conception as the cantatas.

Thus the church doors were closed to Bach. The church
choirs refused to do for the cantatas what the oratorio
societies had done in the concert room for the Passions;
while it did not occur to these societies to bring to light
the treasures hidden in the cantatas, these being works
with nothing of the oratorio about them, and not being
long enough to fill a programme.

Even greater obstacles were placed in the way of the
resuscitation of Bach's music by the controversy upon
modern and classical art that sprang up around the work
of Wagner. The consequent neglect of Bach was almost
the least effect of this controversy, and in itself, indeed,
was quite natural, for nowhere has the present such a
right to be its own arbiter as in art. What did him
harm, however, was the narrow definition of the classical
that was put forward in opposition to the Wagnerian style
and to Wagner's manner of interpreting Beethoven. The
conservative party maintained that true classical music
should concern itself only with perfect form and the expression of indefinite feeling, and prove its true greatness
by avoiding drastic tone-painting and far-reaching poetic
pretensions. Bach was an old musician; therefore he was
a classical musician; therefore he could not have thought
otherwise than as one was entitled to assume the classical
masters thought; thus he was a witness against Wagner.
This thoughtless and polemical attitude was accountable
for people not trying to find the real Bach, — and this
just at the time when his works were at last made accessible to the world.

The earlier history of the publication of Bach's works
is an unpleasant story. None of the hopes were fulfilled
that had been built on the scheme for the publication of
the complete works, at the beginning of the nineteenth
century, by Hoffmeister and Kühnel (afterwards Peters).

Two other publishers, Simrock and Nägeli, had had similar
plans, but their promises were unredeemed. They could
only bring out the works for which there was a market,
i. e., pianoforte and instrumental compositions*. The difficulties in the way of issuing the cantatas were realised
by Breitkopf and Härtel when, in 1821, they published
Ein' feste Burg at $1^1/_3$ thalers per copy. In 1829 Zelter
writes to Goethe that they regarded the work as a "drug"**.
Such was the fate of the first cantata of Bach's that was
offered to the German public. More success fell to the lot
of the six motets which the same firm had published in
1803 at the instance of Schicht, who afterwards became
a St. Thomas cantor. The publication of the Magnificat
(Simrock 1811, in E flat major instead of D major) went
almost unnoticed***.

After the Berlin performance of the *St. Matthew Passion*,
circumstances seemed to improve; in 1830 the score of
this work was published by Schlesinger; in the same year
Simrock printed six cantatas — *Nimm von uns Herr; Herr
deine Augen; Ihr werdet weinen und heulen; Du Hirte*

---

* On the whole subject see Hermann Kretzschmar's account
of the Bachgesellschaft, in his preface to vol. XLVI of the great
Bach Edition.

The Well-tempered Clavichord was first issued by Simrock of
Bonn, in 1800; then came editions by Hoffmeister and Kühnel
(Peters) and Nägeli. It was soon pirated in Paris. In England
F. A. Kollmann, an admirer of Bach, had issued an edition of this
work as early as 1799. About the same time appeared also the
Inventions and the suites, pieces for the violin, and separate organ
works. Peters followed most tenaciously the plan of publishing
the "Œuvres complètes", by which, however, was understood
from the beginning only the instrumental works. It was of the greatest significance that this firm brought out, in the middle of the
forties, the complete organ works in a critically correct edition
by Griepenkerl and Roitsch, by means of which Bach became widely
known among organists.

** *Briefwechsel Goethes und Zelters*, III, 99.

*** In 1818 Nägeli invited subscriptions for the B minor Mass,
but without result. The *Kyrie* and the *Gloria* appeared in 1833;
the second part was issued by Simrock in 1845. Simrock had published the small Mass in A major in 1818.

Israels; Herr, gehe nicht ins Gericht; and *Gottes Zeit:* in 1831 Trautwein brought out the *St. John Passion.* Then the movement was once more checked *.

Thenceforward no doubt could exist among musicians that if it were left to the publishers alone the complete Bach would never appear, but that the work would have to be taken in hand by the community of Bach lovers. Schelble wrote to this effect to Mendelssohn's friend, the singer Franz Hauser (1794—1870), who had a large collection of Bach autographs and copies. In 1837 Schumann, who had done so much for Bach with his pen, inquired in the *Neue Zeitschrift für Musik* whether "it would not be an opportune and useful thing if the German nation were to resolve upon the publication of the complete works of Bach"; and he referred to two letters of Beethoven that had just been made public, in which the composer had congratulated the publisher Hoffmeister on his projected edition of Bach **. When, in 1843, the formation of the English Handel Society was announced, Schumann remarked in his journal that the time was no longer distant "when the plan of a complete Bach edition might be laid before the public." *** In July 1850 the Bachgesellschaft came into being. At its head were Moritz Hauptmann, (then cantor at St. Thomas's), Otto Jahn (the biographer of Mozart, and professor of archaeology at Leipzig), Karl Ferdinand Becker (professor of the organ at the Leipzig

---

* The *Peasant Cantata* and the *Coffee Cantata* were published in 1837 at the instance of Dehn. Between 1840 and 1850 appeared seven other cantatas — *Nimm, was dein ist; Himmelskönig, sei willkommen; Barmherziges Herze;* and *Siehe zu, dass deine Gottesfurcht,* published by Trautwein (1843); *Warum betrübst du dich; Wachet auf;* and *Also hat Gott die Welt geliebt,* published by Breitkopf and Härtel (1847), as supplement to the third volume of Winterfeldt's *Evangelischer Kirchengesang.*

** See Schumann's *Schriften über Musik und Musiker,* II, 103, 104. The two letters of Beethoven appeared in the same volume of the *Neue Zeitschrift für Musik* in which Schumann agitated for the Bach edition.

*** *Neue Zeitschrift für Musik,* XIX, 87.

Conservatoire) and Schumann. The printing and the financial arrangements were undertaken by Breitkopf and Härtel.

From the commencement the undertaking had the greatest difficulties to contend against. There really should have been some years of preparatory labour, in order to sift the material and to draw up a clear plan for the edition *. It was feared, however, that public interest might slacken if something were not issued at once; consequently a start was made with what happened to be ready. In this way an element of disorder crept in that was never afterwards mastered. The editors lived from hand to mouth. Thus the B minor Mass and the French

---

* When Rochlitz was writing about Bach, he expressed the fear that most of the cantatas must be regarded as irretrievably lost. He did not know that Berlin, where the influence of Kirnberger and Marpurg had lasted for a long time, had become the rallying point for Bach manuscripts. This fact was of the utmost significance for the publication of Bach's works. The chief private collectors of Bach manuscripts, besides Forkel and Hauser, were Chr. Fr. Schwenke (1767—1822), the successor of Philipp Emmanuel Bach at Hamburg; J. G. Schicht (1753—1823), cantor of St. Thomas's at Leipzig; and Georg Pölchau (1773—1836), who bought Philipp Emmanuel's library. Pölchau was librarian to the Singakademie from 1833—1836. The Royal Library at Berlin purchased his private collection in 1841 for 8000 thalers; it acquired also the library of the Singakademie, with its rich stores of Bach. The largest private collection of Bach manuscripts and copies at present is that of the singer Joseph Hauser, in Karlsruhe. It is not impossible that there are still some hitherto unpublished works of Bach in private hands in England.

The progress of the Bach cult in the forties may be measured by the rise in the value of manuscripts, which formerly had been so low that in 1824, at the sale of Schwenke's effects, the autograph of the Magnificat could be bought for seven Hamburg marks. Valuable preliminary material for an edition of Bach's works existed in the catalogue of Bachiana of the Royal Library in Berlin, published in 1845 by the custodian of the musical department of the library, S. W. Dehn (1799—1858), in his journal *Caecilia*, and the complete list of Bach's works, comprehending 672 numbers, which Hauser began in the thirties. Mendelssohn took the warmest interest in this work of his friend, and helped him by sending him, in February 1834, a list of all the Bach compositions then in Berlin. This catalogue was not printed.

and English Suites were published without any reference to the oldest versions — for the Mass, the autograph formerly in Nägeli's possession, now in the Royal Library in Berlin — which of course necessitated new and corrected editions.

At first the members of the Committee had thought that voluntary labour would be sufficient to see the edition through; but it soon became evident that the task demanded the whole strength and the whole time of some one. From the ninth year onward the work devolved upon Wilhelm Rust (1822—1892), the grandson of the well-known composer Friedrich Wilhelm Rust of Dresden (1739—1796), who, with Emmanuel Bach, plays an important part in the history of the pianoforte sonata. He superintended the issue with ideal devotion from the ninth until the twenty-eighth year. The prefaces which he contributed to the separate volumes are sometimes masterly. They deal not only with critical and historical matters, but with purely practical questions relating to the manner of performing Bach's music. Towards the end he fell off; the task exceeded the powers of one man; the responsibility also was too great for a single person to bear. In 1882 he surrendered the editorship, in order to be more equal to his new duties as cantor at St. Thomas's, to which post he had been appointed in 1880*. In his place came new forces — Dörffel, Count Waldersee, Naumann, Wüllner. These completed the difficult work in accordance with a pre-arranged scheme.

On the 27th January 1900 the completed final volume —year XLVIth — was laid before the Committee, on which not one of the original founders of the Bachgesellschaft was represented.

---

* Between Hauptmann and Rust, the office had been held by Ernst Friedrich Eduard Richter (1868—1879). Rust's retirement was partly due to some criticisms, not wholly unjustified, by Spitta, (who in 1880 had finished his biography of Bach), in a memorial to the Committee of the Bachgesellschaft. In 1888 Rust left the Committee also. The valuable matter of his prefaces sometimes suffers by his rather obscure and incoherent style.

To the very end the work had been carried on in face of an apathetic public. The number of subscribers, of whom there were three hundred and fifty at the end of the first year, did not increase; without the enthusiastic labours of Franz Liszt and Hauser, who exerted themselves to fill up the gaps as they arose, the number would not even have remained at that. The financial situation was always so bad that the question of the continuance of the Society was raised time after time. Only a few artists realised the magnitude of the undertaking of the Bachgesellschaft. Among them was Brahms, who used to say that the two greatest events during his lifetime were the founding of the German Empire and the completion of the Bach edition. The church choirs, whose help had been counted on, did absolutely nothing.

It must, however, be admitted that the method of publication was the most unpractical that could have been devised. People had to subscribe for the whole edition, and pay for each volume in advance. Single volumes could not be bought separately. The Society thus threw away the good business they might have done with separate issues that were in general request — such as the Passions and the piano and organ works; and the general public was not brought into touch with the weighty undertaking. When at last, in 1869, it was resolved to sell the volumes separately, — at thirty marks per volume, i. e. double the subscription price — it was too late. The press practically ignored the work. The history of the publication of Bach's works is thus a repetition of the history of his own life.

The undertaking of the Bachgesellschaft was supplemented by the work of one man, — Spitta's *Life of Bach*, of which the first volume appeared in 1874, the second in 1880*. For the first time the world had a real biography

---

* Philipp Spitta (1841—1894), son of the poet of *Psalter und Harfe*, was originally a philologist. In 1875 he became professor of musical history at the university of Berlin. His book was translated into English in 1899.

of the master. Before Forkel's book, writers on the subject had simply reproduced the Necrology with more or less of their own fantasy; after Forkel, they were content to gather together the existing information. No one had issued a work adequate to the historical questions involved; Bitter (1813—1885), afterwards Prussian minister of finance, had indeed set himself this aim in his book on Bach (1865), without succeeding in getting beyond dilettantism*. Spitta's work is really a unique performance among artistic biographies. It is rarely that the first scientific investigator of an art epoch leaves so little for his successors to do as in this case. He not only awoke Bach to new life but vivified the whole world in which Bach had worked. It was, indeed, not a work for the average reader, nor a book for musicians to refer to casually. For this it was too exclusively scientific and not always simple and clear enough in its plan, the author having worked too closely together the story of Bach's life, an analysis of his works, and an account of contemporary art. Only those who had the time and the enthusiasm to follow him in his tortuous path could really appreciate the depths and the many beauties of the work. It was predestined to serve as a storehouse of material for writers of Bach biographies of the popular kind.

Nor was it wholly satisfactory to musicians on the æsthetic side. It contains, indeed, many admirable analyses, couched in poetic language; there are some which no one who reads them can ever forget. But the æsthetic view-point is too subordinate to the historical, and owing to the plan of the book the essential artistic quality of Bach's art is never presented as a whole. René de Récy has formulated this reproach most clearly in the *Revue*

---

* Spitta discusses his predecessors in the preface to his first volume, pp. VII ff. C. L. Hilgenfeldt's *J. S. Bach* (Leipzig, 1850) also deserves mention. A second edition of Bitter's *Bach*, in two volumes, appeared in 1880. It must be admitted that this book did a great deal to make Bach better known.

des deux Mondes for 1885. Spitta saw that Bach-æsthetic
was no longer so simple as in the time of Mosewius; he is
too obviously bent on holding up the cantor of St. Thomas's,
as representative of pure music, as an exemplar to the
erring artists of his own day. The historical inquiry had
prejudiced the æsthetic. So it was, again, with the subsequent biographies that were based on Spitta. They do
not complete him on the artistic side in the desired way,
and they are too much under his influence in another
respect, — following him in the plan of mixing up the biography with analyses of the works. There is not the slightest reason for this with Bach. In the case of no other artist
has the external course of his life so little to do with the
origin of his works, or is what we know of his life so insignificant, and, as regards his personal experiences, so
uninteresting. Still we are bound to recognise how much
these popular biographies of Bach have done for him*.

Those whom, according to Hauptmann, the promoters
of the collected edition of Bach's works had principally
in view, actually profited by it least. Though correct
scores of the cantatas were, from the very beginning,
issued at the rate of something like ten each year, performances of them were hardly more frequent than before.

---

* A list of them will be found in the index to Bach literature
given by Schneider in the *Bachjahrbuch* for 1905. Among them
may be mentioned Reissmann's (1880), Otto Gumprecht's (1883),
William Cart's (in French, 1885), R. Batka's (Reclam, 1893), and
H. Barth's (1902). Philipp Wolfrum (1906) deals for the most
part only with the instrumental works, and for the cantatas promises
a future volume — a limitation of scope that should have been
indicated in the title of the book. As it is, it resembles an American
high road, that comes to a sudden end in the middle of a field.
The motto of the book runs thus, — "Only so far as history serves
life will we serve it," — which every artist will echo from his heart.

The latest biography of Bach is the French one by Pirro (1906).
The real progress of historical research is less evident in all these
books than in a number of striking essays that have appeared in
various journals, which have been cited in the preceding pages of
the present work. The "Bachjahrbücher" have latterly become the
rallying point for essays of this kind.

Matters did not improve in this respect until the Bach societies sprang up in various towns. In Vienna, whither the *St. Matthew Passion* had penetrated in 1862, Brahms, as conductor of the local Singverein, exerted himself on behalf of the cantatas. In our own time Robert Franz fought for them with his pen.* The Passions, after about 1860, were taken up in most towns.

For the piano compositions Franz Liszt continued the work that Mendelssohn had begun, and, by brilliant transcriptions of the organ compositions, especially of the G minor and A minor fugues, forced Bach as an organ composer on the public attention. The Peters edition carried the preludes, fugues, and chorale preludes into every church about the middle of the forties. A landmark in the victorious course of Bach was afforded by the inauguration of the Eisenach memorial in 1885, where the reverence of the artists who assembled round Liszt found public expression.

It is well known that Wagner was an admirer of Bach. He regarded him as the great teacher of Beethoven, who cut himself loose from Haydn as the youth developed into the man. He has thus expressed, in his essay "What is German?" the significance of Bach for German spiritual life — "If we would comprehend the wonderful originality, strength and significance of the German mind in one incomparably eloquent image, we must look keenly and discerningly at the appearance, otherwise almost inexplicably mysterious, of the musical marvel Sebastian Bach. He is the history of the inner life of the German mind during the awful century when the German people was utterly extinguished. Look at this head, hidden in its absurd French full-bottomed wig, look at this master, a miserable cantor and organist in little Thüringian towns whose names we hardly know now, wearing himself out in poor

---

* See *Neue Zeitschrift für Musik*, vol. 47, pp. 49—52 (1857) — "Remarks upon Bach's cantatas, occasioned by a performance of several of them by the Halle Singakademie."

situations, always so little considered that it needed a
whole century after his death to rescue his works from
oblivion; even in his music taking up with an art-form
which externally was the complete likeness of his epoch,
dry, stiff, pedantic, like perruques and pigtails in notes;
and see now the world the incomprehensibly great Sebastian built up out of these elements! To these creations
I only refer briefly, since it is impossible to characterise
by any comparison whatever their wealth, their grandeur,
and their all-embracing significance." *

Unfortunately Wagner nowhere discusses the nature of
Bach's art more thoroughly, or fixes his æsthetic im-
pressions of it. Nor must it be overlooked that, for Wagner,
Bach's cantatas hardly ranked as true church music, of
which his own ideal was pure choral song with occasional
organ accompaniment. He regards the addition of instruments as the beginning of the decline of this branch of
the art, — which explains why Wagner often speaks of
Bach's motets, but hardly mentions the cantatas **.

But it was in his works, rather than his words, that he
prepared the way for Bach. From them the world learned
again to look for a profound inner relation between word
and tone in the musical setting of poetry. The outcome
of Wagner's art was a revolution of the whole musical consciousness. The hearer became exigent. Henceforth only
the truly characteristic in music could satisfy him, only
the truly dramatic could move him. Thus a whole mass
of music sank slowly into the abyss of oblivion; and by
the side of the music drama of Wagner the dramatic
religious music of Bach came out in a clear light. Warring
as Wagner did against "the beautiful" in music, he was
at the same time, though unconsciously, fighting for Bach,
whose "pithy and often most poetical conception of the
text" in the motets astonished him. It is only now, after

---

* *Gesammelte Werke*, X, 65, 66. The essay was written in 1865.
** He discusses the Passions in vol. I, p. 169 ff. of his *Gesammelte Werke*.

the strife is over, that we can see the importance of the victory. The magnitude of the change of view makes it wholly incomprehensible to us how the post-Beethovenian epoch could remain insensible to the greatness of Bach, and how even those who planned the great Bach edition could make a distinction between the "pleasing" and the "unpleasing" works.

Bach numbered from the beginning many admirers among French musicians, as was shown by their ardent co-operation in the subscription for the collected edition. Among them were Gounod, — whose understanding of Bach must not be estimated merely by his dubious arrangement of the C major prelude, — and the older school of French organists. Saint-Saëns must indubitably be reckoned among the best Bach connoisseurs; and the same may be said of Gabriel Fauré. Guilmant, Widor and Gigout, the creators of modern French organ music, derive directly from Bach. The violinist Charles Bouvet, with his little Bach Society, worked hard for the instrumental works. The Paris performance of the *St. Matthew Passion* by the Concordia Society under Widor, in 1885, was a decisive point in the public recognition of Bach. The Schola Cantorum, under Vincent d'Indy and Bordès, gave excellent performances of some of the cantatas; this, again, was the special object of the Paris Bach Society, begun under the auspices of Fauré and Widor, the conductor of which, Gustave Bret, is chiefly bent on organising a capable choir — perhaps the most difficult of undertakings in Paris. The lack of mixed choirs is, generally speaking, the greatest obstruction to the diffusion of Bach's works in France; many years may still elapse before a change is made in this respect and the Bach of the cantatas becomes more widely known. Excellent Bach translations have been made by, among others, Maurice Bouchor and Madame Henriette Fuchs*. A uniform translation of

---

* See also Gevaert's French edition of the *St. Matthew Passion* (published by Lemoine, Paris and Brussels).

the whole of the cantatas is being prepared by G. Bret, the conductor of the Bach Society.

In France, as a matter of fact, we can best realise how Wagner had prepared the way for Bach. The enthusiasm for Bach sprang up when the Wagner enthusiasm, that had finally become little more than a fashion, had spent itself, and the conviction arose that there was something alien to French artistic feeling in Wagner's union of poetry and music. It was precisely at this stage that Bach came on the scene. Every year it becomes more obvious how largely his system of musical characterisation coincides with French artistic perceptions. His characterisation is wholly plastic; whereas the monumental formlessness of Wagner sets an ever-widening gulf between him and the French genius. Even French military music has come under the influence of Bach. In order to make the chorale preludes accessible to the people, M. Th. Barnier, *chef de musique* of the 57th regiment of infantry in Bordeaux, has arranged them for military band, and plays them at promenade concerts.

England has this advantage over France, that it possesses exceptionally fine choruses. The future will show how the contest there between Bach and Handel will end. That the musical saint of the English is regarded on the continent as decidedly inferior to Bach cannot be denied; and the general experience is that cultivation of the cantatas of the one leads to something like injustice to the oratorios of the other, which, a couple of decades ago, completely dominated the musical world. Mendelssohn in this respect shares the fate of Handel*.

In Belgium the indefatigable Gevaert fought Bach's battle with great success.

---

* For information as to the progress of Bach's music in England see Grove's *Dictionary of Music and Musicians*, arts. "Bach Society", "Bach Choir", and the appendix (in the fifth edition) to the article on Johann Sebastian Bach. See also the *Musical Times*, Sept. to Dec. 1896. [Translator's note.]

Bach triumphed also in Rome. At first many of his works were produced privately by Herr von Keudell, Frau Professor Helbig, and Frau Dr. Mengarini. Alessandro Costa rehearsed the B minor Mass with a small chorus recruited from these circles. In the spring of 1889 the whole of higher Roman society was invited to a performance of the Mass in the oratory in the Via Belsiana. In his *Trionfo della Morte* (1894), Gabriele d'Annunzio gives a picture of the public at this memorable performance and the impression it made. The Roman Bach Society dates from the year 1895*.

All this, however, constitutes only the external history of Bach's victory; to estimate its true magnitude we must look in the scores of the composers of the nineteenth century. Since Mendelssohn, every composer of any significance has been to school to Bach, not as a pedantic teacher, but to one who impels them to strive after the truest and clearest expression, and to achieve impressiveness not by the wealth of the means they employ but by the pregnancy of their themes. In Wagner, the spirit of Bach is most evident in the score of the *Meistersinger*. An interesting Bach-renaissance is visible in the consummate polyphony of Max Reger. How Bach will influence modern orchestral composition cannot yet be seen; only this much is clear, that he will lead us back to a certain simplicity, and will develop in a quite extraordinary way the sense of form of future generations**.

As regards the present-day esteem of Bach, we must beware of taking all verbal enthusiasm for reality. Since it ceased to be a risk, and became a recommendation, to swear by Bach, lip-service has been plentiful. Much of what is said of him represents no personal experience at all, but is a mere echo of the experience of others. How far have we really got?

---

* *Il Trionfo della Morte*, pp. 41 ff.
** Interesting opinions of leading musicians upon Bach may be seen in the replies to queries in *Die Musik*, Year V, Part I, 1905—1906.

He is clearly influencing domestic music. This is beyond
dispute. The Inventions, the Suites and the *Well-tempered
Clavichord* have become the property of the people. What
the average amateur of the present day lacks in theoretical
musical education is supplied for him by these works of
Bach, from which he unconsciously imbibes certain principles of thematic formation, of part writing, of modulation and of construction, and from which he acquires a
certain unconscious critical faculty, that protects him
against inferior art.

As regards our public music the conditions are not so
satisfactory. To expect to hear the complete Bach in our
concert rooms would be to experience many disappoint-
ments. Our pianoforte virtuosi give us transcriptions of
the organ works rather than original piano compositions, —
on what grounds is not apparent. Why must it always be
the A minor prelude and fugue that is given to the public?
Even in Liszt's arrangement they are merely makeshifts
on the piano. Where can we hear, except rarely, performances of the suites, the *Well-tempered Clavichord*, the
Italian Concerto, the Chromatic Fantasia, the piano concerto in A minor, the C major concerto for two pianos?
Where are the Brandenburg orchestral concertos and the
orchestral suites securely fixed in our programmes? Where
are Bach's secular cantatas regularly given? Statistics
of Bach performances in our concert programmes would
bring some curious facts to light, and would show that there
are not too many towns where the auditor can really get
to know Bach.

The church cantatas stand in a category of their own. Even
where the Passions are regularly given, there are certain
difficulties in the way of producing the cantatas. It looks
as if their title were against them. Many conductors who
have vowed themselves to the service of Bach think it in-
judicious to place cantatas on their programmes, with
the exception of the one or two that have become classics.
They do not strike these people as sufficiently decorative.

When, however, one of them takes it into his head to devote a whole evening to the cantatas, he has to invoke all the muses and all the saints against his choral committee, who are afraid that the programme will not draw, or that it offers too little variety. One often believes oneself back in the days — it was in 1858 — when so excellent an institution as the Hamburg Bach Society, terrified lest there might be too much Bach in the programme, arranged it in this way: An eight-part motet by Bach; Chopin's Berceuse; the "Hall of Song" scene from *Tannhäuser*, (in a piano arrangement); Bach's chorale *Jesu meine Freude**.

Latterly the question has been sharply debated whether the cantatas should be given elsewhere than in church. A paper read at the second Bach Festival (1904) took for its motto: "The church works of Bach for the church"**. The demand seems at bottom just, and yet is false. Bach's cantatas today could only in quite exceptional cases be given in the course of the church service, and it is neither to be expected nor to be wished that the service should be so altered as to restore the old Leipzig conditions. The independent position of music in the ritual at that time was, as a matter of fact, something quite unnatural in itself, and only explicable by peculiar historical circumstances. The evolution of things has led to a separation between the church service and art that is good for both of them, — we have the service on one side and on the other the sacred concert, or whatever name people may prefer to call it by. The ideal for the present day is really a sacred concert, composed of three or four Bach cantatas, selected for the appropriateness of their text to the ecclesiastical season. Pure Bach services of this kind should have the preference over the liturgical celebrations that are grouped round a Bach cantata. Yet here again opinions

---

* See Joseph Sittard's *Geschichte des Musik- und Konzertwesens in Hamburg,* Leipzig, 1890.

** *Bachjahrbuch* 1904, p. 25.

differ*. It should be observed, however, that under these circumstances the church must no longer be regarded as a sacred place. If the church, for any reason, is not available, the performances can be transferred to the concert room without their religious character being affected thereby. How can Bach help it if churches are often so built today that no chorus and no orchestra can be placed in them, or only in such a way that the chorus sings into the backs of the audience? The great point is that Bach, like every lofty religious mind, belongs not to the church but to religious humanity, and that any room becomes a church in which his sacred works are performed and listened to with devotion. It follows that everything that might disturb the audience must be avoided, and that a single cantata in a programme of other works is no use. Either a cantata evening or no cantata at all! Wherever such cantata evenings have been ventured upon, their success has shown that all the fears for them, real or imaginary, were groundless.

In comparison with the cantatas, everything else that Bach has done appears as hardly more than a supplement. So long as the public has heard only the Passions, the Mass and the Christmas Oratorio, we cannot say that the whole Bach is ours again. He is not yet known and will not be until then. History and criticism have done almost all for him that can be done. It is time for the æsthetic to take the place of the historical, time to try to comprehend the nature of Bach's art in its whole depth and its rich multifariousness**. The necessity also becomes more and

---

* Waldemar Voigt, of Göttingen, (see the *Bachjahrbuch* for 1904, pp. 41 and 42), was forced by external circumstances to recognise the "ideal" Bach services as the best. At St. Wilhelm's in Strassburg, under the conductorship of Professor Münch, several musical festivals of this kind, consisting only of Bach's cantatas, have been held annually for more than twenty years.

** See Kretzschmar's preface to Vol. XLVI of the Bachgesellschaft edition. In the introduction to the *Bachjahrbuch* for 1905, Arnold Schering speaks earnestly on this subject to all true lovers of Bach.

more urgent for more exact investigation into the musical practice of Bach's time. From this quarter much interesting light is yet to be thrown. We need it. The deeper we go into the question of how Bach should be performed, the more complicated it becomes. It breaks up into a number of questions of detail, which can be solved only by historical gleanings and by ever-repeated practical trials.

For the elucidation of these questions, as well as for the spreading of a wider general knowledge of Bach, much is to be hoped for from the triennial Bach Festivals planned by the Bachgesellschaft. The hope seems justifiable. The four that have already been held have done much to stimulate interest*. It is certain, however, that Bach Festivals, and everything else that we can do *ad gloriam Bachi*, are not what are finally needed most, but the quiet, modest work of thousands of unknown men, who go to Bach for nothing more than their own inner satisfaction, and love to communicate these riches to their neighbours. Only to people like these will he truly reveal himself.

CHAPTER XIII.

THE ORGAN WORKS.

Bachgesellschaft Edition.

Vol. XV. Sonatas. The great Preludes and Fugues. Toccatas. Passacaglia.
- XXXVIII[1]. Preludes, Fugues, and Fantasias. Eight small Preludes and Fugues.
- XXXVIII[2]. Concertos after Vivaldi.
- XXV[2]. The *Orgelbüchlein*. The Schübler Chorales. The Eighteen Chorales.
- III. The Preludes upon the Catechism Hymns.
- XL. Detached Chorale Preludes and the Chorale Variations.

---

* Berlin 1901, Leipzig 1904, Eisenach 1907, Duisburg 1910. The new Bachgesellschaft was founded on the 27th January 1900, on which date the old Society was dissolved, having fulfilled its task, the publication of Bach's works. The Bach Museum at Eisenach is the property of the new Gesellschaft.

Of all his preludes and fugues for the organ, only the prelude and fugue in E flat, in the third part of the *Klavierübung,* was published by Bach. Everything else of this order has come down to us in manuscript, either in autographs, — comprising about a third, — or in copies, or even in copies of copies.   It is really wonderful that under these circumstances more should not have been lost.   We possess the F minor prelude —

and its fugue, for example, only in a copy made by a pupil of Kittel! We owe the preservation of the great C minor fantasia —

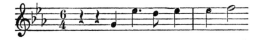

to Krebs, who, as he notes at the end of it, made a copy of it on the 10th January 1751, a few months after the master's death.   This manuscript had almost fallen into the hands of a shopkeeper for use as waste-paper.   Beneficent fate willed that it should be rescued by Reichardt, court organist in Altenburg.   The Russian pianist Palschau, of Petersburg, deserves mention as a kind of unfaithful steward among copyists; he undertook to improve the Dorian toccata, and to this end behaved towards it, as Rust says, like a Russian censor.

The majority of the organ compositions belong to the Weimar and pre-Weimar periods; at Cöthen and in the first Leipzig period Bach appears only occasionally to have written for this instrument. Afterwards, however, about 1735, the first love revives in him, and he writes the gigantic organ works of his latest and maturest period. In the same period he sifted and revised his earlier compositions, during which occupation he was overtaken by death.

It is only in exceptional cases that we can determine precisely the date of composition of the separate preludes and fugues. Spitta thinks that the great G major prelude with its fugue (Peters II, No. 2; B. G. XV, No. 11) belongs to 1724 or 1725, and the C major prelude (Peters II, No. 1; B. G. XV, No. 15) to 1730. He bases this opinion on the fact that the water mark of the paper used for the autograph is the same as that in the scores of the cantatas of those years.

As a rule we have to rely on internal chronological evidences. Fortunately they are fairly clear. For every discriminating player the preludes and fugues, on closer acquaintance, fall into four groups: the works in which Bach is still under the influence of contemporary masters, those in which his independent mastery is evident, the consummate compositions of the Weimar period, and the final works.

There are about a dozen preludes and fugues in which Bach reveals himself as a gifted pupil of Frescobaldi and Buxtehude*. The storm and stress of the whole of the early

---

* Prelude and fugue in G major (Peters IV, No. 2, C minor (Peters IV, No. 5), C major (Peters III, No. 7), G minor (Peters III, No. 5; B. G. XV, No. 5), A minor (Peters III, No. 9), toccata and fugue in E major (B. G. XV, p. 276), fugue in C minor (Peters IV, No. 9), prelude in A minor (Peters IV, No. 13), fugue in C minor on a theme by Legrenzi (Peters IV, No. 6), fugue in B minor on a theme by Corelli (Peters IV, No. 8), fantasia in G major (Peters IV, No. 11), canzona (Peters IV, No. 10), prelude and fugue in D minor (Peters III, No. 4), and pastorale in F major (Peters I, No. 86). The four last-named works rank much above the others, and already have a certain perfection. The theme of the D minor fugue is identical with that on which the fugue in the first sonata for violin solo (G minor) is constructed, the priority belonging to the violin fugue. The charming pastorale was one of Mendelssohn's favorite pieces. In the Peters edition some little piano pieces are appended to it, with which it has no connection.

organ art comes to life again in these works; the preludes
have a kind of dramatic excitement, and are somewhat
spasmodic and lacking in unity; the fugues are often confused; but the proportions on which the works are laid
out give us the feeling that the future promises something
great.

Bach owed his development not only to his perpetually
improving organ technique, but before all to the study of
Legrenzi, Corelli and Vivaldi, whose music was just then
becoming known in Germany. Here he learned what
neither Buxtehude nor Frescobaldi had been able to teach
him — clearness and plasticity of musical structure*. In
the C minor fugue (Peters IV, No. 6; B. G. XXXVIII, No. 14)
upon a theme of Legrenzi —

and in that in B minor (Peters IV, No. 8; B. G. XXXVIII,
No. 19), in which Corelli's fugue on

is expanded from thirty-nine bars to one hundred, we see
his effort to realise a new ideal, and to design in simpler,
broader lines. In the canzona in D minor (Peters IV,
No. 10; B. G. XXXVIII, No. 20), he has entered the
world of beautiful forms, which he never leaves again. In
the G major Fantasia (Peters IV, No. 11; B. G. XXXVIII,
No. 10) there is a lengthy five-part section of tranquil and
finished polyphony, surrounded by quick and brilliant yet
at the same time simplified northern passage-work. Thus
did Bach win his freedom from Buxtehude by means of

---

* On Bach as a pupil of the Italians, and his adaptation of
Vivaldi's violin concertos for organ, see p. 192. These arrangements are in Vol. VIII of the Peters edition, and Vol. XXXVIII[2]
of the B. G. edition.

the Italians, and was enabled to bring to glorious reality the ideals that for two generations had agitated German organ music.

We can only surmise in what order the works came in which he rises to independent mastery*. An important point in Bach's work is no doubt indicated by the small G minor fugue (Peters IV, No. 7; B. G. XXXVIII, No. 18) and the well-known D minor toccata and fugue (Peters IV, No. 4; B. G. XV, p. 267). So vigorously and broadly laid-out a theme as that of the G minor fugue is not to be met with in previous organ music, — to say nothing of the rapid and weighty development of the fugue, in which there is hardly a trace of the ordinary fugal phraseology. Only the second pedal passage, that seems to belong to the older world, is inexpressive.

In the D minor toccata and fugue, the strong and ardent spirit has finally realised the laws of form. A single dramatic ground-thought unites the daring passage work of the toccata, that seems to pile up like wave on wave; and in the fugue the intercalated passages in broken chords only serve to make the climax all the more powerful.

The peculiar charm of these works comes from their spontaneous freshness of invention. They affect the hearer almost more powerfully than any other of Bach's organ works, and to play them is always to experience something of what the master himself must have felt when, for the first time, he exploited the full possibilities of the organ with regard to wealth of tone and variety of combination.

For this reason the wonderful pathos of the prelude and fugue in D major (Peters IV, No. 3; B. G. XV, No. 2) and the toccata and fugue in C major (Peters III, No. 8;

---

* We may cite the fugue in G minor (Peters IV, No. 7), a small fantasia in C minor (Peters IV, No. 12), which Mendelssohn particularly liked to play; the toccatas and fugues in D minor (Peters IV, No. 4; B. G. XV, p. 267) and C major (Peters III, No. 8; B. G. XV, p. 253); the preludes and fugues in D major (Peters IV, No. 3; B. G. XV, No. 2) and C major (Peters IV, No. 1; B. G. XV, No. 1).

B. G. XV, p. 253) is as potent today as it ever was. Perhaps we are able to appreciate these works even more than our ancestors, for the great music of the nineteenth century has certainly had one result — it has given those who have been nourished upon it a clear criterion for distinguishing between true and false pathos, and a doubled sense of enjoyment of the true, which is so rare.

In the brilliant and dashing fugues belonging to these preludes, and again the one belonging to the majestic C major prelude (Peters IV, No. 1; B. G. XV, No. 1) there is an extraordinary display of virtuosity. We must not judge them too strictly by the rule that a fugue should be good in the first part, better in the middle, and excellent in the last, for the two fugues in C major, at any rate, fall off in quality somewhat towards the end.

Between these masterpieces of his youth and his real masterpieces Bach himself has drawn a clearly perceptible line; the former he left as they were; at the others he worked incessantly until he had given them their definite form. Thus it happens that for these works it is not the oldest copies, often not even the autographs, that are the most valuable, but the manuscripts that embody the work in its latest form. The extant autograph of the prelude and fugue in A major (Peters II, No. 3; B. G. XV, No. 6), for example, has no practical value, since it gives us merely an earlier, imperfect form of the work — in $^3/_8$ time instead of $^3/_4$. It should be noted, too, that in the manuscripts the indication of certain preludes as fantasias or toccatas is not uniform. Sometimes they are not even entitled "prelude", but vaguely "pièce d'orgue". There are occasional Italian titles*.

---

* The Weimar (and Cöthen?) masterpieces for organ, some existing in later revisions, are the prelude and fugue in F minor (Peters II, No. 5; B. G. XV, No. 4), D minor (toccata, Peters III, No. 3; B. G. XV, No. 8), F major (toccata, Peters III, No. 2; B. G. XV, No. 10), C major (Peters II, No. 1; B. G. XV, No. 15), G major (Peters II, No. 2) B. G. XV, No. 11), C minor (fantasia, Peters III, No. 6; B. G. XV, No. 7), C minor (Peters II, No. 6;

Bach worked longest at the fugues in A minor (Peters II,
No. 8); B. G. XV, No. 13) and G minor (Peters II, No. 4;
B. G. XV, No. 12).   The original form of the A minor
subject is found in a three-part clavier fugue, in this shape*

The elements of the later theme are already all there, but
the great and simple melodic line that the musician is striving after is as yet hidden by accessories, and is too ab-
breviated to be effective.   Only after long labour did it
attain the calm plasticity of the finished theme, with its
mixture of playfulness and strength in the semiquavers, —

The plan of the fugue and its main incidents are already
prefigured in the first form.

The A minor has also undergone revision.   There is a
copy of it — J. P. Kellner's — in which its essential chromatic line does not come out clearly through the majestic
tread of the opening, —

B. G. XV, No. 16), A major (Peters II, No. 3; B. G. XV, No. 6),
E minor (Peters III, No. 10; B. G. XV, No. 3), G minor (fantasia,
Peters II, No. 4; B. G. XV, No. 12), A minor (Peters II, No. 8;
B. G. XV, No. 13).

* B. G. III, p. 334; Peters ed. of the Clavier Works, Part 4.
See Reinhard Oppel (Bonn) *Die grosse A moll Fuge für Orgel und
ihre Vorlage*, in the *Bachjahrbuch*, 1906, pp. 74—78.

Definite form: —

Original form: —

In the second edition of his great *Generalbassschule*
Mattheson tells us that at an organ examination in 1725
he gave the candidates the following theme to develop
extempore —

He does not mention Bach's name, but says he knows well
to whom the theme belongs and who was the first to work
it out artistically. The most natural assumption is that
he had heard the fugue during Bach's Hamburg journey
of 1720. It would thus be one of the works that the master
played to Reinken at that time, perhaps out of compliment
to him, the theme of the fugue being, in fact, borrowed
from Reinken*.

In Bach's version the theme is much simpler and
more elegant. It runs thus —

* See p. 197.

How is this difference to be explained? Is the form in which Mattheson quotes it the original one, which Bach has altered and improved? Or has Mattheson remembered it wrongly and misquoted it? The probability is that the theme never existed save in its present perfect form. Mattheson knew it, but he could not give it to his candidate in this shape, because according to the rules of fugue it was incorrect. It is laid down in the rules that a fugue theme shall not extend over an octave. The Hamburg examiner therefore thought it necessary to alter Bach's theme in order to bring it into conformity with the eternal laws of the art.*

The fugues in B minor and G minor are virtuoso works, like those in C major and D major, — not, however, like those, merely brilliant streams of notes, but perfect architectonic creations, late-Gothics in music. As in that mediæval form of architecture, the luxuriant detail of the pierced work only serves to unify and vitalise the simple, boldly-flung lines, and to exhibit power in its utmost flexibility. The A minor fugue is the simpler and clearer in construction; that in G minor surpasses it, however, in richness of imagination.

In general, however, in the Weimar fugues virtuosity becomes less and less prominent. The themes become compact, simple, unadorned, almost severe; in the working-out there is no longer any thought of effect. On the border-line stands the G major fugue (Peters II, No. 2; B. G. XV, No. 11), the theme of which, — in a minor form, however, — is used again in the first chorus of the cantata *Ich hatte viel Bekümmernis* (No. 21). The themes of the others no longer proceed by way of rapid passage work, but are built up of massive notes. This similarity groups them into a category of their own. They are the fugues in C major (Peters II, No. 1; B. G. XV, No. 15), C minor (Peters II, No. 6; B. G. XV, No. 16), C minor (Peters III, No. 6;

---

* The author is indebted for this explanation to Herr H. Keller, of Stuttgart.

B. G. XV, No. 7), F minor (Peters II, No. 5; B. G. XV,
No. 4), F major (Peters III, No. 2; B. G. XV, No. 10),
D minor (Peters III, No. 3; B. G. XV, No. 8), and A major
(Peters II, No. 3; B. G. XV, No. 6). Their lack of showy
effects accounts for these works not being so popular with
players and audiences as the A minor and G minor fugues.
But one has only to live with them to prize them more
highly than those, even if at first sight they have not the
same fascination. They represent the pure sublime, not,
as before, the sublime in guise of the pathetic. The C minor
fugue —

and the F minor fugue —

are so tremendously tragic precisely because they have
divested themselves of every shred of passion, and express only great sorrow and deep longing. The theme of
the D minor fugue is indescribably suggestive of tranquil
power; it throws out its limbs like an arch of mighty
stones —

Those who still maintain that Bach's fugues are too
elaborately wrought for church use are apparently ignorant
of this one, or do not feel the Palestrina-like character
of its style, or perceive that all these themes are really
embodiments of religious ideas. An organist who recognised
their true character once declared that he could no longer
hear them without imagining a secret superscription to
each of them. The C minor Fugue —

with its grand victory over its chromatic counter-theme, seemed to him the symbol of confident faith.   Over the sunny and vivacious A major fugue —

he would write "the gladsomeness of faith".   It is worth noting that the same theme, slightly modified, dominates the orchestral introduction to the cantata *Tritt auf die Glaubensbahn* (No. 152).   The curious step-rhythm that runs through it should be noted.

The question of how many of the preludes and fugues originated together is difficult to decide.   The preludes and fugues in A major, D minor (toccata), C major and G major seem to have sprung from the same ideas. This is also the case with the prelude and fugue in E minor (Peters III, No. 10; B. G. XV, No. 3), which are unique in their brevity and concision.   In the A minor fugue the inner kinship of its theme with the motives of the prelude is so obvious that it seems to rise from the foaming prelude like Venus from the waves of the sea.

On the other hand, it looks as if the two C minor preludes and the toccata in F major belonged to a later period than their respective fugues; Bach has apparently substituted these preludes for earlier ones with which he was dissatisfied.   If this be the case, he has nevertheless conceived the substituted preludes in the spirit of the fugues, preserving in each case an inner community between the two pieces. He always conceived preludes and fugues in pairs.   If we find isolated specimens of each, they are works rejected by him at some revision or other.

We may probably assume two dates at which Bach revised his organ works. The first fell in the period when Friedemann and Emmanuel were in a position to play their father's compositions; this would account for the fact that the preludes and fugues in G major and C major, in their definitive form, are written on paper of 1725 and 1730. A later and much more drastic revision probably took place towards the end of his Leipzig period, when Bach, having practically ceased to write cantatas, began to feel a new interest in his organ works. It is possible that he had the idea of making a complete collection of his preludes and fugues, as well as of the larger chorales he had revised. That after his death the basis for such a collection existed is proved by the fact that in a number of manuscript copies the fugues and preludes in A minor and C major and the pair in C minor (Peters II, No. 6; B. G. XV, No. 16), with the three last Leipzig works — the preludes and fugues in C major (Peters II, No. 7; B. G. XV, No. 17), B minor (Peters II, No. 10; B. G. XV, No. 14) and E minor (Peters II, No. 9; B. G. XV, No. 18) — are grouped together as the "six great preludes and fugues".

Besides these three great Leipzig works there is a fourth, — the prelude and triple fugue in E flat major (Peters III, No. 1; B. G. III, pp. 173 and 254) which embody the great chorales that appeared in 1739 as the third part of the *Klavierübung*. The preludes and fugues in C major, B minor and E minor, however, belong to a later date.

The works of this period, apart from the preludes and fugues in C major, show a return to the style of Buxtehude. They are not constructed on a single unified idea, like those of Bach's middle epoch, but are based on the dramatic opposition of different themes. Nevertheless the power and vastness of the design give the works an air of grandeur that is very different from the dramatic restlessness of Buxtehude and Frescobaldi. The old German organ style thus receives its final transfiguration in the symphonic works of Bach's old age, just as his last organ chorale, *"Wenn wir in höchsten Nöten sind"*, brings the Pachelbel style of chorale treatment to perfection.

It is the symphonic character of the latest works that makes it probable that the two preludes in C minor, which are conceived in the same spirit, belong to the same epoch, although they are grouped with fugues of the Weimar period. In the F major toccata and the C major prelude (Peters II, No. 7; B. G. XV, No. 17), there is a return to the virtuoso style, now, however, raised to a higher dignity and simplicity. In each case a single idea is worked out in complete accordance with its own nature. The C major prelude reminds us strongly of the first chorus in the cantata *Sie werden aus Saba alle kommen* (No. 65).

The prelude in E flat major, that introduces the greater chorales, symbolises godlike majesty. The triple fugue at the end of them is a symbol of the Trinity. The same theme recurs in three connected fugues, but each time with another personality. The first fugue is calm and majestic, with an absolutely uniform movement throughout; in the second, the theme seems to be disguised, and is only occasionally recognisable in its true shape, as if to suggest the divine assumption of an earthly form; in the third, it is transformed into rushing semiquavers, as if the Pentecostal wind were coming roaring from heaven.

Perhaps the most striking thing among these Leipzig works is the flowery arabesque of the B minor prelude. The E minor prelude and fugue are so mighty in design, and have so much harshness blended with their power, that the hearer can only grasp them after several hearings. Time is needed, again, before one can feel at home in the quiet world of the B minor and C major fugues. It is not less certain that only by degrees do we find our footing in the majestic monotony of the F major toccata and the C major prelude. This does not imply, however, that these works should not be performed in church and at sacred concerts, but rather that they cannot be played often enough. Nor are they too long for the church service. The few minutes that they take can be found somehow in the liturgy. This is not too much to expect; to play the works with "cuts" is criminal.

The *Eight little preludes and fugues* (Peters VIII, B. G. XXXVIII), and the organ sonata (Peters I, B. G. XV) were written for the instruction of the two eldest sons. Any student with a fairly good piano technique can take up these works at once "in order to perfect [habilitate] himself in pedal-study", as they said in Bach's time. He will reach his goal quicker and better than with modern organ- schools, against which — while fully admitting their merits — the reproach always holds good that they keep the student too long at the elements, and are too pedagogic in plan. Bach, on the other hand, loved to place his pupil at once in the midst of difficulties.

In the strict sense of the term, it is wrong to speak of Bach's "organ sonatas". The two manuscripts in which they have come down to us — one from Friedemann's possession, the other from Emmanuel's — prove that they are really works for the clavicembalo with two manuals and pedal. This instrument was at that time in common use. It was excellently adapted for playing in three real parts, which accounts for the sonatas being in strict trio-form. This does not imply that Bach never played them on the organ also. He intended the last movement of the E minor sonata to come between the prelude and the fugue in G major (Peters II, No. 2; B. G. XV, No. 11) and the largo from the C major sonata to come between the prelude and the fugue in G minor (Peters III, No. 5; B. G. XV, No. 5).

If these sonatas were written for Friedemann, they must have originated towards the end of the second decade of the century. Some sections of them are indeed older, the first movement of the D minor sonata, for example, that occurs among the variants of the first part of the *Well-tempered Clavichord*. This collection was finished in 1722. An older version of the adagio and of the vivace of the sonata in E minor, for oboe d'amore, gamba, and continuo, figures as the introduction to the second part of the cantata *Die Himmel erzählen* (No. 76), which certainly belongs to the year 1723. According to Spitta, the whole of the organ sonatas were in existence as early as 1727; in 1733 Friedemann went to Dresden as organist.

"We cannot say enough of the beauty of these sonatas", writes Forkel. For the connoisseur, indeed, there is hardly a purer æsthetic delight than to pursue these three contra-puntal lines — so free and yet so bound by the laws of beauty — through their delightful intertwinings, to say nothing of the perfection of the themes. The dreamy subject of the *adagio* of the D minor sonata —

made even Bach himself its captive; he took it up again later and made it into a trio, full of longing, for clavier, flute and violin*.

Forkel tells us that Friedemann owed his consummate technique to these sonatas, which is quite credible**. To this very day they are the *Gradus ad Parnassum* for every organist. Whoever has studied them thoroughly will find scarcely a single difficulty in the old or even in modern organ music that he has not met with there and learned how to overcome; and before all he will have attained that absolute precision that is the chief essential for good organ-playing, since in this complicated trio-playing the slightest unevenness in touch is heard with appalling clearness.

It is noteworthy that Friedemann's manuscript of the sonatas, on which the Peters edition is founded, contains many more embellishments than Bach's own autograph copy, which Emmanuel possessed. This belongs to a later

---

* *Adagio* of the concerto in A minor, for flute, violin and clavier, with accompaniment of two violins, viola and continuo. B. G. XVII, No. 8.

** Forkel, p. 60. Forkel speaks of several other separate trios that he knew. Among the pieces of this kind may be mentioned the pastorale in F major (Peters I, p. 86; B. G. XXXVIII, No. 22), and a trio in D minor (Peters IV, No. 14; B. G. XXXVIII, No. 23).

date than Friedemann's copy. We see from this how
Bach became more and more sparing with ornaments; it
is, indeed, one of the reproaches levelled against him by
his critic Scheibe. The edition of the Bachgesellschaft
follows the autograph. Both manuscripts are now in the
Berlin Library.

The passacaglia (Peters I, p. 75; B. G. XV, p. 289) was
also written in the first place for the cembalo with pedal,
and later arranged for the organ. As a matter of fact its
polyphonic structure fits it so thoroughly for the organ
that we can hardly understand nowadays how anyone
could have ventured to play it on a stringed instrument.
On the other hand there is no organ work that makes
such demands as this in the matter of registration. Each
of the twenty sections constructed on the repeated bass
theme must have its characteristic tone-colour, and yet,
if disconnectedness is to be avoided, no colour must be too
sharply differentiated from its predecessor or its successor.

Passacaglia, — in French passecaille — properly denotes
an old Spanish dance. Musicians understood by it a
piece constructed on a recurring bass theme; in the cia-
cona — in French chaconne — which is also developed
like a string of pearls, it was permissible to introduce the
theme in any voice. In Bach's work the theme appears
several times in the upper part, so that it is not a pure
passacaglia, but partakes of the nature of both the passacaglia and the chaconne.

The work was conceived under the influence of Buxtehude, whose organ compositions in this *genre* are of considerable significance. It therefore seems somewhat strange
that there are not a number of youthful works by Bach
in this style. He saw clearly, however, that on the whole
the incoherency of this kind of work was not suitable to
the greatest organ music, and he ventured upon the experiment only with this colossal theme. He follows his
teacher, again, in grouping the passacaglia with a fugue.
Buxtehude, however, placed this at the beginning, while

Bach, with more reason, places it at the end, where it has the effect of rising to a climax. But in the last resort no comparison of Bach's passacaglia with any of Buxtehude's works of the same kind is possible, for the pupil puts into his a dramatic life that was beyond the power of the master.

Both the external and the internal evidence point to the later Weimar period as the date of origin of this work. The autograph was still known to exist about the middle of the nineteenth century. Since then it has disappeared completely, like that of the prelude and fugue in B minor, that must be somewhere in Scotland. Both autographs were used for the Peters edition.

The chorale preludes which he thought worth preserving were grouped by Bach in five collections, containing altogether about ninety of these works. They are, the *Orgelbüchlein*, begun in Weimar and written out in a fair copy at Cöthen; the chorales published in 1739 as the third part of the *Klavierübung*; six chorales published by Schübler, of Zella, about 1747; the canonic variations on the Christmas hymn "Vom Himmel hoch da komm ich her", published about the same time by Balthasar Schmidt of Nuremberg*, which Bach afterwards submitted to the Mizler Society on joining its ranks; and the collection of eighteen great chorales, during the revision of which he was overtaken by death.

Another fifty or so chorale preludes — mostly youthful works — have come down to us** in copies made by pupils and friends. Some of these — e. g. that for double

---

* The approximate date of this edition is determinable by the fact that Emmanuel's clavier concerto in D major, which was issued by the same firm in 1745, bears the publication number 27, while the father's chorale variations are numbered 28. See Spitta, III, 294. Kretzschmar thinks it possible that these variations had already appeared in 1723. (See his preface to Vol. XLVI of the Bach Edition, p. 21). Internal reasons make this date hardly possible.

** B. G. XL, p. 1—102. For chorale works of which Bach's authorship is doubtful, see p. 167 ff.

pedal on "An Wasserflüssen Babylons" (Peters VI, No. 12a) — would certainly have been included by Bach in the collection had he got that far with the revision.

It is not clear what aim he had in view in publishing the six chorales issued by Schübler. They are only arrangements of three-part chorale arias from the cantatas, that have nothing in common with his other chorale preludes, and do not even go particularly well on the organ *. He already had in his portfolio dozens of splendid chorales ready for engraving. Why did he pass these over and issue mere transcriptions?

The chorale partitas upon "Christ, der du bist der helle Tag", "O Gott, du frommer Gott", and "Sei gegrüsset, Jesu gütig" (Peters V, p. 60—91; B. G. XL, p. 107—123)**, in which the number of variations corresponds to that of the verses in the respective hymns, are certainly works of his earliest youth, as is evident from the awkward harmonisation of the chorale melody and the optional use of the pedal. When he wrote these works Bach had not yet found himself; he was still a pupil of Böhm. Where and when he composed them, whether at Lüneburg or at Arnstadt, cannot be determined. In any case they are clever student's exercises, which it is impossible to play without being delighted with the power of original thematic figuration which they exhibit. Bach seems later on to have revised the third partita, as is fairly clear from the improved harmonisation and the obbligato use of the pedal in the last variations. The five-part final variation is a masterpiece. Afterwards Bach no longer writes choralevariations. He was probably led away from the *genre*

---

* For the Schübler chorales see the B. G. XXV, p. 23 ff., and Peters VI, No. 2, VII, Nos. 38, 42, 57, 59, and 63. The chorale prelude on "Wachet auf, ruft uns die Stimme" comes from the cantata of that name (No. 140).

** It may be left undecided whether the partitas upon "Ach, was soll ich Sünder machen" and "Allein Gott in der Höh sei Ehr" (B. G. XL, p. 189—207) are by Bach. It is not impossible. By "partita" here is to be understood a suite of variations.

by purely artistic considerations, though we must not forget that in Weimar and Leipzig he no longer had any practical use for such works, which were only serviceable in places where, according to the old custom, the organ "struck in between the singing" and worked out independently every other verse of the chorale, the singing ceasing*.

When, at the end of his career, Bach once more returned to this form and wrote the variations on "Vom Himmel hoch da komm ich her", his only purpose was to pack into a single chorale the complete art of canon; and in the last variation he could not deny himself the pleasure of introducing all four lines of the melody simultaneously in the last three bars. If this work already shews the tendency to abstract thought that was characteristic of his last years, there is, for all that, a good deal of emotion in these chorale arrangements. They are full of Christmas joyousness and cheeriness. The first variation is of a truly bewitching beauty of tone. It is an interesting fact that besides the engraved copy we possess an original manuscript, that is of later date, and gives the definitive version. It is evident, then, that even in his printed compositions Bach always found something to improve.

In the true chorale prelude, Bach appears to have cultivated chiefly the forms of Pachelbel, Böhm, Buxtehude, and Reinken. Towards the end of the Weimar period, however, he becomes independent of his masters and produces a type of his own — the chorale prelude of the *Orgelbüchlein*. In this the melody is used as a *cantus firmus*, unaltered and uninterrupted, usually in the uppermost voice; round it plays an independently conceived motive, not derived from any of the lines of the melody, but prompted by the text of the chorale, and embodying the poetic idea that Bach regarded as characteristic for music and expressible in musical terms. Thus in the chorale preludes of

---

* See p. 27.

the *Orgelbüchlein* the melody and the text are both represented at the same time, the *cantus firmus* being poetically illustrated by means of the characteristic motive*.

Here Bach has realised the ideal of the chorale prelude. The method is the most simple imaginable and at the same time the most perfect. Nowhere is the Dürer-like character of his musical style so evident as in these small chorale preludes. Simply by the precision and characteristic quality of the line of the contrapuntal motive he expresses all that has to be said, and so makes clear the relation of the music to the text whose title it bears.

The *Orgelbüchlein* is thus not only of significance in the history of the development of the chorale prelude, but is one of the greatest achievements in music. Never before had any one expressed the texts in pure tone in this way; no one afterwards undertook to do so with such simple means. At the same time the essence of Bach's art comes clearly into view for the first time in this work. He is not satisfied with formal perfection and fulness of sound, — otherwise he would have continued to work with the forms and formulæ of his teachers in the chorale prelude. He aims at more than this; he aspires after the plastic expression of ideas, and so creates a tone-speech of his own. The elements of such a speech already exist in the *Orgelbüchlein*: the characteristic motives of the various chorales correspond to many of Bach's later emotional and pictorial tone-symbols. The *Orgelbüchlein* is thus the lexicon of Bach's musical speech. This must be our starting-point if we would understand what he is striving to express in the themes of the cantatas and the Passions. Until the significance of the *Orgelbüchlein* was perceived, the fundamental character of Bach's art remained, almost down to the present day, obscure and disputable.

---

* The form of the chorale prelude in the *Orgelbüchlein* is new only in so far as the independent motive illustrates the text. Regarded from the purely formal standpoint, it is a variety of the Buxtehude *genre* of small chorale fantasia.

The title, indeed, does not indicate the universal significance of this collection. It runs thus: "The Little Organ Book, wherein instruction is given to a beginning organist to work out a chorale in every style, also to perfect himself in the study of the pedal, the pedal being treated quite obbligato throughout in the chorales herein contained. To the honour of the Lord Most High, and that my neighbour may be taught thereby. Autore Joanne Sebast. Bach. p. t. Capellae Magistro S. P. R. Anhaltini-Cothinensis."

The autograph is now in the Royal Library at Berlin. It contains ninety-two leaves, and is bound in paste-board with leather back and corners. At the head of each page Bach wrote the title of the chorale that was to appear thereon, so that if the composition extended beyond the page he had to paste an extra strip of paper below, or make use of the tablature. All these chorales were written in Weimar. Afterwards, in Cöthen, he made a careful fair copy of them. There still exists a Weimar autograph of the *Orgelbüchlein*, that once belonged to Mendelssohn. It lacks the pages containing the first twelve chorales. On the cover is a note to the effect that the owner had cut out three more leaves — two for his bride's album, and one for Clara Schumann*.

The order of the chorales is that of their succession in the church year. This is easily understood when we remember that at that time each Sunday had its own special hymns, allotted to it once for all, and that other organists of the epoch — e. g. B. Walther of Weimar — also wrote similar yearly cycles of chorale preludes. In the details of their grouping, however, especially with regard to the chorales appropriated to feast days, each individual was naturally allowed a certain amount of liberty. Bach made

---

* For further details of this autograph of the *Orgelbüchlein* see Spitta II, 986 (German ed.). It originally contained eight chorales fewer than the Cöthen one. It is not cited in the B. G. edition.

the most ingenious use of this freedom. He disposed of
the chorales in such a way that the Christmas ones formed
a miniature Christmas oratorio, those of the Passion time
a Passion, and those of Easter an Easter oratorio *. He
aimed also at other effects of contrast. The chorale "Das

---

* The following is the original disposition of the chorales for
the various feasts: —

CHRISTMAS ORATORIO

Introduction: Gottes Sohn ist kommen. V, No. 19.
    Herr Christ der einzig Gottessohn. V, No. 22.
    Lob sei dem allmächtigen Gott. V, No. 38.
The Manger: Puer natus in Bethlehem. V, No. 46.
    Gelobet seist du, Jesus Christ. V, No. 11.
    Der Tag, der ist so freudenreich. V, No. 11.
The Appearance of the Angel: Vom Himmel hoch da komm ich
    her. V, No. 49.
    Vom Himmel kam der Engel Schar. V, No. 50.
The Adoration before the Manger: In dulci jubilo (mediæval sacred
    cradle song). V, No. 35.
    Lobt Gott ihr Christen allzugleich. V, No. 40.
The Mystical Adoration: Jesu meine Freude. V, No. 31.
    Christum wir sollen loben schon *(canto fermo in alto)*. V, No. 6.
Final hymns: Wir Christenleut han jetzund Freud. V, No. 55.
    Helft mir Gottes Güte preisen. V, No. 21.

THE PASSION

Introduction: O Lamm Gottes. V, No. 44.
    Christe du Lamm Gottes. V, No. 3.
The Seven Last Words: Da Jesus an dem Kreuze stund. V, No. 9.
Jesus' death: O Mensch bewein dein' Sünde gross. V, No. 45.
Song of Thanksgiving: Wir danken dir, Herr Jesu Christ. V, No. 56.
Meditation: Hilf Gott, dass mirs gelinge. V, No. 29.
    (The chorales on the descent from the cross, the laying in the
tomb, and the departure from the tomb, are not worked out.)

EASTER ORATORIO

Easter Morning: Christ lag in Todesbanden. V, No. 5.
    Jesus Christus unser Heiland, der den Tod überwand. V, No. 32.
    Christ ist erstanden. V, No. 4.
The Announecment of the Resurrection: Erstanden ist der heilge
    Christ. (The text of this chorale represents a dialogue
    between the woman and the angel at the grave.) V,
    No. 14.
    Erschienen ist der herrlich Tag. V, No. 15.
    Heut triumphieret Gottes Sohn. V, No. 28.
    (In the B. G. edition the *Orgelbüchlein* will be found in Vol.
XXV².

alte Jahr vergangen ist" (V, No. 20) is a sorrowful meditation in the twilight as the last evening draws to its close;
it is followed by the jubilant song "In dir ist Freude"
(V, No. 34) that is filled with the light of the new day.
Of the two chorales relating to the presentation in the
temple and Simeon's hymn of praise, the first, "Mit Fried'
und Freud' ich fahr dahin" (V, No. 41), depicts a joyous
longing for death, and the other, "Herr Gott, nun schleuss
den Himmel auf" (V, No. 24), a sorrowful longing. The
sombre hymn on original sin, "Durch Adams Fall" (V,
No. 13), is followed at once by the hymn of salvation in
Christ, "Es ist das Heil uns kommen her" (V, No. 16).

The *Orgelbüchlein* is barely one-third finished. The
Cöthen autograph is planned out for a hundred and sixty-
nine chorales; forty-five of these are complete; for the others
we have only the white pages. What is the explanation
of this? Did the Leipzig appointment come just at this
time and prevent the continuation of the work? In this
case, why did not Bach resume it when later on he turned
his attention again to the chorale prelude? The aban-
donment of the collection in its incomplete state must
have been due to some inward reason. Speaking generally,
it is the grouped chorales relating to the various feast-
times that are finished, and, of the others, those of which
the strong pictorial or characteristic quality seemed to
make them specially suitable for music. The texts of
the numbers not completed lack these musical qualities.
No characteristic theme could be evolved from them; they
could only be developed as pure music, not in their poetic
or pictorial aspects. All the chorales of this collection,
however, were to be little tone-pictures; and as circumstances made this plan impossible, Bach preferred to leave
the collection unfinished. How strictly he adhered to the
characteristic type he had in his mind for the *Orgelbüchlein*
can be seen from the fact that he did not include beautiful
chorales like "Herzlich tut mich verlangen" (V, No. 27)
and "Liebster Jesu wir sind hier" (V, No. 36), which were

quite suitable as regards their size and were certainly in existence at that time, — simply because they were not constructed on a characteristic motive.

When Griepenkerl edited the *Orgelbüchlein* for Peters, about the middle of the forties, he unfortunately altered the original order, in which each chorale is in a position that explains it, and adopted instead a merely alphabetical arrangement, besides inserting "smaller" chorale preludes and chorale fughettas that did not form part of the collection. We get the correct *Orgelbüchlein* by eliminating from the fifth volume of Peters' edition of the organ works Nos. 7, 18, 20, 23, 26, 27, 36, 39, 43, 47, 52, and 53, and arranging the remainder in this order — Nos. 42, 19, 22, 38, 46, 17, 11, 49, 50, 35, 40, 31, 6, 55, 21, 10, 34, 41, 24, 44, 3, 8, 9, 45, 56, 29, 5, 32, 4, 14, 15, 28, 25, 37, 12, 48, 13, 16, 30, 33, 51, 54, 2, 1* . Between Nos. 28 and 25, again, must be inserted the first part of the chorale "Komm Gott Schöpfer, heiliger Geist" (VII, No. 35), which, although Spitta (I, 611) does not think so, was originally part of the *Orgelbüchlein*. The second verse was not added until later. Spitta is of opinion that the treatment of the pedal in the first part is not sufficiently obbligato to authorise our regarding the work as composed for the *Orgelbüchlein*; but every organist will testify that the obbligato character of the pedal part is shown by the fact that it is much more difficult to play than it looks; it is by no means easy always to strike these simple notes on the weakest part of the bar.

The plan of the second collection of chorale preludes is explicable, like the first, from the order of the old hymn books. The *Orgelbüchlein* deals with the *cantica de tempore*, i. e., the hymns grouped according to their order in the church year; the other collection, that appeared in 1739 as the third part of the *Klavierübung*, deals with the

---

* Organists who possess only the Peters edition can reconstruct the original in this way.

catechism hymns*. By these was understood, at that time, a small collection of classical hymns on the main points of the Christian doctrine, that were included in every hymn-book. The arrangement was the same as in the Lutheran catechism. The core of them was formed by Luther's hymns: "Dies sind die heiligen zehn Gebot", "Wir glauben all an einen Gott", "Vater unser im Himmelreich", "Christ, unser Herr, zum Jordan kam", "Jesus Christus unser Heiland" (the communion hymn), and "Aus tiefer Not schrei ich zu dir" (the confessional hymn). Bach chose this catechism in the form of Lutheran hymns for musical treatment. In order to have the dogma complete, he prefaced these five chief hymns with the *Kyrie* and *Gloria* to the Holy Trinity from the Leipzig service, i. e., the three hymns "Kyrie Gott Vater", "Kyrie Gott Sohn", "Kyrie Gott heiliger Geist", and the hymn to the Trinity, "Allein Gott in der Höh sei Ehr", — this last of course, in three versions.

Luther, however, had written a greater and a smaller catechism. In the former he demonstrates the essence of the faith; in the latter he addresses himself to the children. Bach, the musical father of the Lutheran church, feels it incumbent on him to do likewise; he gives us a larger and a smaller arrangement of each chorale, with the exception of "Allein Gott in der Höh sei Ehr". The larger chorales are dominated by a sublime musical symbolism, aiming simply at illustrating the central idea of the dogma contained in the words; the smaller ones are of bewitching simplicity. The whole collection is introduced by the majestic E flat major prelude, and ended by the triple fugue in the same key.

One would have thought this conception at any rate interesting enough to be respected in the various editions. This, however, has never been done except in the original

---

* B. G. III, p. 170—260. The duets on pp. 242—253, however, have nothing to do with the third part of the *Klavierübung*. They were accidentally included during the engraving.

edition of the Bachgesellschaft. Even Naumann, in the practical edition he brought out for Breitkopf and Härtel, mixes these works up with the others without any regard to their special quality and their inner connection. The Peters edition of these catechism chorales can be reconstructed thus —

>   *Introduction:* Prelude in E flat major, III, No. 1.
> *Trinity:* "*Kyrie*". (Large version, VII, Nos. 39a, b, c.; small version, VII, Nos. 40a, b, c.)
>   "Allein Gott in der Höh sei Ehr". (Large version VI, Nos. 5, 6, and 10.)
> *The Ten Commandments.* "Dies sind die heilgen zehn Gebot". (Large version, VI, No. 19; small version, No. 20).
> *Faith:* "Wir glauben all' an einen Gott". (Large version, VII, No. 60; small version, VII, No. 61.)
> *The Lord's Prayer:* "Vater unser im Himmelreich". (Large version, VII, No. 52; small version, V, No. 47.)
> *Baptism:* "Christ unser Herr zum Jordan kam". (Large version, VI, No. 17; small version, VI, No. 18.)
> *Penitence:* "Aus tiefer Not schrei ich zu dir". (Large version, VI, No. 13; small version, VI, No. 14.)
> *The Lord's Supper:* "Jesus Christus unser Heiland, der von uns". (Large version, VI, No. 30; small version, VI, No. 33.)
> *Conclusion:* Triple fugue in E flat major, III, No. 1.

Bach was not correct in placing the penitence between the baptism and the communion, and it is impossible to say why he did so. It should really come last among these doctrinal pieces.

These chorales were probably all composed at the same time, expressly for this collection, towards the end of the thirties. This was certainly the case with the larger versions; in the case of the smaller ones we cannot be sure whether they formed an earlier collection.

It is otherwise with the last collection, the "Eighteen Chorales"*. It contains, for the most part, compositions of the Weimar period, which Bach at the end of his life revised and partly rewrote. Rust, indeed, in the preface to volume XXV of the B. G. edition, maintains against

---

* B. G. XXV, p. 79 ff.

Spitta that they belong to the Leipzig period; but this is hardly probable. They are plainly masterpieces that Bach wrote while still more or less dependent on the forms laid down by Buxtehude, Böhm and Pachelbel. It contains no chorales of the type of those in the *Orgelbüchlein*.

How Bach has polished these works is evident from fifteen older versions that have come down to us *. The autograph of the "Eighteen Chorales" is in the Berlin library; it belonged at one time to Philipp Emmanuel. The last chorale, "Wenn wir in höchsten Nöten sind", is incomplete in the autograph, and must have been completed from the *Art of Fugue*, in which it appeared as Bach's last work **. Here again it is unfortunate that, regardless of Bach's last wishes, these revised chorales are always mixed up in order to get a purely alphabetical arrangement, — although, it is true, this collection is not like the two others, governed by a definite sequence of ideas. The authentic order can be restored in the Peters edition thus: —

(1) Komm, heilger Geist. VII, No. 36.
(2) „ Alio modo. VII, No. 37.
(3) An Wasserflüssen Babylon. VI, No. 12b.
(4) Schmücke dich, o liebe Seele. VII, No. 49.
(5) Herr Jesu Christ, dich zu uns wend'. VI, No. 27.
(6) O Lamm Gottes unschuldig. VII, No. 48.
(7) Nun danket alle Gott. VII, No. 43.
(8) Von Gott will ich nicht lassen. VII, No. 56.
(9) Nun komm der Heiden Heiland. VII, No. 45.
(10) „ Alio modo (Trio). VII, No. 46.
(11) „ Alio modo. VII, No. 47.
(12) Allein Gott in der Höh sei Ehr. VI, No. 9.
(13) „ Alio modo. VI, No. 8.
(14) „ Alio modo (Trio). VI, No. 7.
(15) Jesus Christus unser Heiland. VI, No. 31.
(16) „ Alio modo. VI, No. 32.
(17) Komm, Gott Schöpfer, heiliger Geist. VII, No. 35.
(18) Wenn wir in höchsten Nöten sind (Vor deinen Thron tret' ich allhier). VII, No. 58.

---

* See B. G. XXV², pp. 151—189.
** With regard to Bach's last chorale prelude see pp. 223, 224.

The trio upon "Nun komm' der Heiden Heiland" (VII, No. 46) makes so strange an impression on us that it seems like a transcription of a movement from a cantata. Strictly in the old Pachelbel style is the angular arrangement of "Nun danket alle Gott" (VII, No. 43), that charms both player and hearer more and more as their familiarity with it increases. The chorale "Allein Gott in der Höh sei Ehr" (VI, No. 9), is purely in the style of Böhm; to many people it seems rather youthful. In the prelude on "Nun komm der Heiden Heiland" (VII, No. 45), that is laid out on the same plan, the arabesque-like contour of the melody seems much more mature and perfect. It is full of a dreamy expectancy.

We see the style of Böhm perfected and idealised again in the chorale "An Wasserflüssen Babylon" (VI, No. 12b), in which the melody is given to the tenor. We are reminded of Buxtehude by the arrangement of "Jesus Christus unser Heiland" (VI, No. 32), the brilliant and animated "Komm, heilger Geist, Herre Gott" (VII, No. 36), the "Gott Schöpfer, heiliger Geist" (VII, No. 35), and the "Von Gott will ich nicht lassen" (VII, No. 56).

The most important works in this collection, however, do not conform to any strict type. They are fantasias planned on broad lines, with free thematic use of one or more of the lines of the melody of the chorale. Bach has welded the forms into a new unity, through which the older outlines are only visible as through a fine blue mist. This chorale form might fairly be called the mystic. The chorale themes become veiled, the melodic line more free, as if everything external had been lost, and only the general mood, the fundamental emotional idea, were being expressed. In this style the chorales "Allein Gott in der Höh sei Ehr" (VI, No. 8), "Komm, heilger Geist, Herre Gott" (VII, No. 37), and "Schmücke dich, o liebe Seele" (VII, No. 49) form a category of their own. Mendelssohn was so affected by the mood-painting in the last named chorale that he told Schumann "if life were to deprive him of hope and faith, this one chorale would bring them back"*.

The triple chorale on "O Lamm Gottes" (VII, No. 48) and the arrangement of "Jesus Christus unser Heiland" (VI, No. 31) represent the ideas more in their dramatic aspect, — so much so that one is almost tempted to agree with Rust against Spitta, and date these works from the Leipzig period.

It is difficult to agree with Spitta's division of Bach's chorale arrangements into the three categories of pure chorale preludes, organ chorales, and chorale fantasias. It is more reasonable to group them according to the style of treatment — in the fugued style of Pachelbel, the "coloristic" style of Böhm and Reinken, or free fantasias in the style of Buxtehude. There is further the type of the *Orgelbüchlein*, in which the characteristic motive illustrates the uninterrupted *cantus firmus*, and finally the great chorales, that offer a perfected synthesis of all the forms.

Besides the arrangement of "An Wasserflüssen Babylon" for double pedal (VI, No. 12a), there were several excellent and interesting chorales not included by Bach in any collection, among which may be mentioned the fantasia on "Ein' feste Burg" (VI, No. 22), the sublime fugue on the Magnificat (VII, No. 41), the joyous trio on "Nun freut euch, lieben Christen g'mein" (VII, No. 44), and the expressive chorale "Erbarm' dich mein, o Herre Gott" (B. G. XL, p. 60), which in its kind — the melody is supported by evenly flowing quavers, — is unique among Bach's chorale preludes.

"Christ lag in Todesbanden" (VI, No. 15), "Jesu meine Freude" (VI, No. 29), "Vom Himmel hoch, da komm ich her" (VII, Nos. 54 and 55), and "Wir glauben all' an einen Gott" (VII, No. 62) are all admittedly youthful works,

* Schumann's *Musik und Musiker*, Reclam's edition, I, 153. See also p. 245 of the present volume.

in which we can follow Bach's earliest development. It is not clear why the harmonisation of the chorale "Herr Gott, dich loben wir" (VI, No. 26), that is meant as an accompaniment to the hymn, should figure among the chorale preludes in all editions, even in that of Naumann.

What is needed is a cheap edition of the chorale preludes in their original form, distinguishing the collections planned by Bach himself from the detached chorales that have come down to us, the latter being freely grouped according to their style and their value. With an alphabetical index any one of them could be found in a moment. It is also desirable that the texts should be printed along with the chorales, many of them having by this time disappeared from our hymn-books*.

CHAPTER XIV.

THE PERFORMANCE OF THE ORGAN WORKS.

How did Bach play his organ works, and how should they be played? This practical question is much more important than the historical and æsthetic question. Upon the performance it depends whether these works can really be brought home to the hearers, or whether they are simply to be admired in a kind of respectful wonder, their beauty being taken on trust rather than actually felt. This certainly happens frequently at the present day.

Indications for performance are scarce in Bach's works. Once or twice, as in the D minor toccata (Peters III, No. 3), the changes of manual are indicated; in the *Orgelbüchlein* we are expressly told which pieces are to be played on two keyboards; in the Schübler chorale trios we are told whether eight or four or sixteen feet stops are to be drawn (Peters VII, Nos. 38, 57, 59, 63). That is practically

---

* Chapter XXII of the present volume is devoted to the elucidation of the chorale preludes.

all. We know, from Walther's copy, Bach's manner of playing the chorale prelude "Ein' feste Burg" (Peters VI, No. 22) at the opening of the new organ at Mühlhausen; his unfriendly critic Scheibe informs us that his manner at the organ was extraordinarily quiet; Forkel says that he astonished other organists by the audacity of his tone-combinations*. Otherwise he was distinguished from his contemporaries only by his consistent pursuit of the principle of legato playing. He had no experience of the Venetian shutter swell, which was introduced about that time in England, where Handel took great interest in the invention. In Germany the opposition to this so-called trifling lasted a long time. When Burney, more than twenty years after Bach's death, heard the Berlin organs, he was astonished to find that not one possessed a swell. It no more occurred to Bach than to the rest of his contemporaries that some day organs would be fitted with combination stops, adjustable combinations, and all the rest of the apparatus of the modern organs, especially the so-called "concert" organs.

How do we stand now with regard to the performance of Bach's works on the modern organ? We have achieved infinite possibilities in registration, the power of gradual variation from *pianissimo* to *fortissimo*, and, by means of the swells, a certain power of tone nuance. But we have lost the old tone of the organ that Bach wrote for; and, since the tone is the chief thing, it must be said that the modern organ is not so suitable for Bach playing as is generally supposed**.

----

* "His method of registration was so extraordinary that many organ builders and organists were appalled when they saw him. It seemed to them that such a combination of stops could not possibly sound well; but they wondered greatly when they observed that the organ sounded at its best, though the effect was of an unusual kind that could never have been produced by their own style of registration." (Forkel, p. 20.)

** On the organ of Bach's day see Pirro's *L'Orgue de J. S. Bach* (Paris, 1895); Albert Schweitzer's *Deutsche und französische*

Our registers are all voiced too loudly or too softly. If we pull out the whole of the diapasons and the mixtures, or add the reeds, we get a force of tone that in the end becomes positively unbearable. The lighter manuals are weak in comparison with the great organ; they usually lack the necessary mixtures. Our pedals are coarse and clumsy and also poor in mixtures, as well as in four-feet stops. The trouble comes principally from the change in the disposition of the organs, the relation between diapasons and mixtures having been altered, wholly to the detriment of the latter; but also from the unnaturally strong bellows of the modern organ. In our passion for strength of tone we have forgotten beauty and richness of tone, which depend upon the harmonious blending of ideally voiced stops. The older organs are becoming scarcer and scarcer. There are many organists today who have never heard Bach played on the kind of organ the composer had in view when he wrote. The day is not far distant when the last of our beautiful Silbermann organs will be replaced, or renovated beyond recognition; and then the Bach organ also will be one of the unknown things of the past, like certain orchestral instruments that he uses in his scores.

If we play Bach on an old and well-preserved Silbermann organ, both players and hearers are as little conscious as the master himself was of the need for frequent changes of register, for on such an instrument the diapasons and mixtures give a *forte* so rich, intense, full-coloured, and yet in no wise fatiguing, that we can, if need be, pre-

---

Orgelbaukunst und Orgelkunst (Leipzig, 1906); J. W. Enschedé's *Moderne Orgels en Bachs Orgelmuziek* (in *Caecilia*, Amsterdam, April and May 1907); O. Dienel's *Die Stellung der modernen Orgel zu S. Bachs Orgelmusik* (a lecture, Berlin, 1890); H. Reimann's *Über den Vortrag der Orgelkompositionen Bachs* (*Musikalische Rückblicke*, 1900). Mention may also be made of Isidor Mayrhofer's *Bach-Studien*, Vol. I, *Orgelwerke* (Leipzig, 1901). This work gives æsthetic analyses of all Bach's organ compositions, but does not touch the question of performance.

serve it unchanged throughout a prelude or a fugue*. On such an organ, moreover, both the inner parts and the pedal come out clearly, whereas on the modern organ the inner parts are confused, and the pedal, by reason of its deficiency in four-feet stops and mixtures, and its inferiority in weight to the enormous masses of tone above it, cannot, even at its most brutal, throw out a clear line. And all this on account of the too heavy voicing of our registers! The organs of forty years ago, that are voiced with the normal pressure, — for the simple reason that at that time the electric bellows was unknown, and the wind was consequently sparingly used — are better Bach organs than the modern ones. What a joy it is, for example, to play Bach on the beautiful Walker organs built between about 1860 and 1875!

As a rule Bach kept to the characteristic registration with which he began, getting variety and gradation in his playing by transitions from one manual to another**. It is noteworthy, however, that he played a great many organ pieces throughout on the great organ without any change whatever of manuals and without any gradation of tone,

---

* In Alsace there are still some organs of this kind. I confess that it was these that first put me out of humour with the ultra-modern interpretations of Bach's organ works, and made me long for organs on which one could play the preludes and fugues in their natural, lofty simplicity. Widor afterwards confirmed me in these views.

** The representatives of the old German organ school, that still preserved some traditions from the Bach epoch, played Bach's preludes and fugues throughout on the great organ with diapasons and mixtures. The pedal was sometimes strengthened by reeds. In the last three decades of the nineteenth century this method of performance came to be looked upon as stiff and pedantic. The struggle ended unfavorably to the old tradition, mainly through the fact that this method is really impossible on the brutal organs with the modern voicing. During the last few years a reaction has set in against the false modernisation of the performance of the organ works; the aim is to restore to favour what is legitimate in the old simple style. The Belgian and French organists — Lemmens, Guilmant, Widor, Gigout — always played Bach according to the principles of the old German school. Their organs were voiced more lightly and clearly than the German ones.

the essence of them being the evolution of a single idea, free from any dramatic suggestions. This is especially the case with the works in which the pedal is employed uninterruptedly throughout, — for example, the two preludes in C major (Peters II, Nos. 1 and 7) and A major (II, No. 3) respectively, the majority of the chorales of the *Orgelbüchlein*, and both the larger and smaller ones in the fugal style of Pachelbel. Here any variation of tone-colour or alternation of strong and weak would destroy the ideal unity of the work. The organ sonatas in trio-form, again, are most effective when the tone-colour that has been found to be the best for each of the three obbligato parts is maintained throughout.

As regards the choice of tone-colours, it need only be said that these are sufficiently Bachian when they suit the character of the work. We must not grudge even months of trouble in order to find the right registration. It is still disputable what is meant by the expression "organo pleno" that often figures at the head of a work*. It practically amounts to this, that in passages of this kind Bach desires the main strength of the organ, at any rate diapasons and mixtures. On present-day organs, however, this must be done with discretion, — the tutti of the diapasons and mixtures, thanks to the disagreeably strong quality of the latter, hardly corresponding to what Bach had in his mind.

Should we also use the reeds in Bach's preludes and fugues? His objection to those usually found in modern organs would have been that they are too blaring and that they obscure the polyphony. On the other hand it is probable that he added reeds to his diapasons and mixtures, for he cultivates the metallic tone in the orchestra as well. His pedal timbre was really based on reeds. More-

---

* As bearing on the history of the expression, it may be noted that the Allemannic people still distinguish between the "half" and the "whole" organ. Thus "pro organo pleno" may well have meant originally "for full organ", the reference being to the quality, not to the stops. In point of fact, however, on the old organs the *forte* was used for preludes and fugues.

over we know how highly he valued good reeds in an organ *. What we have to do in future is to restore the old delicate and beautiful reeds, that just add a lustre to the diapasons without overwhelming them as ours do **. Until then we must manage with compromises, and use diapasons, mixtures, and reeds with sufficient discretion to get something like the old quality of tone.

It is interesting to note that Bach's contemporaries complained that the Silbermann brothers voiced their organs too softly, in order to get beauty of tone. Bach evidently did not think so.

The effect that can be made with a fine full *fortissimo* combining all the timbres may be seen in the little prelude in E minor (Peters III, No. 10). If we play it right through without any change, we realise at once that this is how Bach conceived it, and that to play it with any variation of colour or of force is to destroy its dramatic majesty.

We play the chorale preludes of the *Orgelbüchlein* and many others too softly, again, because we do not make sufficient use of beautiful mixtures on the secondary manuals, which would not only sound well in themselves but would permit the use also of one or two reeds. We are thus thrown back, as a rule, on the characterless tone-colour of some eight-feet diapasons — which particularly obscure the polyphonic writing, (the four-feet and two-feet are also generally voiced too strongly) — and we try to make up in sentimentality for what we have lost in richness and quality of tone. It is obviously wrong, for we lose the simple effect of the *cantus firmus*.

---

* See p. 199.
** Even the French reeds, in spite of their beauty, are unfitted for Bach playing. On the other hand, the diapasons and mixtures of the Cavaillé-Coll organs seem made for it, this builder having been particularly anxious to avoid abnormally strong and "solid" voicing. On the organs at St. Sulpice and Notre-Dame, Bach's fugues come out with extraordinary clearness. One of the finest Bach organs in existence is the one, rich in mixtures, that adorns the Cavaillé-Coll *atélier* in Paris (15 Avenue du Maine).

We should carefully consider which chorales are written for two and which for one manual, and not plume ourselves on our cleverness when we play the latter on two manuals*. Bach's own intentions can always be gathered from the style of writing. A part that he intended for one manual cannot be played upon two without seriously marring the grouping and leading of the voices. Conversely, a work conceived for two manuals is written in such a way that each part lies smoothly and clearly on its own manual, down to the smallest detail. This principle can be applied to all the organ works.

If the *cantus firmus* is broken up into coloratura, as in the chorale preludes in Böhm's manner, it often comes out to particular advantage with an oboe or clarinet colouring. Wonderful effects of blending can be obtained by using a small mixture in the swell and adding diapasons and an oboe colouring to it. These chorale preludes in Böhm's style should be played the most delicately of all.

The pedal should not be too heavy, and, at any rate in the chorale preludes, uncoupled wherever possible. It is most effective with its own stops. Frequently only an eight-feet tone should be employed — for example in the chorale preludes "O Lamm Gottes" (Peters V, No. 44) and "Gottes Sohn ist kommen" (Peters V, No. 19). At other times even only a four-feet tone is suitable; e. g. in "In dulci Jubilo" (Peters V, No. 35)**. Where the double pedal is

---

* Most organists succumb to this temptation, e. g., in the little chorale prelude "O Lamm Gottes" (Peters V, No. 44).

** In "Vom Himmel hoch" again (Peters V, No. 50), the pure eight-feet pedal is decidedly better, as it does not cover up the semiquaver figure of the third voice, that often goes very low. It is a mistaken idea that "In dulci Jubilo" requires a pedal with F sharp. Bach writes it thus in order to make the tenor position of the part clear. It is played an octave lower and with a four-feet. Bach would be delighted to know that the latest pedals of Cavaillé-Coll, that go to G, have the natural F sharp; but he would have expressed himself pretty forcibly with regard to the numerous organ builders who think that for the "ordinary" organ a pedal to D is enough.

prescribed throughout, it goes without saying that only eight-feet stops should be employed, with the four-feet for stronger effects. This rule is frequently disregarded. The case is different when the double pedal is used at the end of a work — e. g. in the D major prelude (Peters IV, No. 3); here the sixteen-feet is to be maintained, though it must be admitted that the *fortissimo* of a modern pedal of this kind is far from charming.

The organist should not worry either himself or his hearers too much with the working-out of a canonic passage. The piece is not there for the sake of the canon, but the canon for the sake of the piece, especially in the canons of the *Orgelbüchlein*. If we hear properly the melody of the *cantus firmus*, the other parts can be so far kept in the background that the uninitiated need not even suspect there is a canon in progress.

In chorales to be played on two manuals, experience teaches us that as a rule it is better to let the string character prevail in the left hand and a flute colour in the upper parts, this colour being free from harshness there, but muddy in the lower register.

Special difficulties are offered by the two great chorales with double pedal, "An Wasserflüssen Babylon" (Peters VI, No. 12a) and "Aus tiefer Not schrei ich zu dir" (Peters VI, No. 13). For the first the following registration is recommended — strings in the pedal, in the left hand flutes, in the right hand strings, all soft eight-feet stops*. The chorale prelude "Aus tiefer Not" is very effective when the whole eight and four-feet register — diapasons, mixtures, and reeds, — is used in the pedal; in this way the mixtures and reeds which are often missing can be got from the second and third manuals by coupling, and we can play the four upper parts on the great organ with the full eight and four-feet diapasons, even adding a good mixture later on.

---

* Many organists erroneously imagine that they are bound to use sixteen-feet stops in pieces with double pedal. What then becomes of the fourths, thirds, and seconds in the lower octave!

This solves the problem of bringing out the *cantus firmus* clearly in the upper pedal part. Under certain circumstances it is as well to omit the eight-feet trumpet, and to employ only the four-feet stops for the reed timbre. In truth, however, we can only play these double pedal parts quite legato either on the old narrow Bach pedals or the curved French and English pedals with their circular arrangement. It is impossible on the flat and excessively broad pedal keyboard that is regarded as the only correct thing in Germany.

The foregoing remarks apply to the works that seem to call for neither a change of manuals nor a change of colour. As a rule, however, Bach goes on the presupposition that we shall play his works with the variety suggested by their contents and their style of treatment. He gives no indications on the point, simply because the works carry their own indications. Leading parts on the grand organ, subsidiary parts, (generally recognisable by the omission of the pedal) on the supplementary manuals, — this is what he expects from the player. This can be seen from the D minor toccata (Peters III, No. 3), in which he has specified the changes of manual, probably for a pupil.

In the chorale on "Ein' feste Burg" (Peters VI, No. 22) we can reconstruct Bach's registration from Walther's copy. His indications evidently refer to the Mühlhausen organ, the renovation of which Bach superintended, and which he opened, in all its new glory, in the autumn of 1709, perhaps at the Reformation feast*. First of all, bars 1—20, Bach kept the right hand on the second manual, employing, among others, the sesquialtera, and the left hand on the first manual, defining the tone-quality of this by the fagotto 16″. Bars 20—24 he played on the third

---

* For the specification of the Mühlhausen organ see Spitta I, 355. The registration marks in Walther's copy (Spitta I, 394, 395) are a little confused, owing to the fact that he transferred the registration to his Weimar organ, that had only two manuals. The indications for the Mühlhausen organ can, however, be made out without difficulty.

manual, drawing the soft pedal stops, especially the new sub-bass. During this he strengthened somewhat the other manuals, and came back to them in bars 24—32, in which the assistant — probably Walther, — took advantage of the short pause in the bass in bar 24 to draw the full pedal. In bars 32—37 Bach returned to the third manual, the assistant shutting off the strong pedal registers. The finale, from bar 37, was played on the great organ with all the stops. The registration of the piece could not be simpler or more effective. These two examples show us how ingeniously Bach managed the changes of manual.

The first thing, therefore, is always to look for the simple architectural lines of the work. The registration that brings these out is the right one; any other, no matter how ingenious it may be, is less good, in that it obscures the real configuration of the work. We must keep to the principle that every fugue and every prelude is to begin and end on the great organ. It is quite wrong to give out a fugal theme *piano* or *pianissimo*, and let each voice, as it enters, take it up more loudly. The theme, whether joyous or sad, must always be given out with a certain fullness of tone, leaving the cumulative effect to come from the entries of the different voices. It is painful to hear themes that should enter proudly, like those of the A minor and G minor fugues, given out softly on the third manual in a way that quite obscures their real character — all for the sake of the precious *crescendo*. In many a fugue the whole architectural effect is sacrificed to the desire to render the theme always fully audible, — to which end it and the other voices are transferred from the great organ to one of the others. This is unpermissible. Now and again we hear a Bach fugue played in such a way that it tapers off at the end in the most beautiful *pianissimo*.

This modernisation is partly the product of our present-day way of looking at music. If our organists wish to prove themselves modern musicians, it can only be by transferring the modern orchestral style to these works. They forget that Bach's own orchestral style was the ancient one, not the modern. The effects he aimed at on the organ are the same that he aspires after in the Brandenburg concertos. The organist, therefore, would be well advised to study these works thoroughly, in order to penetrate to the secret of Bach's style and to realise that with him it is a question not so much of a gradual cumulation of effect as of the lucid opposition and combination of two or three bodies of tone. For this reason the modern swell really does our organists a disservice, in that it is always tempting them to indulge in these gradual *crescendi*. The true cumulative effects in Bach are made by the entry at definite moments of two or three new tone-masses, and the *decrescendo* by their departure.

On the other hand the constitution of our organs, that are incapable of the real Bach *forte*, and in which the polyphonic writing does not come out clearly, makes us have recourse to artificial effects instead of natural ones, and we try to make Bach interesting by variations of tone and of colour and by an over-insistence on the theme. Here also, until we begin building ideal Bach organs again, we must resort to a wise compromise. This does not mean that the gradual rise and fall of tone, — effected on a small scale by means of the Venetian shutter swell and on a large scale by means of the cylinder, is always wrong in Bach. Archaistic tendences should not be tolerated in music. Bach would have been the last to set his face against new methods. Many passages — e. g. the conclusion of the A minor fugue — really demand an increase in the *forte* itself. And how happy Bach would have been could he have got a finer *piano* on his third manual by shutting off some of the wind, as is possible by means of the Venetian shutter swell! To refuse to make use of this device in the great episode in the A minor fugue beginning at the fifty-first bar, — employing first a *decrescendo*, then a *crescendo*, — is to be false to Bach. Only the present-day organist must make use of the device in such a way as not

to disturb the original architecture of the fugue, and be
sure that the various episodes of the work come out simply
and clearly. Within these limits he may do what he thinks
necessary. If this principle is generally recognised, there
will be an end of much of the modern pretentious virtuosity
in the performance of Bach's organ works, and people
will come back from the art that merely stimulates interest
to the art that satisfies. And then the hearers will realise
that Bach's organ works are not complicated, but extremely simple.

Organists should particularly avoid the sudden *decrescendo* in the cadences that has gradually become the
fashion under the seductive influence of the cylinder swell.
It is to be hoped also that some day the practice will
cease of employing the cylinder swell at the beginning of
the F major toccata, instead of starting with a good *forte*
and leaving the *crescendo* to the dramatic unfolding of the
canon. For the rest, this toccata is one of the works that
are most effective when played simply with various nuances of the one *forte*.

The works differ greatly with regard to the changes of
manual they require. In many these changes amount
merely to an occasional bar or two on the subsidiary manuals; we may even doubt whether Bach went to these
manuals in the bars where the pedal ceases, — e. g. in the
C major fugue (Peters II, No. 1). Usually, however, the
changes are so important that we cannot be in doubt as
to where the intermezzo begins on the secondary manual,
and where it ends. In a number of fugues the change
comes exactly in the middle, so that they appear to be
triform both in structure and performance: — (1) the
first exposition on the great organ; (2) the intermezzo;
(3) a second exposition extending to the final cadence.
Of this kind are the fugues in G major (II, No. 2), C major
(II, No. 7), F major (III, No. 2), A minor (II, No. 8),
G minor (II, No. 4) and B minor (II, No. 10). The intermezzo on the subsidiary manuals begins each time at the

place where the pedal ceases, (or shortly afterwards) and ends at the re-entry of the pedal (or shortly before). Instead of one big *crescendo*, lasting from the beginning to the end, as we moderns conceive the fugue, the fugue as Bach conceived it consisted of two equipollent main sections, with a subsidiary section between them.

To destroy the character of the intermezzo is to destroy the Bach fugue. The most striking fugues in respect of this simple structure are the three just mentioned, in A minor, G minor and B minor. Here we clearly realise the necessity of a *diminuendo* up to a certain point in the intermezzo. The theme retires to some extent into the innermost and uppermost parts of the organ, there to evolve slowly until the time comes for the re-entry of the pedal, signalised by a return to the tone-colour that prevailed at the commencement of the intermezzo, when the pedal ceased. How the organist manages this, how he passes from one manual to another, how he introduces mixtures and reeds into the diapasons and takes them out again, and brings out this architecture even down to the smallest detail, — that is his affair. He will have to be ruled by the disposition of his organ. The chief thing is for him to recognise the plan of the fugue and bring this out, — not a fantastic plan of his own invention*.

* The following is a suggestion for the registration of the A minor fugue: The manuals are coupled; stops drawn, diapasons 8 and 4 and mixtures of manuals II and III. Begin the fugue on the great organ. On the first beat of bar 44 add the mixtures of the first manual. In bar 51 the left hand remains on the first manual, from which the mixtures are taken off, and the right hand goes to the second; in the second half of bar 59 it is followed by the left; during the sustained F in bar 60 the right hand goes imperceptibly to the third manual; in bar 63 the left follows it; at the same time the mixtures of the third manual are taken off; the swell box slowly closes until bar 70; in bar 71 the right hand goes to the second manual, while on the third, with the swell box closed, the mixtures are again introduced; the swell box is opened slowly; in one of the following bars the left hand goes imperceptibly to the second manual; in the second half of bar 78 it gives out the theme on the first manual, the mixtures of the second entering at

Other fugues exhibit two or more changes. There are two in the following fugues: A major (Peters II, No. 3, bars 59—87 and 121—146); F minor (II, No. 5, bars 43—64 and 96—120); C minor (II, No. 6, bars 59—94 and 118 —143); C minor (III, No. 6, bars 27—50 and 58—67); E minor (III, No. 10, bars 15—19 and 27—33). We meet with more than two intermezzi in the great E minor fugue (Peters II, No. 9), that has, indeed, more the character of a fantasia. It can be properly played only on an organ whose subsidiary manuals are so supplied with mixtures that they do not contrast too markedly with the great organ. The sections dominated by the main theme and the quaver figures are to be played wholly on the great organ, and the passages with the semiquaver figures on the subordinate manuals. The charm depends each time upon the immediate entry of the chief theme and the quaver movement. Here one doubly regrets that Bach has not recorded the change of manuals. An excellent plan is to play the great semiquaver figures, in which the pedal shares, on the first manual, without its own mixtures, but adding those of the other manuals by means of the couplers, and then, at each return of the main theme, bring in the mixtures and finally the reeds of the great organ.

The prelude in E flat major (III, No. 1), which is similarly constructed, must be played in the same way. The triple fugue appended to it is most effective when we play the first part with the full diapasons of the great organ, — perhaps with delicate mixtures of the other manuals coupled to them ,— the second part on the subsidiary manuals with all the mixtures, and in the third

---

the same time; in bar 88 the mixtures of the first manual are added, to which the right hand goes in bar 91; on the sustained E in bar 94 the reeds of the third manual are added, on the first beat of bar 113 those of the second, from bar 132 onwards those of the first, and whatever else is available for a *fortissimo*. The G minor fugue could be registered on the same lines.

part return to the first manual, which has meanwhile been increased to *fortissimo*.

In a number of preludes in which the pedal is used throughout, it is as well to work on a basis of varied *fortes*, relieved one against the other by the intensity of the mixture-tone obtained by adding the coupled manuals to the full diapasons. For the G minor fantasia (II, No. 4), we would propose — at the commencement, the three coupled manuals, diapasons, mixtures and reeds; in bars 9—14 retain only the diapasons; from bar 14 onwards add gradually, each time on the strong beat of the bar, first of all the mixtures, then the reeds in the order III, II, I; in bar 25 take them all off again, so that bars 25—31 are played only with the diapason tone-colour, (of course on the great organ); in bar 31 introduce into the diapason mass first of all the mixtures and reeds on the third manual, two bars later those on the second, and two bars further on those on the first, until the *fortissimo* is reached, which is then retained to the end. This method, by which the player always keeps to the same manual, is perhaps less interesting than many of the modern virtuoso methods; it has, however, the advantage of presenting the work to the hearer in all its grand simplicity.

This gradated *forte* can be employed with the same good effect in the preludes in C minor (II, No. 6) and E minor (II, No. 9), only that here, in the section without pedal, there are episodes that need to be played on the subsidiary manuals.

The fantasia in C minor (III, No. 6) is the despair of every organist. It is almost impossible to reproduce its ideal beauty in material tone. After every attempt we come back to the simplest method, that consists in beginning with a flexible diapason basis, introducing, at the transition from bar 11 to bar 12, almost all the diapasons and mixtures of the subsidiary manuals, returning in bar 21 to the first diapason colour, maintaining this until bar 32, and then gradually introducing, till the end is

reached, the whole of the diapasons of the full organ and
the mixtures of the subsidiary manuals.

One of the works that suffers most at the hands of organists is the B minor prelude (II, No. 10), although its
structure is the simplest possible. We should begin on
the great organ; at bar 17 go to the subsidiary manuals;
in bar 27 the right hand returns to the great organ, followed
by the left hand in bar 28; both remain there until bar 43,
and then move to the other manuals until bar 50, when
they again return to the first manual; from bars 56—60
keep to the great organ, but retain only the diapasons;
during bar 60 introduce mixtures and afterwards reeds
under the cover of the chromatic passage; maintain this
on the great organ until bar 69, when we again take off
the mixtures and the reeds and continue with the diapasons; in bar 73 we come back for the last time to the
subsidiary manuals, which we dexterously bring up to
fortissimo, and return in the course of bars 78 and 79 to
the great organ with all its stops drawn.

In the passacaglia it is very effective to give out the
theme with the complete diapasons of the organ coupled
to the pedal, and then to begin *pianissimo* on the third
manual and to draw more stops at each new variation.
In bar 73 we may perhaps go to the first manual; in the
four variations that follow we may introduce by degrees
the whole of the diapasons and mixtures, and finally some
reeds. In bar 105 we go to the second manual, and afterwards to the third, taking off the mixtures and reeds;
from bar 114 onwards we close the swell box slowly; the
arpeggio passages are played with fine eight, four, and two-
feet registers of the third manual. On the last beat of
bar 129 we revert to the diapasons and mixtures of the
first manual; in the following variations we add reeds and
mixtures of the other manuals; finally we add also the reeds
of the first manual.

To ascertain where the change of manual can be made,
and the way in which it can best be effected, we must

endeavour by continual study of the work to discover the ground principles on which it is constructed. The great art consists in going back with both hands to the great organ at the moment of the pedal entry. From the structure of the passage we must try to infer whether we must go to the first manual with one hand after the other, — in which case it is always best to begin with the left, since this can enter almost imperceptibly in the lower part — or whether Bach demands a decided contrast, for which we must bring both hands simultaneously to the great organ. His own playing must have been characterised by extraordinary refinement, since he expressly desires that the manuals shall lie quite close to each other, so that he may easily pass from one to the other*. There are many critical passages in which sustained notes or harmonies have to be taken with perfect smoothness of transition on another manual.

For changes of manual in accordance with Bach's intentions a certain homogeneous tone-colour must unite the three manuals. On the organs of today, that have scarcely any mixtures on the subsidiary manuals, this is often difficult. It is also regrettable that on our organs the three manuals no longer represent three different and sharply-characterised qualities of tone. Hence the main effect of the change of manuals and of the coupling and uncoupling of them is lost. This causes the organ virtuosi of today to renounce the most natural means of effect and have recourse to the cylinder swell, that finally becomes so monotonous.

If the vital question in Bach playing is that of the coupling and uncoupling of the manuals, and of the entries and exits of different tone-groups, it must be said that the plan of our modern organs does not lend itself greatly to this. The couplers are worked by the pressing of knobs, which means that the player cannot make full use of them, since in Bach playing neither hand can be dispensed with.

------

* See p. 200.

Further, our combination stops and adjustable combinations usually work in such a way that they interfere with the existing registration instead of reinforcing it; and they often have the further disadvantage of not acting separately on each manual, but on the whole organ. The console ought to be so arranged that the couplers can be worked either by the hand or the foot, — the two mechanisms, of course, being connected. The player could then draw the coupler with his hand and release it with his foot, and *vice versâ*, or he could employ only the hand or only the foot, as suited him best. The collective stops and the adjustable combinations should be arranged on a double principle, so that at the will of the organist they could either suspend or supplement the drawn stops. It would be an advantage if they also could be worked both by the hand and the foot. This would imply another much-needed simplification of our organs*.

It looks as if Bach's works were destined not only to instruct the organist but to reform the organ builders of the present day, to emancipate us from the folly of the inventor and lead us back from the complicated to the simple, from the strong-toned organ to the organ of rich and beautiful tone.

The more we play Bach's organ works, the slower we take the tempi. Every organist has this experience. The lines must stand out in calm plasticity. There must be time also to bring out their dovetailing and juxtaposition. At the first impression of obscurity and confusion, the whole effect of the organ piece is gone.

If so many organists imagine that they play Bach "interestingly" by taking him fast, this is because they have not mastered the art of playing plastically, so as to give

---

* The console sketched above is realised in the organ of the new church at Strassburg-Kronenburg, built by the Alsatian firm of Dalstein and Härpfer (Bolchen); the stops of this organ are voiced in the old Silbermann style. The organ at St. Nicholas's in Strassburg is also built on this plan, as a Bach organ.

vitality to the work by bringing out its detail clearly. It is quite a mistaken idea that what Bach chiefly wants is a monotonous smoothness. He certainly favored the legato style. But his legato is not a mere levelling; it is alive. It must be filled by a fine phrasing which the hearer need not perceive as such, but of which he is conscious as a captivating lucidity in the playing. Within the legato, the separate tones must be grouped into living phrases. This intimate style of phrasing breaks up the stiffness of the organ tone. The effect should be as if what is impossible on the organ had become possible, — that is to say, that some notes have a heavy and others a light touch. That is the ideal to be aimed at.

In the old days, when the absolutely uniform legato obtainable by passing under the thumb was not known, so that only a few of the notes were played legato while the others were detached owing to the displacement of the hand, players had a feeling for the artistic grouping of notes within a legato that we have lost, but of which we can form a rough idea by observing how, at that time, runs were divided between the two hands. Even in the introduction to the C major toccata (Peters III, No. 8), or that of the E minor prelude (Peters III, No. 10), there is revealed a whole world of interesting legato combinations. Many organists, indeed, have no idea that this division between the two hands indicates Bach's phrasing; they are even proud of themselves when they play these passages with one hand, or in octaves with both hands, making one monotonous scale passage of them. If we follow the principle indicated by Bach's manner of writing his phrases, we see that he usually conceives four consecutive notes as grouped in such a way that the first is detached from the others by an imperceptible break, and belongs rather to the previous group than to the one that follows. Thus not

In this way there is no sense of monotony in the legato. When we apply this principle we are surprised with what clearness and animation the passages come out. Consequently we must play thus —

Prelude in A minor (Peters II, No. 8):

Toccata in D minor (Peters III, No. 3):

One of the most instructive examples in this regard is the passage-work in the subsidiary section of the B minor prelude. Grouped as a scale it is always unsatisfactory; it only acquires life and form when we play it thus: —

The fresh and healthy prelude in C major, again, (Peters IV, No. 1) with the fine pedal solo, only loses its stiffness when we phrase it on this principle. We have the same experience with the other C major prelude (Peters II, No. 1). This phrasing, however, must never be obtrusively noticeable within the general legato. Its effect must be merely that of an agitation of the main contour. To bring out the phrasing by means of slurs and breath-signs is much too clumsy a method; it should really be done by delicate and inexpressible means.

It is doubtful whether, for the sake of variety, we should now and then play whole quaver or semiquaver passages staccato.

The phrasing of the fugue themes is still in dispute, though we are gradually getting further away from the extravagances of the earlier virtuosi, when they wrought such violence on Bach in the first joy of their virtuosity. A phrasing is fundamentally wrong that is not simple, and cannot be maintained throughout the whole piece, especially whenever the theme enters. Therefore any notes that interrupt the normal flow and are denoted by characteristic leaps, must to some extent be taken out of the group and stand by themselves. Thus: —

Fugue in A minor (Peters II, No. 8):

Fugue in G minor (Peters II, No. 4):

Toccata in F major III (Peters No. 2):

The theme of the E flat triple fugue is interesting, as the transformations it undergoes necessitate changes in its phrasing: —

First fugue:

Second fugue:

Third fugue:

Only when phrased in this way do the themes of the second and third fugues become perfectly clear to the hearer, which is impossible if the notes are grouped evenly.

When the same note is struck repeatedly it should be sustained for only half its time-value, with a pause for the remainder. The repeated notes are thrown into relief by the preceding and following slurs. Thus: —

Fugue in G major (Peters II, No. 2):

Fugue in C minor (Peters III, No. 6).

This rule holds good not only for the phrasing of the themes, but for the treatment of the repeated notes in general. It cannot be observed too strictly. Equally weighty is another rule. If a repeated note occurs on the paper by reason of the same note entering in another voice, the note must be held without repetition; it must not be heard as two notes because one voice takes it over from the other.

In successive chords, the repeated notes are to be detached, and those moving in intervals are to be legato. In this way the leading of the voices is brought out with extraordinary clearness. If one tries to translate these rules into practice, the simplest pieces become difficult.

In order to realise the difficulties and the effect of playing in this strict style, the succession of chords in the middle
section of the little E minor prelude (Peters III, No. 10)
should be studied.

It is upon this plastic style of playing, not on ingenious
registration and virtuosity, that the effect of Bach's organ
works depends.   But everything rests on seeming trifles,
and we organists are much too modest and too indulgent to
ourselves in this respect; moreover so few of us acquire
a technique really adequate to Bach's demands.   Many
do not even acquire absolute precision of touch.

Ornaments occur relatively seldom in the organ works,
yet frequently enough for there to be plenty of opportunities for sins of thoughtlessness*.   It is always forgotten
that the Bach trill, as Emmanuel expressly informs us,
does not begin on the main note but on the secondary
note, and, when it is long, always has a final turn.

Thus the theme of the F minor fugue (Peters II, No. 5)
should be played either: —

Too rapid trills are to be avoided on the organ.

In the opening mordents of the Dorian toccata (Peters
IV, No. 4), the E minor fugue (Peters III, No. 10), and
the E flat prelude (Peters III, No. 1), the ornaments must
be played with a whole-tone interval.   The grace-notes
in the pedal part of the B minor prelude (Peters II, No. 10)
are to be played as quavers; Rust thought he recollected

---

* The following remarks should be supplemented by the
detailed examination of Bach's ornamentation in the chapter on
the performance of the clavier works.

that in the autograph, that unfortunately has disappeared, they were so noted. It is best, however, to separate the two notes, thus:

There remains the question of the organ works for practical use. It is entirely a question of usage. Whoever uses Naumann's instructive collected edition (Breitkopf and Härtel) or Schreyer's collection (Hofmeister, Leipzig) — to mention these alone — certainly gets a good deal of practical information, and no one should neglect to acquaint himself with the brilliant and profound observations and suggestions contained in these and similar works*.

For daily use, however, editions of this kind are not the best. The multitude of fingering, phrasing marks, slurs, tempi marks, and suggestions for registering give the works an overloaded look, and what is really essential remains after all unsaid. What is needed is not these very practical editions so much as thorough separate studies of registration, manual changes, and the like. Here almost everything still remains to be done**.

An organist of the right kind will not take refuge in a practical edition, but will use an original edition, and enter in it his own observations and experiments.

On the structure of Bach's organ themes, again, and on the architecture of the works in themselves and in relation to his clavier music, scarcely anything has been

---

* In Schreyer's edition the phrasing is especially interesting. In Naumann's suggestions we recognise the thoughtful practical organist. One only regrets that he does not give his principal rules and hints in prefaces and notes. A re-issue of them in book form would be welcome.

** An interesting theme, for example, would be a demonstration of the possibilities of the natural manual changes in the B minor prelude (Peters II, No. 10). A special subject for investigation would be the note on which the change is to be made each time.

published as yet that goes to the root of the subject. The
rhythm of the themes of the organ fugues, it may be remarked, is much simpler than that of the clavier fugues.
A few quite elementary syncopations apart, scarcely an
accent falls on the weak part of a bar; the main accent
always falls on the strong beat. Bach sees quite clearly
that any other than this natural accent is impossible on
the organ. For clavier and for orchestra he writes much
more freely. Thus the object of transcribing clavier fugues
for the organ is incomprehensible. No one who really
understands the nature of Bach's organ works can listen
to transcriptions of this kind.

Further, the structure of the works is quite different.
In the organ music Bach works upon much broader and
simpler lines than in the clavier works. We seek in vain
in the organ fugues for the subjective life, so rich in sur-
prises, of the clavier fugues. The former are meant to work
on a certain inner faculty of conception rather than on
the immediate feeling, and to exhibit an idea in lofty simplicity. For this reason Bach's clavier works sound restless on the organ. A satisfactory registration cannot be
discovered for any of them. The difference between the
clavier and the organ styles, in fact, cannot be better
realised than by placing Bach's organ fugues by the side
of his clavier fugues, and studying the musical architecture
of both in detail.

There is, to be sure, one work of Bach's for the organ
that stands on the border-line of the style he has laid
down for his organ works in general. It is the A major
fugue (Peters II, No. 3):

Every organist can convince himself of this. If we play
the theme legato, without the articulation that gives
character to it, it goes very lamely. If we play it as it is

intended to be played, accenting the syncopations by cutting them short, then, no matter how perfectly we play the piece, it has a notably restless effect; this is increased by the fact that the structural interest lies rather in the detail than in the whole, to say nothing of the further fact that sequences of thirds in the bass and a conclusion like that of this fugue are to be found nowhere else in the organ works of Bach.

The interesting point is that we can prove that the theme of this exceptional fugue was originally conceived not for the organ but for the orchestra; in its primary form it was written for the instrumental introduction to the cantata *Tritt auf die Glaubensbahn* (No. 151).

There is more to be said for the transcription of organ works for the piano than for the reverse proceeding, since the piano, as Liszt said, is to music what engraving is to painting; it serves to multiply and disseminate works of art.   When masters like Liszt, Saint-Saëns, Busoni, Reger, Philipp, d'Albert, Vianna da Motta, and Ansorge undertake to arrange Bach's organ works for the pianoforte, the intelligent player has not only the advantage of learning works from which he would otherwise be barred, but the æsthetic pleasure of finding organ effects cleverly realised on the piano. Bach, who was himself passionately devoted to the art of transcription, would have been delighted with the pianoforte apostles of his organ gospel.

There is danger, however, in going to excess.   These transcriptions, even when they are made with the utmost art, cannot in the long run give complete satisfaction. The organ themes lose something on the pianoforte; the simple plan of the works has to be replaced by an artificial one, since the various degrees of strength in the organ tone cannot be reproduced even on the modern pianoforte. When this perception grows, men will some day discover what Bach himself experienced, — it will look back on the age that delighted in transcriptions as on something long passed away, and its joy will not be in the transcription itself but in the education it afforded*. We must not allow these artistic transcriptions, that often surpass the powers of the average player, to make us forget the old German domestic resource of playing the organ works from the original in arrangements for four hands, one player taking the manual parts, the other the pedal parts in octaves.

CHAPTER XV.
THE CLAVIER WORKS.

Bachgesellschaft Edition.

Vol. III. Inventions and Symphonies: *Klavierübung* (Partitas: Italian Concerto: Duets: Goldberg Variations); Toccatas in F sharp minor and C minor; Fugue in A minor.
- XIII². English and French Suites. (As this volume was not critically accurate, the suites were re-issued in Vol. XLV¹.)
- XIV. The Well-tempered Clavichord.
- XXXVI. Suites, Toccatas, Preludes, Fugues, Fantasias. Little Preludes.
- XLII. Sonatas: Sixteen Concertos after Vivaldi.
- XLV¹. Preludes, Fugues, and other pieces. Doubtful Works. Supplementary volume.

The two fugues for two pianos, from the *Art of Fugue*, are contained in Vol. XXV. The *Klavierbüchlein* for Wilhelm Friedemann Bach is given in Vol. XLV¹; Vol. XVIII² contains the two note-books of Anna Magdalena (1722 and 1725).

Peters Edition.

Parts I and II, The Well-tempered Clavichord. III, Sonatas and single Suites. IV, Fantasias, Toccatas, Preludes and Fugues. V and VI, Partitas; Italian Concerto; Goldberg Variations. VII, Little Preludes; Two-Part and Three-Part Inventions; French Suites. VIII, English Suites. IX, Toccatas, Preludes, Fantasias, Fugues, Little Preludes. X, Vivaldi Concertos. XIII, Additional. Supplement I. Series I, Doubtful Works. Pieces from Anna Magdalena's *Klavierbüchlein*. The two fugues for two pianos from the *Art of Fugue* are given in Part XI.

---

* Friedrich Spiro holds the same views upon what is perishable and what is permanent in the epoch of transcriptions. See *Bach und seine Transcriptoren*, in the *Neue Zeitschrift für Musik*, 1904, pp. 680 ff.

The excellent Bischoff edition of the piano works calls for special mention (7 vols, Steingräber edition). The instructive popular edition issued by Ricordi with the coöperation of B. and S. Cesi, Longo, Marciano, Mugellini and Philipp is also very interesting, though unfortunately it gives only a selection, not the complete works.

The piano concertos will be discussed among the instrumental works.

The clavier works, like those for the organ, mostly date from the Weimar and Cöthen periods. Bach, however, published only the great works of the Leipzig period, — six large partitas, the Italian Concerto, four duets, and the Goldberg variations.

Partitas, not suites, — though this is what they really are in form — was the name he gave to the works in the style of his predecessor Kuhnau, who had issued, in 1689 and 1695, two collections of *Klavierübungen*, each containing seven Clavichord "Partitas"*.

The first partita appeared in 1726; it was the first composition that Bach published**. He was at that time forty-one years old. Each following year saw the birth of a new partita of his. When six of them had appeared, he united them under the title of *Klavierübung* (Part I), again in imitation of his predecessor. "Übung" means here, of course, not so much a work for student's practice as one for diversion***.

If Bach's sons informed Forkel correctly, the work made a great sensation in the musical world. "Such excellent clavichord compositions had never before been

---

* See Spitta III, 155.

** The Mühlhausen *Ratswahl* (Council Election) cantata *Gott ist mein König* (No. 71), of the same year, had received the honour of engraving, not at Bach's instance but at that of the Council.

*** The title of the volume is *Klavierübung bestehend in Präludien, Allemanden, Kouranten, Sarabanden, Giguen, Menuetten und andern Galanterien, den Liebhabern zur Gemütsergötzung verfertigt Erster Teil. Im Verlag des Autors, 1731.* (Clavichord exercises, consisting of Preludes, Allemandes, Courantes, Sarabandes, Gigues, Minuets and other Galanteries, composed for the mental recreation of art-lovers. First Part. Published by the author, 1731).

seen or heard. Any one who learned to play a few pieces
out of them well could make a great success with them"*.

The second part of the *Klavierübung*, consisting of the
Italian Concerto and the B minor partita, was published
in Nuremberg in 1735 by Christoph Weigel. Even Scheibe
could not help paying a tribute of admiration to the Italian
Concerto**. It is interesting to note that Bach got the
idea of the work from a sinfonia in Muffat's *Florilegium
primum* (1695). The similarity of the themes is too striking to be explained by mere chance: —

In 1739 the third part of the *Klavierübung* appeared.
It was intended to contain only organ works, — the preludes
on the catechism hymns; the four clavichord duets got
in by mistake. These organ pieces could be played, of
course, on the two-manual pedal-clavicembalo, which
was very popular at that time. How these great works
were received by organists is not recorded.

The fourth part of the *Klavierübung* was also published
in Nuremberg, not by Weigel, however, but by Balthasar
Schmidt, who was also Emmanuel's publisher. It contained the Goldberg Variations. Goldberg was the clavecinist of Count Kayserling, a patron of Bach, who acted
as Russian envoy at the Dresden Court. It was he who
procured Bach the appointment of Court Composer; at
any rate the diploma came through his hands. Goldberg
was a pupil of Friedemann, who was in Dresden at that
time. When he went to Leipzig with his master, which,

---

* Forkel, p. 50.
** See p. 183.

according to Forkel, often happened, he visited Bach to learn what he could from him.   Forkel gives the following account of the origin of the variations:

"Count Kayserling fell very ill and could not sleep at night. Goldberg, who lived with him, had on these occasions to spend the night in an adjoining room, so as to be able to play to him when sleepless. Once the Count said that he would like Bach to write some clavichord pieces for Goldberg, of a quiet and at the same time cheerful character, that would brighten him up a little on his sleepless nights. Bach thought the best thing for the purpose would be some variations, — a form which he had previously thought rather little of, by reason of the persistence of the same basic harmony throughout. .... The Count afterwards always called them *his* variations. He could not hear them often enough, and for a long time, whenever he had a sleepless night, it was "Dear Goldberg, play me one of my variations." Bach was perhaps never so well rewarded for any of his works as for this. The Count gave him a golden goblet, containing 100 louis d'or"*.

That Bach had no particular fondness for the variation form may be gathered from the fact that apart from the Goldberg set, the only variations he wrote were the youthful *Aria variata alla maniera italiana* (B. G. XXXVI, pp. 203—208).   In his organ music also he soon ceased to write variations on chorale melodies.

The theme of the Goldberg variations is found in the *Klavierbüchlein* of Anna Magdalena Bach (1725).   It is the Sarabande that follows the song "Bist du bei mir". It had been in existence at least ten years before he thought of writing variations on it.

The variations, however, are founded less on the theme itself than on its bass.   Over this Bach's imagination plays freely, and the work is in reality more a passacaglia worked out in chiaroscuro than a series of variations.

It is impossible to take to the work at a first hearing. We have to get to know it, and to understand the music of Bach's last period, in which the interest resides not so much in the charm of this or that melodic part, as in the

---

* Forkel, p. 54.

free and masterly working out of the ideas. When once
we arrive at this standpoint, we can savour the gentle,
consoling cheerfulness that gives such warmth to these
seemingly artificial pieces. In the last variation the cheerfulness becomes laughter of the merriest kind. Two folk-
songs disport themselves in it: —

Thus Bach in his old age returns to the quodlibet with which
his ancestors used to enjoy themselves so hugely in their
great family gatherings.

Of all Bach's works this comes the closest to the modern
pianoforte style. If their authorship were not known,
any one would take the penultimate and anti-penultimate
variations, even from the mere look of them on paper, to
be works of Beethoven's last period.

The Goldberg Variations, the Italian Concerto, and the
accompanying partita are written for the clavicembalo
with two keyboards. Even without a positive statement
to this effect any one would soon realise it in performance,
in the difficulty, for one keyboard, of the passages in which
the hands become entangled.

It is strange that Bach did not think of publishing some
of his other clavier works. The *Well-tempered Clavichord*
indeed, was out of the question; it was too large. A copy,
according to the prices of that day, would have cost at least
ten or fifteen thalers. Why, however, were the French

and the English suites not published? Perhaps because they did not strike him as sufficiently difficult and ingenious. As he could permit himself the trouble and luxury of an engraved issue only in a very limited degree, he preferred to expend them on works that would win him honour and recognition among professional musicians and connoisseurs. As compositions in those days, however, were valued less for their æsthetic qualities than for their ingenuity, it would not have benefited Bach to have published these simple suites.

Nevertheless it is a mistake to suppose that his other clavier works were not widely diffused. They were obtainable in manuscript copies. After 1720, indeed, there was scarcely a good German musician anywhere who did not possess at least one work of J. S. Bach. As early as 1717, in his book *Das beschützte Orchester*, Mattheson reckons the "celebrated Weimar organist, Herr Joh. Sebastian Bach", among the leading composers, on the ground of some works of his that he had seen.

Besides the seven partitas that appeared in the *Klavier-übung*, Bach wrote fifteen other suites, — the six French, the six English, and three smaller suites, that may have been sketches for the French*. It is not known how the French and English suites acquired these names. Even Forkel could give no precise information on the point**. He conjectures that the former were so called because they are written in the French style, and the latter "because

---

* The French and English suites are in B. G. XIII²; as the edition of 1863 was not based on the autographs, these works were re-issued in 1895 in Vol. XLV¹. The three youthful suites (in A minor, E flat major, and F major) are in Vol. XXXVI (1866). In the same volume are some fragments of suites and separate dance-pieces. The suite in E major (XLII, pp. 16 ff.) is an arrangement of some instrumental work. The authorship of the suite in B flat major (XLII, pp. 213 ff) and the "sarabande con partita" (XLII, pp. 221 ff.) is doubtful. The passacaglia in D minor (XLII, pp. 234 ff) is certainly not by Bach. It is by Christian Friedrich Witt (d. 1715).

** Forkel, p. 56.

the composer wrote them for an Englishman of quality,"
— which latter was certainly not the case. At a later date
an unsuccessful attempt was made to give the partitas
the title of "German suites".

The French suites figure, though not quite complete,
in the first *Klavierbüchlein* of Anna Magdalena Bach
(1722). There is also an autograph of them with the inscription: "Sex Suiten pur le Clavesin compossee par Mos:
J. S. Bach." The title of the autograph of the English
suites is also in French, but written more correctly. There
is a very valuable copy of the two collections of suites in
Gerber's hand-writing, made between 1725 and 1726,
when he was a pupil of Bach.

The French suites can be proved to be not later in date
than the Cöthen period. The English suites also, in all
likelihood, belong to the same time, though all the manuscripts and the copies that we have of them fall within
the first Leipzig period. In the first year of his work at
St. Thomas's, Bach had to write a new cantata for almost
every Sunday, so that he could have had little time for
other works.

The suite owes its origin to the pipers of the seventeenth
century, who used to string together various national
dances. The German clavichord players adopted the form
from them and developed it. The rule was that it should
consist of at least four pieces, — the allemande, the courante, the sarabande, and the gigue. The allemande is
in easy $4/4$ time, with a quaver or semiquaver up-beat;
the courante or corrente is in $3/2$ time, and is characterised
by its uninterrupted sequences of equal notes; the sarabande is a grave Spanish dance, also in $3/2$ time, the heavy
notes of which are surrounded by coquettish embellishments; the gigue as a rule goes evenly and rapidly, and may
be in all kinds of triple rhythms. It gets its name from
the gigue (ham, or gammon) — the satirical French name
for the older violins; thus a gigue really means a fiddler's
dance.

There was no reason for refusing admission to the suite to other dance forms that cropped up later. The French, especially Marchand and Couperin, made a point of introducing all possible dances. Their suites contain the gavotte, in $^2/_2$ time, with a half-beat up-take; the minuet, in simple triple rhythm; the passepied, a Breton dance similar to the minuet, which, under Louis XIV., made its way into the French ballet; the bourrée, in quick $^4/_4$ time, an angular dance originating in Auvergne. The French also incorporated into their suites the rondeau, the rigaudon, the polonaise, and even independent movements in no particular dance-form.

Bach takes all these rich suite-forms over from his French models, but preserves moderation where they run to extremes[*]. He follows tradition in placing the dances that were not originally part of the suite between the sarabande and the gigue, so that the latter forms the conclusion. He generally places the extraneous movements at the beginning. Thus the English suites open with preludes, and the great partitas in the *Klavierübung* with preludes, symphonies, fantasias, overtures, preambles and toccatas; the French suites, however, begin at once with the allemande.

Naturally some of these dances were somewhat altered in the clavier suite. The gigue, for example, which runs to considerable length in the suite, in its original dance-form consisted merely of two eight-bar phrases with repeats. The Italian composers as a rule retained only the metre and rhythm of the various dances, without troubling to preserve their essential character. The French were more scrupulous in this respect, and made a point of pursuing to its conclusion the rhythmical characteristic of each dance-form[**]. Bach goes still further; he always vitalises

---

[*] On the relation of Bach to the contemporary suite see Spitta II, 84 ff. A full history of the suite will be found in Weitzmann's *Geschichte der Klaviermusik*, 3rd edition by Max Seiffert I, 91 ff.
[**] See Spitta II, 84 ff.

the form, and gives each of the principal dance-forms a definite musical personality. For him the allemande represents vigorous but easy motion; the courante represents a measured haste, in which dignity and elegance go side by side; the sarabande represents a grave and majestic walk; in the gigue, the freest of all forms, the motion is quite fancy-free. He thus raises the suite-form to the plane of the highest art, while at the same time he preserves its primitive character as a collection of dance-pieces.

As with the organ music, so among the clavier works are a number which Bach wrote as teaching pieces for his sons and pupils. His clavier school consisted of the preludes for beginners, the two-part and three-part Inventions, and the *Well-tempered Clavichord*.

Of the preludes for beginners we have altogether eighteen.* Seven are in Friedemann's *Klavierbüchlein*; six more are contained in an old manuscript with the title, *Six Préludes à l'usage des Commençants composés par Jean Sébastien Bach:* they were published for the first time by Forkel**. The others have been handed down to us through pupils.

Even in these little works the overwhelming greatness of Bach is revealed. He merely meant to write a few simple exercises; what he actually wrote were compositions that no one forgets who has once played them, and to which the adult returns with ever new delight. Particularly captivating are the prelude in C minor (p. 119), with its dreamy arpeggio semiquavers; the clear-cut prelude in D major (p. 131); and the jubilant one in E major (p. 132), the intoxication of which must have been one of the richest youthful experiences of any one who thoroughly grasped it.

The title of the principal autograph of the Inventions and symphonies runs thus: "An honest guide, wherewith lovers of the clavier, and especially those anxious to learn,

---

* B. G. XXXVI (1886), pp. 118—127.
** See p. 54 of his book. These were the only six that Forkel knew.

are shown a clear method not only how to learn to play neatly in two parts, but further to play correctly and well in three obbligato parts; and at the same time not only to acquire good *inventiones* [ideas] but to work them out well; but above all to attain a cantabile style of playing, and in addition to get a strong taste for composition. Written by Joh. Seb. Bach, Hochf. Anhalt-Cöthen Kapellmeister. Anno Christi 1723."

Besides this autograph we possess two others, of an earlier date. Friedemann's *Klavierbüchlein*, begun in 1720, contains most of these compositions, but the title is different; instead of "Invention" we have "praeambulum", and instead of "symphony" we have "fantasia" *. When Bach copied them out again he altered the arrangement of the pieces; they still follow each other in the order of their keys, but to each invention he added the corresponding symphony, which is justified by the fact that the two-part and the three-part pieces, as is shown by certain thematic similarities, were, as a rule, written at the same time. In the definitive autograph he again distinguished, on didactic grounds, between two-part and three-part pieces. Here again the final work is a strict selection made by Bach himself from a large number of works of the same kind, relieved by a number of smaller pieces, — splinters, as it were, from the workshop**.

Bach's inability to settle upon the title was due to the absolute novelty of this kind of work. He abandons the binary song-form that was customary for small clavier pieces, and which he himself had used in the six preludes for beginners, and creates a new form of his own, marked by no external divisions, but giving free play to the natural development of the musical idea. The result was that his invention and manner of working became less melodic than thematic and "motival". The same principle would necessarily have led from the *da capo* aria to the freer

---

* See B. G. XLV, pp. 213ff.
** Compare Spitta II, 58 ff.

song-form. Here, however, he never quite won his freedom, though he often seems on the way to it.

The title "Invention" for a clavier piece seems not to have been devised by Bach himself, as was formerly thought, but to have been derived from some unknown composer whose works he copied out at that time for his sons *. He might just as well have called all the pieces simply "preludes"; but he thought this title too general and not sufficiently characteristic for the strict contrapuntal working-out that he had in view.

The Inventions are written not for the clavicembalo but for the clavichord, which at that time was called simply the "clavier". It was only on this instrument that the "cantabile style" of playing was possible that Bach had chiefly in his mind when writing them. Thus in the history of pianoforte playing the Inventions and symphonies are a protest against the dulcimer-like tinkling that was the vogue at that time — and not only at that time. We feel in every bar of these pieces that the idea at the root of them has been the singing and modulatory capacity of the instrument.

When Bach penned the title and expressed the hope that these pieces would give players a strong taste for composition, he could not anticipate how amply his wish would be realised. If the average modern musician, in spite of his possessing less theoretical knowledge of the technique of composition than those of Bach's day, at any rate has a clearer sense of the distinction between true and false art, it is primarily due to these little works of Bach. The child who has once practised them, no matter how mechanically, has acquired a perception of part-writing that he will never lose. He will always instinctively look for the same masterly weaving of the voices in every other piece of music, and feel the poverty of the music where this is lacking. And any one who has studied

---

* Spitta II, 659, 660.

the pieces thoroughly, in their formal and æsthetic aspects, under a capable teacher, has henceforth a criterion of true art, whether he himself becomes a composer or, as in the majority of cases, simply an executant. In any case Bach's title, with its evident desire that clavier study should not be an end in itself but an introduction to composition, is of significance to piano teachers today.

These outwardly similar compositions fall into certain particular types, which are distinguished from each other according as the development of the piece is purely formal or conditioned by an imperative dramatic idea. The first type is represented by the well-known F major Invention, the other by the E minor and F minor symphonies. Closely considered, however, each of these works is a masterpiece *sui generis*, with no exact analogue among the others. Only an infinitely fertile mind could venture to write thirty little pieces of the same style and the same compass, and, without the least effort, make each of them absolutely different from the rest. In face of this inconceivable fertility it seems almost a superfluous question whether any other of the great composers has had an inventive faculty so infinite as Bach's.

The two Parts of the *Well-tempered Clavichord* belong to widely separated periods*. The first was finished in 1722, as appears from the dating of the autograph by Bach himself; the second was compiled in 1744, as we learn from the Hamburg organist Schwenke, who in 1781 made a copy of it from an autograph (now lost) belonging to Emmanuel, the title-page of which bore the date 1744.

In Friedemann's *Klavierbüchlein* of 1720 are found eleven preludes from the First Part, among them the one in C major. Bach's revisions of this and three others (in C minor, D minor, and E minor) made it probable that the majority of the pieces of the *Well-tempered Clavier* did not achieve their present perfection at the first stroke,

---

* B. G. XIV (1866).

but were continually worked over by the composer with a view to giving them a form that would satisfy him.

Gerber, in his Dictionary, says that Bach composed the First Part of the *Well-tempered Clavichord* at a place where time hung heavily on his hands and no musical instrument was available. There may be some truth in this. Gerber's father had been Bach's pupil in the early Leipzig years, so that the tradition may quite well be based on some remark of Bach's, especially as we know that Gerber was studying the *Well-tempered Clavichord* at that time, and Bach himself played it to him thrice*. Bach may well have been in such a situation during some journey with Prince Leopold of Cöthen, when the small portable clavier that figures in the list of the Court instruments would be left behind**. The tradition is at any rate correct to this extent, that the majority of pieces in the *Well-tempered Clavichord* were written in a relatively short time. This manner of production was indeed characteristic of Bach. The Second Part was written after he had practically finished with cantata writing.

A number of preludes and fugues, however, existed for some time before Bach conceived the idea of a collection. This holds good for the Second Part no less than for the First. In both there are pieces which, in their original form, really go back almost to the composer's earliest years. Any one thoroughly conversant with Bach will gradually discover for himself which pieces belong to this category. He will at once see, for example, that of the preludes of the First Part, those in C minor and B flat major do not show the same maturity as most of the others. That the A minor fugue from the same Part is a youthful

---

* The tradition of the origin of the First Part of the *Well-tempered Clavichord* is given on p. 90 of the first volume of the Dictionary, and the account of Bach's teaching of Gerber the elder on pp. 490 ff. of the same volume.

** As a rule the prince took with him, when travelling, a complete sextet of his chamber musicians. See Bunge, *J. S. Bachs Kapelle zu Cöthen*, in the *Bach-Jahrbuch* for 1905, pp. 27 and 42.

work is shewn not only by a certain thematic looseness and lack of design, but also by the fact that it is evidently written for the pedal clavicembalo. The final note in the bass, prolonged through five bars, cannot be sustained by the hands alone, but needs the pedal, as is often the case in the early works. Otherwise the *Well-tempered Clavichord*, like the Inventions and the symphonies, is designed primarily for the clavichord, not for the clavicembalo. Bach himself does not appear to have called the 1744 collection the Second Part of the *Well-tempered Clavichord*, but simply "Twenty-four new preludes and fugues".

He inscribed the work completed in Cöthen the *Well-tempered Clavichord* by way of celebrating a victory that gave the musical world of that day a satisfaction which we can easily comprehend. On the old keyed instruments it had become impossible to play in all keys, since the fifths and thirds were tuned naturally, according to the absolute intervals given by the divisions of the string. By this method each separate key was made quite true; the others, however, were more or less out of tune, the thirds and fifths that were right for their own key not agreeing among each other. So a plan had to be found for tuning fifths and thirds not absolutely but relatively, — to "temper" them in such a way that though not quite true in any one key they would be bearable in all. The question had really become acute in the sixteenth century, when the new custom arose of allotting a separate string to each note on the clavichord; previously the same string had been used for several notes, the tangents dividing the string into the proper length for the desired tone. The organ also imperatively demanded a tempered tuning.

The question occupied the attention of the Italians Giuseppe Zarlino (1558) and Pietro Aron (1529)*. At a later date the Halberstadt organ builder Andreas Werkmeister (1645—1706) hit upon a method of tuning that

---

* See the B. G. XIV, p. 25 of the preface; and the chapter on this question in Weitzmann-Seiffert's *Geschichte des Klavierspiels.*

still holds good in principle. He divided the octave into twelve equal semitones, none of which was quite true. His treatise on Musical Temperament appeared in 1691. The problem was solved; henceforth composers could write in all keys. A fairly long time elapsed, however, before all the keys hitherto avoided came into practical use. The celebrated theoretician Heinichen, in his treatise on thorough-bass, published in 1728, — i. e. six years after the origin of Bach's work — confessed that people seldom wrote in B major and A flat major, and practically never in F sharp major and C sharp major*; which shows that he did not know Bach's collection of preludes and fugues.

At one time it looked as if Bach were to be deprived of the honour of having written the first *Well-tempered Clavichord*. In 1880 there came to light a manuscript of one Bernhard Christian Weber, organist at Tennstedt, bearing a very similar title to that of Bach's work, and with the date "1689" in red crayon. The excitement, however, was soon allayed by Wilhelm Tappert's demonstration that the manuscript was not the work of a forerunner but of a mediocre imitator of the middle of the eighteenth century. If any one can be regarded as a forerunner of Bach it is Mattheson, who, in his *Organistenprobe* (1719), in the article on thorough-bass, advocated the employment of all keys and gave two examples, a difficult one and an easy one, in each**. When this work appeared, however, Bach was already engaged upon the *Well-tempered Clavichord*.

Bach found an imitator in his admirer Georg Andreas Sorge (1703—1788) the Lobenstein organist, who also wrote preludes and fugues in all the twenty-four keys,

---

* See Spitta II, 162. To understand the problem of the twelve equal semitone system we must remember that the octaves had all to be kept true, while the intervals constituting them had to be tempered.
** See Wilhelm Tappert's *Das Wohltemperierte Klavier*, in Eitner's *Monatshefte für Musikgeschichte*, 1899, pp. 123 ff., for an examination of all the pre-Bachian works that claim to make use of all the twenty-four keys.

and issued the work in 1738 through Bach's publisher, Balthasar Schmidt of Nuremberg*.

For a long time it was taken for granted that the autograph of the Second Part of the *Well-tempered Clavichord* was lost. In the middle of the eighteen-nineties Sir George Grove and Ebenezer Prout announced that it still existed and had just passed from private hands into the possession of the British Museum. It had come to England through Muzio Clementi, who had acquired it in some unknown way; after his death it had been bought by a Mr. Emett, at whose house Mendelssohn saw it in 1842 and recognised it as a genuine autograph; his daughter sold it to her friend Miss Eliza Wesley, who bequeathed it to the British Museum on her death in 1895. It is not the original autograph, but a copy carefully made by Bach himself, in which he had continued each prelude and fugue on a separate sheet in such a way that he did not need to turn over when playing it. Unfortunately three of these leaves are lost**.

We have several autographs of the First Part of the *Well-tempered Clavichord.* For each of his two elder sons Bach himself wrote out the work with the utmost care. Friedemann gave his copy to Müller, the cathedral organist at Brunswick, with whom he sometimes stayed after he had given up his post at Halle; it is now in the Berlin Royal Library. Emmanuel's copy was sold in 1802 by his daughter to the Zürich publisher Nägeli, and is presumably still in private hands in that city***. Another auto-

---

* Spitta II, 671 (German edition).

** For a history and description of this autograph see O. Taubmann's *Ein Autograph des zweiten Teils von Bachs Wohltemperierten Klavier*, in the *Allgemeine Musikzeitung* for 1896, (which gives the English authorities), and Alfred Dörffel's remarks in the preface to the B. G. XLV (1895), pp. 68—72.

*** This autograph was not available for the B. G. edition of the *Well-tempered Clavichord.* See Spitta II, 665 ff. In 1885 it belonged to Herr Stadtrat Hagenbuch, president of the Allgemeine Musikgesellschaft of Zürich. Dörffel, who had the opportunity of examining it, regarded it as a fairly rough copy. See his preface to B. G. XLV, pp. 65 ff.

graph of the year 1722 was once in the possession of a
Herr Volkmann, of Pesth, where, in the middle of the
eighteen-forties, it was involved in an inundation of the
Danube, traces of which it still bears. It is called, after
a later owner, the Wagener autograph *.

There was one copyist in particular who thought it his
duty to improve Bach, and tried to do so in every prelude
and fugue in both Parts. His chief concern was to rid
them of all unnecessary complexity, and to give them
the form that Bach himself would have conferred on them
had he lived in another epoch than that of the "Zopf"
(pigtail) and had a more refined taste. He transforms,
for example, the D major fugue of the First Part in this
way —

Forkel had a number of the preludes and fugues from
each part in a still more drastically curtailed form. It
seems almost incredible that he, and after him the Bach
biographers Hilgenfeldt and Bitter, should have regarded
these versions as the authentic ones, and energetically maintained their superiority over those generally accepted **.
The children of Bach's muse slink along in the most miserable shapes, — they are merely skin and bones; and the

* The Imperial Library at Vienna possesses no autograph of
the *Well-tempered Clavichord*, as might be supposed from a somewhat inaccurate article by Bunge in the *Bachjahrbuch* for 1905
(p 32).
** Both these redactions are now in the Berlin Royal Library.
The Forkel form of the C major prelude from the First Part is given
in the supplement to B. G. XIV. It contains only twenty-four
bars instead of thirty-five. It should further be noted that bar 24
(G in the bass), as it is given in most editions, is an error. It is an
interpolation derived from Schwenke's copy of 1781, which is un-
trustworthy in other respects.

man who knew Bach's sons, who had heard them play, and in whom one might presuppose some breath of the Bach spirit, fell a victim to this clumsy deception! Even Zelter had to try his hand at simplifying Bach. So great was the æsthetic suspicion with which people at that time regarded the works of the musical rococo period, even when they bore the name of Bach!

The title of the First Part runs thus in the autograph: —

"The Well-tempered Clavier, or preludes and fugues in all tones and semitones, both with the *tertiam majorem* or Ut, Re, Mi, and the *tertiam minorem* or Re, Mi, Fa. For the profit and use of young musicians desirous of knowledge, as also of those who are already skilled in this *studio*, especially by way of pastime; set out and composed by Johann Sebastian Bach, Kapellmeister to the Grand Duke of Anhalt-Cöthen and Director of his chamber music. Anno 1722."

The first edition of the *Well-tempered Clavichord* was issued by the Englishman Kollmann in 1799*; in the following year the work was issued simultaneously by Nägeli of Zürich and Simrock of Bonn. In the latter edition the Second Part comes before the first**. The first Peters edition appeared in 1801. Breitkopf and Härtel did not bring it out until 1819. The contemporary Paris and London editions are only pirated reprints of the Nägeli version. The first satisfactory text was that of Kroll in the B. G. edition (XIV, 1866)***.

---

* The circle of Kollmann and Wesley was warmly enthusiastic for Bach. Wesley called him simply "The Man". Bach-recitals were given, and a subscription opened for a complete English edition of his works. See Kretzschmar's preface to B. G. XLVI, p. 24. In 1812 Kollmann published "An Analysis of S. Bach's Preludes and Fugues" in the *Quarterly Musical Register*.

** The second Peters edition (1837) was edited by Czerny, and the third (1862/3) by Kroll.

*** Among other editions that of Bischoff, published by Steingräber, calls for special mention. The same firm also published Stade's thoughtful and searching analyses of the fugues of the

The *Well-tempered Clavichord* is one of those works by
which we can measure the progress of artistic culture from
one generation to another. When Rochlitz met with these
preludes and fugues at the beginning of the nineteenth
century, only a few of them really appealed to him. He
placed a tick against these, and was astonished to find
how the number of these ticks increased as he played the
works*. If some one had told this first of Bach prophets
that in another hundred years every musically-minded
man would have regarded each piece in the collection as
perfectly easy to comprehend, he would hardly have
believed it.

The fact that the work today has become common
property may console us for the other fact that an analysis
of it is almost as impossible as it is to depict a wood by
enumerating the trees and describing their appearance.
We can only repeat again and again — take them and
play them and penetrate into this world for yourself.
Aesthetic elucidation of any kind must necessarily be superficial here. What so fascinates us in the work is not the
form or the build of the piece, but the world-view that is
mirrored in it. It is not so much that we enjoy the *Well-
tempered Clavichord* as that we are edified by it. Joy,
sorrow, tears, lamentation, laughter — to all these it gives
voice, but in such a way that we are transported from the
world of unrest to a world of peace, and see reality in a
new way, as if we were sitting by a mountain lake and

Well-tempered Clavichord. We may mention also Carl von Bruyck's
Technische und ästhetische Analysen des Wohltemperierten Klaviers
(Breitkopf and Härtel, 2nd Edition 1889), Jadassohn's *Erläute-
rungen zu ausgewählten Fugen aus J. S. Bachs Wohltemperierten
Klavier,* (the Supplement to his *Lehrbuch des Kanons und der
Fuge,* Leipzig, 1888); Hugo Riemann's *Analyse des Wohltemperierten Klaviers und der Kunst der Fuge* (Leipzig, 1890, 1891, 1894);
E. von Stockhausen's *Die harmonische Grundlage von zwölf Fugen
aus J. S. Bachs Wohltemperiertem Klavier* (Leipzig, W. Weber);
and *Wie studiert man J. S. Bachs Wohltemperiertes Klavier?*, in
the *Neue Musikzeitung,* 1904.
    * See ante, p. 237.

contemplating hills and woods and clouds in the tranquil
and fathomless water.

Nowhere so well as in the *Well-tempered Clavichord* are
we made to realise that art was Bach's religion. He does
not depict natural soul-states, like Beethoven in his sonatas,
no striving and struggling towards a goal, but the reality
of life felt by a spirit always conscious of being superior
to life, a spirit in which the most contradictory emotions,
wildest grief and exuberant cheerfulness, are simply phases
of a fundamental superiority of soul. It is this that gives
the same transfigured air to the sorrow-laden E flat minor
prelude of the First Part and the care-free, volatile prelude
in G major in the Second Part. Whoever has once felt
this wonderful tranquility has comprehended the mysterious spirit that has here expressed all it knew and felt
of life in the secret language of tone, and will render Bach
the thanks we render only to the great souls to whom it
is given to reconcile men with life and bring them peace.

Half a dozen connected preludes and fugues and a dozen
isolated fugues remained over after the compilation of
the *Well-tempered Clavichord*, Bach apparently not thinking them important enough to be included in that collec-
tion*. Two of them, in A major and B minor respectively,
are based on themes by Albinoni**.

Other preludes and fugues were too large and too self-
subsistent for it to be possible to include them in a collection. Of this kind are the fantasia and fugue in A minor***
and the prelude and fugue in the same key†, which are
among the grandest things in piano literature. Later on,
Bach rearranged the prelude and the fugue, with consummate technique, as a concerto for flute, violin and

---

* These preludes and fugues will be found in B. G. XXXVI;
No. 12 is not by J. S. Bach, but by Johann Christoph Bach of
Eisenach.

** B. G. XXXVI, pp. 173 ff. and 178 ff.

*** B. G. XXXVI, p. 81 ff.

† B. G. XXXVI, p. 91 ff.

clavier with orchestral accompaniment, adding, by way of
adagio, an expanded version of the middle movement of
the third organ sonata*.   The prelude begins thus —

and the fugue thus —

He notates the later, in the orchestral concerto, in $^4/_4$
time, and combines it with a broad and free tutti. This
A minor prelude and fugue probably belong, in their
original form, to the Cöthen period; they certainly existed
as early as 1725**.   It was perhaps rearranged as an
orchestral concerto at the beginning of the thirties, when
Bach conducted the performances of the Telemann Musical
Society and had need of concerted pieces.

The fugue in A minor, with its introduction of arpeggio
chords, would perhaps be better described as a fugal fantasia.   The spirited and brilliant work contains no fewer
than one hundred and ninety-eight bars***.

The Chromatic Fantasia and Fugue† was from the first
one of the most popular of Bach's clavier works, as is proved
by the many manuscript copies of it that we possess, dating
from his own and from later times.   The first is found
in a volume bearing the date 1730.   The work, however,
is much older than this; it probably dates from the same
epoch — 1720 — as the great G minor organ fantasia.
It has a kind of inner affinity with this work; not only

---

* The concerto will be found in B. G. XVII, p. 223 ff.
** This date appears on a manuscript copy of Peter Kellner's.
*** B. G. III, p. 334 ff. See also *ante*, p. 271, and Oppel in the
Bachjahrbuch for 1906, pp. 74—78.
† B. G. XXXVI (1886), p. 71 ff.

does the same peculiar fire burn in each of them, but in both the recitative style is carried over into an instrumental medium.

In the C minor fantasia Bach employs the Neapolitan clavier style that had been founded by Alessandro and Domenico Scarlatti, one of the main effects of which consisted in the crossing of the hands*. Bach had already made use of this effect in the gigue in the B flat major suite of the First Part of the *Klavierübung*. The C minor fantasia may belong to the same period as the Italian concerto; perhaps it was written somewhat later, about the end of the thirties. The autograph which we possess points to this period. A fugue was appended to this fantasia, but the autograph unfortunately gives only the first forty-seven bars of this; they are rich in promise**. This does not imply that Bach left it unfinished. It certainly lay before him complete when he made the copy we now have of the C minor fantasia; only he did not get as far as the copying of the whole fugue. By this accident it is lost to us. This is doubly regrettable because, judging by the commencement of it, it was a very individual fugue, more in the form of a fantasia. The theme is constructed on one of those chromatic sequences that we so often meet with in Bach's fugues. It runs thus —

Four larger works of Bach for the clavier, in several movements, have come down to us in the form of clavier sonatas. Two of these, however, must be deducted, — those in A minor and C major — Spitta having discovered in 1881 that they are only arrangements and amplifications

---

of instrumental pieces from Adam Reinken's *Hortus musicus* *.

The D minor sonata is only a transcription for the clavier of the second sonata for solo violin **. The sonata in D major is therefore the only original composition for the clavier ***. In this, however, there is hardly any originality, the youthful composer having written it under the influence of Kuhnau's clavier sonatas. In the final fugue he amuses himself by imitating the cackling of a hen, working out this theme —

and a counter theme —

in merry if not very witty style. A note in Italian tells us what the piece is meant to represent.

Seven clavier compositions in several movements are designated "toccatas". They might with equal propriety have been called sonatas. At that time every piece in several movements for a keyed instrument could be called a toccata, without the title implying anything as to its special form. Of these seven toccatas, five — those in D major, D minor, E minor, G minor and G major —

* These two sonatas are given in B. G. XLII, pp. 29 ff. and 42 ff. In the first edition of his book, Spitta thought they were particularly characteristic of Bach. The essay in which he gives the real facts will be found in his *Musikgeschichtliche Aufsätze* (Berlin, 1894) p. 111 ff. Reinken's *Hortus musicus* has since then been brought out by Riemsdijk. See also *ante*, p. 194; [and Spitta's *Bach* I, 429, 430. TR.]

** B. G. XLII, p. 3 ff. The sonata for solo violin (B. G. XXVII¹, p. 24 ff.) is in A minor.

*** B. G. XXXVI, p. 19 ff. There is another piece in A minor (XLV, p. 168 ff.) called a sonata. It may be an arrangement of some orchestral piece.

belong to the first Weimar period*; the other two — in F sharp minor and C minor — seem to have been composed somewhat later**. As a whole the G minor toccata is the most interesting. The melancholy adagios of the D minor and the G major toccatas are touching in their simplicity. In the two later toccatas the total impression is somewhat weakened by the lack of finish in the design. In the F sharp minor toccata we find already the descending chromatic theme that later dominates the *Crucifixus* of the B minor Mass. It is here in the following form —

Quite *sui generis* is a "capriccio" in B flat major, probably written in Arnstadt in honour of Bach's second brother Johann Jacob***, who had enlisted as oboist in the Swedish guard when Charles XII was in Poland in 1704. The nineteen-year old Johann Sebastian may have written the *Capriccio sopra la lontananza del suo fratello dilettissimo* ("Capriccio on the departure of his beloved brother") for the family leave-taking. It begins with an arioso, inscribed "Cajoleries of his friends, who try to deter him from his journey"; then comes an andante, meant to be "a representation of the diverse accidents that may befall him in foreign lands"; the "general lamentation of his friends" is depicted in a passacaglia-like adagissimo on a descending chromatic theme suggesting that of the *Crucifixus* in the B minor Mass; in the following movement "the friends, seeing that it cannot be otherwise, come

---

* B. G. XXXVI, p. 26 ff. The commencement of the toccata in D major reminds us of the organ work in the same key (Peters IV, No. 3). The toccata in A major (B. G. XLII, p. 243 ff.) is not by Bach, but by Purcell.

** B. G. III, pp. 311 ff. and 322 ff.

*** B. G. XXXVI, pp. 190—196. On the æsthetic significance of this work see the chapter on "Word and Tone in Bach".

and say farewell"; thereupon comes the "Aria of the Postilion"; and a "fugue in imitation of the postilion's horn-
call" ends the delightful work, that follows in the footsteps
of Kuhnau's *Biblical histories represented in clavier sonatas*,
published four years earlier (1700).

A capriccio in E major, that probably belongs to the
same period, is not so interesting. It may have been written
in honour of his eldest brother, Johann Christoph Bach of
Ohrdruf, by whom the composer was brought up*.

Among the clavier pieces are some that Bach designed
also for the lute, and were even, perhaps, written in the
first place for that instrument**. This is the case with the
little prelude in C minor —

Recent researches show that the prelude in E flat major
(B. G. XLV, p. 141), the suite in E minor (B. G. XLV,
p. 149 ff.), that in E major (B. G. XLII, p. 16 ff.), and that
in C minor (B. G. XLV, p. 156 ff.) are also clavier arrangements of compositions for the lute; the fugue of the G minor
sonata for solo violin and the *Suite discordable* for violoncello solo have also come down to us in lute tablature.
The three Bach partitas for lute mentioned in Breitkopf's
catalogue of 1761 are thus not lost, as was almost universally supposed. We may therefore probably answer
in the affirmative the question whether Bach himself
played the lute.

---

* B. G. XXXVI, pp. 197—212.

** The following remarks are based on Wilhelm Tappert's *Se-
bastian Bachs Kompositionen für die Laute*, Berlin, 1901 (reprinted
from the *Redende Künste*, 6th year, Nos. 36—40). In this essay
the author condemns the editors of the B. G. edition for not having
issued the lute compositions separately. His reproof, however, is
only partly justified.

CHAPTER XVI.

THE PERFORMANCE OF THE CLAVIER WORKS.

The ordinary player of Bach finds the ornamentation one of the greatest difficulties. It is a book with seven seals to him. In reality the question is by no means so complicated as it appears at first sight*.

We must start from the explanations which Bach himself gives on the third page of Friedemann's *Klavierbüchlein* (1720), under the heading "Explanation of divers signs, showing how to play certain ornaments neatly". Bach elucidates each sign by writing out in full the manner of playing it, thus —

* On the question of Bach's ornamentation see the following: Rust, Preface to B. G. VII; Franz Kroll, Preface to the *Well-tempered Clavichord*, B. G. XIV; Edward Dannreuther, *Musical Ornamentation*, I, pp. 161—210; H. Ehrlich, *Die Ornamentik in J. S. Bachs Klavierwerken* (Steingräber) dealing mostly with the suites; H. Schenker, *Ein Beitrag zur Ornamentik* (Universal Edition, Vienna); Klee, *Die Ornamentik der klassischen Klaviermusik* (Breitkopf and Härtel); Germer, *Die musikalische Ornamentik* (Hug, Leipzig, 3rd ed. 1899). See also Bischoff's remarks in his edition of Bach's clavier works (Steingräber), and the excellent elucidations of the ornaments in Ricordi's edition.

In addition there is the essay on "Manieren" (ornaments) in Carl Philipp Emmanuel Bach's *Versuch über die wahre Art das Klavier zu spielen* ("Essay on the true way of playing the clavier")*.

The main rules to be observed are the following: —

1. Bach indicates the trill simply by the signs t, tr-, ⌁⌁, ⌁, without specifying every time the particular manner or duration of it. As a rule it occupies the whole or the greater part of the note-value.

2. The trill begins, as a rule, with the upper accessory note, and only in exceptional cases with the principal note. In long trills it is desirable first of all to linger a moment on the principal note, and then begin the trill with the adjoining note, especially where a movement or a theme — see, e. g., the F sharp major fugue in the Second Part of the *Well-tempered Clavichord* — commences with a trill, or when the upper note has just been struck.

3. The Bach trill is further distinguished from the modern trill by the fact that it must be played much more slowly. It is spoiled by being taken quickly. We must bear in mind that the sign ⌁ over a quaver signifies nothing more than that it must be decomposed into two pairs of easy demi-semiquavers; in the same way a crotchet, if the tempo be somewhat fast, will be simply split up into two pairs of semiquavers.

---

* Berlin 1753—1762. Part I, 2nd edition, 1759, pp. 45—100. Daniel Gottlob Türk's *Klavierschule* (1789) is also very valuable in this connection (2nd edition, Leipzig-Halle, 1802, pp. 232—369).

The ornament is best realised when we play it with almost an exaggerated deliberation.

4. If the succeeding note is a descending second, then the sign ∿, as a rule, indicates not an ordinary trill but a *Pralltriller*. This must be carefully observed.

Bach writes the trill with a *Nachschlag* (after-beat) thus ∿ ∿, conceiving it as a trill with a mordent. The downward and upward *Vorschlag* (preliminary grace-note) are denoted by crooks of a similar kind but reverse direction ∿ and ∿. Trills with *Vorschlag* and *Nachschlag* (double cadence and mordent) have both signs, thus, ∿ or ∿. The manner of performance is explained by Bach himself in the above-mentioned examples in Friedemann's *Klavierbüchlein*. According to Emmanuel, long trills must always have a *Nachschlag*; but this is dispensed with when several trills follow each other. The sign ∿ before a descending second thus signifies a *Pralltriller*, i. e. a broken trill; it must be played much faster than the ordinary trill. The final note of it must, to use Emmanuel's expression, be "filliped"; by which he means that the key must be struck quickly, and then jerked up again by an equally rapid drawing inwards of the point of the finger, which gives the note a very marked accent. Thus: —

Partita IV: Aria.

In the case of a practised player, Emmanuel recommends a prolongation of this *Pralltriller* by one or two extra notes.

His view of the *Pralltriller* is that it is simply a very rapid trill, of longer or shorter duration, which is suddenly cut short on the staccato main note in such a way that the whole purpose of the trill seemed to be merely the throwing of a weightier accent on this note.

The mordent also, denoted thus ∿, is an interrupted trill, in which it is less a matter of the number of notes trilled than of throwing the accent on the main note thaf cuts the trill short. Unlike the *Pralltriller*, it is not limited to any particular situation. It takes the next note below, and is thus, as it were, the inverse of the *Pralltriller*. Both, in Emmanuel's phrase, "glide into the second, the mordent above, the *Pralltriller* below".

We may distinguish two chief forms of the mordent, a short and a long. The latter has generally two constituent notes. It can also be represented by the prolonged sign ⌁. Mordents have a preference for the major second.

French Suite: Sarabande in E flat major.

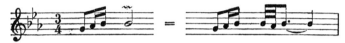

The turn in Bach's music, denoted thus ∿, must as a rule be played in four equal notes, in accordance with the note in Friedemann's book. A longer duration may, however, be given to the principal note if the tempo is not too quick to allow of this. Thus —

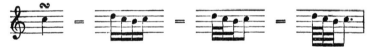

The *Vorschläge* (appoggiature), indicated by slurs or small notes, are sometimes long, sometimes short. In each case, however, the accent falls on them, not on the principal note. The latter is tied with them and struck lightly: Emmanuel calls this the *Abzug* (pulling off).

If the *Vorschlag* is long, it takes half the value of the following note, if equal division is possible; if not, two-thirds fall to the *Vorschlag*, thus —

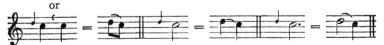

This rule, however, is not to be rigorously adhered to, but must be interpreted with reasonable regard to the requirements of the rhythm at the moment. The *Vorschlag*

before a long note is generally long, and that before a short or passing note is generally short. Yet here again everything depends upon the position and the significance of the note. According to Emmanuel, a *Vorschlag* that takes the interval of a third is always short, even before a long note. The examples are very instructive in which the long and the short *Vorschläge* are met with in the same work, as in the sinfonia in E flat major and the sarabande from the partita in G major. Here the *Vorschläge* on the second and third beats of the bar are best rendered short, and those on the first beat long. Thus: —

Sinfonia in E flat.

To be played:

Partita V: Sarabande.

To be played:

The more we study the nature of the Bach *Vorschlag*, the more we see that the actual note-values are a matter of indifference, and that the real questions are the weight and the energy of the accents. As he always writes the accent as an abbreviation of the note, such passages as these —

only attest that the first note must have a strong accent, while the second must be tied to it and have a diminuendo. The time-values of the notes must be as if written thus —

Conversely, quavers or semiquavers grouped in pairs must always be played in such a way that the second is only a kind of after-breath of the first, and sustained for only a fraction of its time-value. The tie is thus simply an accent-mark.

The *Nachschlag*, indicated by a crook appended to the note or by small notes, is always short, and must merge into the note that follows. Thus when Bach writes —

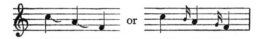

it must be played as if written thus —

When, as in the courante of the first partita, he writes —

this is merely the old, inexact method of notation for —

All through his work we find him using the dot in the old way, that was more summary than exact.

These explanations of Bach's "manieren" can only be regarded as general rules for the average case. If the ornaments accumulate, we soon exhaust the art of explanation, and are thrown back upon our sense of natural euphony as the last authority. This is also Philipp Emmanuel's view. After pursuing the casuistry of the rendering of ornaments into its final subtleties, in the end he submits the decision to artistic feeling, and so disowns the scholasticism at which he has been so seriously labouring all the time. Any one who has made himself familiar with the fundamental principles of Bach's ornamentation will find, by a little reflection, a satisfactory solution of the difficult rhythmical and tonal problems involved. He must always bear in mind that the reason for the ornaments being indicated by signs, instead of written out in notes, is that he may have a certain freedom in the embellishment of the design. If we can get out of some of the beaten tracks of modern piano playing, and acquire a sense of the formal principles underlying the old ornamentation, we shall have achieved a good deal. The question of whether we shall ever agree upon an interpretation of the numerous ornaments in the aria of the Goldberg variations will then be nearer a satisfactory answer*.

Closely considered, the whole system of ornamentation of that epoch indicates the partial surrender of the composer to the virtuoso, who wanted to make his own effect by adding freely to the music. During the last century and a half we have slowly moved away from this conception of the rôle of the executant artist. The first to set his face against it was Bach himself. He could not combat his critic Scheibe's reproach that he left nothing to the player, but wrote out in full what had been formerly indicated by signs**. The reproach is just. As a matter of fact Bach banishes ornaments from his music. In the *Well-tempered Clavichord* we practically never meet with them; even a bravura piece like the Italian Concerto is almost destitute of them. In his vocal music, again, they are almost wholly

---

* Dannreuther (I, 202—204) suggests one interpretation of the aria.

** See *ante*, p. 180.

dispensed with. His music certainly seemed bare to his contemporaries. Only in the *galant* genre, the suite, does he allot the ornaments a rôle which, however, is very trifling in comparison with what was customary at the time. There is thus a certain irony in the fact that the small amount of ornamentation in his work should give such trouble to the average player of today. This is, however, his own fault, not Bach's. Any one who will devote four or five hours to getting a clear idea of the main points here discussed will find that the works have lost their terrors for him, and in the end he will find these "manieren" a source of pleasure.

The question whether our modern piano is the right piano for Bach does not as yet occupy the general public very seriously, as it can form no conception of the instruments Bach used. In more expert circles, however, the question is already being debated with some heat.

What would be Bach's attitude towards the modern piano? Exactly the same as towards the modern organ. He would hail with enthusiasm the perfection of its mechanism, but not be particularly enchanted with its tone qualities. Sebastian Erard's invention in 1823 of the repetition action made possible on the hammer-clavier the finely gradated touch that caused Bach to prefer the weak clavichord to the full-toned cembalo. Henceforth, however, it was towards greatly increased strength of tone that attempts to perfect the piano were directed. The more powerful the tone became, the duller became the *timbre*, so that the piano of today no longer suggests in any way the tone of the instrument of Bach's time, — the result of substituting an iron resonance for the clear and bright wood resonance.

The duller the *timbre* of an instrument, the less suitable is it for polyphonic playing, in which each voice must stand out clearly from the others, and be always perceptible by the hearer without effort. How unsatisfactory our piano is in music with bold obbligato parts, like those of Bach, only becomes evident after we have heard a few preludes and fugues on a good clavichord or clavicembalo. The clavichord is a string quartet in miniature; every detail comes out lucidly on it. On the cembalo every melodic line is quite clear, the plucked tone having a much sharper quality than that of the modern piano.

Whether, however, it is advisable to posit a return to the old instruments as imperative for the true enjoyment of Bach's clavier music is doubtful. The clavichord is put out of court at once, for we could never again accustom ourselves to so weak a tone. It is otherwise with the cembalo. The charm of its sparkling and rustling tone is not so easily resisted, and the variety of tone that it permits, by means of change of keyboards, coupling, uncoupling, and octave coupling, almost makes us forget that no nuance of tone is possible on it. The bass part too, comes out more clearly and beautifully on the cembalo than on any other instrument. Any one who has heard Frau Wanda Landowska play the Italian Concerto on her wonderful Pleyel clavecin finds it hard to understand how it could ever again be played on a modern piano*.

But even in a quite small concert room the cembalo fanatic's enthusiasm has to contend against the unfortunate fact that at a distance of about twenty-five feet the tone that is so rustling when heard at close quarters becomes somewhat feeble and tremulous. Nor do all Bach's works sound equally well on the cembalo. It is best for pieces of unbroken and uniform motion, those that, like the C major prelude of the Second Part of the *Well-tempered Clavichord*, consist of arpeggio-like broken chords, and particularly those in pure two-part form, like the A minor prelude from the Second Part of the *Well-tempered Clavichord*. On the other hand the abruptness of its tone and its inability

---

* See also Richard Buchmayer's article on *Cembalo oder Piano-forte*, in the *Bachjahrbuch* for 1908, pp. 64—93. In Germany Hirl (Berlin) and Rehbock (Duisburg) particularly devote themselves to making cembalos.

to sustain a note make it unsuitable for music that demands a singing quality of tone. The reconstructed cembalo thus seems better fitted for Bach's music in private circles and for certain of his works than to impress the general public with the clavier compositions as a whole. None the less all lovers of Bach owe their gratitude to the scholars, artists and instrument makers who have again brought the cembalo in honour among us; and it is to be hoped that the instrument will be more used for Bach playing. On the other hand we must not imagine that the cry of "back to the cembalo" solves the problem of which instrument we should play Bach upon. For the moment we can only be sure that the modern piano is not so close in character to the one Bach dreamed of as Spitta and his contemporaries thought it was. This is evident from the peculiar demands made by Bach's works, and a certain toning down is already beginning to be noticeable in the modern piano. We are gradually realising that the excessively strong and blunted tone of our grand pianos may be necessary for a large concert room, while in a small music room in a house it is too deafening to be pleasing, and that we must combine our consummate mechanism with a fabric of such a kind that the tone shall again be bright and clear and metallic. When this has been properly realised, and we have again reproduced in perfection the type of the table piano of 1830, as we have done with the cembalo, then we shall be much nearer the solution of the question which piano we ought to play Bach upon — at any rate at home. Until then, any one who would rather play Bach beautifully than powerfully must be content with a well-restored table piano of 1830 or 1840.

But the problem will not be wholly solved even by a reform of the domestic piano, for the reason that Bach had two instruments in his mind's eye. The modern piano is suitable for the music of the clavichord type; while the pieces calculated for the cembalo come out in their true beauty only in the silvery tone of that instrument.

As regards the interpretation of the clavier works, opinions are gradually become clearer. When Liszt and Bülow, in the middle of the nineteenth century, undertook to show the public again the living Bach, they had to fight a tradition that made stiffness, pedantry, and absence of temperament the true requisites for Bach playing. We can therefore easily understand their falling into the other extreme, and thinking that if Bach was to speak intelligibly to us he must be born again in the spirit of modern virtuosity. This was the origin of those Bach arrangements and Bach "interpretations" that aimed at modern effects, in which the aim was not so much to bring out the laws of the works themselves as to make Bach talk like a modern. Later on Bülow himself went astray in his Bach editions — that of the Chromatic Fantasia was a typical case — trying to give the public a simpler idea of Bach's works than the composer had. What he was dimly striving after came into clearer consciousness in a later and more reflective generation of pianists, that had learned to look at Bach's work as a whole. Two typical representatives of this new school are Busoni and Vianna da Motta. These, and the others who see eye to eye with them, do not aim so much in their Bach playing at ingenious dynamic nuances or striking effects as on making the broad plastic lines of the work speak for themselves.

Bach is an organist rather than a "klavierist"; his music is more architectonic than "sentimental". That is to say, his feelings express themselves in a kind of acoustic design. As in his organ works, so in his clavier works, there is little of the imperceptible merging of *piano* into *forte* and *vice versâ*. A certain strength of tone dominates a whole period, and is followed by another period of a contrasted intensity of tone. "Bach's music is always more or less majestic", says Vianna da Motta*. "It always rises in broad

* See his article on *Zur Pflege Bachscher Klavierwerke*, in the *Neue Zeitschrift für Musik*, 1904, p. 678 ff. The article discusses the problem of a new style of Bach playing.

terraces, like the primitive Assyrian temples." It is this
structure that we must look for if we wish to understand
a given work thoroughly; otherwise we shall always come
to it with an arbitrary conception of our own, and try to
force it into conformity with this.

We must begin with the study of the clavier works in
which Bach himself has indicated *forte* and *piano*. These
are the Italian Concerto, the Chromatic Fantasia, — if
we can rely on the copies here — and the last partita, in
B minor. These shew us on what very simple lines Bach conceived the structure of a work. The contrasting periods are
very long. A change only occurs when there comes a salient
episode of a different kind. Even in the echo piece at the
end of the partita the contrasts are not lavishly employed.

This very partita, however, shews us that in many works
Bach did not calculate on *any* variation of tone-strength.
After having made use of the two keyboards in the overture, he adopts only one colour for all the other numbers.
The courante, the sarabande and the gigue are taken *forte*
throughout; likewise the first gavottes, passepieds and
bourrées; to each of these three dances a second is appended
that is to be played on the *piano* manual. This implies
that the dance movements in the other suites are also to
be rendered in a uniform colour. To play them with
emotional transitions from *forte* to *piano* and *vice versâ*
is to destroy their character.

On the other hand it is obvious that the majority of the
long introductions to the English suites and the partitas
demand two tone-colours, and are built on the same plan
as the overture to the last partita. In the prelude to the
English suite in G minor —

the *piano* begins at bar 33 and continues to bar 67. Then
comes a *forte* passage, lasting to bar 99; from this point

the hands play for some bars on different keyboards, the one that has the flying quaver motive derived from the main theme being each time on the *forte* manual; from bar 109 to bar 125 both are on the main manual; the succeeding *piano* passage lasts until bar 161, where the right hand goes to the *forte* manual, while the left stays on the soft manual; in bar 185 this hand also goes to the *forte*.

It is important that in the pieces noted by Bach with *forte* and *piano* we should be quite clear how he goes from one tone-tint to the other — sometimes with both hands at once, sometimes with one following the other. In this connection the organ works should again be studied, which, being laid out on larger and simpler lines, exhibit the "terraces" much more clearly. Nor should the Brandenburg concertos be forgotten; they are most illuminative as to the structure of Bach's works and the employment of different degrees of strength of tone. We must consider too that in the orchestral suites called "overtures" (B. G. XXXI[1]) Bach indicates changes only for the introductions and the free movements, but not for the dances. This accords with the principles exhibited in the last clavier partita.

With the information thus acquired we have some sort of a guide as to the dynamic plan underlying the preludes and fugues of the *Well-tempered Clavichord*. Here again there are a number of pieces, among both the preludes and the fugues, that are intended to be played in one colour throughout. Where the character of the architecture shows no logical necessity for change, where, consequently, alterations of *forte* and *piano* seem arbitrary, it is better to maintain an agreeable and flexible *forte*, — for example, the preludes in C sharp minor, D minor and E major from the First Part. In the fugues we shall still more frequently have the conviction that they are not planned for dynamic variety.

In the pieces that employ two degrees of strength of tone, these degrees are either distributed simultaneously

between two voices or they alternate. To the first order
belong the preludes in D minor, A minor and B minor
from the Second Part; here the proper dynamic is to bring
to the front each time the voice that has the main theme,
while the other voice remains more in shadow, as it were.
Many preludes are laid out in such a way that the one
hand always plays *piano*, the other always *forte*, as it is
prescribed in the middle movement of the Italian Concerto.
A typical specimen of this is the three-part prelude in
F sharp minor from the Second Part, which is written in
such a way that the left hand plays the lower voices, and
the right hand the upper voice alone. To play now *forte*,
now *piano* here would be as wrong as to do so against
Bach's express specifications in the middle movement of
the Italian Concerto.

The clue to the distribution of light and shade in the
A flat major and A major preludes from the First Part is
given by the entry of the theme. Wherever it appears,
whether in one part alone or in the *ensemble*, it must be
given out *forte*; the rest must be kept *piano*.

In the F minor prelude of the Second Part, again, that
is so often maltreated —

the variations of *forte* and *piano* are unequivocally determined, for the first section at any rate, by the entry
of the main theme; in the second section the matter is less
clear, theme and episode not being so clearly marked off
from each other. The most natural way of playing it
would be thus — bars $1—4^1/_2$ *forte*; $4^1/_2—8^1/_2$ *piano*;
$8^1/_2—16^1/_2$ *forte*; $16^1/_2—20^1/_2$ *piano*; $20^1/_2—32^1/_2$ *forte*;
$32^1/_2—40$ *piano*; $40^1/_2—46^1/_2$, right hand *forte*, left *piano*;
$46^1/_2—52^1/_2$ *vice versâ*; $52^1/_2—56^1/_2$ *piano*; then *forte* to
the end.

The prelude in C major from the First Part seems to be
calculated on an echo effect of the kind obtainable on the

two-manual cembalo. The first half of the bar should thus be played *forte*, the second half *piano*. In this way it sounds exquisite on the cembalo. The prelude has then the effect of a cheerful reverie, instead of the pathetic effect we are apt to read into it when we try to bring out the mysterious melody that seems to hover above it. If we play it pathetically on our pianos, with a big and continuous *crescendo*, the effect is unsatisfactory — no matter whether this finishes in a *fortissimo*, or, contrary to Bach's clear intentions, dies away to a *pianissimo* (if indeed it has not done this several times already). The one thing we can be sure of with regard to the modern way of interpreting this prelude is that there has never yet been a pianist who has succeeded in playing it to the satisfaction of another.

The D major fugue in the First Part, which is more on the lines of a fantasia —

makes its natural effect when we play the main theme — the upward-striving demisemiquaver figure — *forte* each time it occurs, contrasting it with the calm, downward-moving semiquaver figure, which must be played *piano*. In this way the powerful final climax becomes particularly effective*.

In the D minor prelude from the Second Part, again —

* The plan may be detailed thus: bars 1—2, *forte*; 3 *piano*; 4 and 5 right hand *forte*, left *piano*; 6—9¹/₄ both hands *forte*; 9²/₄—10, the downward semiquaver answer, *piano*; 10¹/₄ *forte*; the semiquaver answer again *piano*; 11—16 both hands *forte*; 16—19 the first crotchet each time strong, the three others weak; 20 *forte* in both hands; 21 first crotchet *forte*, the others weak; 22 to the end, *forte* in both hands.

the descending answer to the ascending fanfare-like theme should contrast with this by being taken *piano*. If we are to play this prelude in accordance with the sense of it we must conceive it as scored for Bach's orchestra. On closer examination we shall discover only a few quite short sections that are to be given in the *piano* tint. These short *piano* interludes are very characteristic of Bach, as we see from many examples among the organ and orchestral works. Their very brevity makes them doubly effective*.

In the majority of pieces, however, these episodes are to be recognised only from their structural plan, and not as contrasts inherent in the theme itself. It is safest to be guided by the cadences and the incidents of the polyphony. If the segment is preceded by an important cadence, or if one or more voices are resting, then it is a fair assumption that the passage in question is to be played *piano*. The E major fugue from the Second Part may serve as an example; bars 1—22 *forte*; 23—34 *piano;* 35 to the end *forte*. The E flat major fugue from the same Part is similarly laid out: bars 1—30 *forte*; 30—58 *piano;* but with the theme given out *forte*; 59 to the end *forte*. The C sharp minor fugue from the First Part calls for a similar treatment. For increases of intensity within the *forte*, Bach relies only secondarily on dynamic means; he builds up the effect by the fulness of his tone and the way in which the voices co-operate.

The evidence for the inner necessity of a change to *piano* is not always so clear as this; as a rule we have to be satisfied with a certain amount of probability, — for example, when, in the F major fugue from the Second Part, we begin the *piano* at bar 29 and let it cease in the left

---

* The following plan seems the most natural: bars 1—$2^1/_4$ *forte*; $2^3/_4$—$3^1/_{12}$ *piano*; $3^2/_{12}$—$4^1/_4$ *forte*; $4^1/_4$—$5^1/_{12}$ *piano*; $5^1/_4$—16 *forte*; 17—$18^1/_{12}$ *forte*; $18^1/_{12}$—$21^1/_{12}$ *piano*, the left hand playing bar 19 *forte*; $21^1/_{12}$—$32^1/_{12}$ *forte*; $32^1/_{12}$—$41^1/_{12}$ *piano*; $41^1/_{12}$—$42^1/_4$ *forte*; $42^1/_4$—$43^1/_{12}$ *piano*; $43^1/_{12}$—$44^1/_4$ *forte*; $44^1/_4$—$45^1/_{12}$ *piano*; then *forte* to the end.

hand in the second half of bar 66, in the middle voice in the right hand in bar 70, and in the upper voice in the second half of bar 73; or when, in the G minor fugue of the First Part, we end the *forte* at bar $12^1/_4$, take the following bars *piano*, only bringing out the theme *forte* wherever it occurs, and let the final *tutti* begin at bar 28; or when, in the C major fugue from the First Part, we begin the *piano* at bar 14 and let it continue until bar 24; or when, in the D major fugue from the Second Part, we play *forte* until bar 16, *piano* until $27^1/_2$, and then bring in the final *tutti*.

With many preludes and fugues, however, our efforts are in vain; we can discover in them no dynamic plan that could not equally well be replaced by another, and our only recourse is to bring out the theme and avoid marked contrasts. As an example we may cite the F minor fugue from the Second Part. In the G minor fugue from the Second Part it is clear enough that the final *tutti* begins with bar 67; but it is not so clear how far back the previous *piano* extends. One is tempted to begin it in bar 40.

It is a false modernisation to let a cadence that ends a *forte* section die away in a *diminuendo*, so as to lead over into the following *piano*; or to make a *crescendo* at the end of a *piano* section in order to glide imperceptibly into the *forte*. In this way we level the terraces on which everything depends in these works, and destroy the plastic outlines of the piece. The Bach cadence is something solid, and must be given out in the normal tone-strength of the section which it concludes. It is this stark antithesis that gives the music its charm, as can be seen in the Brandenburg concertos. The *tutti* voices suddenly cease, and the *concertino* of the solo voices, after having entered on the last chord of the *tutti*, remains suspended, as it were, in the air.

It is another false modernisation to begin or end *pianissimo*. Just as in a pianoforte piece that Bach himself has marked, or in a Brandenburg concerto, or in an organ work, we have to begin and end in a *forte*, we must so begin and end in the pieces of the *Well-tempered Clavichord*. This

rule will not at first be acquiesced in by players who think
in the modern pianistic way. It will strike them as pedantic. Nevertheless, the longer we play Bach, the more we
revolt against artificialities and clevernesses of every kind,
and feel that the simplest way is the only right one.

Some day we shall even dare to begin and end the E flat
minor and B flat minor preludes from the First Part in a
beautiful but full tone-colour, and to conceive them largely
and pathetically, instead of delicately and sentimentally
as we do now. In the E flat minor prelude all the chords,
whether they lie above or below, should be taken *piano*,
while everything that pertains to the eloquent theme, including the cadences, should be taken *forte*. In the B flat
minor prelude we should begin with a vigorously-shaded
forte, take bars 13 and 14 *piano*, then begin again with a
quiet *forte*, that works up until three bars before the end,
the final cadence being taken in a quiet *forte*.

A further fault, that is likewise grounded in the pianistic
feeling of our time, consists in sacrificing everything in a
fugue to the working-out of the theme, and, as soon as
this enters, clapping the hand as it were over the mouth
of the other obbligato voices, the result being that the
auditor hears the theme but not the fugue. In episodical
passages it is natural to play the theme, whenever possible,
on a separate manual, as it were; but in the logical opening
and final structure of the fugue all the obbligato voices
have equal rights, and the theme can only be considered
as *primus inter pares*.

From the foregoing it is evident that on the piano, as
on the organ, it is wrong to begin a theme *pianissimo* and
then work it up through a continuous *crescendo* to a final
fortissimo, as if we were first presenting it as a cub, and
then showing it in all the stages of its development until
it becomes a lion. Every Bach theme, whether it expresses
joy or grief, has a touch of the sublime about it, and it
must be delivered in this style from the beginning. It
must be confessed, though, that it is difficult for us modern

musicians to emancipate ourselves from the idea of working Bach gradually up to a final climax. There are still
many artists who think that the essence of the fugue in
general, and of the Bach fugue in particular, consists in
a gradual piling-up from *piano* to *fortissimo*.

The laws here laid down for the plastic performance
of Bach's music are not derived from traditions, but are
grounded in the works themselves. They attest that nothing
is gained by besprinkling his compositions with *pianissimo,
piano, mezzoforte, forte, fortissimo, crescendo* and *decrescendo,*
as if they were written for the accordion, but that we must
aim either at the working-out of a broad dynamic plan,
or decide to play the work with a uniform strength of tone.
This view can seem pedantic only to those who think that
it elevates monotony to an artistic principle. The opposite
is really the case. When the one quality of tone is distributed over a segment, large or small, it must be richly
shaded in detail, but in such a way that these shadings do
not overstep the limits of that particular degree of tone.
Bach loved the clavichord so much precisely because he
could produce this shading of detail on it; and the magic
of his playing for his contemporaries came from this vivacity
of detail. We must therefore distinguish in his music
between an architectonic dynamic, that aims at bringing
out the great lines of the piece, and the dynamic of detail
that accompanies it, the object of which is to give life to
these lines. The latter could almost be styled declamatory
dynamic, being somewhat analogous to the cadential
element in musical speech.

Bach's music is Gothic. Just as in Gothic architecture
the great plan develops out of the simple motive, but
enfolds itself in the richest detail instead of in rigid line,
and only makes its effect when every detail is truly vital,
so does the impression a Bach work makes on the hearer
depend on the player communicating to him the massive
outline and the details together, both equally clear and
equally full of life.

If in place of this dual architectonic dynamic we put the uniform modern emotional dynamic, such as we meet with in Beethoven's works, we have simply done our best to make Bach unintelligible, by confounding the great and the small nuances in one*.

Therefore to play the preludes in E flat minor and B flat minor from the First Part with a uniform strength of tone does not mean playing them monotonously, but declaiming them with simple and impressive pathos, avoiding sentimental effects, and trying to get all possible richness by the perfect shading of the normal *forte*. Within our Bach *forte* we must get the relief of a *piano* and a *forte*, and a similar shading in the *piano*. Our *mezzoforte* is unknown to Bach; the sign *mf* is nowhere to be found in his music. He severs the link that binds *piano* to *forte*. On the other hand, as is proved by his markings in the scores of the cantatas, he distinguishes a *pianissimo* within the *piano*. A *mezzoforte* makes a Bach piece uninteresting. This holds good not only for the piano and the organ works but for the orchestral concertos and the cantatas. If an orchestral piece does not make its effect, we may be sure that in half the cases this is the fault of a lack of character in the quality of tone employed. Unfortunately our pianists and instrumentalists can get a *mezzoforte*, but neither a *piano* nor a *forte* that is rich and capable of gradation. For this reason it is no unreasonable demand, curious as it may seem, that whoever wishes to interpret Bach must first of all learn how to play *forte* and *piano*.

---

* This is the case in the Czerny edition of the *Well-tempered Clavichord* (1837). We wonder whether the editor himself used to execute the numerous *crescendi* and *decrescendi* that he has sprinkled over the text. It is interesting to know that he justifies his markings by the practice of Beethoven, by whom he often heard the preludes and fugues played. The Steingräber edition and the Ricordi edition are much more sparing with nuances. In principle, however, their standpoint is that of Czerny, their system of dynamics not springing from the natural plan of the work, but being grafted on to it. The player will never feel these nuances to be "necessary", in the true artistic sense, but merely adventitious.

In Bach, however, the really essential thing is not so much the dynamic shading as the phrasing and accentuation. We soon realise this when we look at one of those precious orchestral scores which he has furnished with indications for performance. Seiffert, in his fine essay on *Praktische Bearbeitungen Bachscher Kompositionen** justly contrasts him in this respect with Handel. "In Handel", he says, "the care for dynamic effects is always uppermost; for the phrasing he is satisfied with incidental hints. Bach gives extremely little in the way of dynamic suggestion; but he all the more carefully phrases the orchestral parts." Seiffert's explanation of this difference — that Handel had at his disposal trained orchestral players, while Bach had only town musicians, — is not convincing. The difference in the two methods is rooted in the dissimilarity of the men's music. Bach's works demand a characteristic and subtle phrasing of the themes and of the parts, on which the effect of the whole almost entirely depends. Handel's themes and passages, on the contrary, run more on the customary lines, and demand no such individuality of phrasing.

In general we may lay down the principle that in Bach every theme and every phrase must be delivered as if we were playing it on a bowed instrument. This holds good for the pianoforte not less than for the wood-wind instruments. We play the preludes and fugues of the *Welltempered Clavichord* in accordance with Bach's intentions when we try to render them as if we were employing not a keyed instrument but a quartet or a quintet. The ideal must be to link the notes in such a way that they do not seem to be struck one after the other, but as if several bows were being simultaneously drawn over the strings.

Bach's omission to record the phrasing and grouping in his clavier works is due partly to the fact that this was not customary at that time, the "executive artist" in our

---

* In the *Bachjahrbuch* for 1904, p. 59.

sense of the term being as yet unknown; and partly to the fact that the players he had in view were almost always his sons and his pupils, who were familiar with his principles. In the works for clavier with other instruments there are often indications of the phrasing in the clavier part, Bach thinking it necessary that the clavier player should phrase precisely like the instrumentalists. Look, for example, at many movements in the violin sonatas, and, among the clavier concertos, at the one in A major (No. 4). The greatest importance, however, attaches to the dots and ties in the orchestral parts of the Brandenburg concertos and of certain cantatas. A study of these will convince any one of the right way to phrase the clavier works.

Legato playing, that is regarded as the characteristic of the Bach school, does not, as we observed in connection with the organ works, mean a uniform style of delivery, but implies an endless variety in the tieing and grouping of single notes of equal value. Four semiquavers are for Bach not four semiquavers, but the raw material for quite varied shapes, according to how he groups them: thus —

The last system of connection, that is almost universal elsewhere, is always subordinated by him to the other and more characteristic systems. He mostly groups the notes in twos when the second and third semiquavers have the same note in common. In these cases he always uses short ties, as if he were afraid of being misunderstood. Thus on the very first page of the Italian concerto —

The same grouping is also found in certain cases where none of the notes is repeated; but it is observable that here, as a rule, the melody moves in seconds. In the B minor fugue from the First Part, Bach indicates this grouping by twos, as it did not seem to him quite self-evident —

In this connection it cannot be sufficiently insisted on that the second of the tied notes should be like a mere breath. A Bach connoisseur like Gevaert advocates writing such passages in this way* —

This accentual rule naturally holds good only for the normal case in which the first of the two tied notes coïncides with the stronger beat. In the opposite case the second gets the strong accent, and the first counts as a preliminary.

Prelude 20 (Second Part).

The rhythm in which the fourth note is detached from the first three appears in the *presto* of the Italian Concerto, where Bach in addition places a dot over the last note, so as to ensure it being properly detached from the others —

The combination most frequently met with, however, is that in which the last three notes are tied and separated from the first. Here again Bach makes sure of the freedom of the first by means of a dot. Thus at the commencement of the Italian Concerto —

---

* In his vocal score of the *St. Matthew Passion* he uses this method for the final chorus of the First Part.

In a longer succession of tied notes, again, the first **must** be detached from the others.   Bach phrases the *presto* of the Italian Concerto sometimes thus —

The dot only signifies that the note does not belong to the same group as those that follow; it is, however, closely bound to the preceding ones.   In our notation this is best expressed by including the detached note in the same tie as the previous notes, thus —

Fugue in B flat (Second Part).

Fugue in G major (Second Part).

In the groups in triple time, again, the first beat is **very** often the end of a tied series, not the commencement **of** a new one.   Bach's phrasing of the theme of the A **major** fugue from the First Part would therefore be this —

Even in pure triplets it is in certain cases **better to** separate the second and third notes from the first as **if** taking a light breath.   The eighth bar of the B flat major prelude from the Second Part should consequently **be** played thus —

This phrasing is so frequent in Bach because his themes and figuration, even where the bar-divisions do not indicate it to the eye, have generally an up-beat character, beginning with an unaccented note that leads into an accented one. It is a great mistake to play successive notes in his music with equal values, in the style of Czerny's "School of Velocity", or Clementi, or Cramer. There the essence of the legato phrasing is that we begin with an accented note and play the remainder as nearly as possible with the same weight. Bach's legato, however, is much less pianistic and much more vital. The large tie in his music embraces numberless smaller ones, that gather the notes into subordinate groups. Neither in his piano runs nor in his violin runs does he desire equivalence in the notes. Each has its relative value, namely that belonging to it from its place in the tie.

This can be explained on historical grounds. The monotonous legato that obsesses our pianoforte schools could only come after the passing-under of the thumb had become recognised as the cardinal principle in playing. A legato of this kind was impossible so long as people simply passed the other fingers over and under each other, or merely moved the hand as a whole, and fingered scale passages 3, 4, 3, 4, 3, 4, or 5, 4, 3, 2, 2, 1, as Bach tells his son to do in the *Klavierübung*. Ties of the second kind grew out of the style of fingering. For this reason Bach's legato, compared with the usual pianistic legato, is as much richer and more varied as his fingering was richer and more diverse than ours. We must not imagine we are playing Bach with the right legato when we have worked out on paper all the passings-under of the thumb and the complicated interchanges of the fingers, and so made sure that every note will be properly sustained even to the last hundred-thousandth of its value. The correct tieing and fingering are those which bring out all the variety intended by Bach in the phrasing and the accents, i. e. those which "tell".

The Bach staccato coincides only in rare cases with our light modern staccato. It is not so much a key pizzicato as the short and heavy stroke of a bow. Its effect is therefore to accentuate the note rather than to lighten it. It would be better indicated in our notation by a short stroke than by a dot.

Long quaver or semiquaver passages in staccato are rarely met with in Bach; when he separates the notes it is only by way of a transient interruption of the legato. Perhaps in passages like this —*

the semiquavers between the two ties are to be played staccato, and this time lightly, not heavily. Certain indications in the orchestral parts make it probable that in the weakest beats of the $^6/_8$ and similar times, when the motion is quite uniform, a light staccato is often intended to break the legato. In general, however, the rule holds good that Bach's staccato does not run a uniform course, and that it is not light but heavy. An interesting case where he makes use of a staccato to accentuate a beat is found in the final allegro of the clavier concerto in A major: —

The transition here is in every respect so abrupt, especially as the orchestra enters on the trill, that the brake must to some extent be put on the triplets. To play them with a light staccato would be to run the risk of negating Bach's intentions.

---

* From the Siciliano of the fourth sonata for clavier and violin, bar 9. The ties are Bach's own.

The only rhythm that must always be given in **staccato** notes is that which Bach uses to express solemnity — ♩. ♩. ♩. We must detach the second note from the first, let it press forward towards the one that follows, and play it rather too heavily than too lightly, in order to preserve the impression of a somewhat formal solemnity, of the kind that Bach wishes to suggest in many of his sarabands and gigues. Thus the bass of the F sharp major prelude from the Second Part should be played thus —

Nor should we be afraid to play whole pieces, — such as the G minor prelude from the Second Part, — if they are wholly in this rhythm, — without a single really legato note.

The rhythms ♪ ♫ and ♫ ♪, and the variants of these, demand a certain emphasis on the short notes, as if there were a fear of their passing unobserved. The shorter they are in actual time-value, the more careful must we be to make them tell. In this way we can detach them somewhat from the main note and play them with the heavy staccato.

For example —

Well-tempered Clavichord. Prelude 17 (Second Part).

Have we any means of knowing whether groups of notes are to be played staccato? In the first place, the staccato is required when the sequence is in characteristic or widely-separated intervals. Under this first rule come all the themes that have anything of a "springy" motion. The

best-known example is perhaps the theme of the **F major
Invention** —

The theme of the chorale fantasia *Jesus Christus unser
Heiland*, again, from the Third Part of the *Klavierübung*,
must be played staccato —

The theme of the A minor fugue from the Second Part
of the *Well-tempered Clavichord* must be given thus —

It seemed self-evident to Bach that the crotchets in this
theme could only be rendered in this way. Some players,
however, might have been in doubt as to whether to play
the quavers legato or staccato. Bach therefore settled
the matter by adding dots to the notes. He could not
foresee that by so doing he would tempt the players of
later generations to play the crotchets legato, as they have
no dots, and to contrast the staccato quavers with them.

The second rule for the employment of the staccato in
Bach might be formulated somewhat thus — that any
note interrupting a uniform motion at once steps out of
the general tie embracing the preceding notes. The examples of this are innumerable; a typical one is the theme
of the D minor fugue from the First Part, in which Bach
himself marks the staccato point throughout the whole
piece —

Here indeed it becomes perfectly clear that the principle of
the Bach phrasing is derived from an ideal bowing. This
general rule, however, has one exception. The interrupting
passage is only to be played staccato if it moves in a zig-zag
line. If it consistently ascends or descends in uniform
and close-lying intervals, it must be played legato.

There are thus two fundamental conceptions from which
the whole of Bach's themes have sprung. The first is
that of the differentiated ties; the second is that of the
staccato as a rhythmic interruption of the legato. Therefore the phrasing of the themes should not be left to the
caprice of genius, but must be deduced from the ground-
rules of legato and staccato in Bach. Every player can
acquaint himself with the typical combinations that arise
from the differentiation of the ties and from the concur-
rence of legato and staccato, and can thus learn to bring
out the various groups of which a Bach theme is composed.

A few examples from the *Well-tempered Clavichord* may
serve to elucidate these points.

Themes consisting purely of differentiated ties: —

Prelude 20 (Part II).

Fugue 6 (Part II).

Fugue 10 (Part I).

Prelude 5 (Part II).

Prelude 2 (Part II).

Themes combining legato and staccato: —

Fugue 2 (Part I).

Fugue 21 (Part I).

Fugue 16 (Part I).

Fugue 1 (Part I).

Fugue 15 (Part I).

Fugue 11 (Part I).

Fugue 5 (Part I).

Fugue 12 (Part I).

Fugue 7 (Part II).

Closely bound up with the question of phrasing is that of accentuation; it is, indeed, solved by the right solution of the other. It has already been remarked, in connection with ties, that Bach's themes are mostly conceived as beginning with a large up-beat. The unaccented notes do not follow, but lead up to, an accented note. Therefore to play Bach rhythmically means accenting not the downbeat but the emphatic beat. With him, more than with any other composer, the bar-divisions are only external divisions of the themes, the real metre of which cannot as a rule be represented in simple time-species. The first to express this clearly was Rudolf Westphal, in his metrical study of the fugues in common time in the *Well-tempered Clavichord*, in which he proves again and again that those who regard the bar-lines in Bach's music as the borders of the rhythmic factors are bound to play him unrhythmically*.

In a Bach theme everything urges forward to a principal accent. Till this comes all is restless, chaotic; when it arrives the tension relaxes, and at one stroke all that went before becomes clear, — we understood why the notes had these intervals and these values. The chaos becomes order, the restlessness becomes peace. The theme lies before the hearer like a good coin, with the milling fresh

---

* See Westphal's *Die C Takt-Fugen des Wohltemperierten Klaviers*, in the *Musikalisches Wochenblatt* for 1883, pp. 237 ff. The justice of his views upon Bach is unassailable, even if we do not share his general opinions upon musical metre.

and sharp. If, however, this emphasis is lacking, and in place of the note that is an integral part of the rhythm of the theme we accent strongly a note that belongs only to the bar-rhythm, the unity and totality of the impression are destroyed; all he has in his hand is a coin of several pieces soldered together, that keep falling asunder. This of course does not mean that in Bach the thematic accent and the bar-accent never coincide. Cases of this kind, however, are more or less accidental.

The superior vitality and lucidity given to Bach's music by throwing the main accent on the characteristic notes can be seen at once by any one who makes a practical trial of it, accenting according to the nature of the theme, instead of taking the phrases with the usual rise and fall. The final *diminuendo*, with all its shadings, that we introduce into everything out of pure habit, is one of the direst enemies of stylistic Bach playing.

The point can be best elucidated by reference to the theme of the E flat minor prelude. It is usually played thus —

It should really go thus —

If we play it in this way, the prelude, couched as it is in dialogue form, acquires a much finer inner coherence.

To these indications for the accentuation of Bach's melodies one is tempted to add another rule, that may seem extrinsic and imperfect, but which does good service in the majority of cases. According to this rule, we should primarily emphasise the notes at the end of a melodic line

running in a certain direction, whether this is carried through
in one piece or breaks off now and then and continues in
separate segments. In the latter case the end notes of each
segment form preliminary accents, that are meant to lead
up to and culminate in the last and principal accent. It is
just these themes built up in periods that are most often
misunderstood. The following is a specimen of correct
accentuation —

Well-tempered Clavichord. Fugue 11 (Part II).

Here, as a rule, we do indeed hear the first two accents;
the third, however, on the F, that ought to crown the others,
is lost, and the theme runs about in the fugue like the
poor ghost that carries its head under its arm.

Fugue 17 (Part II).

This case is similar to the foregoing. The average player
resists the seductive appeal of the third beat for the first
accent; he cannot, however, resist the first beat of the
second bar, — he respects the traditional rights of a note
that occupies so important a position, and gives the A flat
the accent that should be given to the D flat, without
noticing that the succeeding semiquavers are no more
than an ideal retardation of the passage of the D flat into
the C.

In the second place, a main accent must be given to a
note that interrupts a melodic line more or less suddenly,
whether the note be syncopated or not. As a matter of
fact, in the majority of cases it will happen either on a
striking interval or on a syncopation. This sudden holding-
back is a characteristic feature of a number of Bach's
themes. If we efface it, by emphasising the strong beats,

we only torture the outline of the theme; but if we bring it out by proper accentuation, we reveal the great natural line that embraces this angular curve. We should therefore always emphasise with confidence any conspicuous interval or syncopation.

This holds good even in matters of detail. In the B minor prelude of the First Part of the *Well-tempered Clavichord* the natural bar-accent seems demanded by the regular quaver-movement in the bass. If, however, we accent thus —

it will immediately be found that this rhythmical antagonism between the upper parts and the even bass is the very life of the prelude. It is unnecessary to say that here the emphasised notes are to be detached from the preceding ones.

The following are types of themes that call for this syncopated accentuation —

Fugue 19 (Part II).

That the main accent here must be given to the last note, which on the first thought one would hardly venture to do, — is proved by the further course of the piece, and especially its end. The two syncopations are thus only preliminary accents, leading up to the third.

Fugue 16 (Part II).

Here the method of accentuation may be thought **too** venturesome; but with repeated playing it will finally seem more right than the more obvious accentuation on the first beat. A particular result of this syncopated accentuation is to give life to the otherwise monotonous seven quavers on the same note.

Fugue 8 (Part I).

This theme clearly shows how little significance the bar-divisions in Bach have for the thematic emphasis. That the consistent syncopated accentuation here is the only right one is shewn by the composer himself at the finish. As if he had sufficiently played with the performer and the hearer he brings in the theme in augmentation in such a way that the syncopations fall on the strong beats —

In the animated second subject of the Italian Concerto, again, we can see how the syncopation deprives the neighbouring strong beat of its accent. It is usually accented thus —

This, however, does not bring out the essential principle of its structure. The correct way of phrasing is that in which the two syncopations act as preliminary accents, leading up to the final accent, thus —

It may be objected that accentuation on these principles is too harsh and rough to be correct. It is, however, the only accentuation that does justice to the original character of Bach's themes. The hearer will not feel anything disagreeable in the sharp characterisation they thus receive; he will only feel the truth and vitality of it. In any case the fugues will now give him more enjoyment than before, as he will grasp the rhythmic essence of them, instead of regarding them, in the customary way, as mere sequences of intervals. And it is quite certain that the cultivated hearer also pursues a theme in all its developments not as a sequence of intervals, but primarily as a succession of certain characteristic accents, that bring with them the idea of the intervals associated with them.

Reference has been made, in the chapter on the organ works, to the profound distinction between Bach's organ themes and his clavier themes. The former are almost always based on the principle of the accentuation of the strong beat, since it is impossible to bring out any other accent on the organ. It is even impossible to make one note stand out above the others. The possibility of this on the piano, if only in a limited way, is made use of by Bach to the utmost permissible limits. Bowed instruments, again, can individualise the tone much more even than the piano; the themes of Bach's instrumental works are much freer and bolder than those of the clavier works.

Whatever force we give to the accent, the phrasing must be kept discreet and unobtrusive. In the last resort the whole phrase, with its varieties of ties and the *staccati* between them, must be embraced as it were in one large tie, which permits of diversity without restlessness. The hearer really should not be conscious of the phrasing as such; he must only be conscious of it as a self-evident and vital illumination of the whole, down to the smallest detail, so that he is himself surprised at the ease with which he grasps this complicated polyphony.

There is little to be said with regard to the tempo in Bach's clavier works. The better any one plays Bach, the more slowly he can take the music; the worse he plays him, the faster he must take it. Good playing implies fine phrasing and accentuation in every detail in every voice. This of itself sets certain technical bounds to speed. On the other hand, in playing of the right kind the hearer, even if the tempo is not quick in itself, has the feeling of it being quite fast enough, for the reason that at any quicker pace he could not grasp the detail. It should never be forgotten what a complicated process it really means for any musician, — even for one who is not listening to it for the first time, — to follow one of Bach's polyphonic works properly. Of course if we are careless as to our phrasing and accentuation, and so obliterate the greater part of the detail, we can play faster with impunity, so as to give the music another interest of a kind. In general, however, the maxim holds good that the vivacity of a Bach piece depends not on the tempo but on the phrasing and the accentuation. In this sense every one may strive to play him with plenty of temperament.

The tempo marks, where they exist, should not be interpreted in a modern sense. Bach's *adagio, grave,* and *lento* are not so slow as ours, nor his *presto* so fast; therefore we are easily betrayed into making his slow movements too long-drawn and of hurrying his fast ones. The circle of possible tempi in his music is a relatively narrow one*. The question is really one of varied nuances on either side of a moderato. The *presto* of the Italian Concerto is, as a rule, played twice as fast as it should be. Nobody will make this mistake who tries to realise the complicated system of ties that Bach has indicated in the movement. It goes without saying that the *alla breve* sign in Bach

---

* For this reason it is hard to see the use of the unauthentic tempo marks that are sometimes inserted in the works. Metronome marks should be moderately used, and relegated to foot-notes.

implies nothing as regards the tempo, — it does not double the speed of the four-crotchet beat.

The ideal edition of Bach's clavier works would be a critically correct reprint of the original, in which the text is not adorned with ties and dynamic indications. It is hard to say how much mischief has been done by many of the old editions and arrangements. It would be something to establish the principle that the editor should indicate all additions of his own, so that the player who has not the original edition at hand may know what is and what is not by Bach, and can use his own judgment. An inquiry among the piano-playing public would show that the majority have no idea that the ties and dynamic indications in their scores are not Bach's own.

The best thing for our Bach editors to do would be to follow Busoni's example, and publish, not arrangements, but their "interpretations" of the works. Busoni's edition of the Chromatic Fantasia (published by Simrock) is one of the finest achievements of this kind, that fascinates even those who cannot always see eye to eye with Busoni on the question of the permissible limits of modernisation of Bach's music. It is to be hoped that Bülow's arrangement of this work is nowadays relegated to a bygone epoch of Bach interpretation; he himself would wish it to be so, were he alive now.

"Instructive" editions of Bach's clavier works have this difficulty to contend with — that in half of them the text becomes unreadable by reason of the number of ties, staccato dots, and accents that are needed in order to give vitality to the phrasing. Perhaps future editors will adopt the plan of expressing their views in prefaces and foot-notes instead of in the text. After all, the essential things are only the suggestion of the great dynamic lines and the phrasing and accenting of the themes; the details of the development of the work follow of themselves from these. Another advantage of editions of this kind would be that they could discuss various alternative phrasings, instead of peremptorily thrusting one upon the player. It cannot be denied that many editions of piano music do not induce self-reliance, but the lack of it. This does more harm in the case of Bach's music than in any other. No one can play it satisfactorily who is not conscious of the essential principles of its musical structure.

Perhaps even the copious fingerings that adorn our Bach editions are not so beneficial as is generally supposed, for they relieve the player of the trouble and the profit of working them out for himself.

The rules for playing Bach's clavier works here elaborated are open to many objections. The view that the phrasing of the preludes and fugues of the *Well-tempered Clavichord* is primarily to be learned from Bach's own phrasing of orchestral parts will perhaps be thought too drastic; the rules as to accentuation may appear to lay too much stress on characterisation; it will be objected that these dynamic rules insist too strongly on the architectonic side of the music. All this, however, does not in any way invalidate the rules. We may even regard it as a positive necessity to formulate general principles for performing Bach's clavier works; and it may be that these will coincide with the views of a number of our Bach pianists, who are also in revolt against excessive and unintelligent modernisation of the works, and believe that more is to be hoped for from a careful artistic enquiry than from self-satisfied caprice.

The greater or less extent to which these views are adopted, however, is of little consequence. They will have fulfilled their object if they prompt players to more thorough reflection and a more careful examination of the works. In any case, no reader can be so conscious as the author that the framing of rules is more unsatisfactory and more imperfect in art than anywhere else.

CHAPTER XVII.

CHAMBER AND ORCHESTRAL WORKS.

Bachgesellschaft Edition.

Vol. XXVII. Six sonatas for violin solo; six suites for cello solo.
- IX¹. Three sonatas for clavier and flute; one suite and six sonatas for clavier and violin; three sonatas for clavier and gamba; sonata for flute, violin and continuo; sonata for two violins and continuo.
- XLV. Four inventions for violin and clavier.
- XLIII¹. Three sonatas for flute and continuo. Concerto for four claviers with orchestral accompaniment (Vivaldi).
- XVII. Seven concertos for clavier and orchestra; concerto for clavier, flute, violin and orchestra.
- XXI¹. Three concertos for two claviers and orchestra.
- XXXI³. Two concertos for three claviers and orchestra.
- XXXI¹. Overtures for orchestra.
- XIX. Brandenburg concertos.
- XXI¹. Two concertos for violin and orchestra; concerto for two violins and orchestra.

Peters Edition.

Series II. Parts 1—13. Works for clavier with orchestra.
- III. Parts 1—8. Works for violin and flute.
- IV. Parts 1 and 2. Works for cello and gamba.
- VI. Works for orchestra.

Bach seems to have cultivated violin playing from childhood; when he left the gymnasium at Lüneburg he was an accomplished violinist and could take a place as such in the orchestra of Johann Ernst, the brother of the reigning Duke of Weimar*. Nor did he neglect the stringed instruments in later life. In chamber music he played by preference the viola, for in this way he found himself as it were in the centre of the web of tone**.

We have no direct information as to the extent of his proficiency on these instruments. We may be sure, however, that he had a thorough practical knowledge of the technique of the stringed instruments, — otherwise it

---

* See p. 100.
** See p. 209.

would have been impossible for him to take such unique advantage of all the effects that can be obtained on them, as he does in the polyphonic works for violin, gamba and cello solo.

Nor can he quite forget that he is a violinist in the works written for keyed instruments; the violinist is observable on every page. The characteristic of Bach's piano and organ style is precisely this, that he demands from the keyed instruments the same aptitudes for phrasing and modulation as the strings. At bottom he conceived everything for an ideal instrument, that had all the keyed instrument's possibilities of polyphonic playing, and all the bowed instrument's capacities for phrasing. This is how he came to write polyphonically even for a single instrument.

Polyphonic playing on the violin had long been customary in Germany. Bruhns (1666—1697) of Husum, Buxtehude's pupil, used to perform in this way, at the same time playing the bass on the organ pedals*. The Italians were far behind the Northerners in this art.

Although Bach wrote in reality three partitas (suites) and three sonatas, it is customary to speak, for brevity's sake, of his six sonatas for solo violin. As might be guessed from our knowledge of his way of composing, these works were written within a short time of each other. They belong to the Cöthen epoch; the oldest autograph we have of them probably dates from about 1720.

The history of this autograph is told by Pölchau, the gallant manuscript-hunter of the early days of Bach enthusiasm, in a short note on the front page of it: "I found this excellent work, in Bach's own handwriting, in Petersburg in 1814, among a lot of old papers, destined for the butter shop, that had belonged to Palschau, the pianist." At a later date it passed, with the other manuscript trea-

---

* On polyphonic violin-playing in the eighteenth century see Spitta II, 79 ff.

sures of the finder, into the possession of the Berlin Royal
Library.

Pölchau was in error, however, in imagining it to be an
autograph of Bach's. It is from the hand of Anna Magdalena, whose handwriting even at that time was deceptively
like that of her husband. While she was making the copy
she was watching over one of the boys — perhaps Friedemann, — who used a free page for exercises of his own
in making notes, his father having written some examples
for him. There are no blank sheets, for the leaves are
filled on the same principles as the English autograph of
the Second Part of the *Well-tempered Clavichord*, — in
order to avoid the necessity of turning over, each work is
made to occupy one or other side of a page only.

In the later Leipzig period Anna Magdalena made a
new copy of the sonatas for solo violin. She made them
up in one volume with those for violoncello, with the title:
"Pars I. Violino Solo, Senza Basso, composée par Sr.
Jean Seb. Bach. Pars II. Violoncello Solo, Senza Basso,
composée par Sr. J. S. Bach. Maître de la Chapelle et
Directeur de la Musique à Leipsic. Ecrite par Madame
Bachen. Son Epouse." Bach, it will be observed, is not
called Court composer; the copy * must therefore be dated
earlier than 1736.

The sonatas for solo violin were first printed in 1802,
by Simrock of Bonn. In 1854 Robert Schumann edited
them for Breitkopf and Härtel, adding a pianoforte accompaniment to them. This was following in the footsteps

---

* This manuscript also belonged to Pölchau, at whose death
it went to the Royal Library in Berlin. These two "autographs"
are very interesting, as they exhibit a change in Bach's method
of notation that is also met with elsewhere, and helps us somewhat
to date his works. In the older manuscripts, a sharp is usually
cancelled by the ♭ sign, rarely by the natural; later — from about
the first Leipzig period, — the natural is exclusively used for this
purpose.

These sonatas for violin solo exist also in a copy made by Joh.
Peter Kellner in 1726.

of Mendelssohn, who had adopted the same procedure in 1847 with the Chaconne from the second partita *. To us it is incomprehensible that two such great artists could believe that they were thus carrying out Bach's intentions.

The sonatas and partitas are so arranged that each sonata is following by a partita. In both of them we hardly know what to admire most — the richness of the invention, or the daring of the polyphony that is given to the violin. The more we read, hear and play them, the greater our astonishment becomes.

The Chaconne that concludes the second partita has always been regarded as the classical piece for solo violin, — and justly, since both the theme and its development are consummately adapted to the genius of the instrument. Out of a single theme Bach conjures up a whole world. We seem to hear sorrow contending with pain, till at last they blend in a mood of profound resignation.

It is very instructive to compare the Chaconne with the Passacaglia for organ, which is also in reality a chaconne **. For the organ, Bach takes a theme that is accented only on the strong beats of the bar, knowing well that the least syncopation would give the whole work a restlessness that would make it unbearable on the organ. On the violin, however, that permits of every kind of accent, cross-accentuation makes for superior force and vivacity. He therefore employs here a quite unusual amount of syncopation; the instrument, free from the hindrance of an accompaniment, shall for once realise all its powers

---

* He published his arrangement first through Ewer and Co., London, and afterwards (in 1849) through Breitkopf and Härtel. The Leipzig Conservatoire edition, with David's fingering and bowing, was issued by Kistner in 1843. See Dörffel's erudite preface to B. G. XXVII^1.

** See p. 280. The chaconne and passacaglia are derived from old dance forms, and are characterised by the fact that they are developed out of an ever-recurring theme of eight bars in $^3/_4$ time. In the chaconne this theme may appear in all the parts; in the passacaglia it is confined to the bass.

in perfect unrestraint. It is interesting to look at the two
themes, side by side, that between them incarnate the
organ and the violin music of Bach: —

Chaconne for violin.

Passacaglia for organ.

Notice how, in the Chaconne, Bach alternates between
polyphonic and monophonic writing, so as to give the hearer
relief, and to heighten the effect of the polyphony by the
monophony interspersed among it. His music as a whole
is full of these fine calculations of effect.

Every one who has heard these sonatas must have
realised how sadly his material enjoyment of them falls
below his ideal enjoyment. There are many passages in
them that the best player cannot render without a certain
harshness. The arpeggio harmonies sometimes make a particularly bad effect, even in the finest playing. Polyphonic
arpeggio playing is and must be an impossibility. There
is thus some justification for the question whether Bach,
in these sonatas, has not overstepped the bounds of artistic
possibility. If it be so, he has for once acted against his
own principles, for everywhere else he has been careful to
set an instrument only such tasks as it can solve with
satisfaction to the ear.

Recent research seems to show that the traditions of
Bach's own day can throw some light on this. In an
interesting article by Arnold Schering, one of the most
assiduous of the Bach students of our time, some passages
from old works are cited that make it probable that the

old arched bow, with which the tension was effected not by means of a screw but by the pressure of the thumb, was still in use in Germany in Bach's time*. The flat, mechanically stretched Italian bow, the predecessor of that of today, was indeed known in Germany from the beginning of the eighteenth century, but displaced the older one very slowly.

The German violinist of Bach's day could thus stretch the hairs tighter or relax them as he liked. Chords that the virtuosi of today can only play with difficulty and without any beauty of effect by throwing the bow back on the lower strings, gave him no trouble at all; he simply loosened the hairs a little, so that they curved over the strings. This accounts for the fact that the Germans cultivated polyphonic playing on the violin **, while it was almost unknown to the Italians. In Italy, the straight bow with its purely mechanical tension had already established itself by the end of the seventeenth century. This bow permits polyphonic playing only to a limited extent, since it allows of no further tension during the performance, for if the hairs are relaxed they do not arch over the strings, but fall against the stick. With the old German bow, on the other hand, the stick of which was not straight, there was a fair space between the hairs and the bow.

---

* See the "Bachheft" of the *Neue Zeitschrift für Musik,* 1904, p.675 ff, — *Verschwundene Traditionen des Bachzeitalters.* The article appeared in an expanded form in the *Bachjahrbuch* for 1904, pp. 104—115. The chief passage cited by him runs thus: "As regards the small and medium-sized violins, the Germans hold the bow like the Lullists, pressing the hairs together with the thumb, the other fingers resting on the back of the bow .... while the Italians leave the hairs untouched, as also the gambists and others do in the bass, the fingers lying between the wood and the hair" (Georg Muffat's preface to the *Florilegium secundum,* 1698). Caspar Majer testifies to the same thing in his *Neu eröffneter Musik-Saal* (Nuremberg, 1741). Schering's theory has already been mentioned on p. 209.

** Interesting examples of violin chords are given in Joh. Jak. Walther's *Hortus chelicus,* 1694. See Schering's article in the *Neue Zeitschrift für Musik,* 1904, p. 677.

The last representative of chord playing on the violin was the Norwegian, Ole Bull (1810—1880). His bridge was quite flat; he had his bows made in such a way that the stick stood at a considerable distance from the hairs*. It is interesting to know that he always maintained that this method was no new invention of his own, but a return to the true violin method of the past. It is quite possible that in Scandinavia the traditions of the seventeenth century had been retained, along with the old bows, down to Ole Bull's time.

In his sonatas for violin solo Bach has thus demanded of the instrument nothing impossible or even unsatisfactory *per se*, but only what seems so with our excessively arched bridges and our flat Italian bows. To play these sonatas as he did, we need only to file down the arching of the bridge so as to bring the strings almost level, and to use a bow so shaped from nut to point that the hairs can curve towards the stick without touching it**. Still better is a bow with slightly curved stick. In this way violinists will be able once more to play Bach in a correct style. Any one who has heard the chords of the Chaconne played without any restlessness, and without arpeggios, can no longer

---

* His stick was bent downwards considerably at the point. Schering does not mention Ole Bull. A special study of the playing of this notable virtuoso should have some bearing on the question under discussion. Corelli's bow was stretched mechanically, but it was not so flat as ours.

** It is to be hoped that the instrument makers will soon provide us with serviceable bows of the old type. Till then the player must make shift with an old bow, inserting a couple of pieces of wood between the stick and the hairs at top and bottom. A bow reconstructed in this primitive way will do quite well to experiment with. I owe to my friend E. Hahnemann the opportunity of hearing the Chaconne and other works of Bach for solo violin played in the old way by an eminent violinist with a bow thus provisionally arranged. The flat bridge is less disadvantageous than one would think, as in Bach's music we have not to play in the high positions, where the string is pressed down so deeply that there is a danger of the bow touching two strings at once. Ole Bull, according to Spohr, used his A and D strings only in the lower position.

doubt that this is the only correct and, from the artistic standpoint, satisfactory way of playing it. Of course the slackly-stretched bow demands a different technique from the usual one. The pure "springing" bowing is impossible*. But the tone also undergoes a change; it acquires a curious softness. If we play the chords with the hairs of the bow relaxed, we get an almost organ-like tone, somewhat like that of a soft salicional. To get an idea of this tone, unscrew the hairs of an ordinary bow, place the stick under the violin, lay the hairs over the strings, and fasten them again to the stick. If we move this reversed bow, we obtain the organ-like ethereal tone that the relaxed bow produced.

When we have imitated the old bow as best we can, and given the hairs their utmost tension by thumb pressure in the monophonic passages, we still do not get the powerful tone of the modern mechanically-stretched bow. We purchase beauty of tone, that is to say, at the expense of some loss of strength. The reproach was always being levelled against Ole Bull that his tone was weak.

It is a question whether the modern public would accustom itself to this weak tone. In large concert rooms it will scarcely be possible to play the sonatas for solo violin in the old way, as the tone would not "carry" sufficiently. In chamber music performances, on the other hand, the proper style of rendering should suit admirably. If we have once heard the Chaconne in this way we cannot afterwards endure it in any other. Thus the result would be that the works for solo violin would disappear from the programmes of the larger concerts, and be restored to the chamber music to which they really belong.

The movements of the sonatas for the solo violin that exist also for the piano or organ are arrangements of violin

---

* Schering conjectures that the echo passages that play a large part in Bach's orchestral scores were rendered by all the string players suddenly relaxing the hairs of their bows. It would be interesting to experiment with a string orchestra playing with the old bows.

originals*. It is doubtful whether they are all effective in
this form. They show, however, how completely the violin
method of phrasing ranked with Bach as the universal
method, to which the keyed instruments had to try to
conform. When we read the prelude of the third partita
we find it impossible to believe that Bach could have
entertained the idea of asking the organ to perform these
repeated semiquavers, the proper articulation of which
is possible only on a bowed instrument — yet this is what
he actually does in the instrumental prelude to the "Ratswahl" cantata *Wir danken dir, Gott, wir danken dir* (No.29)**.
He could only venture to do so because he himself played
the part on the *Rückpositiv* on the organ at St. Thomas's.

The fugue of the first sonata may have been originally
conceived for the organ. Its theme is derived from the
first movement of the "Veni Sancte Spiritus", and runs
thus —

Mattheson quotes this theme in his *Grosse Generalbassschule,* and sketches a development of it which resembles
Bach's at many points, especially in the employment of
a chromatic counter-subject. As he quotes in the same
place the theme of the great organ fugue in G minor without mentioning Bach's name, it may be taken for granted
that he had also the fugue of the third sonata before him.
Did Bach play it in Hamburg, about 1720, as an organ
fugue? Assuredly not in the present form, for the structure
of the fugue — it reminds us of the Chaconne — has no-

---

* The fugue from the first sonata (G minor) appears as an organ
fugue in D minor (Peters III, No. 4). The second sonata (A minor)
exists as a clavier sonata in D minor. The first movement of the
third sonata (C major) is arranged for the clavier in G major. It
is very interesting to see how Bach has here transformed and vivified the bass part. (B. G. XLII, p. 27 ff.)

** The cantata was written in 1731.

thing whatever in common with those for the organ, but is wholly designed for the violin. Here again, therefore, the violin form must be the original one*.

In two places Mattheson speaks of the fugue of the A minor sonata —

with unreserved admiration**.

The six sonatas for cello solo also belong to the Cöthen period. They are as perfect in their own way as the works for violin solo. Chord-playing, of course, is not used to anything like the same extent; nor does Bach even employ a simple kind of two-part polyphony. This is to be explained by the fact that the Germans played the "big violin" with the non-relaxable bow.

In quality these suites remind us of the French. The last but one is described as "Suitte discordable", and requires the tuning of the A string down to G, thus

For the last, Bach requires a five-stringed instrument, with an E string above the A There may have been five-stringed cellos at that time. It is more probable, however, that Bach wrote the suite for the

---

* On this question see Spitta II, 82 ff.; he supposes that Mattheson heard Bach play the fugue on the organ, as the former knew it in 1727, at a time when he had probably not seen the sonatas and suites for violin. But why not? Why should not Bach have taken these violin works to Hamburg with him in 1720?
** *Kern Melodischer Wissenschaft* (1737), p. 147; *Der Vollkommene Kapellmeister* (1739), p. 369. He quotes the theme incorrectly each time (Spitta II, 79).

"viola pomposa" that he invented, and that was strung in this way. We know from Gerber, who was the son of one of Bach's pupils, that Bach employed this instrument in the orchestra in the early Leipzig years *. "The stiff way", says the lexicographer, "in which the violoncello was played in Bach's time compelled him to invent, for the animated basses in his works, the so-called viola pomposa, which was a little longer and deeper than a viola, and was tuned like a violoncello, with a fifth string, e, and was laid on the arm; on this convenient instrument very high and rapid passages were easier."

In considering the works for a solo instrument with clavier, we must remember the distinction of that day between the obbligato clavier and the accompanying clavier. In a sonata with obbligato clavier, the latter plays the chief rôle, several obbligato parts being given to it, while the solo instrument has only one. In Bach we do not get a "sonata for violin and clavier", or "sonata for flute and clavier", but "sonata for clavier and violin" and "sonata for clavier and flute". A light is thrown on the way of looking at the matter in that epoch by the fact that a work for clavier and violin, if the polyphony was in three parts, was called a trio; they counted, that is to say, not the instruments but the obbligato parts. By sonata for violin and clavier Bach means a composition in which the clavier only supplies the bass and the figured bass. Even Zelter uses the terms in this sense.

Of Bach's works for obbligato clavier and violin we possess a suite in A major** and six sonatas***; for violin with accompanying clavier he wrote a sonata, a fugue† and four Inventions††.

The suite for clavier and violin is not on the same level

---

* See p. 205.
** B. G. IX, p. 43 ff.
*** B. G. IX, p. 69 ff.
† B. G. XLIII¹, p. 31 ff.
†† B. G. XLV¹, p. 172 ff.

as the six sonatas; it is probably an earlier work. Bach incessantly improved the sonatas, as is shown by the various copies of them. The last version is represented by a copy of Altnikol's. The manuscript that belonged to Emmanuel is overloaded with ornaments. In the same way, Friedemann, when transcribing his father's organ sonatas, embellished them according to the taste of the epoch*. This shows us how much reliance is to be placed on the ornaments in any work of Bach's that we possess only in copies, even though these are by his sons.

These sonatas were written at Cöthen. How small, by the side of them, seem the works of Corelli and the other Italian violin composers, at whose feet Bach had sat in Weimar!

Bach's sonatas, like Beethoven's, depict soul-states and inner experiences, but with force in the place of passion. Whether he is sunk in sorrow or in mystical dreams, Bach always recovers himself in a compact fugal finale.

Sorrow predominates; we could almost imagine that Bach wrote these works under the impression of the loss of his first wife. The Siciliano of the fourth sonata is constructed on a theme that closely resembles that of the aria "Erbarme dich" in the *St. Matthew Passion*, and a sob runs through both of them —

Siciliano from the fourth sonata.

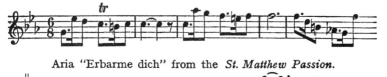

Aria "Erbarme dich" from the *St. Matthew Passion*.

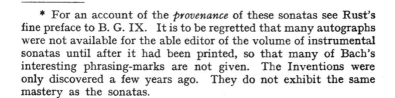

---

* For an account of the *provenance* of these sonatas see Rust's fine preface to B. G. IX. It is to be regretted that many autographs were not available for the able editor of the volume of instrumental sonatas until after it had been printed, so that many of Bach's interesting phrasing-marks are not given. The Inventions were only discovered a few years ago. They do not exhibit the same mastery as the sonatas.

This movement has of course nothing in common with the "Siciliano" of earlier composers except its motion and its rhythm. It has nothing of the lyrical pastoral mood; it is filled with the deepest pathos throughout. It should be played in this spirit, the violin part, as in the corresponding aria in the *St. Matthew Passion*, being heavily rather than lightly accented. The third and sixth quavers should be brought out with some force, and opposed, by means of a certain weight of emphasis, to the following strong beat. If Bach had not conceived it thus he would not have aimed at greater intensity, towards the end, by throwing the accent back on to the weak beat by means of syncopation —

Many of our violinists play these sonatas in a "sentimental" style instead of the "expressive" Bach style. An experienced critic in the *Neue Zeitschrift für Musik* rightly complains that in the practical edition of the new Bachgesellschaft the player will be misled into beginning the proud and energetic themes of the allegro movements in a soft *piano*, in order to get the usual gradual *crescendo* — and will do this even in the theme of the last sonata* —

That this is intended to suggest impetuous motion is shewn by the fact that Bach uses it again, only in fuller form, in the secular cantata *Weichet nur, betrübte Schatten* (B. G. XI²), to illustrate the words "Phoebus flies with swift horses".

---

* See the *Neue Zeitschrift für Musik* for 1904, pp. 686, 687. He also complains with justice that a great number of ties and staccato signs have been inserted in the text.

Of what use are all the *pianos, mezzofortes* and *fortes* that the majority of our players and many editors import into these sonatas? The musician has yet to be born who can convince another where the *piano* or the *forte* or the *crescendo* or *decrescendo* should begin and end in the various movements. Of course the obvious echo effects and the contrast intended between a pianoforte theme in one part and the *tutti* theme in another admit of no question. But what nuances are we to put, for ex-ample, into the first movement of the B minor sonata or that of the E major? Why should we play now softly, now loudly, in the andante of the first sonata? As this alternation is not an essential part of the structure of the works, its only effect must be to create an impression of aimlessness and unrest. What should we say if any one were to paint over fine old steel engravings in modern tints, under the pretext of heightening their effect? Yet there is no such general outcry against the variety of colours that are imposed upon Bach's works.

In general, each movement of the violin sonatas should be played with a uniform strength of tone. This does not mean that they are to be played monotonously. De-clamatory nuances, contained within the range of the general tone-quality, must bring out the detail in the same animated way as in the case of the pianoforte works. But from the architectonic standpoint there should be no insistence, in this music, on variations of tint that will affect the broad plastic lines of it; our modern emo-tional dynamics would obliterate the plan of the work and give a false idea of the co-operation of the three ob-bligato voices*.

We should try to play these sonatas with an eye only to the animated and plastic working-out of the detail, and to a kind of broad declamation, leaving the variety to come from the vivacious interplay of the parts. The

---

* On the principles of the Bachian dynamics see p. 355.

direct impression the pieces make in this way will prove
the rightness of the principle.

As regards the tempo, the andante movements are as
a rule taken rather too slowly, and the allegros much too
fast *. We seldom meet with a player who plays, for example, the theme of the final allegro in the third sonata
in such a way that the hearer receives the impression of
proud strength that should be given by this sequence of
intervals built up on a basis of moving semiquavers —

Even the best performance, however, is not wholly
satisfactory. This is the fault of our pianoforte, the dull
timbre of which does not blend with that of the violin.
It is hopeless to try to blend a modern grand piano and
a stringed instrument; as Wagner, says, the *timbre* of the
piano and that of the violin are incompatible. In a Bach
clavier sonata this is unpleasantly evident, for the composer has calculated on the co-operation of absolutely
homogeneous obbligato parts. This was obtainable in
his day, the cembalo producing the pure tone of a string
vibrating on a wood resonance. It was only slightly
brighter than that of the violin owing to its coming from
a metal string. When the cembalo part is played on a
modern piano the *ensemble* of the equal homogeneous parts
is destroyed; we only hear a solo with pianoforte accompaniment.

Even if, in the future, we should go back to a domestic
instrument that substitutes a pure, silvery *timbre* for the
thick and brutal tone of our huge grands and uprights, the

---

* On the general question of tempo see p. 381.

difficulties with regard to the performance of the sonatas for piano and violin would be only half surmounted. In the clavier parts of these works, Bach counts on the simultaneous doubling of a tone in several octaves, which is possible only on the cembalo. A good cembalo, like that of Friedemann's acquired by Count Voss, had four strings to each note, — two giving the ground tone, one the lower octave, and one the upper octave. According to the couplers he used, the player could strike simply the two ground-tone strings, or these and that of the upper octave, or all four together. The tone was small but very rich. In this respect our modern piano cannot compare for a moment with the sparkling, dashing cembalo. Moreover the player could bring out the theme more pointedly by doubling it in the upper octave, or — if the theme was in the bass — in the lower octave. We can thus imagine how different the adagio of the first sonata, that of the third, and the largo of the fifth, would sound then from what they do on a keyed instrument of today, on which it is impossible to play in three octaves at once. As a matter of fact the adagio of the fifth sonata, with the double stopping in the violin and the arpeggio demisemiquavers in the clavier, is positively unpleasant when performed nowadays. The necesssary vaporousness and at the same time definiteness of the tone can never be got on our grand piano, and the double stopping in the violin is never quite beautiful, for it can only be properly done with the loosened bow. Only in this way can these two violin parts receive the delicate, organ-like tone they need, with the silvery tone of the clavier playing round it*. Nature fortunately is compassionate, and lets us believe that we hear music only with the ears, while in truth we take it in at the same time through the eyes, and correct our hearing accordingly. We enjoy these works because the eye's perception of the

---

* It is an interesting fact that in the original version of this work the piano has semiquavers, not demisemiquavers. See B. G. IX, 250 ff.

beauty of them on the paper, and the mind's conception
of the noble counterpoint, permit the ear to believe that
the works sound well in performance; and the delusion
continues even if both players indulge in senseless alternations of *pianissimo* and *fortissimo*. But any one who has
the misfortune to hear only with the ears is bound to admit
that Bach's sonatas for clavier and violin imperatively
demand the cembalo. This was insisted upon by Rust
in his preface to the original edition (1860)*. He could
not foresee that forty years later the demand would be
still more peremptory, and that an attempt would be made
to meet it by the construction of the new cembali. We
would not deprive those who have only a modern piano
of their pleasure in these sonatas; only we must be quite
clear as to what an ideal performance of the works would
sound like, and not seek this ideal in a false modernisation
of them.

We must not omit to mention the tradition that in performing sonatas of this kind the cembalo bass was helped
by a stringed instrument. We shall, in fact, find that a
discreet violoncello does good service in these works of
Bach, especially where the theme has to be brought out in
the lowest voice. This can be tested, for example, in the
largo of the F minor sonata. An old manuscript — partly
autograph — of the sonatas categorically recommends the
use of an optional gamba to strengthen the bass. It bears
the title: "Sei Suonate à Cembalo certato è Violino Solo
col Basso per Viola da Gamba accompagnato se piace.
Composte da Giov. Sebast. Bach."

The chords to be struck between the obbligato voices
are only rarely figured. They must be added, however, in
every place where the contrapuntal web is thin — for
example, when only the violin part and the bass are at
work, or when the clavier alone is playing in two parts.
If the movement begins with only a bass note, it goes with-

* B. G. IX.

out saying that the whole chord is to be struck, but in such a way as if it were being sounded by another clavier, not by the one that is playing the obbligato parts. In this discreet way the harmonic basis of the whole can be indicated throughout, even when three or more voices are going together. But to handle the piano part in this way requires exceptional skill, and a knowledge of the peculiarities of Bach's figuring, otherwise the harmony will not be correctly filled in. Kirnberger appears to have employed two claviers when playing the sonatas; one played the obbligato parts, the other strengthened the bass and supplied the harmonies*.

We also possess the following instrumental sonatas by Bach: three wonderful ones for clavier and gamba (B. G. IX, p. 175 ff.); three for obbligato clavier and flute (B. G. IX, p. 3 ff.); three for flute with clavier accompaniment (B. G. XLIII[1], p. 3 ff.); one for two violins with clavier accompaniment (B. G. IX, p. 231 ff.); one for two flutes with clavier accompaniment (B. G. IX, p. 260 ff.), which Bach afterwards re-wrote as the first sonata for clavier and gamba, though it sounds better for two flutes**.

The end of the first movement of the third sonata for clavier and flute (A minor) is lacking. Bach wrote it on the same sheet as one of the concertos for two claviers with orchestral accompaniment, employing, in his usual economical way, the three vacant staves at the bottom of each page. From six of these leaves the lower part has been cut away, so that we lack some fifty bars of the sonata***. The autograph was already in this mutilated state when von Winterfeld bought it for a few groschen from an antiquary in Breslau.

The sonata for flute, violin and accompanying clavier

---

* See Rust's remarks on the existence of two clavier parts in Kirnberger's copy of the sonatas (B. G. IX, Preface, p. 17).
** A sonata for violin and clavier in G minor (B. G. IX, p. 274), if it be genuine, is a youthful work.
*** The fragment is given in B. G. IX, 245 ff.

(G major)* is written for the "violino discordato"; Bach desires the player to tune the two upper strings a tone lower, and consequently writes the part out a tone higher. As there is nothing in the violin part that could not equally well be played with the strings tuned in the ordinary way, Bach's purpose in prescribing the peculiar tuning can only have been to get a softer *timbre*, that would blend better with that of the flute.

Of Bach's orchestral works probably scarcely any have been lost; we possess four large suites** and six concertos***.

It cannot be settled whether the suites were written in Cöthen or in Leipzig. In any case Bach performed them not only before the Prince of Cöthen but also in the Telemann Musical Society at Leipzig, which he conducted from 1729 to 1736. He calls these works overtures, not suites or partitas, this being the customary name at that time for an orchestral suite in which the introduction played the chief part. They are, however, just as much real partitas as those in the *Klavierübung*, except that the old dances, — the allemande, the courante and the sarabande, — retire in favour of the newer and freer movements.

The introductions are monumental movements, all constructed on the plan of the French overture. They begin with a stately section; to this succeeds a long and brilliant allegro; at the end the slow section returns. When Mendelssohn, in 1830, played to the old Goethe, on the piano, the overture of the first of the two suites in D major, the poet thought he saw a number of well-dressed people walking in stately fashion down a great staircase†. In 1838 Mendelssohn succeeded in getting them performed by the orchestra at the Gewandhaus, Leipzig. It was the

---

* B. G. IX, 221 ff.
** B. G. XXXI¹ (1881).
*** B. G. XIX (1868).
† See ante, p. 241.

first performance of any of these splendid works since Bach's death*.

In the dance melodies of these suites a fragment of a vanished world of grace and elegance has been preserved for us. They are the ideal musical picture of the rococo period. Their charm resides in the perfection of their blending of strength and grace.

The celebrated "aria" is found in the first D major overture.

The six concertos are known as the "Brandenburg", having been written for the Margrave Christian Ludwig (1677—1734). He was the youngest son of the great Electoral Prince by the latter's second marriage; he was passionately devoted to music, and maintained an excellent orchestra. He made Bach's acquaintance about 1719, perhaps at the Meiningen court, — with which he had relations through his sister, — or perhaps in Karlsbad, when Bach accompanied Prince Leopold there. Enchanted by Bach's playing, he asked him to compose some works for his orchestra. Bach fulfilled this wish and sent him two years later these six concertos with the following dedication: —

A son Altesse Royalle, Monseigneur Crêtien Louis, Marggraf de Brandebourg.

Monseigneur

Comme j'eus il y a une couple** d'années, le bonheur de me faire entendre à Votre Altesse Royalle, en vertu de ses ordres, & que je remarquai alors, qu'Elle prennoit quelque plaisir aux petits talents que le Ciel m'a donnés pour la Musique, et qu'en prennant Conge de Votre Altesse Royalle, Elle voulut bien me faire l'honneur de me commander de Lui envoyer quelques pieces de ma Composition: j'ai donc selon ses tres gracieux ordres, pris la liberté de rendre de mes tres-humbles devoirs à Votre Altesse Royalle,

* They were published, but only in part, by Peters in 1853. The firm did not venture to print the second D major overture until 1881, — not being sure till then, in default of an autograph, that the work was really Bach's!

** This can only mean two years. It is inconceivable that Bach should allow a longer time to elapse before he carried out the wishes of the Prince.

par les presents Concerts, que j'ai accomodés à plusieurs Instruments; La priant tres-humblement de ne vouloir pas juger leur imperfection, à la rigueur du gout fin et delicat, que tout le monde scait qu'Elle a pour les pièces musicales; mais de tirer plutot en benigne Consideration, le profond respet, & la tres-humble obéissance que je tache à Lui témoigner par là. Pour le reste, Monseigneur, je supplie tres humblement Votre Altesse Royalle, d'avoir la bonté de continuer ses bonnes graces envers moi, et d'être persuadée que je n'ai rien tant à cœur, que de pouvoir être employé en des occasions plus dignes d'Elle et de son service, moi qui suis avec une zele sans pareil

Monseigneur   De Votre Altesse Royalle
Le tres humble & tres obeissant serviteur
Jean Sebastien Bach.
Coethen, d. 24 Mar (Mars? Mai?)
1721.

(To his Royal Highness, Monseigneur Crêtien Louis, Margrave of Brandenburg.

Monseigneur,

As I had the honour of playing before Your Royal Highness a couple of years ago, and as I observed that You took some pleasure in the small talent that heaven has given me for music, and in taking leave of Your Royal Highness You honoured me with a command to send You some pieces of my composition, I now, according to Your gracious orders, take the liberty of presenting my very humble respect to Your Royal Highness, with the present concertos, which I have written for several instruments, humbly praying You not to judge their imperfection by the severity of the fine and delicate taste that every one knows You to have for music, but rather to consider benignly the profound respect and the very humble obedience to which they are meant to testify. For the rest, Monseigneur, I very humbly beg Your Royal Highness to have the goodness to continue Your good graces towards me, and to be convinced that I have nothing so much at heart as the wish to be employed in matters more worthy of You and Your service, for with zeal unequalled

Monseigneur,
I am
Your Royal Highness's most humble and most obedient servant
Jean Sebastian Bach.
Coethen, 24 Mar (March? May?)
1721.)

How the Prince received this gift, and how he rewarded Bach for it, we do not know. When he died, these concertos, together with the rest of his large musical collection, were inventoried and valued. They do not, however, figure in the inventory under the composer's name, like those of Vivaldi and other Italians, but are included in two lots, one containing seventy-seven concertos by various writers, the other a hundred. Each of these concertos was valued at four groschen*. Thus in the year 1734 the six Brandenburg concertos were worth twenty-four groschen. At a later date the autograph score which Bach had sent to the Margrave came into the possession of Kirnberger, who left it to his pupil Princess Amalie of Prussia. She bequeathed it to the library of the Joachimsthal Gymnasium, whence it afterwards came to the Royal Library in Berlin. In elegance and cleanness this autograph surpasses even the famous score of the *St. Matthew Passion.* The barlines are drawn throughout with a ruler**.

In spite of all this care, the score contains an error. In the eleventh bar of the fifth concerto the semiquavers of the viola descend in fifths with those of the obbligato cembalo. It is interesting to see that the error is due to a correction made by Bach in the fair copy. He noticed, that is to say, that the viola in the original version — which we have in the orchestral parts, that have been accidentally preserved — ascended in hidden octaves with the solo violin. He at once erased this sequence, which he had already written in the fair copy, and inserted in place of it the descending semiquavers, without observing that in this way he was falling out of the frying-gan into the fire***. This is presumably the passage referred to by Zelter in a passage on Mendelssohn in one of his letters to Goethe. "In the score of a splendid concerto by Sebastian Bach," he says, "the lynx eye of my Felix, when he was ten years old, detected six consecutive fifths, which I perhaps

---

* Spitta discovered this inventory in the Royal domestic archives in Berlin. See his *Bach*, II, 129.

** The concertos were first printed by Peters, in 1850.

*** See Rust's preface to B. G. XIX, p. 17. The Bachgesellschaft editors have elected to print the older version as the lesser evil.

would never have discovered, as I do not bother about these things in large works, and the passage is in six parts *."

The Brandenburg concertos are the purest products of Bach's polyphonic style. Neither on the organ nor on the clavier could he have worked out the architecture of a movement with such vitality; the orchestra alone permits him absolute freedom in the leading and grouping of the obbligato voices. When we said, in another connection that Bach's mode of expression is to be conceived as a plastic one, and deduced from this certain principles for performance, there was a danger of our being misunderstood, as if our object were to try to re-introduce the old, stiff way of playing his music. But one has only to go through these scores, in which Bach has marked all the nuances with the utmost care, to realise that the plastic pursuit of the musical idea is not in the least formal, but alive from beginning to end. Bach takes up the ground-idea of the old concerto, which develops the work out of the alternation of a larger body of tone — the *tutti* — and a smaller one — the *concertino*. Only with him the formal principle becomes a living one. It is not now a question merely of the alternation of the *tutti* and the *concertino*; the various tone-groups interpenetrate and react on each other, separate from each other, unite again, and all with an incomprehensible artistic inevitability. The concerto is really the evolution and the vicissitudes of the theme. We really seem to see before

* *Briefwechsel zwischen Zelter und Goethe,* ed. Reclam II, 394; letter of 25 May 1826. There is another error in the hundred and eighty-second bar (B. G. XIX, p. 120, bar 4). The last three quavers of the first flute descend in octaves with the bass. Spiro's ingenious and unquestionably correct "Bach-conjecture" is well known; he regards the error as simply a clerical one and proposes to play these three quavers a third higher. (See the *Sammelbände der Internationalen Musikgesellschaft,* 1900—1901, pp. 651—653.) It may be less well known that the mistake must be laid not at Bach's door but at that of the editors, as Professor Ludwig, of Strassburg, kindly informs me. See the somewhat confused correction in the following year's issue, — B. G. XXXVIII, p. 45.

us what the philosophy of all ages conceives as the fundamental mystery of things, — that self-unfolding of the idea in which it creates its own opposite in order to overcome it, creates another, which again it overcomes, and so on and on until it finally returns to itself, having meanwhile traversed the whole of existence. We have the same impression of incomprehensible necessity and mysterious contentment when we pursue the theme of one of these concertos, from its entry in the *tutti*, through its enigmatic struggle with its opposite, to the moment when it enters into possession of itself again in the final *tutti*.

In Bach we often have not one but several groups of solo instruments, that are played off against each other in the development of the movement. The wind instruments are used with the audacity of genius. In the first concerto Bach employs, besides the strings, a wind-*ensemble* consisting of two horns, three oboes and bassoon; in the second, flute, oboe, trumpet and violin are used as a kind of solo quartet against the body of the strings; in the third he aims at no contrast of *timbres*, but employs three string trios, all constituted in the same way; in the fourth concerto the *concertino* consists of one violin and two flutes; in the fifth it consists of clavier, flute and violin; in the sixth, Bach employs only the *timbre* effects to be had from the strings, — two violas, two gambas, and cello.

The study of Bach's nuances in these works is a continual source of delight. They are all so simple, and yet so full and rich. Observe, for example, how, in the first movement of the fourth concerto, from the twenty-seventh bar before the end, the *piano* comes down in a wavy line from top to bottom, following the line of the *forte* theme, that winds downwards and lies, as it were, in violent convulsions on the ground, till suddenly a bold *forte* of the whole orchestra puts an end to the unrest that began with the first entry of this subsidiary theme in the violins, and leads into the victorious conclusion.

Many conductors, indeed, are still of opinion that Bach

ought to be corrected here and there; they think that the nuances should not be sharply defined against each other, but should merge into each other by a *crescendo* or *diminuendo*. This, of course, quite destroys the terrace-like plan of Bach's music to which Vianna da Motta has called attention. There are also conductors who try to get a better effect by making a final *tutti* dribble out to a *pianissimo*.

The same rules hold good for the tempo here as in the organ and clavier works; the better the playing, the slower the tempo can be, because when the hearer perceives all the expressive detail a quite moderate tempo has the effect on him of a quick one, while in the faster tempo he could scarcely grasp the rich polyphony.

Are the Brandenburg concertos suitable for our concert halls? No one can doubt this who has heard one of them — say under Steinbach, — and observed the effect on the audience. These works should become popular possessions in the same sense as the Beethoven symphonies are. Spiro finely says, in a glowing article in which he affirms the right of the modern public to Bach's orchestral works, that these concertos in reality are not concertos but symphonies*. It is to be hoped that the overtures also will come into their own before long. Our instrumentalists would profit greatly by going to school to Bach. There are no insuperable difficulties in the way of performance. It is not for the best that the *flutes à bec* in the fourth concerto should have to be replaced by our traverse flutes, but the total effect really does not suffer. Viola players who can also play the gamba will probably be found before long in nearly every orchestra, so that the sixth concerto may some day be freed from its Babylonian captivity. For the second concerto the instrument-makers Alexandre Brothers, of Mainz, have made a small F trumpet, on which

---

* *Bach und seine Transkriptoren*, in the *Neue Zeitschrift für Musik*, 1904, p. 680 ff.

it is possible for any good trumpeter, with a little practice, to play the original Bach part, so that for the future it will not be necessary to modify the part or give it to the clarinet. Mendelssohn had recourse to the latter device when he produced the first D major overture; and it is retained in David's edition of the work for the Gewandhaus concerts. The small *Quartgeige*, giving the four-feet tone, for which Bach writes in the first concerto, must also find cultivators again.

Too large an orchestra is rather a disadvantage to these concertos, as it destroys the natural proportion between the solo instruments and the *tutti*. We are on the very border-line between chamber music and orchestral music. The wood-wind in the *tutti* must of course be increased in proportion to the strings. The accompanying clavier must not be omitted, even when the orchestra is a large one. In a small room a cembalo can be employed; in a large one it is best to have a good table piano, or a small Erard grand of the old style. A modern grand is too dull harmonically. For the "concertising" piano, however, we should always employ a modern grand, as here it must play the part of a solo voice; the harmonies should be given on another piano. It is most desirable also that the basses in the *tutti* be accompanied in octaves by a piano, as this will bring them out more clearly than exaggerated emphasis in the double basses. It will always be noticed that to force the tone anywhere in these works is to spoil the effect.

When once the Brandenburg concertos and the overtures have established themselves in the concert room, the question will arise as to how far some of the preludes to the cantatas can win the same rights of naturalisation. It is already settled, in principle, by the fact that Bach himself does not hesitate to transfer movements from his overtures and concertos into his cantatas. He used the introduction to the first Brandenburg concerto as the "sinfonia" for the cantata *Falsche Welt, dir trau ich nicht*

(No. 52)*, and the first movement of the third concerto
as the prelude to the cantata *Ich liebe den Höchsten von
ganzem Gemüte* (No. 174); but as a piece for strings alone
did not seem to him rich enough for the church, especially
in a festal cantata on Whit Monday, he added in the latter
case three obbligato oboes and two horns, without altering
the original composition. This would be regarded as an
astounding technical feat, had he not eclipsed it by another.
He made the splendid chorus of the Christmas cantata,
Unser Mund sei voll Lachens (No. 110) by simply adding
vocal parts to the allegro of the second overture in D major
(B. G. XXXI, p. 66 ff.). One would almost suppose he
had written the overture and the cantata together; the
allegro theme of the overture is so characteristic a musical
representation of laughter that it seems to have been
prompted by the text of the cantata —

A cantata prelude particularly fitted for performance
as an independent orchestral piece is the wonderful orchestral mood-picture from *Am Abend aber desselbigen
Sabbats* (No. 42), in which Bach paints the silence and the
peace in which the slowly descending twilight envelops
the earth**.

---

  * It is given in the latter form as a supplement to B. G. XXXI¹,
p. 96 ff. The small *Quartgeige* is omitted. The whole of the first
Brandenburg concerto has come down to us in a somewhat shortened
form, in a copy of 1760, also as a "sinfonia", consisting only of
Allegro, Adagio, Minuet, Trio I, and Trio II. See Dörffel's introduction to B. G. XXXI¹, p. 19.
  ** Others are: the vigorous C major symphony from the Easter
cantata *Der Himmel lacht, die Erde jubilieret* (No. 31); the "sonata"
of the cantata *Himmelskönig, sei willkommen* (No. 182); the introduction to the cantatas *Tritt auf die Glaubensbahn* (No. 152) and

The arrangement of Bach's clavier and organ works for orchestra must be regarded as superfluous and imperfect, even when they are as sensitively done as Raff's arrangement of the G minor English suite.

It is misleading to speak of Bach's clavier concertos and violin concertos, as these works have nothing in common with the modern concerto, in which the rôle of the orchestra is largely that of an accompanist. With Bach it is only a matter of giving a specially brilliant obbligato part to the solo instrument. If this happens to be the cembalo it may also play the bass in order to employ both hands.

That Bach thought in the first place of the obbligato part, and only secondarily of the instrument that was to play it, is evident from the fact that the majority of the seven clavier concertos are not primarily planned for the clavier. Almost all are arrangements; six probably come from violin concertos *.

Gleichwie der Regen und Schnee (No. 18); and the orchestral chorale fantasia on *Was Gott tut, das ist wohlgetan*, from the cantata *Die Elenden sollen essen* (No. 75). On a smaller scale are the splendid preludes to *Gottes Zeit* (No. 106), *Nach dir, Herr, verlanget mich* (No. 150), *Ich hatte viel Bekümmernis* (No. 21) and *Ich steh mit einem Fuss im Grabe* (No. 156).

* The concertos will be found in B. G. XVII (1867). No. 1 (D minor) is taken from the lost violin concerto. The first two movements are used again in the jubilee cantata, *Wir müssen durch viel Trübsal* (No. 146). Bach uses the first movement, enriched with three (in part) obbligato oboes, as the introduction to the cantata. On the second movement, the adagio, he super-imposes the main chorus, — an achievement that can be set by the side of the transformation of the D major overture into the opening chorus of the Christmas cantata *Unser Mund ist voll Lachens* (No. 110).

No. 2 (E major). The introduction and the Siciliano of this concerto are used again in the cantata *Gott soll allein mein Herze haben* (No. 169); the finale serves as introduction to the cantata *Ich geh' und suche mit Verlangen* (No. 49). This concerto may have been originally conceived for the clavier.

No. 3 (D major) is a transformation of the violin concerto in E major (B. G. XXI¹, No. 2).

No. 4 (A major) seems also from its *facture* to have been derived from a violin work, although it is somewhat more pianistic in form than the others. The original is unknown.

Bach needed clavier concertos when he directed the
Telemann Society. The arrangements are often made with
quite incredible haste and carelessness; either time was
pressing, or he felt no interest in what he was doing. Violin
effects to which he could easily have given a pianistic turn
are not re-modelled at all; later on he improves them here
and there in the score, but leaves them as they are in
the clavier part *. The reason for this was that he himself
played the cembalo part, and did as he pleased with the
notes before him, making a new part out of them.

We are under no special obligation to incorporate these
transcriptions in our concert programmes. It is otherwise
with the triple concerto for clavier, flute and violin in
A minor, which we are accustomed to regard as *the* Bach
clavier concerto. No audience, surely, could help being
carried away by this work even at a first hearing. It
would certainly occupy the first place in the repertory of
every earnest pianist if the co-operation of the two other
solo instruments and the whole style of the work did not
demand more rehearsals than the majority of concert
directors are in the habit of allowing to a piano concerto.

As is well known, this concerto has grown out of the
clavier prelude and fugue in A minor. On comparing the
sketch with the masterly expansion of it we seem to share
the pride that Bach must have felt when he saw the new

No. 5 (F minor) is an arrangement of a lost violin concerto in
G minor, as is shown beyond question by the nature of the work.

No. 6 (F major) is identical with the fourth Brandenburg concerto (B. G. XIX, p. 85 ff., G major).

No. 7 (G minor) is the A minor violin concerto (B. G. XXI[1],
No. 2). In the last six empty staves of the G minor concerto we
find the commencement of a second D minor concerto for piano,
that has come down to us complete as the introduction to the cantata *Geist und Seele wird verwirret* (No. 35).

For further information see Rust's preface to B. G. XVII.

* Rust gives the oldest originals of the arrangements in B. G.
XVII, p. 273 ff. The first transcription of the D minor concerto
is particularly interesting.

work arise in all its majesty out of the old. The middle movement is taken from the organ sonata in D minor*.

Of the three concertos for two claviers and orchestra, two — the first and the third — are arrangements of concertos for two violins**. The original of the first, in C minor, no longer exists; the third, also in C minor, is identical with the D minor concerto for two violins***. How Bach could venture to transfer the two cantabile violin parts in the largo of this work to the cembalo, with its abrupt tone, must be left to himself to answer. Had he not done it himself, we should be protesting in his name today against so un-Bach-like a transcription. This is not the only case in which he makes it hard for his prophets to go forth in his name against the evil transcribers.

The one original concerto, however — No. 2, in C major — compensates us for all our disappointed expectations in the two others, — if we can speak of disappointment in connection with Bach. The fact that it was originally conceived for two claviers is shown at once not only by the rich writing for the two solo parts, (in the third section of the splendid fugue they are in three parts throughout,) but also by the subordinate position given to the orchestra. It is not an orchestral concerto with two soli cembali, but a concerto for two claviers with orchestral accompaniment. Perhaps, indeed, the first movement existed at one time without instrumental accompaniment. Certain

---

* The concerto is given in B. G. XVII, p. 223, where it is styled the eighth clavier concerto. On the question of its relation to the prelude and fugue in A minor and the middle movement of tho third organ sonata, see ante p. 339. The fifth Brandenburg concerto (D major), that is on the same lines, might be called the second of Bach's original concertos for clavier. For both there exist, besides the part for the solo cembalo, one for the accompanying cembalo, which adds the harmonies in the *tutti* passages. But even for the ordinary clavier concertos Bach made use of two claviers, as is shown by the fourth concerto (A major), for which he wrote out with his own hand the part for the accompanying clavier.

** B. G. XXI² (1871).

*** B. G. XXI¹, p. 41.

indications go to show that this was added later, and that Bach wrote it out at first not in score but in parts. Otherwise we cannot explain how it happens that in two places of this first allegro, — bars 83 and 108 — the orchestra enters with the major third, while the clavier parts maintain the minor third, — which grows logically out of what has gone before, — and do not make it major until the following crochet. Bach would certainly have noticed this error had he had the clavier and orchestral parts before him in the score. The curious thing is that the mistake was not noticed in performance, and at once corrected in the clavier parts[*].

An accompanying piano is not necessary here, the two solo claviers themselves supplying the most essential harmonies. The *cembalo accompagnato* is here really the orchestra, consisting of a simple string quartet, which in reality only plays a figured bass that has a good deal of rhythmical interest. In a performance in a small room it can be quite well replaced by a third piano. An ordinarily good player could easily play the part direct from the orchestral score. We could even arrange for the two pianos all that is really indispensable in the orchestral accompaniment[**].

The two concertos for three claviers (B. G. XXXI[3]) are constructed on the principle that underlies the original works for two claviers. In them also the string quartet retires into the background. For the most part it only supplies the harmonies, and aims at supporting and throwing into relief the leading part in the *ensemble* of the three

---

[*] The observation is Rust's; see his preface to B. G. XXI[2], p. 8. The error is of course corrected in the B. G. edition. Rust's hypothesis that Bach resorted to this concerto form from the desire to omit the third (accompanying) clavier from the other concertos for two claviers, — in which, however, it is a necessity — cannot be regarded as proved.

[**] This had been already observed by Forkel (p. 58). He also mentions that Pachelbel had written a toccata for two claviers. Spitta conjectures that Bach knew Couperin's allemande for two pianos. No works of importance for two claviers belonging to that epoch seem to be known, except those of Bach.

claviers. The second concerto — it is not agreed whether the original key is C major or D major — is planned on larger lines than the first (D minor), and the orchestra plays a more important part in it. In the adagio there are even *tutti* passages in which the three claviers merely accompany the orchestra. The tonal and rhythmical effects that Bach has achieved with three claviers are indescribable. At every hearing of these works we stand amazed before the mystery of so incredible a power of invention and combination.

An old tradition has it that Bach wrote these two concertos in order to play them with his two eldest sons. If this be true, they must date from about 1730—1733.

The concerto for four claviers (A minor) is based upon a Vivaldi concerto for four violins*.

Of the violin concertos we possess only the half — those left by Philipp Emmanuel; those belonging to Friedemann are probably lost for ever. We have three concertos for violin and orchestra (A minor, E major and G major)**; an important fragment of an allegro movement from a work for violin and large orchestra (D major)***; and a concerto for two violins with simple string orchestra (D minor)†. Of lost violin concertos at least three — two for one violin and one for two violins — have come down to us in clavier arrangements††.

---

* B. G. XLIII[1], p. 71 ff. The Italian original is printed after it. From the middle of the nineteenth century it has been regarded as lost, though Hilgenfeld had seen it.

** A minor and E major in B. G. XXI[1], pp. 3 ff. and 21 ff.; as clavier concertos (G minor and D major) in B. G. XVII, pp. 199 ff. and 81 ff. The G major concerto figures as the fourth of the Brandenburgs in B. G. XIX, p. 85 ff.; as a clavier concerto (F major) in B. G. XVII, p. 153 ff.

*** B. G. XXI[1], p. 65 ff. The end has been added by another hand.

† B. G. XXI[1], p. 41 ff.; as a concerto for two claviers (C minor) in B. G. XXI[2], p. 83 ff.

†† The clavier concerto in D minor (B. G. XVII, p. 3 ff.) corresponds to a violin concerto in D minor; that in F minor (B. G. XVII, p. 135 ff.) to a violin concerto in G minor; the concerto for

The concertos for violin and orchestra that have survived are among the works of Bach to which it is useless to employ the method of analysis; we must put them in the category of which Forkel briefly and eloquently observes: "One can never say enough of their beauty." The A minor and E major concertos are beginning to win a place in our concert halls. Modern audiences are enthralled by the two adagio movements, in which the violin moves about over a *basso ostinato*. We involuntarily associate them with the idea of Fate. The beauty of the A minor concerto is severe, that of the E major full of an unconquerable joy of life, that sings its song of triumph in the first and last movements.

The concerto for two violins, in D minor, is perhaps more widely known still. It can be played at home, as its orchestral part can be easily transcribed for the piano. Every amateur should know the wonderful peace of the *largo ma non tanto* in F major.

The concerto in E major was regularly given in the Berlin Singakademie even in Zelter's time. This Bach-improver — for such he is shewn to be by his revision of the parts and the marks of expression he has added — thought it necessary to have more alternations of solo and *tutti* than Bach had indicated. Emmanuel seems to have performed this concerto in Hamburg, otherwise he would not have had the parts copied so carefully.

Forkel has a notable passage to the effect that Bach had instrumental soli played during the communion, and wrote most of his own for this purpose[*]. Of the violin

two claviers in C minor (B. G. XXI[2], p. 3 ff.) points to the existence of a concerto for two violins in the same key. This list, however, must comprise only a few of the lost compositions for violin and orchestra. A re-arrangement of these clavier concertos for violin is desirable.

[*] Forkel, p. 60. The theory is only mentioned here to be scouted. It is a pure conjecture of Forkel's, who confesses, in his chapter on the instrumental works, that he knows hardly anything of them, and finds it more interesting to lament as lost a genus of Bach composition that he himself cannot imagine.

concertos, however, he could have used only the largo from the concerto for two violins.

In modern performances of the two concertos for single violin the orchestra is generally too large. This becomes unpleasantly noticeable when the *basso ostinato* in the middle movements is played in an intolerably heavy style by half a dozen contrabasses and twice as many cellos. The accompanying piano is usually omitted, without regard for those hearers who are conscious of gaps in the passages where only the violin and the bass are playing. Ysaye plays these concertos in captivating style, even though at times he modernises them too much; but his habit of having the general bass performed on a harmonium is inexplicable either on historical, or logical, or musical grounds.

CHAPTER XVIII.

THE MUSICAL OFFERING AND THE ART OF FUGUE.

The Musical Offering: B. G. XXXI^2; Peters Ed. of the Clavier Works, Part XII.
The Art of Fugue: B. G. XXV^1; Peters Ed. of the Clavier Works, Part XI.

Bach wrote *The Musical Offering* on his return from Potsdam in 1747. He had been received by the King on May 7th; on July 7th he sent him his gift. The composition and the engraving of it had therefore been a matter of less than two months. Nor did the engraver even live in Leipzig. It was Schübler, of Zella, through whom Bach had already published several clavier works and six organ chorales.

The copy with the dedication passed from the possession of Princess Amalie into that of the Joachimsthaler Gymnasium, and is now in the Royal Library at Berlin. Bach's dedication runs thus: —

Allergnädigster König

Ew. Majestät weyhe hiermit in tieffster Unterthänigkeit ein Musicalisches Opfer, dessen edelster Theil von Deroselben hoher Hand selbst herrührt. Mit einem ehrfurchtsvollen Vergnügen erinnere ich mich annoch der ganz besonderen Königlichen Gnade, da vor einiger Zeit, bey meiner Anwesenheit in Potsdam, Ew. Matestät selbst, ein Thema zu einer Fuge auf dem Clavier mir vorzuspielen geruheten, und zugleich allergnädigst auferlegten, solches alsobald in Deroselben höchsten Gegenwart auszuführen. Ew. Majestät Befehl zu gehorsamen, war meine unterthänigste Schuldigkeit. Ich bemerkte aber gar bald, dass wegen Mangels nöthiger Vorbereitung, die Ausführung nicht also gerathen wollte, als es ein so treffliches Thema erforderte. Ich fassete demnach den Entschluss, und machte mich sogleich anheischig, dieses recht Königliche Thema vollkommen auszuarbeiten, und sodann der Welt bekannt zu machen. Dieser Vorsatz ist nunmehro nach Vermögen bewerkstelliget worden, und er hat keine andere als nur diese untadelhafte Absicht, den Ruhm eines Monarchen, ob gleich nur in einem kleinen Puncte, zu verherrlichen, dessen Grösse und Stärke, gleich wie in allen Kriegs- und Friedens-Wissenschaften, also auch besonders in der Musik, jedermann bewundern und verehren muss. Ich erkühne mich dieses unterthänigste Bitten hinzuzufügen: Ew. Majestät geruhen gegenwärtige wenige Arbeit mit einer gnädigen Aufnahme zu würdigen, und Deroselben allerhöchste Königliche Gnade noch fernerweit zu gönnen

Ew. Majestät

allerunterthänigst gehorsamsten Knechte,

Leipzig, den 7. Julii.

1747.   dem Verfasser.

("Most gracious King:

To Your Majesty I dedicate herewith, in deepest submissiveness, a Musical Offering, the noblest part of which comes from your own exalted hand. It is with respectful pleasure that I remember still the very special royal favour with which, on my recent visit to Potsdam, Your Majesty Yourself deigned to give me on the clavier a theme for a fugue, and most graciously imposed on me the command to develop it at once in Your Majesty's exalted presence. It was my most humble duty to obey Your Majesty's command. I soon observed however, that owing to the lack of necessary preparation, the working-out was not as successful as so excellent a theme demanded. Therefore I resolved, and set to work immediately, to work out fully this truly royal theme, and then make it known to the world. This undertaking has now been accomplished to the best of my ability, and it has no other object than the irreproachable one of exalting, if even in only a small degree, the fame of a Monarch whose greatness and power in all the arts both of war and of peace, but especially in music, everyone must admire and honour. I make bold to add this most humble request, that Your Majesty will deign to honour this small work with Your gracious acceptance, and continue to bestow Your most exalted kindly favour on Your Majesty's most humble and obedient servant,

The Author."

Leipzig, 7th July 1747.)

Along with this dedication, however, he sent only the first third of the work, as far as the six-part ricercare*; the two remaining parts he probably sent to the King by the hands of his son.

Five leaves in brown leather binding with gold tooling form the bulk of the portion sent first. The paper is of uncommon fineness and strength. The dedication occupies two leaves; then follows the three-part ricercare and a canon. Afterwards comes a separate large folio-sheet with the *Canon perpetuus*, five *Canones diversi*, and the *Fuga canonica in Epidiapente*, all upon the *Thema regium*.

The ricercare is rather a fugal three-part fantasia than a fugue, and contains many surprising things**. We ask, for instance, what is the meaning of the triplet passage that enters unmotived at the thirty-first bar, especially as it is at once abandoned, and twice again emerges only to disappear at once. Why did not Bach open his work with a larger and stricter piano fugue upon the royal theme? The most natural explanation is that he wished to keep to the improvisation that he had made before the monarch. The "complete working-out" of which the dedication speaks must consequently be taken to mean, with regard to the first piece, only a fundamental revision of the fugue actually played on the 7th May. We thus possess one of Bach's improvisations, written down by his

---

* Ricercare was originally the term for all imitative and fugal pieces, even when they were very freely developed. Etymologically the word signifies a piece of music in which we have to "seek" something — namely, the theme. In Bach's day it signified a fugue worked out with particular ingenuity.

** It is inscribed: *Regis Jussu Cantio et Reliqua Canonica Arte Resoluta* — an acrostic on the word "ricercare".

own hand. That this is so is further suggested by the unusual freedom and animation of the fugue*. It is regrettable that this splendid work, not being included among the clavier compositions, is almost unknown to the majority of players.

The royal theme runs thus —

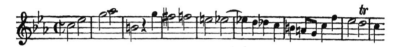

Frederick had desired Bach to extemporise a six-part fugue for him. Bach did so, not, however, on the King's theme but on one of his own, giving as his excuse that it was not every theme that lent itself to six-part treatment. Afterwards he made it a point of honour to work out the King's theme also in six parts. Thus originated the ricercare, which, with two supplementary canons, constituted the second consignment. This is not so luxuriously got up as the first; it consists of four ordinary leaves, held together by a pin.

The six-part ricercare is Bach's richest piece of fugal writing. In order to allow of a more comprehensive view of it, he wrote it out in score on six staves. It is, however, as playable on the piano as any of the fugues of the *Welltempered Clavichord***.

From the technical standpoint the work is unique; but we seek in vain in it for the inspiration and the poetry that make the fugues of the *Well-tempered Clavichord* so beautiful. No matter how often we play it, it affords no lasting satisfaction. It is a product of Bach's last creative period, in which the contrapuntal technique, though not

---

* Observe, for example, the almost wanton play he makes with the diminution of the theme.

** In the autograph that Bach sent to the engraver, the fugue is compressed into two staves. In this form, which is more convenient for the player, it is given as a supplement to B. G. XXXI² p. 45 ff.

actually an aim in itself, nevertheless plays the leading part, the invention taking a subordinate place.

The *Musical Offering* ends with a sonata for flute, violin, and accompanying clavier, to which there is added a *canon perpetuus*. It is in four movements, — largo, allegro, andante, allegro. In the largo the royal theme is merely suggested; in the fugued allegro it is used as the *cantus firmus*; the andante harks back to motives from the three-part ricercare; the royal theme forms the basis of the finale in this form —

Bach thus wrote two sonatas for flute, violin and accompanying clavier; one in the Weimar or the Cöthen period*, the other three years before his death. The difference between the two works is enormous. The first belongs to his naïve period, when he was solely intent on beauty of sound. When we listen to it we seem to be wandering by a woodland brook, over meadows that the morning dew has studded with diamonds. The later sonata transports us to great mountain heights, where vegetation ceases, and peaks, rising one above the other, stand out in sharp outlines against the blue sky. The beauty of the trio-sonata of the *Musical Offering* is of this quality. It is profound and severe, without any of the gracious charm that distinguishes the work of the youthful period**.

We have a manuscript copy of the *Musical Offering* in which the figured bass of the clavier part is written out by

---

* In G major: largo, vivace, adagio, presto. B. G. IX, p. 221 ff.
** The first re-issue of the *Musical Offering* was made by Breitkopf and Härtel in 1832; Peters brought it out in 1866.

Kirnberger *. This work by a pupil of Bach is invaluable as showing us how simply and correctly the composer wished the figured bass to be worked out.

The *Musical Offering* contains in all ten canons, including the *fuga canonica* at the end of the first part. They are not canons in the ordinary sense of the word, aiming at a definite musical effect, but clever musical charades, of the kind that the musicians of that time were fond of propounding to each other. The solutions of the first six canons are given by Kirnberger in his *Kunst des reinen Satzes***. In two of them, — the fourth and the fifth — Bach aims at a certain musical symbolism. Over the fourth, in which the theme is treated in augmentation in contrary motion, he writes: "Notulis crescentibus crescat Fortuna Regis", ("May the good fortune of the King increase like that of the note-values"). The fifth, a circle canon ascending through the scale, is inscribed: "Ascendenteque Modulatione ascendat Gloria Regis", ("And as the modulation ascends, so may it be with the glory of the King").

It was the custom to indicate the way to the solution of the canon by showing the notes of the theme on which the other parts had to enter. In the two canons that precede the sonata, Bach omits this hint. "Quaerendo invenietis" ("Seek, and ye shall find!") runs his inscription. The first is in two parts, the second in four. While the latter is clear enough, the former permits of several solutions, which were put forward by Agricola, Kirnberger, and the Freiburg cantor Fischer — the latter in the *Allgemeine musikalische Zeitung* of 1806***.

Besides these we have five other canons by Bach. One is given by Marpurg in his *Abhandlung von der Fuge*; another, belonging to the year 1713, was inscribed to an

---

* It is reproduced in B. G. XXXI², p. 52 ff.
** Vol. II, p. 45 ff.; reproduced in B. G. XXXI², p. 41 ff. See also Spitta III, 195.
*** B. G. XXXI², pp. 12 and 13 (Preface) and 49. Spitta III, 195.

unknown person, probably his Weimar colleague and friend
Walther; he paid the same honour, during his Hamburg
journey of 1727, to an amateur of that town, a "Monsieur
Houdemann", who returned the compliment with a poem
on Bach*; another canon, also given in Marpurg's *Abhandlung von der Fuge*, was inscribed, so Spitta conjectures,
to Schmidt, the organist at Zella; the fifth canon is found
on Hausmann's picture of Bach, belonging to St. Thomas's
school**.

While engaged on the *Musical Offering*, Bach resolved
to carry out systematically a plan which he had here undertaken somewhat unsystematically, — to write a complete
work on a single theme. The new work was to be a practical
illustration of the art of fugue.

It is an error to say he did not complete the *Art of Fugue*.
He died before the engraving was completed; hence the
work has come down to us in a seemingly incomplete form.
During the last weeks of Bach's life none of the elder sons
was with his father. After his death they went on with
the engraving in ignorance of what his plan had been.
The plates were prepared by Schübler, of Zella, to whom
Bach had also entrusted the engraving of the *Musical
Offering***. Perhaps Bach had originally intended to etch
the work himself on copper; three pages of the autograph,
written in such a way that they could be reproduced directly on the plate, point to this intention.

How little Schübler and the sons were acquainted with
Bach's design is evident from the fact that they paid no
regard to a list of errors, carefully made by Bach, that
has fortunately come down to us. They were not even
clear as to the arrangement of the pieces. Moreover they

---

* See p. 185.
** These canons and their solutions are given in B. G. XLV[1]
(1895), pp. 131—138. See also Spitta I, 387; III, 228, 229, 265.
*** Four copies of the original edition still exist, as well as an
autograph of Bach's of an earlier date. The work was first issued
afresh by Nägeli, of Zürich, and afterwards by Peters, of Leipzig.

inserted a simple variant as a new piece, — fugue No. 14 is identical with fugue No. 10, except that it lacks the first twenty-two bars.   Rust thinks that the whole style of the edition indicates that none of the elder sons had anything to do with it.   That is not so; they merely attended to it in a hurry.

Among Bach's papers was found also a large fugue upon three themes, at which he had worked until the last, without finishing it.   Emmanuel and Friedemann thought it had been intended for the *Art of Fugue*, and printed it there, unfinished as it was.   In order, however, that the work might not end in this incomplete way, they added the organ chorale "Wenn wir in höchsten Nöten sind", which Bach had dictated to Altnikol.   No one can say whether it had really been his intention to end the *Art of Fugue* with these two works.   In a sense they belong to it, in another sense not.   They have nothing to do with the specimen fugues, for they are not based on the same subject.   On the other hand, they are so skilfully worked out, — see, for example, Bach's constant manipulation of the theme in inversion in the organ chorale, — that he may well have written them with a view to their forming an appendix to the *Art of Fugue*.

The three themes of the unfinished fugue run thus: —

The three separate fugues on these themes are completed; Bach is just about to combine them at the point
where the manuscript breaks off.

The theme of the last fugue spells Bach's name. In the
Weimar days Bach had remarked to his colleague Walther
upon the peculiarity of the four letters of his name, as
accounting for the musical aptitudes of the Bach family.
Walther mentions this at the end of the meagre little
article that he devotes to his former friend in his musical
dictionary (1732), and expressly says that the "remarque"
came from Herr Kapellmeister Bach himself*. This makes
it all the more curious that Bach should have waited until
the last year of his life before making a fugue on this interesting theme. Friedemann, when questioned by Forkel
upon this point, said positively that his father had never
written any fugue but this upon the family name**. The
various fugues on B A C H, that claim to have been composed by Johann Sebastian, therefore cannot be his. There
are four of these. One of them, if not like Bach, is not
uninteresting. Spitta tries to preserve the ascription of
at least two of these fugues. They are not printed in the
B. G. edition, however, even among the doubtful works;
only the themes are given***.

The theme B A C H is a favorite one with the moderns.
Liszt and Schumann have written fugues upon it. In
Reger's music we fancy we can often detect it even where
it is not expressly indicated. Nor must we forget Barblan's
accomplished organ passacaglia on B A C H.

The *Art of Fugue* was published some months after Bach's
death, at the price of four thalers. It had, however, no sale;
then, at Emmanuel's request, Marpurg (1718—1795) wrote
a preface to it; and the work was re-issued with a new cover

---

* See also p. 186.
** Forkel told this to Griepenkerl, by whom it was communi-
cated to Roitzsch, from whom the tradition comes.
*** Spitta III, 206, 207. For the themes of the four apocryphal
fugues on B A C H, see B. G. XLII (1892), Preface, p. 34.

and the recommendation of the celebrated theoretician at the Leipzig Easter fair of 1752. Its worth was recognised; Mattheson praised it warmly*; but still it did not sell. In 1756 Emmanuel had sold barely thirty copies. The hundred and thirty thalers received did not cover the cost; and the disappointed son sold the plates of his father's last work for the value of the metal. Such was the fate of the *Art of Fugue*.

In his biography Forkel says indignantly, "If a work of this kind, by so exceedingly famous a man as Bach, had appeared anywhere but in Germany, perhaps ten fine editions would have been taken up out of pure patriotism. In Germany there were not sold even enough copies to pay for the copper-plates and the engraving**."

Perhaps Forkel's exasperation with his countrymen carries him too far. It was not the fault of individuals, but of the epoch, that the great cantor's work had no success. Music had struck into new paths that led it away from the fugal style, and those who were still interested in it were not fugue masters but fugue schoolmasters, and incompetent to understand the true Bach, however much they swore by him. We get this impression even from Marpurg's preface, which partly consists of only a moderately clever polemic against the new tendency that refuses to recognise the fugue as the vital cornerstone of music***.

The *Art of Fugue* consists of fourteen fugues and four canons on the theme —

The theme cannot strictly be called interesting; it is not a stroke of genius, but has plainly been made with

---

* For his remarks upon it see p. 226.
** p. 53.
*** See B. G. XXV¹, prefatory notes, pp. 15 and 16.

an eye to its manifold "workableness" and capacity for inversion. Nevertheless it grows upon us after repeated hearings. It introduces us to a still and serious world, deserted and rigid, without colour, without light, without motion; it does not gladden, does not distract; yet we cannot break away from it.

We get the same impression from the first four fugues, that deal with the theme itself and its inversion. With the fifth fugue, however, the monotony of the theme is broken. The regular pace of the first four notes becomes more varied rhythmically; the theme acquires a grave movement –

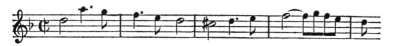

From the eighth fugue onwards it becomes more and more animated, until, in the eleventh, it assumes the following form —

All the possible fugue types, including those of which Bach himself had never made use, are represented in the *Art of Fugue*. We do not know which to wonder at most — that all these combinations could be devised by one mind, or that, in spite of the ingenuity of it all, the parts always flow along as naturally and freely as if the way were not prescribed for them by this or that purely technical necessity.

His purpose in this work being a purely theoretical one, Bach writes the fugues out in score, and calls them "counterpoints".

The last four fugues are grouped in pairs, each of a pair being note for note an exact inversion of the other, as if we were reading it in a mirror. They are in three parts; the negative stands immediately under the positive. Here again Bach soars playfully above every technical difficulty. The pieces are bright and animated from beginning to end, as if it were a pure accident that one of them happened to be the reflection of the other.

Bach himself must have felt the purest pride in them. He arranged the last pair for two claviers, adding a fourth obbligato part so that both instruments should be fully occupied. In this form the last two pieces of the *Art of Fugue* were given as a supplement, and when the work was republished in the nineteenth century this part of it was fastened on by the pianists and soon became the most popular of all. The theme runs thus —

A CATALOGUE OF SELECTED DOVER BOOKS
IN ALL FIELDS OF INTEREST

A CATALOGUE OF SELECTED DOVER BOOKS
IN ALL FIELDS OF INTEREST

WHAT IS SCIENCE?, *N. Campbell*
The role of experiment and measurement, the function of mathematics, the nature of scientific laws, the difference between laws and theories, the limitations of science, and many similarly provocative topics are treated clearly and without technicalities by an eminent scientist. "Still an excellent introduction to scientific philosophy," H. Margenau in *Physics Today.* "A first-rate primer . . . deserves a wide audience," *Scientific American.* 192pp. 5⅜ x 8.
Paperbound $1.25

THE NATURE OF LIGHT AND COLOUR IN THE OPEN AIR, *M. Minnaert*
Why are shadows sometimes blue, sometimes green, or other colors depending on the light and surroundings? What causes mirages? Why do multiple suns and moons appear in the sky? Professor Minnaert explains these unusual phenomena and hundreds of others in simple, easy-to-understand terms based on optical laws and the properties of light and color. No mathematics is required but artists, scientists, students, and everyone fascinated by these "tricks" of nature will find thousands of useful and amazing pieces of information. Hundreds of observational experiments are suggested which require no special equipment. 200 illustrations; 42 photos. xvi + 362pp. 5⅜ x 8.
Paperbound $2.00

THE STRANGE STORY OF THE QUANTUM, AN ACCOUNT FOR THE GENERAL READER OF THE GROWTH OF IDEAS UNDERLYING OUR PRESENT ATOMIC KNOWLEDGE, *B. Hoffmann*
Presents lucidly and expertly, with barest amount of mathematics, the problems and theories which led to modern quantum physics. Dr. Hoffmann begins with the closing years of the 19th century, when certain trifling discrepancies were noticed, and with illuminating analogies and examples takes you through the brilliant concepts of Planck, Einstein, Pauli, Broglie, Bohr, Schroedinger, Heisenberg, Dirac, Sommerfeld, Feynman, etc. This edition includes a new, long postscript carrying the story through 1958. "Of the books attempting an account of the history and contents of our modern atomic physics which have come to my attention, this is the best," H. Margenau, Yale University, in *American Journal of Physics.* 32 tables and line illustrations. Index. 275pp. 5⅜ x 8.
Paperbound $1.75

GREAT IDEAS OF MODERN MATHEMATICS: THEIR NATURE AND USE, *Jagjit Singh*
Reader with only high school math will understand main mathematical ideas of modern physics, astronomy, genetics, psychology, evolution, etc. better than many who use them as tools, but comprehend little of their basic structure. Author uses his wide knowledge of non-mathematical fields in brilliant exposition of differential equations, matrices, group theory, logic, statistics, problems of mathematical foundations, imaginary numbers, vectors, etc. Original publication. 2 appendixes. 2 indexes. 65 ills. 322pp. 5⅜ x 8.
Paperbound $2.00

The Music of the Spheres: The Material Universe — From Atom to Quasar, Simply Explained, *Guy Murchie*
Vast compendium of fact, modern concept and theory, observed and calculated data, historical background guides intelligent layman through the material universe. Brilliant exposition of earth's construction, explanations for moon's craters, atmospheric components of Venus and Mars (with data from recent fly-by's), sun spots, sequences of star birth and death, neighboring galaxies, contributions of Galileo, Tycho Brahe, Kepler, etc.; and (Vol. 2) construction of the atom (describing newly discovered sigma and xi subatomic particles), theories of sound, color and light, space and time, including relativity theory, quantum theory, wave theory, probability theory, work of Newton, Maxwell, Faraday, Einstein, de Broglie, etc. "Best presentation yet offered to the intelligent general reader," *Saturday Review*. Revised (1967). Index. 319 illustrations by the author. Total of xx + 644pp. 5⅜ x 8½.
Vol. 1 Paperbound $2.00, Vol. 2 Paperbound $2.00,
The set $4.00

Four Lectures on Relativity and Space, *Charles Proteus Steinmetz*
Lecture series, given by great mathematician and electrical engineer, generally considered one of the best popular-level expositions of special and general relativity theories and related questions. Steinmetz translates complex mathematical reasoning into language accessible to laymen through analogy, example and comparison. Among topics covered are relativity of motion, location, time; of mass; acceleration; 4-dimensional time-space; geometry of the gravitational field; curvature and bending of space; non-Euclidean geometry. Index. 40 illustrations. x + 142pp. 5⅜ x 8½.
Paperbound $1.35

How to Know the Wild Flowers, *Mrs. William Starr Dana*
Classic nature book that has introduced thousands to wonders of American wild flowers. Color-season principle of organization is easy to use, even by those with no botanical training, and the genial, refreshing discussions of history, folklore, uses of over 1,000 native and escape flowers, foliage plants are informative as well as fun to read. Over 170 full-page plates, collected from several editions, may be colored in to make permanent records of finds. Revised to conform with 1950 edition of Gray's Manual of Botany. xlii + 438pp. 5⅜ x 8½.
Paperbound $2.00

Manual of the Trees of North America, *Charles Sprague Sargent*
Still unsurpassed as most comprehensive, reliable study of North American tree characteristics, precise locations and distribution. By dean of American dendrologists. Every tree native to U.S., Canada, Alaska; 185 genera, 717 species, described in detail—leaves, flowers, fruit, winterbuds, bark, wood, growth habits, etc. plus discussion of varieties and local variants, immaturity variations. Over 100 keys, including unusual 11-page analytical key to genera, aid in identification. 783 clear illustrations of flowers, fruit, leaves. An unmatched permanent reference work for all nature lovers. Second enlarged (1926) edition. Synopsis of families. Analytical key to genera. Glossary of technical terms. Index. 783 illustrations, 1 map. Total of 982pp. 5⅜ x 8.
Vol. 1 Paperbound $2.25, Vol. 2 Paperbound $2.25,
The set $4.50

IT'S FUN TO MAKE THINGS FROM SCRAP MATERIALS,
Evelyn Glantz Hershoff
What use are empty spools, tin cans, bottle tops? What can be made from
rubber bands, clothes pins, paper clips, and buttons? This book provides
simply worded instructions and large diagrams showing you how to make
cookie cutters, toy trucks, paper turkeys, Halloween masks, telephone sets,
aprons, linoleum block- and spatter prints — in all 399 projects! Many are easy
enough for young children to figure out for themselves; some challenging
enough to entertain adults; all are remarkably ingenious ways to make things
from materials that cost pennies or less! Formerly "Scrap Fun for Everyone."
Index. 214 illustrations. 373pp. 5⅜ x 8½. Paperbound $1.50

SYMBOLIC LOGIC and THE GAME OF LOGIC, *Lewis Carroll*
"Symbolic Logic" is not concerned with modern symbolic logic, but is instead
a collection of over 380 problems posed with charm and imagination, using
the syllogism and a fascinating diagrammatic method of drawing conclusions.
In "The Game of Logic" Carroll's whimsical imagination devises a logical game
played with 2 diagrams and counters (included) to manipulate hundreds of
tricky syllogisms. The final section, "Hit or Miss" is a lagniappe of 101 additional puzzles in the delightful Carroll manner. Until this reprint edition,
both of these books were rarities costing up to $15 each. Symbolic Logic:
Index. xxxi + 199pp. The Game of Logic: 96pp. 2 vols. bound as one. 5⅜ x 8.
Paperbound $2.00

MATHEMATICAL PUZZLES OF SAM LOYD, PART I
selected and edited by M. Gardner
Choice puzzles by the greatest American puzzle creator and innovator. Selected
from his famous collection, "Cyclopedia of Puzzles," they retain the unique
style and historical flavor of the originals. There are posers based on arithmetic,
algebra, probability, game theory, route tracing, topology, counter and sliding
block, operations research, geometrical dissection. Includes the famous "14-15"
puzzle which was a national craze, and his "Horse of a Different Color" which
sold millions of copies. 117 of his most ingenious puzzles in all. 120 line
drawings and diagrams. Solutions. Selected references. xx + 167pp. 5⅜ x 8.
Paperbound $1.00

STRING FIGURES AND HOW TO MAKE THEM, *Caroline Furness Jayne*
107 string figures plus variations selected from the best primitive and modern
examples developed by Navajo, Apache, pygmies of Africa, Eskimo, in Europe,
Australia, China, etc. The most readily understandable, easy-to-follow book in
English on perennially popular recreation. Crystal-clear exposition; step-by-
step diagrams. Everyone from kindergarten children to adults looking for
unusual diversion will be endlessly amused. Index. Bibliography. Introduction
by A. C. Haddon. 17 full-page plates, 960 illustrations. xxiii + 401pp. 5⅜ x 8½.
Paperbound $2.00

PAPER FOLDING FOR BEGINNERS, *W. D. Murray and F. J. Rigney*
A delightful introduction to the varied and entertaining Japanese art of
origami (paper folding), with a full, crystal-clear text that anticipates every
difficulty; over 275 clearly labeled diagrams of all important stages in creation.
You get results at each stage, since complex figures are logically developed
from simpler ones. 43 different pieces are explained: sailboats, frogs, roosters,
etc. 6 photographic plates. 279 diagrams. 95pp. 5⅝ x 8⅜. Paperbound $1.00

PRINCIPLES OF ART HISTORY,
H. Wölfflin
Analyzing such terms as "baroque," "classic," "neoclassic," "primitive,"
"picturesque," and 164 different works by artists like Botticelli, van Cleve,
Dürer, Hobbema, Holbein, Hals, Rembrandt, Titian, Brueghel, Vermeer, and
many others, the author establishes the classifications of art history and style
on a firm, concrete basis. This classic of art criticism shows what really
occurred between the 14th-century primitives and the sophistication of the
18th century in terms of basic attitudes and philosophies. "A remarkable
lesson in the art of seeing," *Sat. Rev. of Literature.* Translated from the 7th
German edition. 150 illustrations. 254pp. 6⅛ x 9¼.   Paperbound $2.00

PRIMITIVE ART,
Franz Boas
This authoritative and exhaustive work by a great American anthropologist
covers the entire gamut of primitive art. Pottery, leatherwork, metal work,
stone work, wood, basketry, are treated in detail. Theories of primitive art,
historical depth in art history, technical virtuosity, unconscious levels of pat-
terning, symbolism, styles, literature, music, dance, etc. A must book for the
interested layman, the anthropologist, artist, handicrafter (hundreds of unusual motifs), and the historian. Over 900 illustrations (50 ceramic vessels,
12 totem poles, etc.). 376pp. 5⅜ x 8.   Paperbound $2.25

THE GENTLEMAN AND CABINET MAKER'S DIRECTOR,
Thomas Chippendale
A reprint of the 1762 catalogue of furniture designs that went on to influence
generations of English and Colonial and Early Republic American furniture
makers. The 200 plates, most of them full-page sized, show Chippendale's
designs for French (Louis XV), Gothic, and Chinese-manner chairs, sofas,
canopy and dome beds, cornices, chamber organs, cabinets, shaving tables,
commodes, picture frames, frets, candle stands, chimney pieces, decorations, etc.
The drawings are all elegant and highly detailed; many include construction
diagrams and elevations. A supplement of 24 photographs shows surviving
pieces of original and Chippendale-style pieces of furniture. Brief biography
of Chippendale by N. I. Bienenstock, editor of *Furniture World.* Reproduced
from the 1762 edition. 200 plates, plus 19 photographic plates. vi + 249pp.
9⅛ x 12¼.   Paperbound $3.50

AMERICAN ANTIQUE FURNITURE: A BOOK FOR AMATEURS,
Edgar G. Miller, Jr.
Standard introduction and practical guide to identification of valuable
American antique furniture. 2115 illustrations, mostly photographs taken by
the author in 148 private homes, are arranged in chronological order in extensive chapters on chairs, sofas, chests, desks, bedsteads, mirrors, tables, clocks,
and other articles. Focus is on furniture accessible to the collector, including
simpler pieces and a larger than usual coverage of Empire style. Introductory
chapters identify structural elements, characteristics of various styles, how to
avoid fakes, etc. "We are frequently asked to name some book on American
furniture that will meet the requirements of the novice collector, the beginning dealer, and . . . the general public. . . . We believe Mr. Miller's two
volumes more completely satisfy this specification than any other work,"
Antiques. Appendix. Index. Total of vi + 1106pp. 7⅞ x 10¾.
        Two volume set, paperbound $7.50

The Bad Child's Book of Beasts, More Beasts for Worse Children, and A Moral Alphabet, *H. Belloc*
Hardly and anthology of humorous verse has appeared in the last 50 years without at least a couple of these famous nonsense verses. But one must see the entire volumes — with all the delightful original illustrations by Sir Basil Blackwood — to appreciate fully Belloc's charming and witty verses that play so subacidly on the platitudes of life and morals that beset his day — and ours. A great humor classic. Three books in one. Total of 157pp. 5⅜ x 8.
Paperbound $1.00

The Devil's Dictionary, *Ambrose Bierce*
Sardonic and irreverent barbs puncturing the pomposities and absurdities of American politics, business, religion, literature, and arts, by the country's greatest satirist in the classic tradition. Epigrammatic as Shaw, piercing as Swift, American as Mark Twain, Will Rogers, and Fred Allen, Bierce will always remain the favorite of a small coterie of enthusiasts, and of writers and speakers whom he supplies with "some of the most gorgeous witticisms of the English language" (H. L. Mencken). Over 1000 entries in alphabetical order. 144pp. 5⅜ x 8.
Paperbound $1.00

The Complete Nonsense of Edward Lear.
This is the only complete edition of this master of gentle madness available at a popular price. *A Book of Nonsense, Nonsense Songs, More Nonsense Songs and Stories* in their entirety with all the old favorites that have delighted children and adults for years. The Dong With A Luminous Nose, The Jumblies, The Owl and the Pussycat, and hundreds of other bits of wonderful nonsense. 214 limericks, 3 sets of Nonsense Botany, 5 Nonsense Alphabets, 546 drawings by Lear himself, and much more. 320pp. 5⅜ x 8.
Paperbound $1.00

The Wit and Humor of Oscar Wilde, *ed. by Alvin Redman*
Wilde at his most brilliant, in 1000 epigrams exposing weaknesses and hypocrisies of "civilized" society. Divided into 49 categories—sin, wealth, women, America, etc.—to aid writers, speakers. Includes excerpts from his trials, books, plays, criticism. Formerly "The Epigrams of Oscar Wilde." Introduction by Vyvyan Holland, Wilde's only living son. Introductory essay by editor. 260pp. 5⅜ x 8.
Paperbound $1.00

A Child's Primer of Natural History, *Oliver Herford*
Scarcely an anthology of whimsy and humor has appeared in the last 50 years without a contribution from Oliver Herford. Yet the works from which these examples are drawn have been almost impossible to obtain! Here at last are Herford's improbable definitions of a menagerie of familiar and weird animals, each verse illustrated by the author's own drawings. 24 drawings in 2 colors; 24 additional drawings. vii + 95pp. 6½ x 6.
Paperbound $1.00

The Brownies: Their Book, *Palmer Cox*
The book that made the Brownies a household word. Generations of readers have enjoyed the antics, predicaments and adventures of these jovial sprites, who emerge from the forest at night to play or to come to the aid of a deserving human. Delightful illustrations by the author decorate nearly every page. 24 short verse tales with 266 illustrations. 155pp. 6⅝ x 9¼.
Paperbound $1.50

THE PRINCIPLES OF PSYCHOLOGY,
William James
The full long-course, unabridged, of one of the great classics of Western literature and science. Wonderfully lucid descriptions of human mental activity, the stream of thought, consciousness, time perception, memory, imagination, emotions, reason, abnormal phenomena, and similar topics. Original contributions are integrated with the work of such men as Berkeley, Binet, Mills, Darwin, Hume, Kant, Royce, Schopenhauer, Spinoza, Locke, Descartes, Galton, Wundt, Lotze, Herbart, Fechner, and scores of others. All contrasting interpretations of mental phenomena are examined in detail—introspective analysis, philosophical interpretation, and experimental research. "A classic," *Journal of Consulting Psychology.* "The main lines are as valid as ever," *Psychoanalytical Quarterly.* "Standard reading . . . a classic of interpretation," *Psychiatric Quarterly.* 94 illustrations. 1408pp. 5⅜ x 8.
Vol. 1 Paperbound $2.50, Vol. 2 Paperbound $2.50,
The set $5.00

VISUAL ILLUSIONS: THEIR CAUSES, CHARACTERISTICS AND APPLICATIONS,
M. Luckiesh
"Seeing is deceiving," asserts the author of this introduction to virtually every type of optical illusion known. The text both describes and explains the principles involved in color illusions, figure-ground, distance illusions, etc. 100 photographs, drawings and diagrams prove how easy it is to fool the sense: circles that aren't round, parallel lines that seem to bend, stationary figures that seem to move as you stare at them — illustration after illustration strains our credulity at what we see. Fascinating book from many points of view, from applications for artists, in camouflage, etc. to the psychology of vision. New introduction by William Ittleson, Dept. of Psychology, Queens College. Index. Bibliography. xxi + 252pp. 5⅜ x 8½.   Paperbound $1.50

FADS AND FALLACIES IN THE NAME OF SCIENCE,
Martin Gardner
This is the standard account of various cults, quack systems, and delusions which have masqueraded as science: hollow earth fanatics. Reich and orgone sex energy, dianetics, Atlantis, multiple moons, Forteanism, flying saucers, medical fallacies like iridiagnosis, zone therapy, etc. A new chapter has been added on Bridey Murphy, psionics, and other recent manifestations in this field. This is a fair, reasoned appraisal of eccentric theory which provides excellent inoculation against cleverly masked nonsense. "Should be read by everyone, scientist and non-scientist alike," R. T. Birge, Prof. Emeritus of Physics, Univ. of California; Former President, American Physical Society. Index. x + 365pp. 5⅜ x 8.   Paperbound $1.85

ILLUSIONS AND DELUSIONS OF THE SUPERNATURAL AND THE OCCULT,
D. H. Rawcliffe
Holds up to rational examination hundreds of persistent delusions including crystal gazing, automatic writing, table turning, mediumistic trances, mental healing, stigmata, lycanthropy, live burial, the Indian Rope Trick, spiritualism, dowsing, telepathy, clairvoyance, ghosts, ESP, etc. The author explains and exposes the mental and physical deceptions involved, making this not only an exposé of supernatural phenomena, but a valuable exposition of characteristic types of abnormal psychology. Originally titled "The Psychology of the Occult." 14 illustrations. Index. 551pp. 5⅜ x 8.   Paperbound $2.25

FAIRY TALE COLLECTIONS, *edited by Andrew Lang*
Andrew Lang's fairy tale collections make up the richest shelf-full of traditional children's stories anywhere available. Lang supervised the translation of stories from all over the world—familiar European tales collected by Grimm, animal stories from Negro Africa, myths of primitive Australia, stories from Russia, Hungary, Iceland, Japan, and many other countries. Lang's selection of translations are unusually high; many authorities consider that the most familiar tales find their best versions in these volumes. All collections are richly decorated and illustrated by H. J. Ford and other artists.

THE BLUE FAIRY BOOK. 37 stories. 138 illustrations. ix + 390pp. 5⅜ x 8½.
Paperbound $1.50

THE GREEN FAIRY BOOK. 42 stories. 100 illustrations. xiii + 366pp. 5⅜ x 8½.
Paperbound $1.50

THE BROWN FAIRY BOOK. 32 stories. 50 illustrations, 8 in color. xii + 350pp. 5⅜ x 8½.
Paperbound $1.50

THE BEST TALES OF HOFFMANN, *edited by E. F. Bleiler*
10 stories by E. T. A. Hoffmann, one of the greatest of all writers of fantasy. The tales include "The Golden Flower Pot," "Automata," "A New Year's Eve Adventure," "Nutcracker and the King of Mice," "Sand-Man," and others. Vigorous characterizations of highly eccentric personalities, remarkably imaginative situations, and intensely fast pacing has made these tales popular all over the world for 150 years. Editor's introduction. 7 drawings by Hoffmann. xxxiii + 419pp. 5⅜ x 8½.
Paperbound $2.00

GHOST AND HORROR STORIES OF AMBROSE BIERCE,
edited by E. F. Bleiler
Morbid, eerie, horrifying tales of possessed poets, shabby aristocrats, revived corpses, and haunted malefactors. Widely acknowledged as the best of their kind between Poe and the moderns, reflecting their author's inner torment and bitter view of life. Includes "Damned Thing," "The Middle Toe of the Right Foot," "The Eyes of the Panther," "Visions of the Night," "Moxon's Master," and over a dozen others. Editor's introduction. xxii + 199pp. 5⅜ x 8½.
Paperbound $1.25

THREE GOTHIC NOVELS, *edited by E. F. Bleiler*
Originators of the still popular Gothic novel form, influential in ushering in early 19th-century Romanticism. Horace Walpole's *Castle of Otranto*, William Beckford's *Vathek*, John Polidori's *The Vampyre*, and a *Fragment* by Lord Byron are enjoyable as exciting reading or as documents in the history of English literature. Editor's introduction. xi + 291pp. 5⅜ x 8½.
Paperbound $2.00

BEST GHOST STORIES OF LEFANU, *edited by E. F. Bleiler*
Though admired by such critics as V. S. Pritchett, Charles Dickens and Henry James, ghost stories by the Irish novelist Joseph Sheridan LeFanu have never become as widely known as his detective fiction. About half of the 16 stories in this collection have never before been available in America. Collection includes "Carmilla" (perhaps the best vampire story ever written), "The Haunted Baronet," "The Fortunes of Sir Robert Ardagh," and the classic "Green Tea." Editor's introduction. 7 contemporary illustrations. Portrait of LeFanu. xii + 467pp. 5⅜ x 8.
Paperbound $2.00

EASY-TO-DO ENTERTAINMENTS AND DIVERSIONS WITH COINS, CARDS, STRING, PAPER AND MATCHES, *R. M. Abraham*
Over 300 tricks, games and puzzles will provide young readers with absorbing fun. Sections on card games; paper-folding; tricks with coins, matches and pieces of string; games for the agile; toy-making from common household objects; mathematical recreations; and 50 miscellaneous pastimes. Anyone in charge of groups of youngsters, including hard-pressed parents, and in need of suggestions on how to keep children sensibly amused and quietly content will find this book indispensable. Clear, simple text, copious number of delightful line drawings and illustrative diagrams. Originally titled "Winter Nights' Entertainments." Introduction by Lord Baden Powell. 329 illustrations. v + 186pp. 5⅜ x 8½. Paperbound $1.00

AN INTRODUCTION TO CHESS MOVES AND TACTICS SIMPLY EXPLAINED, *Leonard Barden*
Beginner's introduction to the royal game. Names, possible moves of the pieces, definitions of essential terms, how games are won, etc. explained in 30-odd pages. With this background you'll be able to sit right down and play. Balance of book teaches strategy — openings, middle game, typical endgame play, and suggestions for improving your game. A sample game is fully analyzed. True middle-level introduction, teaching you all the essentials without oversimplifying or losing you in a maze of detail. 58 figures. 102pp. 5⅜ x 8½. Paperbound $1.00

LASKER'S MANUAL OF CHESS, *Dr. Emanuel Lasker*
Probably the greatest chess player of modern times, Dr. Emanuel Lasker held the world championship 28 years, independent of passing schools or fashions. This unmatched study of the game, chiefly for intermediate to skilled players, analyzes basic methods, combinations, position play, the aesthetics of chess, dozens of different openings, etc., with constant reference to great modern games. Contains a brilliant exposition of Steinitz's important theories. Introduction by Fred Reinfeld. Tables of Lasker's tournament record. 3 indices. 308 diagrams. 1 photograph. xxx + 349pp. 5⅜ x 8. Paperbound $2.25

COMBINATIONS: THE HEART OF CHESS, *Irving Chernev*
Step-by-step from simple combinations to complex, this book, by a well-known chess writer, shows you the intricacies of pins, counter-pins, knight forks, and smothered mates. Other chapters show alternate lines of play to those taken in actual championship games; boomerang combinations; classic examples of brilliant combination play by Nimzovich, Rubinstein, Tarrasch, Botvinnik, Alekhine and Capablanca. Index. 356 diagrams. ix + 245pp. 5⅜ x 8½. Paperbound $1.85

HOW TO SOLVE CHESS PROBLEMS, *K. S. Howard*
Full of practical suggestions for the fan or the beginner — who knows only the moves of the chessmen. Contains preliminary section and 58 two-move, 46 three-move, and 8 four-move problems composed by 27 outstanding American problem creators in the last 30 years. Explanation of all terms and exhaustive index. "Just what is wanted for the student," Brian Harley. 112 problems, solutions. vi + 171pp. 5⅜ x 8. Paperbound $1.35

SOCIAL THOUGHT FROM LORE TO SCIENCE,
H. E. Barnes and H. Becker
An immense survey of sociological thought and ways of viewing, studying, planning, and reforming society from earliest times to the present. Includes thought on society of preliterate peoples, ancient non-Western cultures, and every great movement in Europe, America, and modern Japan. Analyzes hundreds of great thinkers: Plato, Augustine, Bodin, Vico, Montesquieu, Herder, Comte, Marx, etc. Weighs the contributions of utopians, sophists, fascists and communists; economists, jurists, philosophers, ecclesiastics, and every 19th and 20th century school of scientific sociology, anthropology, and social psychology throughout the world. Combines topical, chronological, and regional approaches, treating the evolution of social thought as a process rather than as a series of mere topics. "Impressive accuracy, competence, and discrimination . . . easily the best single survey," *Nation.* Thoroughly revised, with new material up to 1960. 2 indexes. Over 2200 bibliographical notes. Three volume set. Total of 1586pp. 5⅜ x 8.
Vol. 1 Paperbound $2.75, Vol. 2 Paperbound $2.75, Vol. 3 Paperbound $2.50
The set $8.00

A HISTORY OF HISTORICAL WRITING, *Harry Elmer Barnes*
Virtually the only adequate survey of the whole course of historical writing in a single volume. Surveys developments from the beginnings of historiography in the ancient Near East and the Classical World, up through the Cold War. Covers major historians in detail, shows interrelationship with cultural background, makes clear individual contributions, evaluates and estimates importance; also enormously rich upon minor authors and thinkers who are usually passed over. Packed with scholarship and learning, clear, easily written. Indispensable to every student of history. Revised and enlarged up to 1961. Index and bibliography. xv + 442pp. 5⅜ x 8½. Paperbound $2.50

JOHANN SEBASTIAN BACH, *Philipp Spitta*
The complete and unabridged text of the definitive study of Bach. Written some 70 years ago, it is still unsurpassed for its coverage of nearly all aspects of Bach's life and work. There could hardly be a finer non-technical introduction to Bach's music than the detailed, lucid analyses which Spitta provides for hundreds of individual pieces. 26 solid pages are devoted to the B minor mass, for example, and 30 pages to the glorious St. Matthew Passion. This monumental set also includes a major analysis of the music of the 18th century: Buxtehude, Pachelbel, etc. "Unchallenged as the last word on one of the supreme geniuses of music," John Barkham, *Saturday Review Syndicate.* Total of 1819pp. Heavy cloth binding. 5⅜ x 8.
Two volume set, clothbound $13.50

BEETHOVEN AND HIS NINE SYMPHONIES, *George Grove*
In this modern middle-level classic of musicology Grove not only analyzes all nine of Beethoven's symphonies very thoroughly in terms of their musical structure, but also discusses the circumstances under which they were written, Beethoven's stylistic development, and much other background material. This is an extremely rich book, yet very easily followed; it is highly recommended to anyone seriously interested in music. Over 250 musical passages. Index. viii + 407pp. 5⅜ x 8. Paperbound $2.00

THREE SCIENCE FICTION NOVELS,
John Taine
Acknowledged by many as the best SF writer of the 1920's, Taine (under the name Eric Temple Bell) was also a Professor of Mathematics of considerable renown. Reprinted here are *The Time Stream*, generally considered Taine's best, *The Greatest Game*, a biological-fiction novel, and *The Purple Sapphire*, involving a supercivilization of the past. Taine's stories tie fantastic narratives to frameworks of original and logical scientific concepts. Speculation is often profound on such questions as the nature of time, concept of entropy, cyclical universes, etc. 4 contemporary illustrations. v + 532pp. 5⅜ x 8⅜.

Paperbound $2.00

SEVEN SCIENCE FICTION NOVELS,
H. G. Wells
Full unabridged texts of 7 science-fiction novels of the master. Ranging from biology, physics, chemistry, astronomy, to sociology and other studies, Mr. Wells extrapolates whole worlds of strange and intriguing character. "One will have to go far to match this for entertainment, excitement, and sheer pleasure . . ."*New York Times.* Contents: The Time Machine, The Island of Dr. Moreau, The First Men in the Moon, The Invisible Man, The War of the Worlds, The Food of the Gods, In The Days of the Comet. 1015pp. 5⅜ x 8.

Clothbound $5.00

28 SCIENCE FICTION STORIES OF H. G. WELLS.
Two full, unabridged novels, *Men Like Gods* and *Star Begotten*, plus 26 short stories by the master science-fiction writer of all time! Stories of space, time, invention, exploration, futuristic adventure. Partial contents: *The Country of the Blind, In the Abyss, The Crystal Egg, The Man Who Could Work Miracles, A Story of Days to Come, The Empire of the Ants, The Magic Shop, The Valley of the Spiders, A Story of the Stone Age, Under the Knife, Sea Raiders,* etc. An indispensable collection for the library of anyone interested in science fiction adventure. 928pp. 5⅜ x 8.

Clothbound $4.50

THREE MARTIAN NOVELS,
Edgar Rice Burroughs
Complete, unabridged reprinting, in one volume, of Thuvia, Maid of Mars; Chessmen of Mars; The Master Mind of Mars. Hours of science-fiction adventure by a modern master storyteller. Reset in large clear type for easy reading. 16 illustrations by J. Allen St. John. vi + 490pp. 5⅜ x 8½.

Paperbound $1.85

AN INTELLECTUAL AND CULTURAL HISTORY OF THE WESTERN WORLD,
Harry Elmer Barnes
Monumental 3-volume survey of intellectual development of Europe from primitive cultures to the present day. Every significant product of human intellect traced through history: art, literature, mathematics, physical sciences, medicine, music, technology, social sciences, religions, jurisprudence, education, etc. Presentation is lucid and specific, analyzing in detail specific discoveries, theories, literary works, and so on. Revised (1965) by recognized scholars in specialized fields under the direction of Prof. Barnes. Revised bibliography. Indexes. 24 illustrations. Total of xxix + 1318pp.
Vol. 1 Paperbound $2.00, Vol. 2 Paperbound $2.00, Vol. 3 Paperbound $2.00,

The set $6.00

HEAR ME TALKIN' TO YA, *edited by Nat Shapiro and Nat Hentoff*
In their own words, Louis Armstrong, King Oliver, Fletcher Henderson, Bunk Johnson, Bix Beiderbecke, Billy Holiday, Fats Waller, Jelly Roll Morton, Duke Ellington, and many others comment on the origins of jazz in New Orleans and its growth in Chicago's South Side, Kansas City's jam sessions, Depression Harlem, and the modernism of the West Coast schools. Taken from taped conversations, letters, magazine articles, other first-hand sources. Editors' introduction. xvi + 429pp. 5⅜ x 8½.   Paperbound $2.00

THE JOURNAL OF HENRY D. THOREAU
A 25-year record by the great American observer and critic, as complete a record of a great man's inner life as is anywhere available. Thoreau's Journals served him as raw material for his formal pieces, as a place where he could develop his ideas, as an outlet for his interests in wild life and plants, in writing as an art, in classics of literature, Walt Whitman and other contemporaries, in politics, slavery, individual's relation to the State, etc. The Journals present a portrait of a remarkable man, and are an observant social history. Unabridged republication of 1906 edition, Bradford Torrey and Francis H. Allen, editors. Illustrations. Total of 1888pp. 8⅜ x 12¼.
                                   Two volume set, clothbound $25.00

A SHAKESPEARIAN GRAMMAR, *E. A. Abbott*
Basic reference to Shakespeare and his contemporaries, explaining through thousands of quotations from Shakespeare, Jonson, Beaumont and Fletcher, North's *Plutarch* and other sources the grammatical usage differing from the modern. First published in 1870 and written by a scholar who spent much of his life isolating principles of Elizabethan language, the book is unlikely ever to be superseded. Indexes. xxiv + 511pp. 5⅜ x 8½.   Paperbound $2.75

FOLK-LORE OF SHAKESPEARE, *T. F. Thistelton Dyer*
Classic study, drawing from Shakespeare a large body of references to supernatural beliefs, terminology of falconry and hunting, games and sports, good luck charms, marriage customs, folk medicines, superstitions about plants, animals, birds, argot of the underworld, sexual slang of London, proverbs, drinking customs, weather lore, and much else. From full compilation comes a mirror of the 17th-century popular mind. Index. ix + 526pp. 5⅜ x 8½.
                                               Paperbound $2.50

THE NEW VARIORUM SHAKESPEARE, *edited by H. H. Furness*
By far the richest editions of the plays ever produced in any country or language. Each volume contains complete text (usually First Folio) of the play, all variants in Quarto and other Folio texts, editorial changes by every major editor to Furness's own time (1900), footnotes to obscure references or language, extensive quotes from literature of Shakespearian criticism, essays on plot sources (often reprinting sources in full), and much more.

HAMLET, *edited by H. H. Furness*
Total of xxvi + 905pp. 5⅜ x 8½.   Two volume set, paperbound $4.75

TWELFTH NIGHT, *edited by H. H. Furness*
Index. xxii + 434pp. 5⅜ x 8½.   Paperbound $2.25

LA BOHEME BY GIACOMO PUCCINI,
translated and introduced by Ellen H. Bleiler
Complete handbook for the operagoer, with everything needed for full enjoyment except the musical score itself. Complete Italian libretto, with new, modern English line-by-line translation—the only libretto printing all repeats; biography of Puccini; the librettists; background to the opera, Murger's La Boheme, etc.; circumstances of composition and performances; plot summary; and pictorial section of 73 illustrations showing Puccini, famous singers and performances, etc. Large clear type for easy reading. 124pp. 5⅜ x 8½.
Paperbound $1.00

ANTONIO STRADIVARI: HIS LIFE AND WORK (1644-1737),
W. Henry Hill, Arthur F. Hill, and Alfred E. Hill
Still the only book that really delves into life and art of the incomparable Italian craftsman, maker of the finest musical instruments in the world today. The authors, expert violin-makers themselves, discuss Stradivari's ancestry, his construction and finishing techniques, distinguished characteristics of many of his instruments and their locations. Included, too, is story of introduction of his instruments into France, England, first revelation of their supreme merit, and information on his labels, number of instruments made, prices, mystery of ingredients of his varnish, tone of pre-1684 Stradivari violin and changes between 1684 and 1690. An extremely interesting, informative account for all music lovers, from craftsman to concert-goer. Republication of original (1902) edition. New introduction by Sydney Beck, Head of Rare Book and Manuscript Collections, Music Division, New York Public Library. Analytical index by Rembert Wurlitzer. Appendixes. 68 illustrations. 30 full-page plates. 4 in color. xxvi + 315pp. 5⅜ x 8½.
Paperbound $2.25

MUSICAL AUTOGRAPHS FROM MONTEVERDI TO HINDEMITH,
Emanuel Winternitz
For beauty, for intrinsic interest, for perspective on the composer's personality, for subtleties of phrasing, shading, emphasis indicated in the autograph but suppressed in the printed score, the mss. of musical composition are fascinating documents which repay close study in many different ways. This 2-volume work reprints facsimiles of mss. by virtually every major composer, and many minor figures—196 examples in all. A full text points out what can be learned from mss., analyzes each sample. Index. Bibliography. 18 figures. 196 plates. Total of 170pp. of text. 7⅞ x 10¾.
Vol. 1 Paperbound $2.00, Vol. 2 Paperbound $2.00,
The set $4.00

J. S. BACH,
Albert Schweitzer
One of the few great full-length studies of Bach's life and work, and the study upon which Schweitzer's renown as a musicologist rests. On first appearance (1911), revolutionized Bach performance. The only writer on Bach to be musicologist, performing musician, and student of history, theology and philosophy, Schweitzer contributes particularly full sections on history of German Protestant church music, theories on motivic pictorial representations in vocal music, and practical suggestions for performance. Translated by Ernest Newman. Indexes. 5 illustrations. 650 musical examples. Total of xix + 928pp. 5⅜ x 8½. Vol. 1 Paperbound $2.00, Vol. 2 Paperbound $2.00,
The set $4.00

THE METHODS OF ETHICS, *Henry Sidgwick*
Propounding no organized system of its own, study subjects every major methodological approach to ethics to rigorous, objective analysis. Study discusses and relates ethical thought of Plato, Aristotle, Bentham, Clarke, Butler, Hobbes, Hume, Mill, Spencer, Kant, and dozens of others. Sidgwick retains conclusions from each system which follow from ethical premises, rejecting the faulty. Considered by many in the field to be among the most important treatises on ethical philosophy. Appendix. Index. xlvii + 528pp. 5⅜ x 8½.
Paperbound $2.50

TEUTONIC MYTHOLOGY, *Jakob Grimm*
A milestone in Western culture; the work which established on a modern basis the study of history of religions and comparative religions. 4-volume work assembles and interprets everything available on religious and folkloristic beliefs of Germanic people (including Scandinavians, Anglo-Saxons, etc.). Assembling material from such sources as Tacitus, surviving Old Norse and Icelandic texts, archeological remains, folktales, surviving superstitions, comparative traditions, linguistic analysis, etc. Grimm explores pagan deities, heroes, folklore of nature, religious practices, and every other area of pagan German belief. To this day, the unrivaled, definitive, exhaustive study. Translated by J. S. Stallybrass from 4th (1883) German edition. Indexes. Total of lxxvii + 1887pp. 5⅜ x 8½.   Four volume set, paperbound $10.00

THE I CHING, *translated by James Legge*
Called "The Book of Changes" in English, this is one of the Five Classics edited by Confucius, basic and central to Chinese thought. Explains perhaps the most complex system of divination known, founded on the theory that all things happening at any one time have characteristic features which can be isolated and related. Significant in Oriental studies, in history of religions and philosophy, and also to Jungian psychoanalysis and other areas of modern European thought. Index. Appendixes. 6 plates. xxi + 448pp. 5⅜ x 8½.
Paperbound $2.75

HISTORY OF ANCIENT PHILOSOPHY, *W. Windelband*
One of the clearest, most accurate comprehensive surveys of Greek and Roman philosophy. Discusses ancient philosophy in general, intellectual life in Greece in the 7th and 6th centuries B.C., Thales, Anaximander, Anaximenes, Heraclitus, the Eleatics, Empedocles, Anaxagoras, Leucippus, the Pythagoreans, the Sophists, Socrates, Democritus (20 pages), Plato (50 pages), Aristotle (70 pages), the Peripatetics, Stoics, Epicureans, Sceptics, Neo-platonists, Christian Apologists, etc. 2nd German edition translated by H. E. Cushman. xv + 393pp. 5⅜ x 8.   Paperbound $2.25

THE PALACE OF PLEASURE, *William Painter*
Elizabethan versions of Italian and French novels from *The Decameron*, Cinthio, Straparola, Queen Margaret of Navarre, and other continental sources — the very work that provided Shakespeare and dozens of his contemporaries with many of their plots and sub-plots and, therefore, justly considered one of the most influential books in all English literature. It is also a book that any reader will still enjoy. Total of cviii + 1,224pp.
Three volume set, Paperbound $6.75

THE WONDERFUL WIZARD OF OZ, *L. F. Baum*
All the original W. W. Denslow illustrations in full color—as much a part of
"The Wizard" as Tenniel's drawings are of "Alice in Wonderland." "The
Wizard" is still America's best-loved fairy tale, in which, as the author expresses
it, "The wonderment and joy are retained and the heartaches and nightmares
left out." Now today's young readers can enjoy every word and wonderful picture of the original book. New introduction by Martin Gardner. A Baum
bibliography. 23 full-page color plates. viii + 268pp. 5⅜ x 8.
Paperbound $1.50

THE MARVELOUS LAND OF OZ, *L. F. Baum*
This is the equally enchanting sequel to the "Wizard," continuing the adventures of the Scarecrow and the Tin Woodman. The hero this time is a little
boy named Tip, and all the delightful Oz magic is still present. This is the
Oz book with the Animated Saw-Horse, the Woggle-Bug, and Jack Pumpkin-
head. All the original John R. Neill illustrations, 10 in full color. 287pp.
5⅜ x 8.
Paperbound $1.50

ALICE'S ADVENTURES UNDER GROUND, *Lewis Carroll*
The original *Alice in Wonderland*, hand-lettered and illustrated by Carroll
himself, and originally presented as a Christmas gift to a child-friend. Adults
as well as children will enjoy this charming volume, reproduced faithfully
in this Dover edition. While the story is essentially the same, there are slight
changes, and Carroll's spritely drawings present an intriguing alternative to
the famous Tenniel illustrations. One of the most popular books in Dover's
catalogue. Introduction by Martin Gardner. 38 illustrations. 128pp. 5⅜ x 8½.
Paperbound $1.00

THE NURSERY "ALICE," *Lewis Carroll*
While most of us consider *Alice in Wonderland* a story for children of all
ages, Carroll himself felt it was beyond younger children. He therefore provided this simplified version, illustrated with the famous Tenniel drawings
enlarged and colored in delicate tints, for children aged "from Nought to
Five." Dover's edition of this now rare classic is a faithful copy of the 1889
printing, including 20 illustrations by Tenniel, and front and back covers
reproduced in full color. Introduction by Martin Gardner. xxiii + 67pp.
6⅛ x 9¼.
Paperbound $1.50

THE STORY OF KING ARTHUR AND HIS KNIGHTS, *Howard Pyle*
A fast-paced, exciting retelling of the best known Arthurian legends for young
readers by one of America's best story tellers and illustrators. The sword
Excalibur, wooing of Guinevere, Merlin and his downfall, adventures of Sir
Pellias and Gawaine, and others. The pen and ink illustrations are vividly
imagined and wonderfully drawn. 41 illustrations. xviii + 313pp. 6⅛ x 9¼.
Paperbound $1.50

Prices subject to change without notice.

Available at your book dealer or write for free catalogue to Dept. Adsci,
Dover Publications, Inc., 180 Varick St., N.Y., N.Y. 10014. Dover publishes more
than 150 books each year on science, elementary and advanced mathematics,
biology, music, art, literary history, social sciences and other areas.